Becoming a master student

EIGHTH EDITION

Tools, techniques, hints,

ideas, illustrations,

examples, methods,

procedures, processes,

skills, resources, and

suggestions for success.

Houghton Mifflin Company
Boston   New York

DAVE ELLIS

Printed in the U.S.A.

Library of Congress Catalog Card Number: 96-76895

Student text ISBN: 0-395-83054-0
Instructor's edition ISBN: 0-395-83056-7

4 5 6 7 8 9 - VH -00 99 98 97

Notice: *Becoming a Master Student* was previously entitled *Survival Skills for Students* and before that *Survival Tools for College.*

This book is available in Spanish (fifth edition) and French (sixth edition). A Canadian edition (eighth edition) is also available. Contact your Houghton Mifflin sales representative or College Survival for more information.

> College Survival
> A Program of Houghton Mifflin Company
> 2075 Foxfield Road, Suite 100
> St. Charles, IL 60174

Portions of the "Power Processes" are excerpted from *Human Being: A Manual for Happiness, Health, Love, and Wealth* by David Ellis and Stan Lankowitz.

As part of Houghton Mifflin's ongoing commitment to the environment, this text has been printed on recycled paper.

FOR THE MOST PART, STUDENTS HAVE CREATED THIS BOOK. The First Edition of *Becoming a Master Student* came from notes that I collected while teaching a course to students. They ended up teaching me more than I ever imagined there was to learn about student success while I was supposed to be teaching them. Since that edition, hundreds of thousands of students have used this book, and their continuing input has dramatically changed it. To all of those students of different ages and from a variety of cultures and ethnic groups, I send my heartfelt thanks.

In previous editions of this book, I have listed many of the educators who have contributed significantly to the strategies and insights offered to students. Unfortunately, this list has gotten so long that I cannot list, by name, the hundreds of significant contributors. Some educators have offered an idea or two as a part of an article. Others have provided the inspiration and much of the content for entire articles. Still others have offered suggestions that have totally rearranged the structure and outline of this text. Thank you all.

During the last 16 years, I have worked day to day with dozens of people who have contributed dramatically to the creation of this text. They have lent ideas, logistical support, project management, consultation, and design. To all of those people, I want you to know that I know that this book would never have been produced without you. There are a few people out of the dozens I have worked with who have made such a difference in this book that to leave them unnamed would border on unethical. In particular, I thank and acknowledge the work of Doug Toft, Jeff Swaim, Stan Lankowitz, Larry David, Bill Rentz, Adel Brown, Ellen Whalen, Mary Maisey-Ireland, Robbie Murchison, Bill Fleming, Bill Harlan, Judy Maisey, James Anderson, Wayne Zako, Karen Marie Erickson, and Shirley Wileman-Conrad.

CA COLLEGE SURVIVAL
Committed to Student Success

I want your feedback. When you see ways to improve this book, please write to me. More than ever, I recognize the value of your ideas. I want to know what works and what doesn't work for you.

Dave Ellis

P.O. BOX 8396 • RAPID CITY, SD 57709 8396

For the photography and illustration in this book, I thank Mike Wolforth, Sid Spelts, Lee Christianson, John Backlund, Tim Blough, Mike Speiser, and Teresa Verburg. Thanks also for art direction, layout, and design, to the staff of Amherst & Reeves, particularly Doug Garcia, Susie Griggs, and Jenny Kendall.

For their contribution to my life and personal growth, I thank my wife, Trisha Waldron, and my friends Stan Lankowitz and Barb Churchill. I also treasure what I have learned from my children, Sara, Elizabeth, Snow, and Berry, and the constant encouragement of my parents, Maryellen and Ken.

I know that no book and no set of ideas comes from a single person, and my intention is to continue to share with others what all of the people I have mentioned here shared with me.

Dave Ellis

Table of Contents

introduction

As you begin...

consider one way to ensure that this book is worthless—and seven ways you can benefit instead. Also do a textbook reconnaissance and discover options for getting the most out of this book. You can declare what you want from your education and commit to making this book a partner in your success.

EXERCISE #1
TEXTBOOK RECONNAISSANCE

Start becoming a master student right now by doing a 15-minute "textbook reconnaissance" of this book. Here's how:

First, read the table of contents. Do it in three minutes or less. Next, look at every page in the book. Move quickly. Scan headlines. Look at pictures. Notice forms, charts, and diagrams.

A textbook reconnaissance shows you where a course is going. It gives you the big picture. That's useful because brains work best when going from the general to the specific. Getting the big picture before you start makes details easier to recall and understand later on.

Your textbook reconnaissance will work even better if, as you scan, you look for ideas you can use. When you find one, write the page number and a two-word description of it in the space below. The idea behind this technique is simple: It's easier to learn when you're excited, and it's easier to get excited about a course if you know it's going to be useful, interesting, or fun.

When you have found five interesting ideas, stop writing and continue your survey. Remember, look at every page, and do it quickly. And here's another useful tip for the master student: Do it now.

Page Number	Description
1.	
2.	
3.	
4.	
5.	

T HE FIRST EDITION OF THIS BOOK began with the sentence: *This book is worthless.*

Many students thought this was a trick to get their attention. It wasn't. Others thought it was reverse psychology. It wasn't that, either. Still others thought it meant that the book was worthless if they didn't read it. It's more than that.

The book is worthless even if you read it, if reading is all you do.

This book is worthless

What was true of that first edition is true of this one. Until you take action and use the ideas in it, *Becoming a Master Student* really is worthless.

You probably won't take action and use the ideas until you are convinced that you have something to gain. The main purpose of this introduction is to sell you on the value of committing yourself to spend the energy to use this book actively. Before you stiffen up and resist, the purpose of this sales pitch is not to separate you from your money. You already bought the book. Now you can get something for your money by committing yourself to take action—in other words, commit yourself to become a master student. Here's what's in it for you.

Pitch #1: You can save money now and make more later.

Start with money. Your college education is one of the most expensive things you will ever buy. Typically, it costs students $30 to $70 an hour to sit in class. (See Exercise #6 on page 21.) Unfortunately, many students think their classes aren't even worth 50 cents an hour.

> " "
> *Change and growth take place when a person has risked himself and dares to become involved with experimenting with his own life.*
> –HERBERT OTTO

> " "
> *The human ability to learn and remember is virtually limitless.*
> –SHEILA OSTRANDER & LYNN SCHROEDER

As a master student, you control the value you get out of your education, and that value can be considerable. The joy of learning aside, college graduates make about $1 million more during their lifetimes than their nondegreed peers. It pays to be a master student.

Pitch #2: You can rediscover the natural learner in you.

Joy is important too. As you become a master student, you will learn how to learn in the most effective way possible by discovering the joyful, natural learner within you.

Children are great natural students. They quickly learn complex skills, such as language, and they have fun doing it. For them, learning is a high-energy process involving experimentation, discovery, and sometimes, broken dishes. Then comes school. For some students, drill and drudgery replace discovery and dish breaking. Learning can become a drag. You can use this book to reverse that process and rediscover what you knew as a child—that laughter and learning are not mutually exclusive.

Sometimes learning does take effort, especially in college. As you become a master student, you will learn how to get the most out of that effort.

Pitch #3: You can choose from hundreds of techniques.

Becoming a Master Student is packed with hundreds of practical, nuts-and-bolts techniques. And you can begin using them immediately. For example, during your textbook reconnaissance on page vi you practiced three powerful learning techniques in one 15-minute exercise. (If you didn't do the textbook reconnaissance, it's not too late to get your money's worth. Do it now.) If you doze in lectures, drift during tests, or dawdle on term papers, you can use the ideas in this book to become a more effective student.

Not all these ideas will work for you. That's why there are so many of them in *Becoming a Master Student*. You can experiment with the techniques. As you discover what works, you will develop a unique style of learning that you can use for the rest of your life.

Pitch #4: You get the best suggestions from thousands of students.

The concepts and techniques in this book are not here because learning theorists, educators, and psychologists say they work. They are here because tens of thousands of students from all kinds of backgrounds tried them and say they work. These are people who dreaded giving speeches, couldn't read their own notes, and couldn't remember where the ileocaecal valve was. Then they figured out how to solve these problems, which was the hard part. Now you can use their ideas.

Pitch #5: You can learn about you.

The process of self-discovery is an important theme in *Becoming a Master Student*. Throughout the book you can use Discovery Statements and Intention Statements for everything from organizing your desk to choosing long-term goals. Studying for an organic chemistry quiz is a lot easier with a clean desk and a clear idea of the course's importance to you.

Pitch #6: You can use a proven product.

The first seven editions of this book were successful for tens of thousands of students. In schools where it was widely used, the dropout rate decreased as much as 25 percent and in some cases, 50 percent. Student feedback has been positive. In particular, students with successful histories have praised the techniques in this book.

Pitch #7: You can learn the secret of student success.

If this sales pitch still hasn't persuaded you to actively use this book, maybe it's time to reveal the secret of student success. (Provide your own drum roll here.) The secret is, there are no secrets. Perhaps the ultimate formula is to give up formulas and keep inventing.

The strategies and tactics that successful students use are well known. You have hundreds of them at your fingertips right now, in this book. Use them. Modify them. Invent new ones. You're the authority on what works for you.

However, what makes any technique work is commitment—and action. Without them, the pages of *Becoming a Master Student* are just 2.1 pounds of expensive mulch. Add your participation to the mulch, and these pages are priceless.

JOURNAL ENTRY #1
DISCOVERY STATEMENT

Success is a choice. Your choice. To get to what you want, it helps to know what you want. That is the purpose of this Journal Entry.

Select a time and place when you know you will not be disturbed for at least 20 minutes. (The library is a good place to do this.) Relax for two or three minutes, clearing your mind. Then complete the following sentences and keep writing. Write down everything you want to get out of school. Write down everything you want your education to enable you to do after you finish school.

When you run out of things to write, stick with it just a bit longer. Be willing to experience a little discomfort. Keep writing. What you discover might be well worth the extra effort. You can begin choosing success right now by choosing a date, time, and place to complete this Journal Entry. Write your choice here and block out the time on your calendar.

Date: _____

Time: _____

Place: _____

What I want from my education is . . .

_____

_____

_____

When I complete my education, I want to be able to . . .

_____

_____

_____

I also want . . .

_____

_____

JOURNAL ENTRY #2
DISCOVERY STATEMENT

On a separate piece of paper, write a description of a time in your life when you learned or did something well. This situation need not be related to school. Describe the details of the situation, including the place, time, and people involved. Describe how you felt about it, how it looked to you, how it sounded. Describe the physical feelings you associate with the event. Do the same for emotions.

Get ∞ the most out of this book

1. Rip 'em out. The pages of *Becoming a Master Student* are perforated because some of the information here is too important to leave in the book and some of it your instructor may want to see. For example, Journal Entry #1 asks you to write some important things you want to get out of your education. To keep yourself focused, you could rip that page out and post it on your bathroom mirror or some place where you'll see it several times a day.

You can reinsert the page by just sticking it into the spine of the book; it will hold. A piece of tape will fix it in place.

2. Skip around. You can use this book in several different ways. Read it straight through, or pick it up, turn to any page, and find an idea you can use. Look for ideas you can use right now. For example, if you're having trouble listening to boring lectures, skip directly to Chapter Five: Notes.

As you skip around, keep in mind that *Becoming a Master Student* is organized into two major sections. The first six chapters are about core study skills such as reading and taking notes; the last six focus on skills that apply in many areas of life.

3. If it works, use it. If it doesn't, lose it. If there are sections of the book that don't apply to you at all, skip them—unless, of course, they are assigned. Then, see if you can gain value from these sections anyway. When you are committed to getting value from this book, even an idea that seems irrelevant or ineffective at first can turn out to be a powerful tool. Topics that aren't relevant now may be just what you want in the next year or three years from now.

4. Rewrite this book. Here's an alternative strategy to the one above. If an idea doesn't work for you, rewrite it. Change the exercises to fit your needs. Create a new technique by combining several others. Create a technique out of thin air!

5. Put yourself into the book. As you read about techniques in this book, invent your own examples, starring yourself in the title role. For example, as you were reading the explanation of Exercise #1, you might have pictured yourself using this technique on your world history textbook. Sometimes it pays to let your mind wander.

6. Work with others. Talk with your classmates about what works and what doesn't. Peer pressure is often characterized as negative. You can turn that idea around. Form a group of students who support each other in mastering the art of learning.

7. Yuk it up. Going to school is a big investment. The stakes are high. It's OK to be serious about that, but you don't have to go to school on the deferred-fun program. A master student celebrates learning, and one of the best ways to do that is to have a laugh now and then.

8. Own this book. Write your name and address on the first page of this book now, and don't stop there. As you complete Journal Entries and exercises, you create a record of what you want to get out of school and how you intend to get it. Every time your pen touches a page, you move closer to mastery of learning.

Another way to own this book is to write summaries of each chapter. Experiment with several different techniques, including outlines, mind maps, and concept maps. For details, see Chapter Five.

9. Do the exercises. Action makes this book work. To get the most out of an exercise, read the instructions carefully before you begin. To get the most out of this book, do most of the exercises. More important, avoid feeling guilty if you skip some. And by the way, it's never too late to go back and do those.

These exercises invite you to write, touch, feel, move, see, search, ponder, speak, listen, recall, choose, commit, and create. You might even sing and dance. Learning works best when it involves action.

True education is not about cramming material into your brain. Education is the process of expanding your capabilities, of bringing yourself out into the world. Doing the exercises brings you into the heart of that process.

10. Get used to a new look and tone. This book looks different from traditional textbooks. *Becoming a Master Student* presents major ideas in magazine-style articles. You will discover lots of lists, blurbs, one-liners, pictures, charts, graphs, cartoons, and even a joke or two. The book is colorful throughout not only to provide visual interest but also to underscore in a graphic way the importance of racial diversity—one of the subjects of Chapter Seven.

The icons and key visuals in this book carry special meanings. Journal Entries are introduced by a drawing of a twisted pencil. This is a sign of infinity, symbolizing the idea that journaling is a process that never ends. The picture of the running shoe that accompanies the exercises throughout this book indicates the action that makes for effective learning.

One more note: As a strategy for avoiding sexist language, this book alternates the use of feminine and masculine pronouns.

11. Practice critical thinking. Throughout this book are activities labeled "Practicing Critical Thinking." Look for them next to the icon of the "thinker" inside a light bulb, who's there to encourage contemplation and constant problem solving. Also note that other elements of this text promote critical thinking, including exercises and Journal Entries.

12. Learn about learning styles. Check out the Learning Style Applications at the end of each chapter. These are included to increase your awareness of your preferred learning styles and to help you explore new styles. Each exercise will guide you through experiencing four specific learning styles as applied to the content of the chapter. The four-color icon for these applications represents those styles. For a detailed explanation of these styles, see "Learning styles—Discovering how you learn" in Chapter One.

**EXERCISE #2
COMMITMENT**

This book is worthless without your action. One powerful way to begin taking action is to make a commitment. Conversely, without commitment, sustained action is unlikely. The result is a worthless book. Therefore, in the interest of saving your valuable time and energy, this exercise gives you a chance to declare your level of involvement up front. From the choices below, choose the sentence that best reflects your commitment to using this book. Write the number in the space provided at the end of the list.

1. *"Well, I'm reading this book right now, aren't I?"*
2. *"I will skim the book and read the interesting parts."*
3. *"I will read the book and think about how some of the techniques might apply to me."*
4. *"I will read the book, think about it, and do the exercises that look interesting."*
5. *"I will read the book, do exercises, and complete some of the Journal Entries."*
6. *"I will read the book, do exercises and Journal Entries, and use some of the techniques."*
7. *"I will read the book, do most of the exercises and Journal Entries, and use some of the techniques."*
8. *"I will study this book, do most of the exercises and Journal Entries, and use some of the techniques."*
9. *"I will study this book, do most of the exercises and Journal Entries, and experiment vigorously with most of the suggestions in order to discover what works best for me."*
10. *"I promise to get value from this book, beginning with Exercise #1: 'Textbook Reconnaissance,' even if I have to rewrite the sections I don't like and even if I have to invent new techniques of my own."*

Enter your commitment level and today's date here:

Commitment level_____   Date_____

If you selected commitment level 1 or 2, you might consider passing this book on to a friend. If your commitment level is a 9 or 10, you are on your way to terrific success in school. If you are somewhere in between, experiment with the techniques; and if you find they work, consider returning to this exercise and raising your level of commitment.

first step

In this chapter...

■ take a **First Step** to personal change: tell the truth about your current abilities. Doing so allows you to **change habits** and to set goals that you can reach. In the process, keep yourself on track with the **Discovery and Intention Journal Entry System.** Also discover and expand your learning styles, reflect on the value of higher education, and find ways to pay for school.

JOURNAL ENTRY #3
DISCOVERY STATEMENT

Perhaps you know people who've tried to repair their cars without knowing what parts they needed. Or maybe you've tried to buy clothes for someone without knowing that person's size and preferred styles. In such cases we can be more effective when we know what the specific problem is or what the people involved truly want.

On a separate sheet of paper, describe a time when you wanted to solve a problem but lacked specific information about the nature of that problem. This could also be a time when you had no clear idea of the outcome you desired.

Now describe a time when, based on your diagnosis and desired results, you were able to accurately diagnose a problem and efficiently solve it.

Succeeding in this course—and in school—uses the same process. It begins with identifying the skills you already have, along with the new skills you want to acquire. It also involves telling the truth about any problem you face right now and creating a plan to solve it.

Take time now to preview the Discovery Wheel exercise on page 14. Then list several specific benefits you can gain by reading and applying this chapter.

I discovered that I . . .

_____

_____

_____

_____

_____

_____

First Step : Truth is a key to mastery

THE FIRST STEP TECHNIQUE IS SIMPLE: Tell the truth about who you are and what you want. End of discussion. Now proceed to Chapter Two.

Well, it's not quite that simple.

The First Step is one of the most powerful tools in this book. It magnifies the power of all the other techniques. It is a key to becoming a master student.

Unfortunately, a First Step is easier to explain than it is to use, and it's not that easy to explain. "Telling the truth" sounds like pie-in-the-sky moralizing, but there is nothing pie-in-the-sky about a First Step. It is a practical, down-to-earth way to change behavior. No technique in this book has been field-tested more often or more successfully— or under tougher circumstances. Just ask almost any recovering alcoholic.

A fundamental principle of Alcoholics Anonymous is that alcoholics must tell the truth about their drinking before they can begin to change. This is an essential ingredient in AA's "First Step" and in its entire Twelve Step program. Today people recovering from addictions to food, drugs, sex, work, and whatever else human beings can abuse, employ the same principle. They use First Steps to change their behavior for one reason: First Steps work.

Compared to conquering addictions, training to be a master student is a snap. But let's be truthful. It's not easy to tell the truth about ourselves. We might have to admit that we're afraid of algebra or that we never complete term papers on time. It's tough to admit weaknesses.

> " "
> No one can make you feel inferior without your consent.
> –ELEANOR ROOSEVELT

> " "
> You either change things or you don't. Excuses rob you of power and induce apathy.
> –AGNES WHISTLING ELK

> " "
> In oneself lies the whole world, and if you know how to look and learn, then the door is there and the key is in your hand. Nobody on earth can give you either that key or the door to open, except yourself.
> –J. KRISHNAMURTI

For some people, it's even harder to admit strengths. Maybe they don't want to brag. Maybe they're attached to poor self-images. The reasons don't matter. The point is, using the First Step system in *Becoming a Master Student* means telling the truth about your good qualities too.

Making this technique work also means telling the truth about what you want.

Sounds easy, you say? Many people would rather eat nails. If you don't believe it, find three other students and ask them what they want to get out of their educations. Be prepared for hemming and hawing, vague generalities, and maybe even a helping of pie-in-the-sky 'a la mode.

On the other hand, if one of them tells you she wants a degree in journalism with double minors in earth sciences and Portuguese so she can work as a reporter covering the environment in Brazil, chances are, you've found a master student.

The details of her vision are a clue to her mastery. Goals are more powerful when they are specific. So are First Steps, whether they are verbal or written. For example, if you want to improve your note-taking skills, you might write, "I am an awful note taker." It would be more effective to write, "I can't read 80 percent of the notes I took in American Constitutional History last week and I have no idea what was important in that class."

Be just as specific about what you want. You might declare, "I want to take legible notes that help me predict what questions will be on the final exam."

In Exercise #5: "The Discovery Wheel" and Exercise #3 you can take a giant First Step. You can tell the truth about what kind of student you are and what kind of student you want to become. If that prospect puts a knot in your stomach, that's good. Notice that knot. It is your friend. It is reminding you that telling the truth about yourself takes courage, which is an important characteristic of a master student.

Your courage will be rewarded. The Discovery Wheel and the rest of the exercises in this book are your First Steps to tapping resources you never imagined you had. You can even take a First Step to mapping out the rest of your life with a detailed career plan.

They're all First Steps—no kidding. It's just that simple. The truth has power.

JOURNAL ENTRY #4
INTENTION STATEMENT

Review Exercise #1: "Textbook reconnaissance." Consider the articles in this book that you thought might be valuable. Choose the one from which you think you can get the most immediate, practical benefit and scan that article until you come to a specific technique you can use. Write an Intention Statement in this space concerning how you will use that technique within the next week. Include when you intend to use it.

For example, if you listed the article called "When reading is tough," you could use any of the techniques suggested for difficult reading assignments. If you have a tough computer science course, you might choose to form a support group to discuss reading assignments. In that case, you might write, "I intend to contact four other students after class tomorrow about forming a group to study computer science."

I intend to use the study technique . . .

_____

_____

_____

_____

I will use it at these times . . .

_____

_____

_____

_____

EXERCISE #3
TAKING THE FIRST STEP

The purpose of this exercise is to give you a chance to discover the positive as well as the negative aspects of yourself. It is the most difficult exercise in this book. To make the exercise worthwhile, do it with courage.

Some people suggest that looking at negative aspects is counter to positive thinking. Well, perhaps. Positive thinking is a great technique. So is seeing the truth, especially when we see the whole picture—even though a realistic picture of ourselves may include some extremely negative points.

If you admit that you can't read, and that's the truth, then you have taken a strong positive First Step to becoming a successful reader. On the other hand, if you say that you are a terrible math student, and that's not the truth, then you are programming yourself to accept unnecessary failure. The point is, tell the truth.

This exercise is similar to each Journal Entry–Discovery Statement appearing throughout this text. The difference is that in this case, for reasons of confidentiality, you don't write your discoveries in the book.

Be brave. If you approach this exercise with courage, you are likely to write down some things you don't want others to read. You may even write down some truths about yourself that could get you into trouble. Do this exercise on separate pieces of paper; then hide or destroy them.

To make this exercise work, follow these three suggestions:

1. Be specific. It is not effective to write, "I could improve my communication skills." Of course you can. Instead, write down precisely what you can do to improve your communication skills. For example: "I can spend more time really listening while the other person is talking, instead of thinking about what I'm going to say next."

2. Look beyond the classroom. What goes on outside school often has the greatest impact on your ability to be an effective student.

3. Be courageous. This exercise is a waste of time if done halfheartedly. Be willing to risk. Sometimes you may open a door that reveals a part of yourself that you didn't want to admit was there. The power of this technique is that once you know what the "it" is, you can do something.

Part 1
Time yourself, and for 10 minutes, write as fast as you can and complete the following sentences with anything that comes to mind. Complete each sentence at least 10 times. If you get stuck, don't stop; just write something—even if it's crazy.

It is ineffective when I . . .
It doesn't work when I . . .
I could change . . .

Part 2
When you have completed the first part of the exercise, review what you have written and cross off things that don't make any sense. The sentences that remain represent possible goals for your experience as a master student.

Part 3
Here's the tough part. Time yourself, and for 10 minutes, write as fast as you can. Complete the following sentences with anything that comes to mind. As in Part 1, complete each sentence at least 10 times and just keep writing, even if it sounds silly.

I am very good at . . .
It is effective when I . . .
Something very positive about me is . . .

Part 4
Review your list and circle the things that really fit. This is a good list to keep for those times when you question your own value and worth.

The Discovery and Intention

One way to become a better student is to grit your teeth, grunt, and try harder. There is another way. You can use the Discovery and Intention Journal Entry System to increase your effectiveness with the least possible struggle. It's a way to focus your energy, and it's closely related to the idea of taking a First Step.

The Discovery and Intention Journal Entry System is a little like flying a plane. Airplanes are seldom exactly on course. Human and automatic pilots are always checking and correcting the heading. The resulting path looks like a zigzag. The plane is almost always flying in the wrong direction, but because of constant observation and course correction, it arrives at the right place.

The same system can be used by students. In fact, you have already used it if you completed Journal Entries on pages 3 and 8. (If you haven't, consider doing one right now.) Journal Entries throughout this book are labeled either "Discovery Statement" or "Intention Statement." Each Journal Entry will contain a short set of directions and space in which you can write.

Through Discovery Statements, you can learn "where you are." They are a record of what you learn about yourself as a student—both strengths and weaknesses.

Discovery Statements can also be declarations of what you want, descriptions of your attitudes, statements of your feelings, transcripts of your thoughts, and chronicles of your behavior.

Intention Statements can be used to alter your course. They are statements of your commitment to do a specific task, to take a certain action. An intention arises out of your choice to direct your energy toward a particular goal.

The purpose of this system is not to get you pumped up and excited to go out there and try harder. Discovery and Intention Statements keep you focused on what you want and how you intend to get it.

The Journal Entry process is a cycle. You can write Discovery Statements about where you are and where you want to go. Then you can write Intention Statements about the specific steps you will take to get there.

GOAL

AIRPORT

Journal Entry System

Then you can write Discovery Statements about whether you completed those steps and what you learned in the process, followed by more Intention Statements, and so on. Sometimes the statements will be long and detailed. Usually they will be short, maybe just a line or two. Practice it, and the cycle can become automatic.

Don't panic when you fail to complete an intended task. Straying off course is normal. Simply make the necessary corrections. Miraculous progress may not come immediately. Do not be concerned. Stay with the cycle. Use Discovery Statements to get clear about your world and what you want out of it. Then use Intention Statements to direct your actions. When you notice progress, record it.

The following statement might strike you as radical, but it is true: It often takes the same amount of energy to get what you want in school as it takes to get what you don't want. Sometimes getting what you don't want takes even more effort.

An airplane burns the same amount of fuel flying away from its destination as it does flying toward it, so it pays to stay on course.

You can use the Discovery and Intention Journal Entry System to stay on your own course and get what you want out of school. Consider the guidelines for Discovery Statements and Intention Statements on pages 12 and 13, then develop your own style. Once you get the hang of it, you might discover you can fly.

EXERCISE #4
DEFACE THIS BOOK

Some books should be preserved in pristine condition. This isn't one of them.

There are valid reasons for not writing in any book. For one thing, it decreases the resale value. However, the benefit of writing in your books outweighs that consideration.

Becoming a Master Student is about learning, and learning is an active pursuit, not a passive one. Something happens when you reach out and touch a book with your pen. When you make notes in the margin, you can hear yourself talking with the author. When you doodle and underline, you can see the author's ideas take shape. You can even argue with an author or create your own ideas.

While you're at it, create symbols for reviewing the text later, such as Q for questions or an * for important points. You could also circle words to look up in a dictionary.

To complete this exercise, find something you agree with or disagree with on this page and write a short note in the margin about it. Or draw a diagram. Better yet, do both. Let creativity be your guide. Have fun.

Begin defacing now.

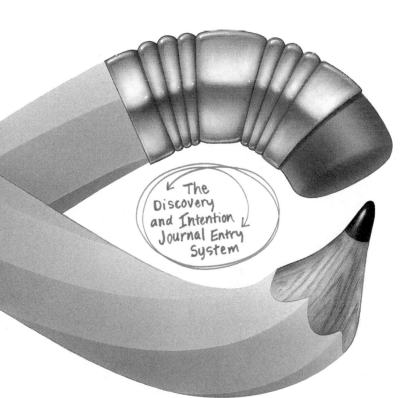

The Discovery and Intention Journal Entry System

Hello Author I Agree

Seven Discovery & Intention

Discovery Statements

1. Discover what you want. You can have more energy when what you're doing leads to what you want. Many students quit school simply because they are unclear about what they want. Writing it can make it clear.

2. Record the specifics. Observe your actions and record the facts. If you spent 90 minutes reading a spy novel instead of your anatomy text, write about it and include the details, such as when you did it, where you did it, and how it felt.

3. Notice your inner voices and pictures. We talk to ourselves constantly in our heads, and our minds manufacture pictures faster than television.

When you notice internal chatter getting in your way, write down what you are telling yourself. If this seems difficult at first, just start writing. The act of writing can trigger a flood of thoughts.

Our mental pictures are especially powerful. Picturing yourself flunking a test is like a rehearsal to do just that, and resisting or ignoring negative images can make them even more powerful. One way to deflate negative images is to describe them in detail.

4. Notice physical sensations. When you avoid a certain kind of accounting problem, note the physical symptoms— a churning stomach, perhaps, or shallow breathing or yawning. Record your observations quickly, as soon as you make them.

Also notice how you feel when you function well. Use Discovery Statements to pinpoint exactly where and when you learn most effectively.

5. Use discomfort as a signal. When you are writing a Discovery Statement and you begin to feel uncomfortable, bored, or tired, that may be a signal that you are about to do valuable work. Stick with it. Tell yourself you can handle the discomfort just a little bit longer. You will be rewarded.

6. Suspend self-judgment. When you are discovering yourself, be gentle. If you continually judge your behaviors as *bad* or *stupid* or *galactically imbecilic*, sooner or later your mind will revolt. Rather than put up with the abuse, it will quit making discoveries. Be kind.

7. Tell the truth. "The truth will set you free" is a cliché. Practice telling the truth, and you might find out why the phrase is so well-worn. The closer you get to the truth, the more powerful your Discovery Statements will be.

And remember, telling the truth requires courage and vigilance. Don't blame yourself when you notice you avoid the truth. Just tell the truth about it.

Intention Statements

1. Make your intentions positive. Instead of writing "I will not fall asleep while studying accounting" write, "I intend to stay awake when studying accounting."

Also avoid the word *try*. Trying is not doing. When we hedge our bets with *try* we can always tell ourselves, "Well, I tried to stay awake." The result is, we fool ourselves into thinking we succeeded.

Statement guidelines

2. Make intentions small and keepable.
Give yourself the opportunity to succeed. Break large goals into small, specific tasks you can accomplish quickly. If you want to get an "A" in biology, ask yourself, "What can I do today?" You might choose to study biology for an extra hour. Make that your intention.

Experience success by choosing your intentions with care. Set goals you can accomplish.

3. Use observable criteria for success.
Experiment with an idea from trainer Robert Mager[1], who suggests that you define your goals through behaviors that can be observed and measured. Rather than writing "I intend to work harder on my history assignments," write, "I intend to review my class notes, and I intend to make summary sheets of my reading." Then, when you review your progress, you can determine more precisely whether you accomplished what you intended.

4. Set time lines. Time lines can focus your attention, especially if used in conjunction with suggestion #2. For example, if you are assigned a term paper, break the assignment into small tasks and set a precise time line for each one. You might write, "I intend to select a topic for my paper by 9 a.m. Wednesday." And remember, you create time lines for your own benefit, not to make yourself feel guilty.

5. Be careful of intentions that depend on others. Your intention might depend on the actions of other people. If you write that you intend for your study group to complete the assignment by Monday, your success depends on other students. Make such intentions carefully; then ask for the assistance of the people they depend on.

6. Anticipate self-sabotage. Be aware of what you might do, consciously or unconsciously, to undermine your intentions. If you intend to study differential equations at 9 p.m., notice when you sit down to watch a two-hour television movie at 8 p.m.

7. Identify your rewards. Rewards that are an integral part of a goal are the most powerful. For example, your reward for earning a degree might be the career you want.

External rewards, such as a movie or an afternoon in the park, are valuable too. These rewards work best when you're willing to withhold them. If you intend to take a nap on Sunday afternoon whether you finish your English assignment or not, the nap is not an effective reward.

Another way to reward yourself is to sit quietly after you have finished your task and savor the feeling. One reason why success breeds success is that it feels good.

PRACTICING CRITICAL THINKING #1

The purpose of this exercise is to explore how your feelings can inhibit your ability to think objectively.

For each of us there are certain issues that trigger strong emotional reactions. For some people, these topics include abortion, gay and lesbian rights, capital punishment, and funding for welfare programs. Your list could include these topics or others.

Create your list in a two-column format on a separate sheet of paper. In one column, write a word or short phrase describing each issue. In the other column, describe the way you typically respond when each issue comes up in conversation or writing.

COLUMN 1	COLUMN 2
Issue	*Response*

Now list what you can do to remain more objective when one of your "hot button" issues comes up.

The *Practicing Critical Thinking* exercises included throughout this book incorporate ideas from Peter Facione, Dean of the College of Arts and Sciences, Santa Clara University. Mr. Facione provided substantial suggestions for these exercises and edited them. He can be contacted through the California Academic Press on the World Wide Web: http://www.calpress.com.

EXERCISE #5
THE DISCOVERY WHEEL

The Discovery Wheel is an opportunity to tell the truth to yourself about the kind of student you are and the kind of student you want to become. This is not a test. There are no trick questions, and the answers will have meaning only for you.

Here are two suggestions to make this exercise more effective.

First, think of it as the beginning of an opportunity to change. There is another Discovery Wheel at the end of this book. You will have a chance to measure your progress, so be honest about where you are now.

Second, lighten up. A little laughter can make self-evaluations a lot more effective.

Here's how the Discovery Wheel works. By the end of this exercise, you will have filled in a circle similar to the one on this page. The Discovery Wheel circle is a picture of how you see yourself as a student. The closer the shading comes to the edge of the circle, the higher the evaluation. In the above example, the student has rated her reading skills low and her note-taking skills high.

It is dangerous, however, to think of these evaluations in terms of "higher" and "lower" if those designations reflect a negative judgment. The Discovery Wheel is not a picture of who you are. It is a picture of how you view your abilities as a student today.

To begin this exercise, read the following statements and award yourself points for each one, using the point system below. Then add up your point total for each section and shade the Discovery Wheel on page 17 to the appropriate level.

5 points
This statement is always or almost always true of me.

4 points
This statement is often true of me.

3 points
This statement is some-times true of me (about half the time).

2 points
This statement is seldom true of me.

1 point
This statement is never or almost never true of me.

1._____I start each term highly motivated, and I stay that way.

2._____I know what I want to get from my education.

3._____I enjoy learning.

4._____I study even when distracted by activities of lower priority.

5._____I am satisfied with how I progress toward achieving goals.

6._____I budget my money and I am in control of my personal finances.

7._____I am excited about the courses I take.

8._____I have a clear idea of the benefits I expect to get from my education.

_____Total score (1) Motivation

1._____I periodically refine my long-term and short-term goals.

2._____I can efficiently use a computer to promote my success in school.

3._____I write a plan for each day and each week.

4._____I assign priorities to what I choose to do each day.

5._____I plan review time so I don't have to cram before tests.

6._____I plan regular recreation time.

7._____I adjust my study time to meet the demands of individual courses.

8._____I have adequate time each day to accomplish what I plan.

_____Total score (2) Time

1._____ I am confident in my ability to remember.

2._____ I remember people's names.

3._____ At the end of a lecture, I can summarize what was presented.

4._____ I apply techniques that enhance my memory skills.

5._____ I can recall information when I'm under pressure.

6._____ I remember important information clearly and easily.

7._____ I can jog my memory when I have difficulty recalling.

8._____ I can relate new information to what I've already learned.

_____ Total score (3) Memory

1._____ I preview and review reading assignments.

2._____ When reading, I underline or highlight important passages.

3._____ When I read, I ask questions about the material.

4._____ When I read textbooks, I am alert and awake.

5._____ I relate what I read to my life.

6._____ I select a reading strategy to fit the type of material I'm reading.

7._____ I take effective notes when I read.

8._____ When I don't understand what I'm reading, I note my questions and find answers.

_____ Total score (4) Reading

1._____ When I am in class, I focus attention.

2._____ I take notes in class.

3._____ I am aware of various methods for taking notes and choose those that work best for me.

4._____ My notes are valuable for review.

5._____ I review class notes within 24 hours.

6._____ I distinguish important material and notice key phrases in a lecture.

7._____ I copy material the instructor writes on the board or overhead projector.

8._____ I can put important concepts into my own words.

_____ Total score (5) Notes

1._____ I feel confident and calm during an exam.

2._____ I manage my time during exams and I am able to complete them.

3._____ I am able to predict test questions.

4._____ I can examine essay questions in light of what I know and come to new and original conclusions during a test.

5._____ I adapt my test-taking strategy to the kind of test I'm taking.

6._____ I understand what essay questions ask and can answer them completely and accurately.

7._____ I start reviewing for tests at the beginning of the term and review regularly.

8._____ My sense of personal worth is independent of my test scores.

_____ Total score (6) Tests

1._____ I am aware of my cultural biases and open to understanding people with different backgrounds.

2._____ I build rewarding relationships with people from other cultures and races.

3._____ I can point out examples of discrimination and effectively respond to them.

4._____ I study in a way that draws on my preferred learning styles.

5._____ I practice using several different learning styles when I study.

6._____ I take specific steps to make a successful transition into higher education.

7._____ I am in regular contact with instructors and students who share my academic interests.

8._____ I effectively integrate schooling with my family and work lives.

_____ Total score (7) Diversity

1._____ I have flashes of insight, and solutions to problems appear to me at unusual times.

2._____ I use brainstorming to generate solutions to a variety of problems.

3._____ When I get stuck on a creative project, I use specific methods to get unstuck.

4._____ I see problems and decisions as opportunities for learning and personal growth.

5._____ I am willing to consider different points of view and alternative solutions.

6._____ I can state the assumptions that underlie a series of assertions.

7._____ I can detect common errors in logic.

8._____ I approach courses in mathematics and science with confidence.

_____ Total score (8) Thinking

1._____I approach writing with confidence.

2._____I can effectively plan and research a large writing assignment.

3._____I create first drafts without stopping to edit or criticize my writing.

4._____I revise my writing for clarity, accuracy, and coherence.

5._____My writing affirms women and is free of sexist expressions.

6._____When writing, I accurately credit ideas and facts from other people.

7._____I know ways to prepare and deliver effective speeches.

8._____I am confident when I speak before others.

_____Total score (9) Writing

1._____I develop and maintain mutually supportive relationships.

2._____I am candid with others about who I am, what I feel, and what I want.

3._____Other people tell me that I am a good listener.

4._____I communicate my upset and anger without blaming others.

5._____I make and keep promises that stretch me to meet my potential.

6._____I am able to learn from various instructors with different teaching styles.

7._____I have the ability to make friends and create valuable relationships in a new place.

8._____I am open to being with people I don't especially like in order to learn from them.

_____Total score (10) Relationships

1._____I have enough energy to study and still fully enjoy areas of my life.

2._____I exercise regularly.

3._____My emotional health supports my ability to learn.

4._____If the situation calls for it, I have enough reserve energy to put in a long day.

5._____I accept my body the way it is.

6._____I notice changes in my physical condition and respond effectively.

7._____I am in control of any alcohol or drugs I put into my body.

8._____The food I eat contributes to my health.

_____Total score (11) Health

1._____I see learning as a lifelong process.

2._____I relate school to what I plan to do for the rest of my life.

3._____I learn by contributing to others.

4._____I revise my plans as I learn, change, and grow.

5._____I am clear about my purpose in life.

6._____I know that I am responsible for my own education.

7._____I take responsibility for the quality of my life.

8._____I am willing to accept challenges even when I'm not sure how to meet them.

_____Total score (12) Purpose

Filling in your Discovery Wheel

Using the total score from each category, shade in each section of the Discovery Wheel. Use different colors if you want. For example, you could use green to denote areas you want to work on. When you have completed the wheel, complete the following Journal Entries.

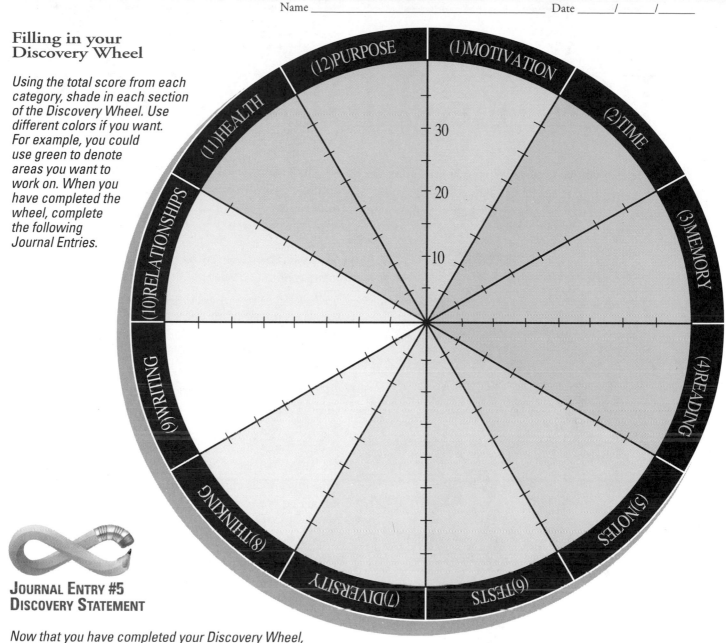

JOURNAL ENTRY #5
DISCOVERY STATEMENT

Now that you have completed your Discovery Wheel, spend a few minutes with it. Get a sense of its weight, shape, and balance. How would you feel if you ran your hands around it? How would it sound if it rolled down a hill? How would it look? Would it roll at all? Is it balanced? Make your observations without judging the wheel as good or bad. Simply be with the picture you have created.

After you have spent a few minutes studying your Discovery Wheel, on a separate sheet of paper, complete the following sentences. Don't worry if you can't think of something to write. Just write whatever comes to mind. Remember, this is not a test.

> *This wheel is an accurate picture of my ability as a student because . . .*
> *My self-evaluation surprises me because . . .*
> *The two areas in which I am strongest are related because . . .*
> *The areas in which I want to improve are . . .*
> *I want to concentrate on improving these areas because . . .*

JOURNAL ENTRY #6
INTENTION STATEMENT

Select one of your discoveries from Journal Entry #5 and plan how you intend to benefit from it.

To gain some practical benefit from this discovery, I will . . .

_____

_____

_____

_____

_____

THE VALUE OF
HIGHER EDUCATION

When you're waist-deep in reading assignments, writing papers, and studying for tests, you might well ask yourself, "Is all this effort going to pay off someday?"

That's a fair question. It gets to a core issue—the value of getting an education beyond high school.

Reassure yourself. The potential benefits of higher education are enormous. To begin, there are economic benefits. Over their lifetimes, college graduates on the average earn more than high school graduates, and that's just one potential payoff. Consider the others explained below.

Learn skills that apply across careers

Jobs that involve responsibility, prestige, and higher incomes depend on self-management skills. These include knowing ways to manage time, resolve conflict, set goals, learn new skills, and control stress. Higher education is a place to practice such skills.

Judging by recent trends, most of us will have multiple careers in our lifetimes. In this environment of constant change, it makes sense to learn skills that apply across careers.

Master the liberal arts

According to one traditional model of education, there are two essential tasks for people to master: use of language and use of numbers. To acquire these skills, students once immersed themselves in seven subjects: grammar, rhetoric, logic, arithmetic, geometry, music, and astronomy. These subjects were called the "liberal" arts. They complemented the fine arts, such as poetry, and the practical arts, such as farming.

This model of liberal education still has something to offer. Today we master the use of language by using the basic processes of communication: reading, writing, speaking, and listening. In addition, courses in mathematics and science help us understand the world in quantitative terms. The abilities to communicate and calculate are essential to almost every profession. Excellence at these skills has long been considered a hallmark of an educated person.

The word *liberal* comes from the Latin verb *libero*, which means "to free." Liberal arts are those that promote critical thinking. Studying them can free us from irrational ideas, half-truths, racism, and prejudice. Beyond this, the liberal arts grant us freedom to explore alternatives and create a system of personal values. Such benefits are priceless, the very basis of political freedom.

Gain a broad vision

It's been said that a large corporation is a collection of departments connected only by a plumbing system. The quip makes a point: As workers in different fields become more specialized, they run the danger of forgetting how to talk to each other.

Higher education can change that. One benefit of studying the liberal arts is the chance to gain a broad vision. Liberally educated people know something about the various kinds of problems tackled in psychology and theology, philosophy and physics, literature and mathematics. They understand how people in all these fields arrive at conclusions and how these fields relate to each other.

Discover your values

We do not spend all of our waking hours at our jobs. That leaves us with a decision that affects the quality of our lives: how to spend leisure time. By cultivating our interest in the arts and community affairs, the liberal arts provide us with many options for activities outside work. These studies add a dimension to life that goes beyond having a job and paying the bills.

Practical people are those who focus on time and money. Yet it's impossible to manage either of these effectively without a clear sense of values. Our values define what we commit our time and money to.

Vocational education is about how to do things that we can get paid for. Through a liberal education, we discover what's worth doing—what activities are worthy of our energy and talents. Both types of education are equally important. No matter where they've attended school, liberally educated people can state what they're willing to bet their lives on.

Discover new interests

Taking a broad range of courses has the potential to change your direction in life. A student previously committed to a career in science might try out a drawing class and eventually switch to a degree in studio arts. Or, a person who swears that she has no aptitude for technical subjects might change her major to computer science after taking an introductory computer class.

To make effective choices about your long-term goals, base those choices on a variety of academic and personal experiences. Even if you don't change majors or switch career directions, you could discover an important avocation or gain a complementary skill. For example, science majors who will eventually write for professional journals can gain value from English courses.

Hang out with the great

Today we enjoy a huge legacy from our ancestors. The creative minds of our species have given us great works of art, systems of science, and technology that defies the imagination. Through higher education, you can gain firsthand knowledge of humanity's greatest creations.

Poet Ezra Pound[2] defined literature as "news that stays news." Most of the writing in newspapers and magazines becomes dated quickly. In contrast, many of the books you read in higher education have passed the hardest test of all—time. Such works have created value for people for decades, sometimes for centuries. These creations are inexhaustible. We can return to them time after time and discover something new. These are the works we can justifiably call great. Hanging out with these works transforms us. Getting to know them exercises our minds as running exercises our bodies.

Through studying the greatest works in many fields, we raise our tastes. We learn ways to distinguish what is superficial and fleeting from what is lasting and profound.

What constitutes a great novel, poem, painting, or piece of music or dance may be different for you than for someone else. Differences in taste reflect the differences in our backgrounds. The point is to find those works that have enduring value for you—and enjoy them for a lifetime.

Join the conversation

In ancient times—long before printing presses, televisions, and computers—people educated themselves by conversing with each other. Students in ancient Athens were often called *peripatetic* (a word that means "walking around") because they were frequently seen strolling around the city, engaged in heated philosophical debate.

Since then, the debate has deepened and broadened. Our finest scientists and artists are voices in a conversation that spans centuries and crosses cultures. This is a conversation about the nature of truth and beauty, knowledge and compassion, good and evil—ideas that form the very basis of our society. Robert Hutchins[3], former president of the University of Chicago, called this the "great conversation." By studying this conversation, we take on the most basic human problems: coping with death and suffering, creating a just society, living with meaning and purpose.

Our greatest thinkers left behind visible records. You'll find them in libraries, concert halls, museums, and scientific laboratories across the world. Through higher education, you gain a front-row seat for the great conversation—and an opportunity to add your own voice.

Education's worth it . . .

A college education is one of the most durable and worthwhile investments you can make. It's also one of the safest investments possible. When you are clear about what you want, education is usually a way to get it.

Education is a unique purchase—one of the few things you can buy that will last your lifetime. It can't rust, corrode, break down, or wear out. Education can't be stolen, burned, repossessed, or destroyed. Education is a purchase that becomes a permanent part of you. Once you have it, no one can take it away.

Investing money in your abilities is also one of the safest investments you can make. Money invested in land, gold, oil, or stocks can easily be lost. When you invest in yourself, you can't lose. Over a lifetime, a college graduate can expect to earn about $1 million more on the average than a person whose education stops with high school. Education also pays off in job promotions and career satisfaction.

The list of possible benefits continues. Higher education has been suggested as the source of everything from better health to happier marriages. With higher education, you can:

- grasp world events with more ease.
- have more economic and social opportunities.
- be better equipped to be a parent.
- learn how to learn—and how to thrive on change.
- enjoy increased flexibility on the job (with tight supervision less likely).
- enjoy improved retirement benefits.
- have greater travel opportunities.
- improve the likelihood that your children will further their education.

In short, education is a good deal. It is worth investing in again and again as circumstances change and you update your skills.

There are many ways to pay for school, and several ideas are listed in the article that follows. The kind of help you get depends on your background and needs.

Applying for financial aid has little to do with "being poor." Your prospects for aid depend greatly on the costs of the school you attend. Do not assume that your application for financial aid will be rejected.

A plan for paying for your entire education makes staying to the end a more realistic possibility. If you start every term wondering where you are going to get the money, you are more likely to drop out. Create a master plan—a long-term budget listing how much you need to complete your education and where you plan to get the money.

When you know precisely how much you need, ask for help. Every college has someone to assist with this. You can also get help from publications in financial aid offices and most public and college libraries. One useful publication is *The Student Guide*, published yearly; for a copy, write to the U.S. Department of Education, Office of Student Financial Assistance, Washington, D.C. 20202-5464. Another source of information is the Federal Student Aid Information Center, P. O. Box 84, Washington, D.C. 20044, 1-800-433-3243.

JOURNAL ENTRY #7
DISCOVERY STATEMENT

On a separate piece of paper write a one-sentence statement of your mission for taking part in higher education. Allow yourself to write many drafts of this mission statement, and review it periodically as you continue your education.

You might find it difficult to boil this statement down to one sentence. If so, write a paragraph or more. Then look for the sentence that seems most charged with energy for you. Some possible examples:

- *My purpose for being in school is to gain skills I can use to contribute to others.*
- *My purpose for being in school is to live an abundant life that is filled with happiness, health, love and, wealth.*
- *My purpose for being in school is to enjoy myself, make lasting friendships, and follow the lead of my interests.*

. . . and you can pay for it

SEVENTEEN PLACES TO FIND MONEY

1. Pell Grants are financed by the federal government and do not have to be repaid.

2. Supplemental Educational Opportunity Grants (SEOG) are designed to complement other forms of financial aid.

3. College work-study arranges for jobs on or off campus. Your hours of work will be based on your class schedules and your academic progress.

4. Perkins Loans are long-term loans based on financial need and have low interest rates.

5. Federal Family Education Loan Programs offer low-interest loans from banks and credit unions. Ask about Stafford Loans, Supplemental Loans, and the PLUS program.

6. Scholarships are available through most colleges for outstanding performance in athletics, academics, or the arts. Also inquire at fraternal, service, educational, and social organizations.

7. The Veterans Administration has money available for some veterans and their dependents.

8. Active military personnel can take advantage of various financial aid programs by contacting their local personnel office.

9. Company assistance programs, provided by employers, might offer financial aid for employees to attend school while working.

10. Social Security payments are available up to age 18 for unmarried students with a deceased parent, or a parent who is disabled or drawing Social Security benefits.

11. State governments often provide grants and other forms of aid.

12. The U.S. Bureau of Indian Affairs has financial aid available for some Native American students.

13. The local branch of your state employment office provides information about government programs that are set up to train the unemployed. Ask about the JTPA (Job Training Partnership Act) and WIN (Work Incentive) programs.

14. Relatives will often provide financial help for a dedicated student.

15. Personal savings comprise the bulk of money spent on higher education.

16. Employment is another way students can get additional money. Working in a job related to your future career field can supplement your education as well as your finances.

17. Selling something might be an option of last resort, but it is an option. Consider the money you have tied up in a car, motorcycle, horse, piano, house, or hobby.

Note: Programs listed in this article change constantly. In some cases, money is limited and application deadlines are critical. Be sure to get the most current information.

EXERCISE #6
EDUCATION BY THE HOUR

Determine exactly what it costs you to go to school. Fill in the blanks. Use totals for a semester, quarter, or whatever term system your school uses.

Tuition	$_____
Books	$_____
Fees	$_____
Transportation	$_____
Clothing	$_____
Food	$_____
Housing	$_____
Entertainment	$_____
Other (e.g., insurance, medical, child care)	$_____
Subtotal:	$_____
Salary you could earn per term if you weren't in school	$_____
Total (A)	$_____

Figure out how many classes you attend in one term. This is the number of your scheduled class periods per week multiplied by the number of weeks in your school term Put that figure here:

Total (B)	$_____

Divide the Total (B) into the Total (A) and put that amount here: $_____

This is what is costs you to go to one class one time.

Ways to
Change a habit

When people talk about how difficult it is to change a behavior they don't like, they often resort to an explanation: "Well, that's just my nature." Often what's implied by this statement is "And because it's my nature, don't expect me to change."

Perhaps none of us can do much about human nature, especially our individual natures. It could be that we're pretty much stuck with them. Yet the "it's just human nature" school of thought robs us of the opportunity to change. There's another perspective we can take—one that opens up far more possibilities for the quality of our lives.

Instead of talking about human nature, we can talk about habits. We can speak of our ability to control habits. We can change habits by eliminating unwanted ones and adding new ones. People stop smoking, drinking, and overeating. People also start to exercise, fasten seat belts, and develop scores of other effective habits.

Thinking about ourselves as creatures of habits instead of as creatures defined by our nature gives us power. Then we are not faced with the monumental task of changing our very nature. Rather, we can take on the difficult yet doable job of changing our habits.

Success in school and life is largely a matter of cultivating effective habits. At the same time, the new habit that you choose does not have to make headlines. It can be one simple, small change in behavior.

Following are some steps in changing a habit.

Tell the truth

If you completed the First Step exercise in this chapter, you already know about telling the truth. The Discovery Statements you write throughout this book are also examples of truth telling.

Facing the truth about any habit—from falling asleep in class to cheating on tests—frees people. Without taking that step, our efforts to change may be as ineffective as rearranging the deck chairs on the *Titanic.* Telling the truth allows us to see what's actually sinking the ship.

When we admit what's really going on in our lives, our defenses are down. We're open to help from others. The support we need to change the habit has a place to enter.

Commit to use the new behavior

After choosing a new habit, promise to use it and make a plan for when and how. Answer questions such as these: When will you apply the new habit? Where will you be? Who will be with you? What will you be seeing, hearing, touching, saying, or doing? How, exactly, will you think, speak, or act differently?

Take the person who always snacks when she studies. Each time she sits down to read, she positions a bag of potato chips within easy reach. For her, opening a book is a cue to start chewing. Snacking is especially easy given the place she chooses to study: the kitchen. She chooses to

change this habit by studying at a desk in her bedroom instead of at the kitchen table. What's more, she plans to store the potato chips in an inconvenient place: a shelf she can't reach without standing on a chair. And every time she feels the urge to bite into a potato chip, she decides to drink from a glass of water instead.

Affirm your intention

You can pave the way for a new behavior by clearing a mental path for it. To do so, see yourself carrying out your plan. Before you apply the new behavior, rehearse it in your mind. Mentally picture what actions you will take and in what order.

Say that you plan to improve your handwriting when taking notes. Imagine yourself in class with a blank notebook poised before you. See yourself taking up a finely crafted pen. Notice how comfortable it feels in your hand. See yourself writing clearly and legibly. You can even picture how you will make individual letters—the *e*'s, *i*'s, and *r*'s. Then, when class is over, see yourself reviewing your notes and taking pleasure in how easy they are to read.

Such scenes are more vivid if you include all your senses. Round out your mental picture by adding sounds, textures, and colors.

In short, you can act as if your intention is already a reality, as if the new habit is already a part of you. Be the change you want to see—today. In some cases, this may be enough to change the old habit completely.

Start with a small change

You can sometimes rearrange a whole pattern of behaviors by changing one small habit. If you have a habit of being late for class, and if you want to change that process, then be on time to one class. As soon as you change the old pattern by getting ready and going on time to one class, you'll likely find yourself arriving at all of your classes on time. You may even start arriving everywhere else on time.

If you know that you are usually nervous, you don't have to change how you react in all situations at all times. Just change your nervous behavior in one setting. Like magic, watch the rest of your nervousness lessen or even disappear. The joy of this process is watching one small change of habit ripple through your whole life.

Get feedback and support

This is a crucial step and a place where many plans for change break down. It's easy to practice your new behavior with great enthusiasm for a few days. After the initial rush of excitement, however, things can get a little tougher. We begin to find excuses for slipping back into an old habit: "One more cigarette won't hurt." "I can get back to my diet tomorrow." "It's been a tough day. I deserve this beer."

One way to get feedback is to bring other people into the picture. Ask others to remind you when you are changing your habit. If you want to stop an old behavior, such as cramming for tests, then it often works to tell everyone you know that you intend to stop. When you want to start a new behavior, though, consider telling only a few people—those who truly support your efforts. Starting new habits may call for the more focused, long-lasting support that close friends or family members can give.

Support from others can be as simple as a quick phone call: "Hi. Have you started that outline for your research paper yet?" Or it can be as formal as a support group that meets once weekly to review everyone's goals and action plans.

You are probably the most effective source for your own support and feedback. You know yourself better than anyone else and can design a system to monitor your behavior. You can create your own charts or diagrams to track your behavior or you can write about your progress in your journal. Figure out a way to monitor your progress.

Practice, practice, practice . . . without reproach

Psychologists such as B.F. Skinner[4] define learning as a stable change in behavior that comes as a result of practice. This idea is key to changing habits. Act on your intention. If you fail or forget, let go of any self-judgment. Just keep practicing the new habit and allow whatever time it takes to make a change.

Accept the feelings of discomfort that may come with a new habit. Keep practicing the new behavior, even if it feels unnatural. Trust the process. You will grow into the new behavior. Keep practicing until it becomes as natural as breathing. However, if this new habit doesn't work, simply note what happened (without guilt or blame), select a new behavior, and begin this cycle of steps again.

Going back to square one doesn't mean you've failed. Even when you don't get the results you want from a new behavior, you learn something valuable in the process. Once you understand ways to change one habit, you understand ways to change many habits.

JOURNAL ENTRY #8
INTENTION STATEMENT

Choose one behavior you want to change. Review the article "Ways to change a habit." Then select one or two suggestions and on a separate sheet of paper, write how you will use them to change your behavior. Begin by writing: I intend to . . .

Ideas are tools

There are many ideas in this book. Don't believe any of them. Instead, think of them as tools. For example, you use a hammer for a purpose—to drive a nail. When you use a new hammer, you might notice its shape, its weight, and its balance. You don't try to figure out whether the hammer is "right." You use it. If it works, you use it again. If it doesn't work, you get a different hammer.

This is not the attitude most people adopt when they encounter new ideas. The first thing most people do with new ideas is measure them against old ones. If a new idea conflicts with an old one, the new one is likely to be rejected.

People have plenty of room in their lives for different kinds of hammers, but they tend to limit their capacity for different kinds of ideas. A new idea, at some level, is a threat to their very being—unlike a new hammer, which is simply a new hammer.

Most of us have a built-in desire to be right. Our ideas, we often think, represent ourselves. And when we identify with our ideas, they assume new importance in our lives. We put them on our mantels. We hang them on our walls. We wear them on our T-shirts and display them on our bumpers. We join associations of people who share our most beloved ideas. We make up rituals about them, compose songs about them, and write stories about them. We declare ourselves dedicated to these ideas. Sometimes, we are even willing to die for them.

Some ideas are worth dying for. But please note: This book does not contain any of those ideas. The ideas on these pages are strictly "hammers."

Imagine someone defending a hammer. Picture this person holding up a hammer and declaring, "I hold this hammer to be self-evident. Give me this hammer or give me death. Those other hammers are evil. There are only two kinds of people in this world: people who believe in this hammer and infidels."

That ridiculous picture makes a point. This book is not a manifesto. It's a toolbox, and tools are meant to be used. This approach to ideas is much like one advocated by psychologist and philosopher William James[5]. His approach to philosophy, which he called *pragmatism*, emphasized the usefulness of ideas as a criterion of truth. James liked to talk about the "cash value" of an idea—whether it leads to new actions and new results.

If you read about a tool in this book that doesn't sound "right" or one that sounds a little goofy, remember that the ideas here are for using, not believing. Suspend your judgment. Test the idea for yourself.

If it works, use it. It if doesn't, don't.

Ask: What if that's true?

When presented with a new idea, many people take pride in being critical thinkers. They look for problems. They continue to doubt the idea until there's clear proof. They probe for weaknesses. Their main question seems to be "What's wrong with this idea?"

This approach can be useful at times, and it is just one approach. When we constantly look for what's wrong with new ideas, we may miss how they can be useful.

A different and potentially more powerful approach is to ask "What if that idea were true?" This opens all sorts of new possibilities and variations. Rather than looking for what's wrong, we can look for what's potentially valuable. Faced with a new idea, we can stay in the inquiry, look deeper, and go further.

Keep looking for answers

The airplane, the light bulb, the notion of the unconscious, the invention of the transistor and the computer chip—these and many other tools became possible when their inventors practiced the art of continually looking for additional answers.

Another way to expand your toolbox is to keep looking for answers. Much of your education will be about finding answers to questions. Every subject you study—from algebra to history to philosophy—poses a unique set of questions. Some of the most interesting questions are those that admit many answers: How can we create a just society? How can we transmit our values to the next generation? What are the purposes of higher education? How can we prevent an ecological crisis?

Other questions are more personal: What career shall I choose? Shall I get married? Where shall I live and how shall I spend my leisure time? What shall I have, do, and be during my time on earth?

Perhaps you already have answers to these questions. Answers are wonderful, especially when they relate to our most persistent and deeply felt questions. Answers can also get in the way. Once we're convinced that we have the answer, it's easy to stop looking for more answers. We then stop learning. Our range of possible actions becomes limited.

Instead of latching on to one answer, we can look for more. Instead of being content with the first or easiest options that come to mind, we can keep searching. Even when we're convinced that we've finally handled a problem, we can brainstorm until we find five more solutions.

When we keep looking for answers, we uncover fresh possibilities for thinking, feeling, and behaving. Like children learning to walk, we experience the joy of discovery.

A caution

A word of caution: Any tool—whether it's a hammer, a wrench, or a study technique—is designed to do a specific job. A master mechanic carries a variety of tools because no single tool works for all jobs. If you throw a tool away because it doesn't work in one situation, you won't be able to pull it out later, when it's just what you need. So if an idea doesn't work for you and if you are satisfied you gave it a fair chance, don't throw it away. File it away instead. The idea might come in handy sooner than you think.

And remember, this book is not about figuring out the "right" way. Even the "ideas are tools" idea is not "right." It's a hammer... (or maybe a saw).

**PRACTICING
CRITICAL THINKING #2**

This exercise is an experiment in creative thinking suggested by Power Process #1: "Ideas are tools." When we see ideas as tools, one of our aims can be to create many possible solutions when we're faced with a problem. That way, we have a bigger "tool box"—more options from which we can choose.

Describe in writing a problem you face in your academic or personal life right now—anything from handling conflict with an instructor to finding a new day care provider. Perhaps you already have a possible solution to this problem in mind. Great. Now create at least five more solutions. Whenever possible, list solutions that seem to contradict each other.

Describe your problem and list your possible solutions on a separate sheet of paper.

Next, write about any change in the way you see this problem after creating alternative solutions.

**EXERCISE #7
MAYBE IT'S YOUR BREATH**

The way you breathe affects the way you think, and the way you think affects the way you breathe. A good supply of oxygen to the brain is essential for focused concentration. The next time you find your mind wandering, take a short break and do the following exercise. Read all the directions; then take a moment to practice this technique.

1. Sit up in your chair in a relaxed position, head straight and hands uncrossed in your lap.

2. Close your eyes and take 20 or 30 seconds to relax. Let go of any tension in your face, neck, and shoulders.

3. Inhale, breathing deeply into your abdomen. Your stomach will expand when you breathe deeply.

4. When you have filled your lungs with air, pause; purse your lips as if you were about to whistle; then exhale evenly and forcefully through the small hole between your lips.

5. At the end of your exhalation, pause; then push out the last bit of remaining air in three short, forceful puffs.

6. Repeat this process three to five times.

7. When finished, sit quietly for a minute, observing the rise and fall of your abdomen as you breathe normally.

Learning Styles—

Discovering how you learn

The theory that people learn differently is a fairly new topic in educational psychology, one that's generated a lot of research activity in the last decade. Today many teachers realize that these findings can make a difference in their ability to reach students. As a student, you can also take advantage of this research to promote your own success.

You have already learned thousands of things in your life. Much of this learning took place naturally, outside a classroom, and without any conscious knowledge of learning styles. Some of this learning took place in the classroom, though that experience might not have reflected your natural learning style. In this case, knowing more about how you learn can help you take charge of your education and create effective learning anytime, anyplace.

When you read the article titled "The master student" later on in this chapter and wonder how to apply these ideas to your own life, you may want to revisit *this* article. Knowing about learning styles is one way to make learning—both inside and outside the classroom— a seamless activity in your quest to unleash the master student inside you.

Four stages of learning

There are many theories about learning styles. This article focuses on one that has had a wide acceptance and influence—the experiential learning theory explained by David Kolb[6], a professor at Case Western Reserve University. When we learn naturally and learn well, explains Kolb, we tend to go through four stages in understanding our experience:

Stage 1: Some of us want to know why we are learning things. We seek a purpose for information and a personal connection with the content. This occurs during Stage 1 of the learning cycle.

Stage 2: Some people crave the kind of ideas and facts presented in the classroom. Often, such people are not so concerned about how this material will relate to their personal lives. Instead, these students are eager to learn for the sheer pleasure of learning. This occurs during Stage 2 of the learning cycle.

Stage 3: Some people hunger for an opportunity to experiment with the knowledge they gain in the classroom. They want to see if the facts they learn actually work in daily life. These learners ask: Does this idea make sense? Is it usable? Such questions occur during Stage 3 of the learning cycle.

Stage 4: Some people are more concerned about how they can use what they learn in making a difference in their lives and the world as a whole. These people do well in mixing with others, enjoy group activities, create "on their feet," and are usually vocal in a group.

The Learning Style Inventory

Complete the Learning Style Inventory that follows to discover more about your preferred learning stages. On the following page are 12 sentences with choices of endings. Rank the endings for each sentence according to how well you think each one fits the way you go about learning something.

Recall some recent situations where you learned something new, perhaps in a job or at school. Then, using the spaces provided, write a "4" next to the sentence ending that seems most like the way you learn. Continue ranking the sentence endings down to "1" for the ending that seems least like the way you learn.

Please do not make ties. This is a forced-choice inventory that does not allow for ties. You must choose a 4, 3, 2, or 1 for each sentence. Before you begin, remove the blank sheet of paper following page LSI-2. Press firmly so your number is copied on the page underneath the questions.

Do this inventory quickly. Time yourself and complete the 12 sentences in about six minutes. Allow another 15 to 20 minutes to score the inventory. Remember, this is not a test. There are no "right" answers.

Here's an example of a completed sentence set:

A. When I learn:

  _2_ I am happy.   _3_ I am fast.   _4_ I am logical.   _1_ I am careful.

Remove the blank sheet of paper following this page. Then, press firmly while completing the sentences below.

REMEMBER: 4 = MOST LIKE YOU   3 = SECOND MOST LIKE YOU   2 = THIRD MOST LIKE YOU   1 = LEAST LIKE YOU

1. When I learn:

_____ I like to deal with my feelings.   _____ I like to think about ideas.   _____ I like to be doing things.   _____ I like to watch and listen.

2. I learn best when:

_____ I listen and watch carefully.   _____ I rely on logical thinking.   _____ I trust my hunches and feelings.   _____ I work hard to get things done.

3. When I am learning:

_____ I tend to reason things out.   _____ I am responsible about things.   _____ I am quiet and reserved.   _____ I have strong feelings and reactions.

4. I learn by:

_____ feeling.   _____ doing.   _____ watching.   _____ thinking.

5. When I learn:

_____ I am open to new experiences.   _____ I look at all sides of issues.   _____ I like to analyze things, break them down into their parts.   _____ I like to try things out.

6. When I am learning:

_____ I am an observing person.   _____ I am an active person.   _____ I am an intuitive person.   _____ I am a logical person.

7. I learn best from:

_____ observation.   _____ personal relationships.   _____ rational theories.   _____ a chance to try out and practice.

8. When I learn:

_____ I like to see results from my work.   _____ I like ideas and theories.   _____ I take my time before acting.   _____ I feel personally involved in things.

9. I learn best when:

_____ I rely on my observations.   _____ I rely on my feelings.   _____ I can try things out for myself.   _____ I rely on my ideas.

10. When I am learning:

_____ I am a reserved person.   _____ I am an accepting person.   _____ I am a responsible person.   _____ I am a rational person.

11. When I learn:

_____ I get involved.   _____ I like to observe.   _____ I evaluate things.   _____ I like to be active.

12. I learn best when:

_____ I analyze ideas.   _____ I am receptive and open-minded.   _____ I am careful.   _____ I am practical.

Interpreting your Learning Style Graph

When you connect the X's on the Learning Style Graph (page LSI-5), you create a learning profile. This profile indicates the stages of learning you prefer. The four learning stages are Diverging, Assimilating, Converging, and Accommodating.

If you prefer Diverging (Stage 1), your profile probably looks like one of these:

You like to consider a situation from different points of view. While in this stage of the learning cycle, you determine why it is important to learn a new concept, strategy, idea, technique, or method.

If you prefer Assimilating (Stage 2), your profile resembles one of these:

You enjoy absorbing the information you have learned into a complete understanding. When you are in this stage of the learning cycle, you are interested in knowing what strategies, ideas, techniques, or methods are important. You value learning lots of facts and then arranging these facts in a logical and concise manner.

If you prefer Converging (Stage 3), your profile looks like one of these:

You like to take the information you've gathered and try it out to see if it works. You ask: Does what I learned make sense? Can I use this information to improve my current situation? While you are in this stage of the learning cycle, you want to know how the strategy, idea, technique or method works. During this stage, it is important to find practical applications for what you learn.

If you prefer Accommodating (Stage 4), your profile looks like one of these:

You like to take what you've practiced and find other uses for it. While in this stage of the learning process, you ask: Where else in my life could I use this newly gained skill or information? During this stage, you seek ways to relate what you've learned to other areas of your life.

Some profiles combine portions of all four stages. The profile below reflects a learner who is focused primarily on gathering information—lots of information! People with this profile often like to gather information. They tend to ask for additional facts from an instructor, or ask where can they go to discover more about a subject:

The following profile indicates a learner who focuses more on understanding what he or she learns and less on gathering lots of information. People with this profile often like smaller chunks of information with plenty of time to digest them. Long lectures can be difficult for these learners:

The profile below indicates a learner who is fairly well balanced. People who have this profile can be highly adaptable. They tend to learn no matter what the instructor does in the classroom. These people generally enjoy learning and do well in school:

NOTE: While you may have higher scores in some areas than in others, remember that you use all four ways of learning.

Scoring your inventory

Now that you have taken the Learning Style Inventory, it is time to interpret the results and create your learning profile.

1. Add up all the numbers you gave to the items marked with brown F-shaped letters. Then write that total to the right in the blank titled "BROWN F" TOTAL. Also total all the numbers for the "TEAL W's", "PURPLE T's", and "ORANGE D's."

"BROWN F" TOTAL _____   "TEAL W" TOTAL _____

"PURPLE T" TOTAL _____   "ORANGE D" TOTAL _____

2. Add the four totals together to arrive at a Grand Total. This Grand Total should equal 120. If you have something other than 120, go back and re-add the colored letters. It was probably just an addition error.

GRAND TOTAL _____

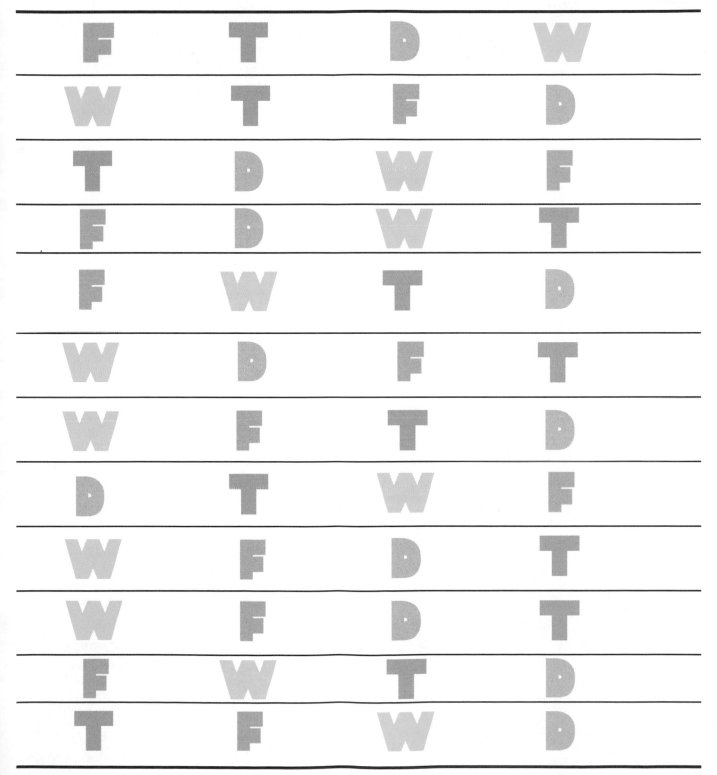

3. So that your scores can be used to compile data about students' learning preferences, please provide the following information about yourself. Place a check next to the following items that apply to you:

GENDER:
❑ Male
❑ Female

AGE:
❑ 15-20
❑ 21-30
❑ 31-40
❑ 41-50
❑ 51-60
❑ Over 60

ATTEND SCHOOL:
❑ Full-time
❑ Part-time

TYPE OF SCHOOL:
❑ Technical
❑ Community college
❑ Four-year college
❑ University

SIZE OF SCHOOL:
❑ Under 5,000
❑ 5,000-10,000
❑ Over 10,000

WORK:
❑ Full-time
❑ Part-time
❑ Do not work

4. Tear out this page in order to transfer your totals from page LSI-3 to the Learning Style Graph on the following page (see instruction number 5). Then, give this page to your instructor so your group's scores can be nationally tabulated.

IMPORTANT: Tear out the blank sheet of paper following page LSI-5 before continuing this exercise.

Instructors, please mail a collection of these student forms to:

College Survival
2075 Foxfield Road, Suite 100
St. Charles, IL 60174

The Learning Style Graph

5. After removing the blank piece of paper that follows this page, transfer your totals to the lines on the Learning Style Graph below. On the brown (F) line, find the number that corresponds to your "BROWN F" total on page LSI-3. Then write an "X" on this number. Do the same for your "TEAL W", "PURPLE T", and "ORANGE D" totals.

6. Now, draw straight lines to connect the four X's. For an example, see the illustration to the right.

Each line on this graph stands for a different aspect of learning.

CE stands for Concrete Experience ("Feeling"). Your number on this line indicates your preference for learning things that have personal meaning. If you prefer concrete experience, you like to learn things that you feel are important and relevant to you today.

RO stands for Reflective Observation ("Watching"). Your number on this line indicates how important it is for you to think about the things you are learning. If you prefer reflective observation, you probably find it important to watch others as they learn about a topic you are studying. You like to plan things out and take time to make sure that you understand a topic accurately.

AC stands for Abstract Conceptualization ("Thinking"). Your number on this line indicates your preference for learning ideas, facts, and figures. If you enjoy abstract conceptualization, you like to think, to absorb many concepts and lots of information on a new topic.

AE stands for Active Experimentation ("Doing"). Your number on this line indicates your preference for applying ideas, trial and error, and practicing what you have learned. You enjoy doing—hands-on activities.

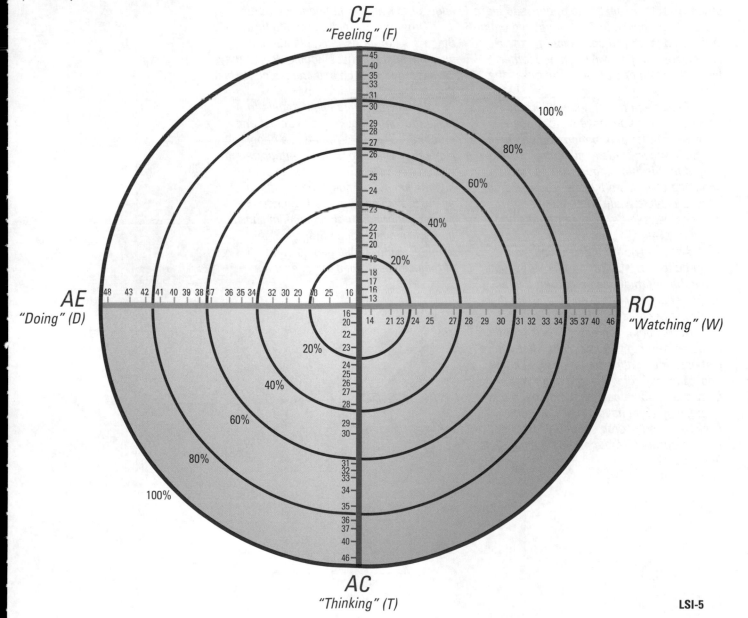

One way to understand the four stages is to see how they relate to actual examples of learning. Consider two activities: learning to ride a bicycle and learning to bungee jump.

Example 1:
Learning to ride a bicycle

When you learn to ride a bicycle, your learning begins with developing an interest in the task. This is natural. Unless otherwise coerced, people seldom take the time to learn a skill they find uninteresting. As children, people become interested in riding a bicycle for many reasons—to keep up with their friends or to find a way to travel that's faster than walking or riding a tricycle.

The cycle of learning begins with a choice—in this case, a choice about whether to learn to ride a bicycle. To make this choice, you first see or hear about a bicycle, reflect on this experience, and think about what to do next. One option is to learn more about riding a bicycle. A second option is to decide that you don't want to ride a bicycle, or that you will learn at another time. Choosing one of these options is the focus of Stage 1.

If you decide that riding a bicycle is important, then you move on to Stage 2. Here you gather information that can help you succeed in actually riding the bicycle. To gather this information, you can watch someone else ride a bicycle. You can also sit on a bicycle while someone else explains what to do with your hands and feet while riding.

After you gather information, you proceed to Stage 3. During this stage, you see if the information you gathered can actually help you ride a bicycle. To do this, you must get on a bicycle and ride.

At this point you enter Stage 4. In this stage of learning you integrate what you've just practiced with other things you know about bicycle riding. Even though you understand some basic mechanics of bike riding, you might have other questions: What if I need to stop suddenly? How do I turn a corner? What can I do if a dog gets in my path?

In turn, these questions create an interest (Stage 1) in gathering more information (Stage 2) that you can experiment with (Stage 3) and combine with your working knowledge of bicycle riding (Stage 4). This illustrates how one learning experience generates similar experiences, leading you through the learning cycle many times.

Example 2:
Learning to bungee jump

Perhaps you've experienced bungee jumping yourself or watched someone else do it. Many people prefer to watch this activity rather than participate. They witness a bungee jump and come to a conclusion: "This is one thing that I don't need to learn!" If this is true for you, then your learning ends with Stage 1. You choose not to gather information—a Stage 2 activity. For example, you don't climb up onto a platform, look over the edge, or ask how to put on ankle straps.

Other people might proceed through Stage 2. After gathering facts about bungee jumping, some of these people decide they have learned enough and choose not to take the plunge.

However, others might decide to make the jump, moving on to action and practice—Stage 3. When these people jump, they will automatically integrate the experience with what they know about bungee jumping. And if they decide to jump again, they might even add some new movement or flair to their jump. In short, they will move through Stage 4 of the learning cycle. These people can truly say of themselves, "I'm a bungee jumper."

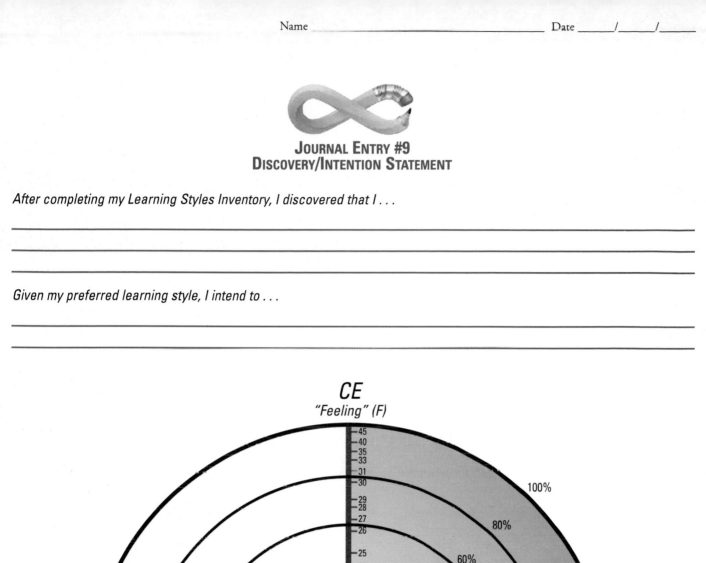

JOURNAL ENTRY #9
DISCOVERY/INTENTION STATEMENT

After completing my Learning Styles Inventory, I discovered that I . . .

_____

_____

_____

Given my preferred learning style, I intend to . . .

_____

_____

_____

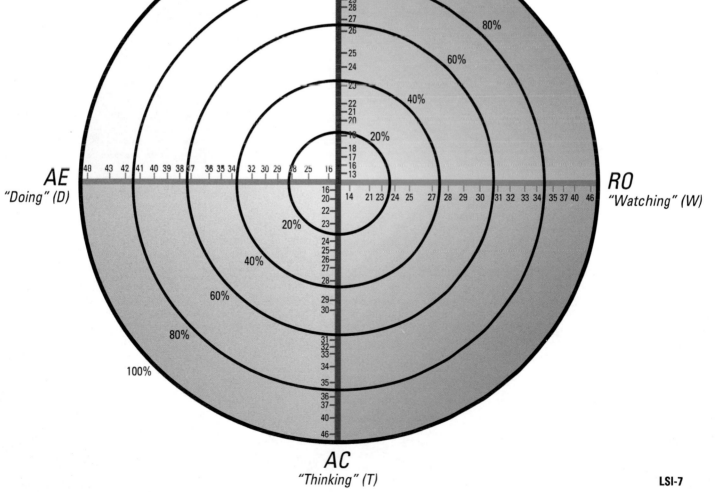

Tear out this page and give it to your instructor.

Using Your Learning Profile to Succeed in School

To get the most value from your learning profile, find benefits in knowing more about how you learn. Look for ways to apply this knowledge in school and at work. Consider the suggestions that follow.

Tolerate discomfort

Discomfort is a natural part of the learning process. If you struggle during a particular stage of learning, allow yourself to feel the discomfort. Low performance during certain stages of the learning cycle is okay.

Also keep in mind that the learning cycle includes all four stages. Neglecting certain stages or moving too quickly through them can interrupt your learning. With appropriate practice, you can expand your preferences and skills to include all four stages.

Match activities to your learning profile

Use your learning profile when choosing your major or planning your career. In either case, you can focus on courses or activities that match your learning preferences. Delegate other tasks to people with appropriate preferences, or ask these people for help.

Adjust your learning strategies

Kolb's work reminds us of a common-sense truth: We prefer to learn things that are important to us—ideas and skills that have some personal meaning in our lives. Sometimes this fails to happen in school, when teachers and students operate without creating *personal meaning* (as in Stage 1), providing adequate time for *practice* (Stage 3), or *integrating* the content with personal meaning (Stage 4). Many teachers do excel at *delivering content* and facts (Stage 2).

You can compensate for this in at least two ways. One is to find out more about your learning preferences. You did this when you completed the Learning Style Inventory. To build on this knowledge, you can adjust your learning strategies in the following ways:

- If you have a strong preference for Stage 1, you are likely to spend time observing others and planning before taking action. You probably also enjoy working with other students. To assist yourself in school, ask questions that help you understand why it is important for you to learn about a specific topic.

- If you have a strong preference for Stage 2, you are skilled at understanding theories and concepts. When in a learning situation, you are likely to enjoy lectures and individual class assignments. Chances are that you also enjoy solitary time and are not fond of working in groups. To assist yourself in school, ask questions that help you gather enough information to understand what you're learning.

  At this point you might increase your effectiveness by choosing not to concentrate equally on all the material in a chapter or content area. Ask your instructor to point out the topics of highest priority. For example, when you complete reading assignments, you might focus primarily on specific parts of a chapter or book.

- If you have a strong preference for Stage 3, you probably excel at working with your hands and at laboratory stations. You're likely to be a pragmatic learner. When in a learning situation, you're interested in knowing how things work. In addition, you probably enjoy working alone or with a small group. To assist yourself in school, ask questions that help you understand how something works and experiment with new ideas.

  Allow time to practice and apply what you learn. You can conduct experiments, do projects, complete homework, create presentations, conduct research, tabulate findings, or even write a rap song that summarizes key concepts. Such activities provide an opportunity to internalize your learning through hands-on practice.

- If you have a strong preference for Stage 4, you are skilled at teaching others what you've learned and helping others see the importance of this new learning. When in a learning situation, you like to apply facts and theories in everyday life. You probably enjoy carrying out plans and having new, challenging experiences. You also enjoy working with others and are likely to have a large social circle. To assist yourself in school, ask questions that help you determine where else in your life you can apply new learning.

Ask for opportunities to demonstrate your understanding. You could teach what you've learned to someone else, present findings from your research, report results from your experiments, demonstrate how your project works, or sing the rap song you wrote.

Stay in charge of your learning

When they experience difficulty in school, some students say: "This instructor can't teach me." "The classroom is not conducive to the way I learn." "This teacher creates tests that are too hard for me." "In class we never have time for questions." "The instructor doesn't teach to my learning style."

Such statements can become a mental crutch, a set of beliefs that prevent you from taking charge of your learning. To support your self-responsibility, make statements such as: "I will find a way to apply this idea." "I can find other people to answer my questions." "I am discovering new ways to learn."

Associate with students who have different learning profiles

If your instructors ask you to form groups to complete assignments, avoid joining a group where everyone shares your learning profile. Instead, join with students whose learning preferences differ from yours. This is one way you can develop skills in all stages of the learning cycle.

Use this book with the stages of learning in mind

Each stage of learning is part of a natural cycle. Skilled students learn in all four ways. If you strongly prefer one stage, then experiment with the others. *Becoming a Master Student* can help. This book is designed to move you through all four stages of learning:

- At the beginning of each chapter you are asked to complete a Journal Entry designed to stimulate your thinking and connect the chapter content to your current life experience (Stage 1).

- Next you are provided with the ideas, information, and suggestions that can help you succeed in school (Stage 2).

- You are also asked to practice new skills with exercises provided throughout each chapter (Stage 3).

- Finally, at the end of each chapter is a Learning Styles Application with four items to help you tie together the chapter content and your previous learning (Stage 4).

You can also look to other articles for ways to expand your learning preferences. For example, read "Ways to change a habit" in this chapter, and then adopt habits that take you through all stages of learning.

As you use this book, think long-term. Look for payoffs over months and years rather than days or weeks. Celebrate your mistakes, seeing them simply as feedback on your current skills, and reward yourself for reaching new mastery as a learner.

EXERCISE #8
RECALL AN ENJOYABLE LEARNING EXPERIENCE

Take three minutes to remember a time when you enjoyed learning something. In the space below, make a brief list of the things you enjoyed about that experience. Within the next 24 hours, share your list with another person or a small group.

_____

_____

_____

_____

_____

_____

_____

_____

_____

_____

_____

_____

_____

_____

_____

More than likely, you'll find that your list has items in common with others. This discovery echoes a principle of psychology—that learning occurs in a similar way for all of us.

At the same time, you might make a related discovery—that people prefer different aspects of learning. Some people enjoy learning things that are important in daily life. Others enjoy learning for the pure pleasure of gaining knowledge and skill. Still others excel when they can take what they learn and experiment with it. Other people enjoy finding new ways to apply what they know to everyday life, and some enjoy all these stages of learning.

Resources on learning styles

Experiential Learning: Experience as the Source of Learning and Development by David A. Kolb (Englewood Cliffs, NJ: Prentice–Hall,1984). Explains the theory of experiential learning, with applications to education, work, and personal development. Contains information on the validity of the *Learning Style Inventory.*

User Guide for the Learning Style Inventory by Donna Smith and David A. Kolb (Boston: McBer, 1985). A manual for teachers and trainers.

Personal Learning Guide by Richard Baker, Nancy Dixon, and David A. Kolb (Boston: McBer, 1985). A practical guide to using training programs to increase learning.

Adaptive Style Inventory by David A. Kolb and Richard Boyatzis (distributed by McBer & Company, Boston, MA 02116). An inventory to assess your adaptability in different learning situations.

Learning Skills Profile by David A. Kolb and Richard Boyatzis (distributed by McBer & Company, Boston, MA 02116). An instrument to compare your learning style to your job skill demands.

Bibliography of Research on Experiential Learning and the Learning Style Inventory (Boston: McBer, 1992). References to recent studies.

The *Learning Style Inventory* is distributed by McBer & Company, Inc.—a human resources, management consulting company located at 116 Huntington Ave., Boston, MA 021116.

Wayne Zako, an educational consultant, contributed to this article on learning styles. He can be reached at Human Options, 4606 South Canyon Road, Rapid City, SD 57702.

the master student

In 1482, Leonardo da Vinci wrote a letter to a wealthy baron, applying for work. In excerpted form, he wrote,

"I can contrive various and endless means of offense and defense. . . . I have all sorts of extremely light and strong bridges adapted to be most easily carried. . . . I have methods for destroying every turret or fortress. . . . I will make covered chariots, safe and unassailable. . . . In case of need I will make big guns, mortars, and light ordinance of fine and useful forms out of the common type. . . ." And then, he added, almost as an afterthought, "In times of peace I believe I can give perfect satisfaction and to the equal of any other in architecture . . . can carry out sculpture . . . and also I can do in painting whatever may be done."

The Mona Lisa, for example.

This book is about something that cannot be taught. It's about becoming a master student. A master is a person who has attained a level of skill that goes beyond technique. For a master, methods and procedures are automatic responses to the needs of the task. Work is effortless; struggle evaporates. The master carpenter is so familiar with her tools, they are part of her. To a master chef, utensils are old friends. Because these masters don't have to think about the details of the process, they bring more of themselves to their work.

Mastery can lead to flashy results—an incredible painting, for example, or a gem of a short story. In basketball, mastery might result in an unbelievable shot at the buzzer. For a musician, it might be the performance of performances, the night when everything comes together.

More often, the result of mastery is a sense of profound satisfaction, well-being, and timelessness. Work seems self-propelled. The master is in control by being out of control. She lets go and allows the creative process to work. That's why after a spectacular performance, it is often said of an athlete or a performer, "She was playing out of her mind."

Likewise, the master student is one who "learns out of her mind." Of course, that statement makes no sense. Mastery, in fact, doesn't make sense. It cannot be captured with words. It defies analysis. Mastery cannot be taught, only learned and experienced.

Examine the following list of characteristics of master students in light of your own experience. The list is not complete. It merely points in a direction. No one can teach us to be master students; we already are master students. We are natural learners by design. As students, we can discover that every day.

As you read, look for yourself. Following are some traits shared by master students.

Inquisitive

The master student is curious about everything. By posing questions she can generate interest and aliveness in the most mundane, humdrum situations. When she is bored during a biology lecture, she thinks to herself, "I always get bored when I listen to this instructor. Why is that? Maybe it's because he reminds me of my boring Uncle Ralph who always tells those endless fishing stories.

He even looks like Uncle Ralph. Amazing! Boredom is certainly interesting." Then she asks, "What can I do to get value out of this lecture, even though it seems boring?" And she finds an answer.

Able to focus attention

Watch a 2-year-old at play. Pay attention to the eyes. The wide-eyed look reveals an energy and a capacity for amazement that keep his attention absolutely focused in the here and now. The master student's focused attention has a childlike quality. The world, to a child, is always new. Because the master student can focus attention, to him the world is always new.

Willing to change

The unknown does not frighten the master student. In fact, she welcomes it—even the unknown in herself. We all have pictures of who we think we are, and these pictures can be useful. They also can prevent learning and growth. The master student is open to changes in her environment and changes in herself.

Able to organize and sort

The master student can take a large body of information and sift through it to discover relationships. He can play with information, organizing pieces of data by size, color, order, weight, and a hundred other categories.

Competent

Mastery of skills is important to the master student. When she learns mathematical formulas, she studies them until they become second nature. She practices until she knows them cold, then practices an extra few minutes. She also is able to apply what she learns to new and different situations.

Joyful

More often than not, the master student is seen with a smile on his face—sometimes a smile at nothing in particular other than amazement at the world and his experience of it.

Able to suspend judgment

The master student has opinions and positions, and she is able to let go of them when appropriate. She realizes she is more than her thoughts. She can quiet her internal dialogue and listen to an opposing viewpoint. She doesn't let judgment get in the way of learning. Rather than approaching discussions with a "Prove it to me and then I'll believe it" attitude, she asks, "What if this were true?" and explores possibilities.

Energetic

Notice the student with a spring in his step, the one who is enthusiastic and involved in class. When he reads, he often sits on the very edge of his chair, and he plays with the same intensity. He is a master student.

Well

Health is important to the master student, though not necessarily in the sense of being free of illness. Rather, she values her body and treats it with respect. She tends to her emotional and spiritual health, as well as to her physical health.

Self-aware

The master student is willing to evaluate himself and his behavior. He regularly examines his life.

Responsible

There is a difference between responsibility and blame, and the master student knows it well. She is willing to take responsibility for everything in her life—for events that most people would blame on others. For example, if she is served cold eggs in the cafeteria, the master student chooses to take responsibility for getting cold eggs. This is not the same as blaming herself for cold eggs. Rather, she looks for ways to change the situation and get what she wants. She could choose to eat breakfast earlier, or she might tell someone in the kitchen that the eggs are cold and request a change. The cold eggs might continue. Even then, the master student takes responsibility and gives herself the power to choose her response to the situation.

Willing to risk

The master student often takes on projects with no guarantee of success. He is willing to participate in class dialogues at the risk of looking foolish. He is willing to tackle difficult subjects in term papers. He welcomes the risk of a challenging course.

Willing to participate

Don't look for the master student on the sidelines. She's in the game. She is a player who can be counted on. She is willing to make a commitment, and she can follow through.

A generalist

The master student is interested in everything around him. He has a broad base of knowledge in many fields and can find value that is applicable to his specialties.

Willing to accept paradox

The word *paradox* comes from two Greek words, *para* (beyond) and *doxen* (opinion). A paradox is something which is beyond opinion or, more accurately, something that may seem contradictory or absurd yet may actually have meaning. For example, the master student can be totally committed to managing money and reaching her financial goals. At the same time, she can be totally detached from money, realizing that her real worth is independent of how much money she has. The master student recognizes the limitations of the mind and is at home with paradox. She can accept that ambiguity.

Courageous

The master student admits his fear and fully experiences it when appropriate. For example, he approaches tough exams as opportunities to explore feelings of anxiety and tension related to the pressure to perform. He does not deny fear— he embraces it.

Self-directed

Rewards or punishments provided by others do not motivate the master student. Her motivation to learn comes from within.

Spontaneous

The master student is truly in the here and now. He is able to respond to the moment in fresh, surprising, and unplanned ways.

Relaxed about grades

Grades make the master student neither depressed nor euphoric. She recognizes that sometimes grades are important, and grades are not the only reason she studies. She does not measure her value as a human being by the grades she receives.

Intuitive

The master student has a sense that is beyond logic. He has learned to trust his feelings, and he works to develop that sense.

Creative

Where others see dullness and trivia, the master student sees opportunities to create. She can gather pieces of knowledge from a wide range of subjects and put them together in a new way. The master student is creative in every aspect of her life.

Willing to be uncomfortable

The master student does not place comfort first. When discomfort is necessary to reach a goal, he is willing to experience it. He can endure personal discomfort and can look at unpleasant things with detachment.

Accepting

The master student accepts herself, the people around her, and the challenges that life offers.

Willing to laugh

The master student might laugh at any moment, and her sense of humor includes the ability to laugh at herself.

Hungry

Human beings begin life with a natural appetite for knowledge. In some people it soon gets dulled. The master student has tapped that hunger, and it gives him a desire to learn for the sake of learning.

Willing to work

Once inspired, the master student is willing to follow through with sweat. Genius and creativity, she recognizes, are mostly the result of persistence and work. When she is in high gear, the master student works with the intensity of a child at play.

The master student in you

The master student is in all of us. By design, human beings are learning machines. We have an innate ability to learn, and all of us have room to grow and improve.

It also is important to note the distinction between learning and being taught. Human beings can resist being taught anything. Carl Rogers[8] goes so far as to say that anything that can be taught to a human being is either inconsequential or just plain harmful. What is important in education, Rogers asserts, is learning. And everyone has the ability to do that.

Unfortunately, people also learn to hide that ability. As they experience the pain sometimes associated with learning, they shut down. If a child experiences feeling foolish in front of a group of people, he could learn to avoid those situations. In doing so, the child restricts his possibilities.

Some children "learn" that they are slow learners. If they learn it well enough, their behavior comes to match that label.

As people grow older, they accumulate a growing list of ideas to defend, a fat catalog of experiences that tell them not to risk learning.

Still, the master student within survives. To tap that resource you don't need to acquire anything. You already have everything you need. Every day you can rediscover the natural learner within you.

In each chapter of this text there is an example of a person who embodies several qualities of a master student.

As you read about these people and others like them, ask, "How can I use this?" Look for the timeless qualities in the people you read about. Many of the strategies used by master students from another time or place are tools you can use.

No list of master students can be complete. The master students in this book were chosen because they demonstrate novel ways to learn—not because they are the best or the only role models. Round out the profiles in this book with other master students you've read about or know personally. As you meet new people, look for those who excel at learning. The master student is not a vague or remote ideal. Rather, master students move freely among us. In fact, there's one living inside your skin.

JOURNAL ENTRY #10
DISCOVERY STATEMENT

After reading "The master student," consider your own strengths and list the qualities of a master student that you observe in yourself.

This is no easy task. Most of us are competent self-critics, but we tend to discount our strong points. If you get stuck trying to complete this Journal Entry, warm up by brainstorming all your good points on a separate sheet of paper. Remember to consider experiences both in and out of school.

The master student qualities I observe in myself include . . .

_____

_____

_____

_____

_____

_____

_____

_____

_____

_____

_____

_____

In the space below, write a specific example of how you model one of these qualities.

_____

_____

_____

_____

_____

_____

_____

_____

master student

benjamin franklin

printer, author, philanthropist, inventor, statesman, diplomat, and scientist was born in 1706 and died in 1790

A question was once somehow or other started between Collins and me on the propriety of educating the female sex in learning and their abilities to study. He was of the opinion that it was improper and that they were naturally unequal to it. I took the contrary side, perhaps a little for dispute's sake. He was naturally more eloquent, having a greater plenty of words, and sometimes, as I thought, I was vanquished more by his fluency than by the strength of his reasons. As we parted without settling the point and were not to see one another again for some time, I sat down to put my arguments in writing, which I copied fair and sent to him. He answered and I replied. Three or four letters on a side had passed, when my father happened to find my papers and read them. Without entering into the subject in dispute, he took occasion to talk with me about my manner of writing,

observed that though I had the advantage of my antagonist in correct spelling and pointing [punctuation]. . . I fell far short in elegance of expression, in method and in perspicuity—of which he convinced me by several instances. I saw the justice of his remarks and thence grew more attentive to my manner of writing, and determined to endeavor to improve my style.

About this time I met with an odd volume of *Spectator*. It was the third. I had never before seen any of them. I bought it, read it over and over, and was much delighted with it. I thought the writing excellent and wished if possible to imitate it. With that view, I took some of the papers, and making short hints of the sentiment in each sentence, laid them by a few days, and then without looking at the book, tried to complete the papers again by expressing each hinted sentiment at length and as fully as it had been expressed before, in any suitable words that should occur to me. Then I compared my *Spectator* with the original, discovered some of my faults and corrected them. . . . I sometimes jumbled my collections of hints into confusion, and after some weeks endeavored to reduce them into the best order before I began to form the full sentences and complete the paper. This was to teach me method in the arrangement of the thoughts. By comparing my work afterwards with the original, I discovered many faults and corrected them; but I sometimes had the pleasure of fancying that in certain particulars of small import I had been lucky enough to improve the method or the language, and this encouraged me to think that I might possibly in time come to be a tolerable English writer, of which I was extremely ambitious.

From Benjamin Franklin's memoirs, available in L. Jesse Lemisch's Benjamin Franklin: The Autobiography and Other Writings *(New York: Signet Classic, 1961), 28-29, by permission of the Regents of the University of California, Berkeley Reprinted by permission*

1 Give at least two examples of First Steps described in the excerpt from Benjamin Franklin's autobiography.

2 Describe a benefit of writing Discovery Statements.

3 The purpose of the Discovery and Intention Journal Entry System is to keep you at a constant level of excitement about learning. True or False. Explain your answer.

4 Our internal chatter and mental pictures can assist or hamper our success. What is one way to minimize negative images?

5 Which one of the following best illustrates the suggestion to choose observable criteria for success?

   (A) Work harder at math.
   (B) Create 10 flash cards covering the main points in Tuesday's lecture on the Spanish Civil War.
   (C) Find a tutor sometime this quarter.

6 The guidelines for writing Discovery Statements do not include:

   (A) Record the specifics.
   (B) Notice your inner voices and pictures.
   (C) Notice physical sensations.
   (D) Trust expectations about what you will discover.
   (E) Use discomfort as a signal.

7 List at least five guidelines for writing Intention Statements.

8 *The suggestions for changing a habit do not include:*

   (A) Tell the truth.
   (B) Start with small changes.
   (C) Affirm that you can change your basic nature.
   (D) Commit to use the new behavior.
   (E) Get feedback and support.

9 *Name at least three ways to find money for school.*

10 *If you want the ideas in this book to work, you must believe in them, says Power Process #1.*
   True or False. Explain your answer.

JOURNAL ENTRY #11
DISCOVERY/INTENTION STATEMENT

Review your experience of this chapter and complete the following sentence.

   In reading and doing this chapter, I discovered that I . . .

_____

_____

   Now, write a plan about something specific that you learned and intend to use from this chapter. Include how and when you intend to use it.

   I intend to use the following strategy . . .

_____

_____

   In order to use this strategy, I will . . .

_____

_____

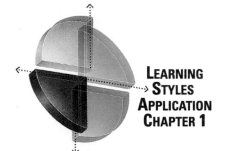

**LEARNING
STYLES
APPLICATION
CHAPTER 1**

*Even though each of us has preferred styles for learning new material, it is useful
to review that material using several styles of learning. Each question below will
"cycle" you through four learning styles. A similar learning style application
appears at the end of every chapter in this book. Write your responses to these
exercises on a separate sheet of paper. For more information about learning styles,
reread the article "Learning styles—Discovering how you learn" on page 26.*

Style 1
*On a separate sheet of paper, write a short paragraph explaining 1) any ways
you have applied the following ideas in your life prior to reading this chapter
and 2) how further mastering these ideas could make a positive difference in
your education.*

- *Telling the truth about your current abilities*
- *Writing a journal focused on self-discovery and intention*
- *Changing habits*
- *Motivation*
- *Considering ideas as tools*

Style 2
*After reviewing the above topics, list 15 new ideas or suggestions you learned
from this chapter. Include those that you already knew about but have never used.*

Style 3
*Using the 15 items you just listed, rank them from (1) most important idea I taught
myself to (15) least important idea I taught myself. After you have ranked them,
write an Intention Statement describing how you plan to put each idea into
practice.*

Style 4
*Now consider your commitment to these ideas by evaluating the amount of
effort you gave to learning each one. Use the following priority scale.*

- *A = I gave "above and beyond" effort to learning this idea.*
- *B = I gave my best effort to learning this idea.*
- *C = I did what I could to learn this idea.*

*Finally, go beyond the classroom. Describe ways to use these ideas that can
make your work life or relationships more rewarding.*

Bibliography

■ Endnotes

[1] Robert Mager, *Preparing Instructional Objectives* (Belmont, CA: Fearon, 1975).

[2] Ezra Pound, *The ABC of Reading* (New York: New Directions, 1934).

[3] Robert Hutchins, "The Great Conversation: The Substance of a Liberal Education," *Great Books of the Western World,* vol. 1 (Chicago: Encyclopædia Britannica, 1952).

[4] B.F. Skinner, *Science and Human Behavior* (New York: Macmillan, 1953).

[5] William James, *Pragmatism and Other Essays* (New York: Washington Square, 1963).

[6] David A. Kolb, *Experiential Learning: Experience as the Source of Learning and Development* (Englewood Cliffs, NJ: Prentice-Hall, 1984).

[7] Abraham Maslow, *The Further Reaches of Human Nature* (New York: Viking, 1971).

[8] Carl Rogers, *Freedom to Learn* (Columbus, OH: Merrill, 1969).

■ Additional Reading

Department of Energy. *The Car Book*, Pueblo, CO: Consumer Information, n.d.

Dominguez, Joe, and Vicki Robin. *Your Money or Your Life: Transforming Your Relationship with Money and Achieving Financial Independence*, New York: Viking, 1992.

Elgin, Duane. *Voluntary Simplicity*, New York: Morrow, 1981.

James, William. *Talks to Teachers on Psychology and to Students on Some of Life's Ideals*, New York: Norton, 1958.

Matheson, Maureen, ed. *College Handbook*, New York: College Board, 1983.

Porter, Sylvia. *Sylvia Porter's Your Financial Security*, New York: Avon, 1990.

time

In this chapter...

■ move from "I don't have enough time" to "I have plenty of time for what matters." Begin by **monitoring** your time. Then adopt some tools for **right-brained time management**, use **computers** to save time, and **overcome procrastination**. Find new connections between **time and money** along with ways to make both work for you. Also develop the skill of **focused attention**— a powerful tool for getting anything done—and discover how **planning** sets you free.

**JOURNAL ENTRY #12
DISCOVERY STATEMENT**

List five times during the past year when you rushed to finish a project or when you did not find time for an activity that was important to you.

_____
_____
_____
_____
_____
_____

Now preview this chapter, looking for five ideas that could help you avoid such situations in the future. List those suggestions here, along with their related page numbers.

Strategy	Page Number

THE WORDS *TIME MANAGEMENT* CAN call forth images of restriction and control. You might visualize a prune-faced Scrooge hunched over your shoulder, stopwatch in hand, telling you what to do every minute. Bad news.

Good news: You do have enough time for the things you want to do. All it takes is learning a few ways to manage time.

Time is an equal opportunity resource. All people, regardless of gender, race, creed, or national origin have exactly the same number of hours in a week. True, some people have enough money to delegate tasks or hire them out to others. Yet no matter how important you are, no matter how rich or poor, you get 168 hours to spend each week—no more, no less.

Time is also an unusual commodity. It cannot be saved. You can't stockpile time like wood for your stove or food for the winter. It can't be seen, felt, touched, tasted, or smelled. You can't sense time directly. Even brilliant scientists and philosophers aren't sure how to describe it.

Because time is so elusive, it is easy to ignore. That doesn't bother time at all. Time is perfectly content to remain hidden until you are nearly out of it. And when you are out of it, you are out of it.

Time is a nonrenewable resource. If you are out of wood, you can chop some more. If you're out of money, you can earn a little extra. If you're out of love, there is still hope. If you're out of health, it can often be restored. But when you're out of time, that's it. When this minute is gone, it's gone.

You've got the time

" "

Even if you are on the right track, you'll get run over if you just sit there.
WILL ROGERS

" "

Dost thou love life, then do not squander time, for that's the stuff life is made of.
–BENJAMIN FRANKLIN

Time seems to pass at varying speeds. Sometimes it crawls and sometimes it's faster than a speeding bullet. On Friday afternoons, classroom clocks can creep.

After you've worked a 10-hour day, reading the last few pages of an economics assignment can turn minutes into hours. A year in school can stretch out to an eternity. At the other end of the spectrum, time flies. These are magic times when you are so absorbed in what you're doing that hours disappear in minutes.

You can manage this commodity so you won't waste it or feel regretful about how you spent it.

Approach time as if you are in control. Sometimes it seems that your friends control your time, that your boss controls your time, that your teachers or your parents or your kids or somebody else controls your time. Maybe that is not true. When you say you don't have enough time, you may really be saying that you are not spending the time you do have in the way that you want.

Time management gives you a chance to spend your most valuable resource in the way you choose. Start by observing how you use time.

You can do so in the next exercise.

EXERCISE #9
THE TIME MONITOR/TIME PLAN PROCESS

The purpose of this exercise is to transform time into a knowable and predictable resource. You can do this by following a two-phase cycle of monitor-plan, monitor-plan, monitor-plan . . . .

This exercise takes place over two weeks. During the first week, you can monitor your activities to get a detailed picture of how you spend your time. Then you can plan the second week thoughtfully. Monitor your time during the second week, compare it to your plan, and discover what changes you want to make in the following week's plan.

Monitor your time in 15-minute intervals, 24 hours a day, for seven days, recording how much time you spend sleeping, eating, studying, traveling to and from class, working, watching television, listening to music, sitting in lectures, taking care of the kids, running errands— everything.

If this sounds crazy, hang on for a minute. This is not about keeping track of the rest of your life in 15-minute intervals. Complete the monitor-plan cycle only for as long as it is useful to you. Most of us have little idea where our time really goes. This exercise offers us an opportunity to find out how we spend our time, our lives.

The point is to become conscious of how you use time. When you know how your time is spent, you can find ways to adjust and manage it so that you spend your time doing the things that are most important to you. Monitoring your time is a critical First Step toward putting you in control of your time.

Some students choose to track their time on 3x5 cards, calendars, or computer software designed for this purpose. You may even develop your own form for monitoring your time.

1. Getting to know the Time Monitor/Time Plan

Look at the Time Monitor/Time Plan on page 41. Notice that each day has two columns, one labeled "plan" and another labeled "monitor." During the first week, use only the "monitor" column. After that, you use both columns simultaneously to continue the monitor-plan process.

Here is an idea that is an eye-opener for many students. If you think you already have a good idea of how you manage time, then guess how many hours you spend in each of the categories listed on page 42. Do this before your first week of monitoring. After you monitor, see how close you were.

To become familiar with the form, look at the example on this page. When beginning an activity, write it next to the time you begin and put a line just above that spot. Round off to the nearest 15 minutes. If, for example, you begin eating at 8:06, enter your start at 8:00. Over time, it will probably even out. In any case, you will be close enough to realize the benefits of this exercise. On Monday, the student in this example got up at 6:45 a.m. and showered and got dressed. He finished this activity and began breakfast at 7:15. He put this new activity in at the time he began and drew another line just above it. He ate from 7:15 to 7:45. It took him 15 minutes to walk to class (7:45 to 8:00), and he attended classes from 8:00 to 11:00.

Keep your Time Monitor/Time Plan with you every minute you are awake for one week. Take a few moments every two or three hours to record what you've done. Or enter a note each time you change activities.

2. Remembering to use your Time Monitor/Time Plan

It may be easy to forget to fill out your Time Monitor/Time Plan. One way to remember is to create a visual reminder for yourself. You can use this technique for any activity you want to remember.

Relax for a moment, close your eyes, and imagine that you see your Time Monitor/Time Plan, only imagine it with arms and legs and as big as a person. Imagine the form sitting at your desk at home. Picture it sitting in your car or sitting in one of your classrooms. Visualize this form sitting in your favorite chair. Picture it sitting wherever you're likely to sit.

When you sit down, the picture of the Time Monitor/Time Plan will get squashed.

You can make this image more effective by adding imaginary noise. The Time Monitor/Time Plan might scream, "Get off me!" Or, since time is money, as the saying goes, you might associate the Time Monitor/Time Plan with the sound of a cash register. Imagine that every time you sit down, a cash register rings.

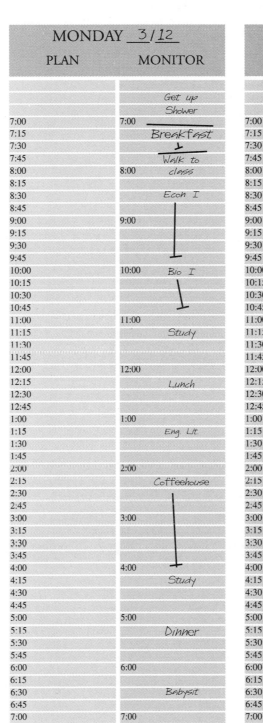

3. Analyzing the Time Monitor/Time Plan

After you've monitored your time for one week, group your activities together by categories. The form below includes the categories "sleep," "class," "study," and "meals." Another category, "grooming," might include showering, putting on makeup, brushing teeth, getting dressed. "Travel" can include walking, driving, taking the bus, and riding your bike. Other categories could be exercise, entertainment, work, television, domestic, and children. Write in the categories that work for you, and then add up how much time you spent in each of your categories. Make sure the grand total of all categories is 168 hours.

In several months, you may want to take another detailed look at how you spend your life. Combine it with planning your time, following the suggestions in this chapter. This sets up a continuous cycle: monitor, evaluate, plan; monitor, evaluate, plan. When you make it a habit, this cycle can help you get the full benefits of time management for the rest of your life. Then time management becomes more than a technique. It's transformed into a habit, a constant awareness of how you spend your lifetime.

WEEK OF ___/___/___

CATEGORY	PLANNED	MONITORED
Sleep		
Class		
Study		
Meals		

MONDAY ___/___/___		TUESDAY ___/___/___		WEDNESDAY ___/___/___	
PLAN	MONITOR	PLAN	MONITOR	PLAN	MONITOR
7:00	7:00	7:00	7:00	7:00	7:00
7:15		7:15		7:15	
7:30		7:30		7:30	
7:45		7:45		7:45	
8:00	8:00	8:00	8:00	8:00	8:00
8:15		8:15		8:15	
8:30		8:30		8:30	
8:45		8:45		8:45	
9:00	9:00	9:00	9:00	9:00	9:00
9:15		9:15		9:15	
9:30		9:30		9:30	
9:45		9:45		9:45	
10:00	10:00	10:00	10:00	10:00	10:00
10:15		10:15		10:15	
10:30		10:30		10:30	
10:45		10:45		10:45	
11:00	11:00	11:00	11:00	11:00	11:00
11:15		11:15		11:15	
11:30		11:30		11:30	
11:45		11:45		11:45	
12:00	12:00	12:00	12:00	12:00	12:00
12:15		12:15		12:15	
12:30		12:30		12:30	
12:45		12:45		12:45	
1:00	1:00	1:00	1:00	1:00	1:00
1:15		1:15		1:15	
1:30		1:30		1:30	
1:45		1:45		1:45	
2:00	2:00	2:00	2:00	2:00	2:00
2:15		2:15		2:15	
2:30		2:30		2:30	
2:45		2:45		2:45	
3:00	3:00	3:00	3:00	3:00	3:00
3:15		3:15		3:15	
3:30		3:30		3:30	
3:45		3:45		3:45	
4:00	4:00	4:00	4:00	4:00	4:00
4:15		4:15		4:15	
4:30		4:30		4:30	
4:45		4:45		4:45	
5:00	5:00	5:00	5:00	5:00	5:00
5:15		5:15		5:15	
5:30		5:30		5:30	
5:45		5:45		5:45	
6:00	6:00	6:00	6:00	6:00	6:00
6:15		6:15		6:15	
6:30		6:30		6:30	
6:45		6:45		6:45	
7:00	7:00	7:00	7:00	7:00	7:00
7:15		7:15		7:15	
7:30		7:30		7:30	
7:45		7:45		7:45	
8:00	8:00	8:00	8:00	8:00	8:00
8:15		8:15		8:15	
8:30		8:30		8:30	
8:45		8:45		8:45	
9:00	9:00	9:00	9:00	9:00	9:00
9:15		9:15		9:15	
9:30		9:30		9:30	
9:45		9:45		9:45	

THURSDAY __/__/__		FRIDAY __/__/__		SATURDAY __/__/__	
PLAN	MONITOR	PLAN	MONITOR	PLAN	MONITOR
7:00	7:00		7:00		
7:15					
7:30		7:30			
7:45		7:45			
8:00	8:00	8:00	8:00		
8:15		8:15			
8:30		8:30			
8:45		8:45			
9:00	9:00	9:00	9:00		
9:15		9:15			
9:30		9:30			
9:45		9:45			
10:00	10:00	10:00	10:00		
10:15		10:15			
10:30		10:30			
10:45		10:45			
11:00	11:00	11:00	11:00		
11:15		11:15			
11:30		11:30			
11:45		11:45			
12:00	12:00	12:00	12:00		
12:15		12:15			
12:30		12:30			
12:45		12:45			
1:00	1:00	1:00	1:00		
1:15		1:15			
1:30		1:30			
1:45		1:45			
2:00	2:00	2:00	2:00		
2:15		2:15			
2:30		2:30			
2:45		2:45			
3:00	3:00	3:00	3:00		
3:15		3:15			
3:30		3:30			
3:45		3:45			
4:00	4:00	4:00	4:00		
4:15		4:15			
4:30		4:30			
4:45		4:45		SUNDAY __/__/__	
5:00	5:00	5:00	5:00	PLAN	MONITOR
5:15		5:15			
5:30		5:30			
5:45		5:45			
6:00	6:00	6:00	6:00		
6:15		6:15			
6:30		6:30			
6:45		6:45			
7:00	7:00	7:00	7:00		
7:15		7:15			
7:30		7:30			
7:45		7:45			
8:00	8:00	8:00	8:00		
8:15		8:15			
8:30		8:30			
8:45		8:45			
9:00	9:00	9:00	9:00		
9:15		9:15			
9:30		9:30			
9:45		9:45			

JOURNAL ENTRY #13
DISCOVERY STATEMENT

By analyzing the result of one week of monitoring my time I discovered that . . .

_____

I want to spend more time on . . .

_____

I want to spend less time on . . .

_____

I was surprised that I spent so much time on . . .

_____

I was surprised that I spent so little time on . . .

_____

I had strong feelings about (describe the feeling and the situation) . . .

_____

EXERCISE #10
CREATE A LIFE LINE

On a large sheet of paper draw a horizontal line. This line will represent your lifetime. Now add key events in your life to this line in chronological order. Examples are birth, graduation from high school, and enrollment in higher education.

Now extend into the future. Write down key events you would like to see occur in one year, five years, and 10 years or more from now. Choose events that are in line with your core values. Work quickly in the spirit of a brainstorm. This is not a final plan.

Afterward, take a few minutes to review your life line. Select one key event for the future as a goal. List any actions you could take in the next month to bring yourself closer to that goal. Do the same with other key events on your life line.

You now have the rudiments of a comprehensive plan for your life.

Finally, extend your time line another 50 years beyond the year when you would reach age 100. Describe in detail what changes in the world you'd like to see as a result of the goals you attained in your life.

ways to get the most out of now

The following time management techniques are about when to study, where to study, ways to handle the rest of the world, and things you can ask yourself when you get stuck. As you read, underline, circle, or otherwise note the suggestions you think you can use.

Pick two or three techniques to use now. When they become habits, come back to this article and pick a couple more.

When to study

1. Study difficult (or "boring") subjects first.
If your chemistry problems put you to sleep, get to them first, while you are fresh. We tend to study what we like first, yet the courses we find most difficult often require the most creative energy. Save the subjects you enjoy for later. If you find yourself avoiding a particular subject, get up an hour early to study it before breakfast. With that chore out of the way, the rest of the day can be a breeze.

Continually avoiding a subject might indicate a trouble area. Further action is called for. Clarify your feelings about the course by writing about those feelings in a journal, talking to an instructor, or asking for help from a friend or counselor. Consistently avoiding study tasks can also be a signal to re-examine your major or course program.

2. Be aware of your best time of day.
Many people learn best in daylight hours. If this is true for you, schedule study time for your most difficult subjects when the sun is up.

Unless you grew up on a farm, the idea of being conscious at 4 a.m. might seem ridiculous. Yet many successful business people begin the day at 5 a.m. or earlier. Athletes and yogis use this time too. Some writers complete their best work before 9 a.m.

Some people experience the same benefits by staying up late. They flourish after midnight.

If you aren't convinced, then experiment. When you're in a time crunch, get up early or stay up late. The new benefits you discover might even include seeing a sunrise.

3. Use waiting time.
Five minutes waiting for a bus, 20 minutes waiting for the dentist, 10 minutes between classes—waiting time adds up fast. Have short study tasks ready to do during these times. For example, carry 3x5 cards with facts, formulas, or definitions and pull them out anywhere.

A tape recorder can help you use commuting time to your advantage. Make a cassette tape of yourself reading your notes. Then play these tapes in a car stereo as you drive, or listen through your earphones as you ride on the bus or exercise.

Where to study

4. Use a regular study area. Your body and your mind know where you are. When you use the same place to study, day after day, they become trained. When you arrive at that particular place, you can focus your attention more quickly.

5. Study where you'll be alert. In bed, your body gets a signal. For most students, it's more likely to be "Time to sleep" than "Time to study!" For that reason, don't sleep where you study. Just as you train your body to be alert at your desk, you also train it to slow down near your bed.

Easy chairs and sofas are also dangerous places to study. Learning requires energy. Give your body a message that energy is needed. Put yourself into a situation that supports that message.

6. Use a library. Libraries are designed for learning. The lighting is perfect. The noise level is low. Materials are available. Entering a library is a signal to quiet the mind and get to work. Most people can get more done in a shorter time at the library. Experiment for yourself.

Ways to handle the rest of the world

7. Pay attention to your attention. Breaks in concentration are often caused by internal interruptions. Your own thoughts jump in to tell you another story about the world. When that happens, notice the thoughts and let them go.

Perhaps the thought of getting something else done is distracting you. One option is to handle that task now and study later. Or write yourself a note about it, or schedule a specific time to do it.

8. Agree with living mates about study time. This includes roommates, parents, spouses, and kids. Make the rules clear, and be sure to follow them yourself. Explicit agreements—even written contracts—work well. One student always wears a colorful hat when she wants to study. When her husband and children see the hat, they respect her wish to be left alone.

9. Get off the phone. The telephone is the ultimate interrupter. People who wouldn't think of distracting you might call at the worst times because they can't see that you are studying. You don't have to be a telephone victim. If a simple "I can't talk, I'm studying" doesn't work, use dead silence. It's a conversation killer. Or short-circuit the whole problem: Unplug the phone. Get an answering machine or study at the library.

10. Learn to say no. This is a timesaver and valuable life skill for everyone. Many people feel it is rude to refuse a request. But saying no can be done effectively and courteously. Others want you to succeed as a student. When you tell them that you can't do what they ask because you are busy educating yourself, most people will understand.

11. Hang a "do not disturb" sign on your door. Many hotels will give you one free, just for the advertising. Or you can make a creative one. They work. Using signs can relieve you of making a decision about cutting off each interruption—a timesaver in itself.

12. Get ready the night before. Completing a few simple tasks just before you go to bed can help you get in gear faster the next day. If you need to make some phone calls first thing in the morning, look up those numbers, write them on 3x5 cards, and set them near the phone. If you are set to drive to a new location, make note of the address and put it next to your car keys. If you plan to spend the afternoon writing a paper, get your materials together: dictionary, notes, outline, paper, and pencil (or disks and computer). Pack your lunch or gas up the car. Organize the diaper bag, briefcase, or backpack.

13. Call ahead. Often we think of talking on the telephone as a prime time-waster. Used wisely, the telephone can actually help you manage time. Before you go shopping, call the store to see if it carries the items you're looking for. If you're driving, call for directions to your destination. A few seconds on the phone can save hours in wasted trips and wrong turns.

14. Avoid noise distractions. To promote concentration, avoid studying in front of the television and turn off the stereo. Many students insist they study better with background noise, and that may be true. Some students report good results with carefully selected and controlled music. The overwhelming majority of research indicates that silence is the best form of music for study.

At times noise may seem out of your control. A neighbor or roommate decides to find out how far he can turn up his stereo before the walls crumble. Meanwhile, your concentration on the principles of sociology goes down the tubes.

To get past this barrier, schedule study sessions for times when your living environment is usually quiet. If you live in a residence hall, ask if study rooms are available. Or go somewhere else, where it's quiet, such as the library. Some students have even found refuge in quiet restaurants, laundromats, and churches.

15. Notice how others misuse your time. Be aware of repeat offenders. Ask yourself if there are certain friends or relatives who consistently interrupt your study time. If avoiding the interrupter is impractical, send a clear message. Sometimes others don't realize they are breaking your concentration. You can give them a gentle yet firm reminder. If your message doesn't work, there are ways to make it more effective. For more ideas, see Chapter Ten.

Things you can ask yourself when you get stuck

16. Ask: What is one task I can accomplish toward my goal? This is a useful technique to use on big, imposing jobs. Pick out one small accomplishment, preferably one you can complete in about five minutes; then do it. The satisfaction of getting one thing done often spurs you on to get one more thing done. Meanwhile, the job gets smaller.

17. Ask: Am I being too hard on myself? If you are feeling frustrated with a reading assignment, noticing that your attention wanders repeatedly, or falling behind on problems due for tomorrow, take a minute to listen to the messages you are giving yourself. Are you scolding yourself too harshly? Lighten up. Allow yourself to feel a little foolish and get on with it. Don't add to the problem by berating yourself.

Worrying about the future is another way people beat themselves up: "How will I ever get this all done?" "What if every paper I write turns out to be this hard?" "If I can't do the simple calculations now, how will I ever pass the final?" Instead of promoting learning, such questions fuel anxiety.

Labeling and generalizing weaknesses are other ways people are hard on themselves. Being objective and specific will eliminate this form of self-punishment and will likely generate new possibilities. An alternative to saying "I'm terrible in algebra" is to say "I don't understand factoring equations." This suggests a plan to improve.

18. Ask: Is this a piano? Carpenters who build rough frames for buildings have a saying they use when they bend a nail or hack a chunk out of a two-by-four: "Well, this ain't no piano." It means perfection is not necessary.

Ask yourself if what you are doing needs to be perfect. You don't have to apply the same standards of grammar to review notes that you apply to a term paper. If you can complete a job 95 percent perfectly in two hours, and 100 percent perfectly in four hours, ask yourself whether the additional 5 percent improvement is worth doubling the amount of time you spend.

Sometimes it *is* a piano. A tiny mistake can ruin an entire lab experiment. Computers are notorious for turning little errors into monsters. Accept lower standards only where they are appropriate.

A related suggestion is to weed out low-priority tasks. The to-do list for a large project can include dozens of items. Not all of them are equally important. Some can be done later on, and others could be skipped altogether if time is short.

Apply this idea when you study. In a long reading assignment, look for pages you can skim or skip. When it's appropriate, read chapter summaries or article abstracts. When reviewing your notes, look for material that may not be covered on a test and decide whether you want to study it.

19. Ask: Would I pay myself for what I'm doing right now? If you were employed as a student, would you be earning your wages? Ask yourself this question when you notice that you've taken your third popcorn break in 30 minutes. Most students are, in fact, employed as students. They are investing in their own productivity and paying a big price for the privilege of being a student. Sometimes they don't realize what a mediocre job may cost them.

20. Ask: Can I do just one more thing? Ask yourself this question at the end of a long day. Almost always you will have enough energy to do just one more short task. The overall increase in your productivity might surprise you.

21. Ask: Am I making time for things that are important but not urgent? If we spend most of our time putting out fires, we may feel drained and frustrated. According to Stephen R. Covey[1], this happens when we forget to take time for things that are truly important but not urgent. Examples are regular exercise, reading, prayer or meditation, quality time with friends and family,

solitude, traveling, and cooking nutritious meals. Each of these can contribute directly to a long-term goal or life mission. Yet when schedules get tight, it's tempting to let these things go for that elusive day when we'll "finally have more time."

That day won't come until we choose to make time for what's truly important. Knowing this, we can use some of the suggestions in this chapter to free up more time.

22. Ask: Can I delegate this? Instead of slogging through complicated tasks alone, you can draw on the talent and energy of other people. Busy executives know the value of delegating tasks to coworkers. Without delegation, many projects would flounder or die.

You can apply the same principle. Instead of doing all the housework or cooking by yourself, for example, assign some of the tasks to family members or roommates. Rather than making a trip to the library to look up a simple fact, call and ask a library assistant to do it. Instead of driving across town to deliver a package, hire a delivery service to do it. All these tactics can free up extra hours for studying.

It's not practical to delegate certain study tasks, such as writing term papers or completing reading assignments. However, you can still draw on the ideas of other people in completing such tasks. For instance, form a writing group to edit and critique papers, brainstorm topics or titles, and develop lists of sources.

If you're absent from a class, find a classmate to explain the lecture, discussion, and any assignments due. Presidents depend on briefings. You can use the technique too.

23. Ask: How did I just waste time?

Notice when time passes and you haven't accomplished what you planned. Take a minute to review your actions and note the specific ways you wasted time. We operate by habit and tend to waste time in the same ways over and over again. When you are aware of things you do that kill your time, you are more likely to catch yourself in the act next time. Observing one small quirk may save you hours. One reminder: Noting how you waste time is not the same as feeling guilty about it. The point is not to blame yourself but to increase your skill. That means getting specific information about how you use time.

24. Ask: Could I find the time if I really wanted to?

Often the way people speak rules out the option of finding more time. An alternative is to speak about time with more possibility.

The next time you're tempted to say, "I just don't have time," pause for a minute. Question the truth of this statement. Could you find four more hours this week for studying? Suppose that someone offered to pay you $10,000 to find those four hours. Suppose, too, that you will get paid only if you don't lose sleep, call in sick for work, or sacrifice anything important to you. Could you find the time if vast sums of money were involved?

Remember that when it comes to school, vast sums of money *are* involved.

25. Ask: Am I willing to promise it?

This may be the most powerful time management idea of all. If you want to find time for a task, promise yourself—and others— that you'll get it done. To make this technique work, do more than say that you'll try or that you'll give it your best shot. Take an oath, as you would in court. Give your word.

One way to accomplish big things in life is to make big promises. There's little reward in promising what's safe or predictable. No athlete promises to place seventh in the Olympics. Chances are that if we're not making large promises, we're not stretching ourselves.

The point of making a promise is not to chain ourselves to rigid schedules or impossible expectations. We can also promise to reach goals without unbearable stress. We can keep schedules flexible and carry out our plans with ease, joy, and satisfaction.

At times we can go too far. Some promises are truly beyond us and we may break them. However, failing to keep a promise is just that—failing to keep a promise. A broken promise is not the worst thing in the world.

Promises can work magic. When our word is on the line, it's possible to discover reserves of time and energy we didn't know existed. Promises can push us to a breakthrough.

Extracurricular activities
Reap the benefits

There's a saying: If you want it done, ask a busy person to do it. The idea is that the busiest people are often the most skilled at managing their time.

Many students in higher education are busier than they've ever been before. Often that's due to the variety of organizations and clubs available on campus: athletics, fraternities, sororities, student newspapers, debate teams, study groups, political action groups, and many more.

With this kind of involvement comes a host of potential benefits. People involved in extracurricular activities are often excellent students as well. Such activities help them bridge the worlds inside and outside the classroom. Through campus organizations they develop new skills, explore possible careers, build contacts for jobs, and add experiences to their résumés. They make new friends among both students and faculty, work with people from other cultures, and sharpen their skills at conflict resolution.

Getting involved in campus organizations comes with some risks as well. When students don't balance extracurricular activities with class work, their success in school can suffer. They can also compromise their health through losing sleep, neglecting exercise, skipping meals, or relying on fast food. These costs are easier to avoid if you keep a few suggestions in mind:

- Enter any commitment outside class consciously, with your eyes open. Decide up front how many hours each week or month you can devote to a campus organization. Leave room in your schedule for relaxing and unplanned events.

- Learn new skills in managing your time. This chapter is teeming with ideas waiting to be used.

- Make commitments from the biggest possible picture of your time—not only the coming days and weeks but the coming months and years. Write down the three or four biggest goals you'd like to achieve in your lifetime. Then choose extracurricular activities that directly support those goals.

- Remember your priorities. Facing a calendar that's filled with commitments and page-long to-do lists can be unsettling. Cut through the confusion by constantly ranking your activities according to importance. Decide what tasks you can delegate and what tasks you can postpone or eliminate.

- Notice when your actions fail to match your promises. You might consistently agree to show up for meetings and find yourself forgetting them or showing up late. If that happens, write a Discovery Statement about the way you're using time. Follow that with an Intention Statement about ways to keep your agreements.

- Say no to activities that fail to create value for you. Avoid joining groups only because you feel guilty, or obligated to join.

- Check out the rules for joining any campus organization. Ask about dues and attendance requirements.

- Do a trial run. Attend one or two meetings of an organization before you decide to join. Explain that you're in the process of making a decision and that you want to find out what the group is about before you make a full commitment.

Debate teams
Honor societies
Language clubs
Peer counseling
    programs
Student government
Professional
    organizations
    for students in
    medicine, law,
    business,
    journalism, etc.
Varsity basketball
Student newspaper
    or yearbook
Community service
    programs
Study groups
Sand volleyball
Ethnic music
groups
Marching bands
Tutoring programs
Work-study
Campus film
    societies
Concert bands
Dance ensembles
Drawing and
    painting clubs
Jazz bands and
    combos
Opera companies
Pottery studios
Chamber music
    groups
Religious groups
Theater groups
Swimming lessons
Programs and
    services for
    students of
    color
Golf team
Fraternities
    and Sororities
Football
Orchestras
Political action
    groups

Divide & Conquer Your Goals

This exercise offers a chance for you to use two essential thinking skills—the ability to generate and the ability to evaluate. You will translate a broad goal into specific, concrete behaviors, making the goal as real as a typewriter or a chain saw.

Many of us have vague, idealized notions of what we want out of life. These notions float among the clouds in our heads. They are wonderful, fuzzy, safe thoughts like "I want to be a good person," "I want to be financially secure," or "I want to be happy." Such goals are possible beginnings for more tangible plans. Left in a generalized form, these goals can leave us confused about how to use them in choosing what to do this weekend.

In contrast, there is nothing vague or fuzzy about chain saws. You can see them, feel them, and hear them. They have a clear function.

Goals can operate the same way—if you make them real. One way to do that is to examine goals up close. Find out what they look like; listen to what they sound like. Pick them up and feel how heavy they are. That's what this exercise is about. It's a chance to inspect the switches, valves, joints, cogs, and fastenings of one of your long-term goals. You will do this by choosing a long-term goal and breaking it into smaller segments until you have taken it completely apart.

Disassembled, a goal might look different to you. When you look at it closely, a goal you thought you wanted might not be something you want after all. Or you might discover you want to choose a new path to a goal you are sure you want. Perhaps you will also see how your education relates to your long-term goal.

For this exercise, you will use a pen, extra paper, and a watch with a second hand. (A digital watch with a built-in stopwatch is even better.) Timing is an important part of the brainstorming process, so follow the stated time limits. This entire exercise takes about an hour.

Part one: Long-term goals

Long-term goals represent major targets in your life. These goals can take five to 20 years to achieve. In some cases, they will take a lifetime. They can include goals in education, careers, personal relationships, travel, financial security, whatever is important to you. Include answers to the following questions in your long-term goals: What do you want to accomplish in your life? Do you want your life to make a statement? What is it?

Brainstorm

Begin with an eight-minute brainstorm. For eight minutes, write down everything you think you want in your life. Write as fast as you can, and write whatever comes into your head. Leave no thought out. Don't worry about accuracy. The object of a brainstorm is to generate as many ideas as possible. Use a separate sheet of paper for this part of the exercise.

Evaluate

After you have finished brainstorming, spend the next six minutes looking over your list. Analyze what you wrote. Read the list aloud. If something is missing, add it. Look for common themes or relationships between goals. Then select three long-term goals that are very important to you—goals that will take many years to achieve. Write these goals in the space provided.

Long-term goal

Long-term goal

Long-term goal

Before you go on, take a minute to reflect on the process you've used so far. What criteria did you use to select your top three goals? For example, write some of the core values (such as love, wealth, or happiness) underlying these goals.

Part two: Mid-term goals

Mid-term goals are objectives you can accomplish in two to five years. They include goals such as completing a course of education or achieving a specific career level. These goals usually support your long-term goals.

Brainstorm

Read aloud the three long-term goals you selected in Part one. Choose one of them. Then brainstorm a list of goals you might achieve in the next one to five years that would lead to the accomplishment of that one long-term goal. These are mid-term goals. Spend eight minutes on this brainstorm. Remember, neatness doesn't count. Go for quantity.

Evaluate

Analyze your brainstorm of mid-term goals. Then select three that you estimate to be most important in meeting the long-term goal you picked. Allow yourself five minutes for this part of the exercise. Write your selections below.

Mid-term goal

Mid-term goal

Mid-term goal

Again, pause for reflection before going on to the next part of this exercise. Why do you see these three goals as more important than the other mid-term goals you generated?

Part three: Short-term goals

Short-term goals are the ones you can accomplish in a year or less. These goals are specific achievements, such as completing a particular course or group of courses. A short-term financial goal probably would include an exact dollar amount. Whatever your short-term goals are, they will require action now or in the near future.

Brainstorm

Review your list of mid-term goals and select one. In another eight-minute brain-storm, generate a list of short-term goals—those you can reach in a year or less that will lead to the accomplishment of that mid-term goal. Write down everything that comes to mind. Do not evaluate or judge these ideas yet. For now, the more ideas you write down, the better.

Evaluate

Analyze your list of short-term goals. The most effective brainstorms are conducted by suspending judgment, so you might find some bizarre ideas on your list. That's fine. Now is the time to cross them out. Next, evaluate your remaining short-term goals to determine which ones you can accomplish and are willing to accomplish. Select three and write them in the space provided.

Short-term goal

Short-term goal

Short-term goal

Part four: Next steps

Take a few minutes to reflect on all the goals you selected in this exercise. Look for relationships. For example, goals could fall in the same category (career or health). Or they could fall in a time sequence, such as goals to be accomplished in one year, five years, and 10 years.

Also think about what accomplishing these goals can mean to you. Think about how the process of choosing them felt.

To make this process even more powerful, write a list of small, achievable steps you can take to accomplish each short-term goal. Make these steps specific enough to include a time line. Then return to this list of steps in a few weeks and note your progress.

The more you practice, the more effective you can be at choosing goals that have meaning for you. You can repeat this exercise, using the other long-term goals you generated, or you can create new ones. Use the process to make long-term goals real in the here and now.

Time management for right-brained people -------------------

Ask some people about managing time and a dreaded image appears in their minds. They see a person with a 50-item to-do list clutching a calendar chock full of appointments. They imagine a robot who values cold efficiency, compulsively accounts for every minute, and is too rushed to develop actual relationships. Often this image is what's behind the comment, "Yeah, there are some good ideas in those time management books, but I'll never get around to using them. Too much work."

The stereotypes about time management present us with a kernel of truth. Sometimes people who pride themselves on efficiency are merely busy. In their rush to check items off their to-do lists, they might be fussing over things that don't need doing—tasks that create little or no value in the first place.

If this is one of your fears, relax. The point of managing time is not to load ourselves down with extra obligations. Instead, the aim is to get the important things done and still be human. An effective time manager is the person who's productive and relaxed at the same time.

Personal style enters the picture too. Many of the suggestions in this chapter appeal to "left-brained" people—those who thrive on making lists, scheduling events, and handling the details first. They may not work for people who like to see wholes and think visually. Remember that the strategies presented in this chapter represent just one set of options for managing time. There are as many different styles for managing time as there are people. The trick is to discover what suits you.

Do give the strategies a fair trial. Some may work for you with a few modifications. Instead of writing a conventional to-do list, for instance, you can plot your day on a mind map. (Mind maps are explained in Chapter Five.) Or write to-do's, one per 3x5 card, in any order in which tasks occur to you. Later you can edit, sort, and rank those cards, choosing which ones to act on.

Strictly speaking, time cannot be managed. Time is a mystery, an abstract concept that cannot be captured in words. The minutes, hours, days, and years march on whether we manage anything or not. What we can do is manage ourselves in respect to time. A few basic principles can do that as well as a truckload of cold-blooded techniques. Among those principles are the following.

Know your values

Begin managing time from a bigger picture. Instead of thinking in minutes or hours, view your life as a whole. Consider what that expanse of time is all about.

As a thought-provoking exercise, write your own obituary. Describe the way you want to be remembered. List the contributions you intend to make during your lifetime. If this is too spooky, write a short mission statement for your life—a paragraph that describes your values and the kind of life you want to lead. Periodically, during the day, stop to ask if what you're doing is contributing to that life.

Do less

Managing time is as much about dropping worthless activities as about adding new ones. The idea is to weed out activities that deliver little reward.

One tool for purging your schedule is a "not-to-do" list. On this list include the notorious time wasters in your life—tasks that are just as well left undone. Examples are activities motivated only by obligation, such as compulsively keeping up with the latest fashions or television shows.

Decide right now to eliminate activities with a low payoff. When you add a new activity to your schedule, consider dropping a current one.

Slow down

Sometimes it's useful to hurry, such as when you're late for a meeting or about to miss a bus. At other times, haste is a choice that serves no real purpose. If you're speeding through the day like a launched missile, consider what would happen if you got to your next destination a little later than planned. Gaining a few minutes might not be worth the added strain.

Remember people

Few people on their deathbeds ever say, "I wish I'd spent more time at the office." They're more likely to say, "I wish I'd spent more time with my family and friends." The pace of daily life can lead us to neglect the people we cherish.

Efficiency is a concept that applies to things—not people. When it comes to relationships, we can often benefit from loosening up our schedules. We can allow extra time for spontaneous visits, free-ranging conversation, and conflict resolution.

Focus on outcomes

You may feel guilty if you spend two hours napping or watching soap operas. But if you're regularly meeting your goals and leading a fulfilled life, there's probably no harm done. When managing time, it's the overall goal of personal effectiveness that counts—more than the means we use to get there. This can be true even when your style of managing time doesn't conform to the experts' advice.

Buy less

Before you purchase an item, ask how much time and money it will take to locate, assemble, use, repair, and maintain. You might be able to free up hours by doing without. If the product comes with a 400-page manual or 20 hours of training, beware.

Remember that inexpensive, "low-tech" tools can actually save time. Keeping track of your appointments and to-do lists on a computer might actually take more time than using pencil, paper, and the old-fashioned appointment book. Before rushing to the store to add another possession to your life, see if you can use or adapt something you already own.

Forget about time

Schedule "downtime" every day—a period when you're accountable to no one else and have nothing to accomplish. This is time to do nothing, free of guilt. Even a few minutes spent this way can yield a sense of renewal.

Also, experiment with decreasing your awareness of time. Leave your watch off for a few hours each day.

Or—What to do if to-do lists are not your style

Likewise, there are many methods for planning your time. Some people prefer a written action plan that carefully details each step leading to a long-range goal. Others just note the due date for accomplishing the goal and periodically assess their progress as the date approaches. Either strategy can work.

Visualizing the desired outcome can be as important as having a detailed action plan. Here's an experiment. Write a list of your goals for the next six months. Then create a vivid mental picture of yourself attaining them and enjoying the resulting benefits. Do this several times in the next few weeks. File the list away, making a note on your calendar to review it in six months. At that time, note how many of your goals you actually accomplished.

Handle it now

A backlog of unfinished tasks can result from postponing decisions or procrastinating. An alternative is to handle the task or decision immediately—to answer that letter now or make that phone call as soon as it occurs to you. You can also save time by graciously saying no to projects that you don't want to take on. Saying "I'll think about doing that and get back to you later" may only mean that you'll take more time to say no later.

Spend time in an area that's free of clocks. Notice how often you glance at your watch, and make a conscious effort to do that less often.

If you still want some sense of time, then use alternatives to the almighty, unforgiving clock. Measure your day with a sundial, hourglass, or eggtimer. Or synchronize your activities with the rhythms of nature—for example, rising at dawn and going to bed at sundown.

You can also plan activities to harmonize with the rhythms of your body. Schedule your most demanding tasks for times when you're normally most alert. Eat when you're hungry, not according to the clock. Scrap schedules when it's appropriate. Sometimes the best-laid plans are best laid to rest.

In summary, take time to retreat from time. Create a sanctuary, a haven, a safe place in your life that's free from any hint of schedules, lists, or accomplishments. One of the most effective ways to manage time is to periodically forget about it.

Keep experimenting

The ideas in the rest of this chapter can also work, sometimes with a little modification, for people who are the most creative among us.

Planning sets you free

One kind of thinking has the power to lift the quality of our lives almost immediately: planning. When you plan, you are the equal of the greatest sculptor, painter, or playwright. More than creating a work of art, you are designing a life. Seeing it this way can draw us into the passion, energy, and excitement of planning.

Planning allows us to glimpse new possibilities. More than that, it brings possibilities into the arena of action. Planning is the art of transforming dreams into realities, the ideal into the real.

When you plan, you can create freedom. This contrasts with the common fear of planning: "Me? Plan? No way. I don't want to be uptight. I don't want to be restrained. I don't want to lose my spontaneity. I don't want to be some tense person who never gets to have any fun. I want to be free. I want to be me."

Great. Then plan.

"No, no," goes the reply. "If I plan, I'll be trapped. I won't be able to just let loose and have a good time. I won't be able to get what I want in life. I'll be boxed in by this plan."

Actually, planning is a way to freedom. One path to feeling calm, peaceful, fun-loving, joyful, and powerful is to have a plan. What we think of as restraint in planning is not really restraint at all. When people are uptight, worried, and hassled—when they're not feeling free—it's often because they have no plan.

Planning increases our freedom in specific ways. This becomes clear as we remember the following ideas.

You set the plan

One freedom in planning stems from the simple fact that you set the plan. The course and direction are yours.

Often, particularly at work or in school, people do not feel this way. They feel the plan is coming from someone else—their employer, supervisor, or teacher.

Consider that this view is inaccurate. If we look ahead far enough into the future, we can choose to see any circumstance as part of a plan for our whole lives. Even when we don't like parts of a job, for example, working provides income and helps us develop useful skills for the next job. When we think far enough in advance, the job no longer has to feel limiting.

You can change the plan

Another freedom in planning is the freedom to change. Any effective plan is flexible, not carved in stone.

Tell people that you have a 20-year plan for your career. Often they'll ask, "Well, is it fair to change the plan?" "Yes," you reply. "I change it every year." Then comes the laughter: "Well, it really isn't a 20-year plan if you change it every year. It's actually a one-year plan."

In reality, we can change our plans often and still preserve the advantages of planning. Those advantages come from choosing our direction and taking charge of our lives.

You choose how to achieve the plan

Planning increases freedom when it creates choices. Suppose you take a new job, and with it comes a detailed list of goals to achieve in one year. You might say, "I didn't choose these goals. There are things in this plan I don't like. I like the rest of the job, though, and all these goals just come with it. I guess I'll have to put up with them."

Even when others select the goals, you can decide whether to accept them. What's more, you can choose ways to achieve any goal.

It's easy to start depending on other people not only for goals but also for ways to achieve them. We start looking to others for hour-by-hour direction, something a lot of companies promote when they "manage" people. There's little freedom in that—little creativity or choice.

If we're without a plan, we let others make our choices for us. We can easily become the victim of our circumstance. Planning allows us to choose, moment to moment, on our own, ways to achieve a goal.

When there's a plan, there's a chance

Planning makes reaching our goals more likely, and that offers another source of freedom. We have a goal. We've laid out the necessary actions in logical steps. And we've decided on a time to perform each action. Now the goal seems possible when it seemed impossible before.

Much of what people undertake at school, at work, in relationships, and at home is simply "digging in"— frantic action with no plan. "Sure, we may never reach the goal," they say. "But at least we were out there trying." In this statement we hear a loss of hope. Planning replaces that despair with a purpose and a time line.

Planning frees you from constant decisions

When you plan, you set aside a time for choosing. That is when you look, decide, commit, promise, and set a direction. In effect, you say, "This is my life, my month, my week, my day. I'll take some time to be responsible for it."

Remember, though, that we don't need to spend all our time planning. Planning by itself is totally ineffective. Nothing in our lives will change until there is action. The value of planning is that it promotes action. After we plan, we are free to act. We're released from the dilemma of always wondering what's supposed to happen next.

When we operate without a plan, we may change our minds often: "Hmmm . . . . That chocolate cake smells great. Maybe I'll have a piece—but maybe I shouldn't. It's a lot of calories. I don't know . . . ." That debate takes up a lot of time and energy.

But suppose you plan to stop eating chocolate cake. What's more, you write down this plan. You speak about this plan to friends, even commit yourself to it in their presence. Temptation still occurs: "Gee, that cake smells great." But then you remember: "Wait. I don't have to make this decision now. I'll just follow my plan and avoid chocolate cake."

Planning makes adjustments easier

With a plan, you are free to handle unexpected change. You've got a timetable and your actions for the day are ranked in order of importance. If something happens that calls for a change in the plan, there's no crisis. In fact, having a written plan makes adjustments easier.

Suppose you are scheduled to give a talk in your speech class next week. Suddenly you find out there was a misprint in the course schedule. You're supposed to speak two days from now, not seven. Without a plan, you would face a lengthy mental process, a whole series of questions: "What will I do now?", "When will I have time to get that speech done?", " How will this affect the rest of my schedule?"

With a plan, things are different. You might say, "I don't have to worry about this. I've done my plan for the week, and I know I have free time tomorrow night between 7 and 10 p.m. I can finish the speech then." Planning frees us to respond to crisis or opportunity. With a plan, we're not so reactive. Planning prevents things from taking our time. Rather, we can give our time to them.

Planning is about creating our own experience. When we plan, our lives do not just "happen" to us. Instead, they flow from choices we've consciously made for ourselves. This self-direction is a fundamental freedom in planning—and one of the most valued freedoms of all.

Strategies for Scheduling

Schedule fixed blocks of time first. Start with class time and work time, for instance. These time periods are usually determined in advance. Other activities must be scheduled around them. Then schedule essential daily activities like sleeping and eating. No matter what else you do, you will sleep and eat. Be realistic about how much time you take for these functions.

Include time for errands. The time we spend buying toothpaste, paying bills, and doing laundry is easy to overlook. These little errands can destroy a tight schedule and make us feel rushed and harried all week. Plan for them and remember to allow for travel time between locations.

Schedule time for fun. Fun is important. Brains that are constantly stimulated by new ideas and new challenges need time off to digest them. Take time to browse aimlessly through the library, stroll with no destination, ride a bike, or do other things you enjoy. Recreation deserves a place in your priorities. It's important to "waste" time once in a while.

Set realistic goals. Don't set yourself up for failure by telling yourself you can do a four-hour job in two hours. There are only 168 hours in a week. If you schedule 169 hours, you lose before you begin.

Allow flexibility in your schedule. Recognize that unexpected things will happen and plan for the unexpected. Leave some "holes" in your schedule; build in blocks of unplanned time. Consider setting aside time each week marked "flextime" or "open time." These are hours to use for emergencies, spontaneous activities, catching up, or seizing new opportunities.

Study two hours for every hour in class. It's standard advice that you allow two hours of study time for every hour you spend in class. Students making the transition from high school to higher education are often unaware that more is expected of them. If you are taking 15 credit hours, plan to spend 30 hours a week studying. The benefits of following this rule will be apparent at exam time.

This guideline is just that—a guideline, not an absolute rule. Consider what's best for you. If you do the Time Monitor/ Time Plan exercise in this chapter, note how many hours you actually spend studying for each hour of class. Then ask how your schedule is working. You may want to allow more study time for some subjects.

Also keep in mind that the "two hours for one" rule doesn't distinguish between focused time and unfocused time. In one four-hour block of study time, it's possible to use up two hours for phone calls, breaks, daydreaming, and doodling. Quality time counts as much as quantity.

Avoid scheduling marathon study sessions. When possible, study in shorter sessions. Three three-hour sessions are usually far more productive than one nine-hour session. In a nine- or 10-hour study marathon, the percentage of time actually spent on a task can be depressingly small. With 10 hours of study ahead of you, the temptation is to tell yourself, "Well, it's going to be a long day. No sense getting in a rush. Better sharpen about a dozen of these pencils and change the light bulbs." In the nine-hour sitting you might spend only six or seven hours studying, whereas three shorter sessions will likely yield much more productive time.

When you do study in long sessions, stop and rest for a few minutes every hour. Give your brain a chance to take a break.

Finally, if you must study in a large block of time, work on several subjects and avoid studying similar subjects back-to-back. For example, if you plan to study sociology, psychology, and computer science, sandwich the computer course between psychology and sociology.

Set clear starting and stopping times. Tasks often expand to fill the time we allot for them. "It always takes me an hour just to settle into a reading assignment" may become a self-fulfilling prophecy.

An alternative is to plan a certain amount of time for that reading assignment, set a timer, and stick to it. People often discover they can decrease study time by forcing themselves to read faster. This can usually be done without sacrificing comprehension.

The same principle can apply to other tasks. Some people find they can get up 15 minutes earlier and still feel alert throughout the day. Plan 45 minutes for a trip to the grocery store instead of one hour. Over the course of a year, those extra minutes can add up to hours. Over a lifetime, they can add up to days.

Feeling rushed or sacrificing quality is not the aim here. The point is to push ourselves a little and discover what our time requirements really are.

Plan for the unplanned. The best-laid plans can be foiled by the unexpected. Cars break down in winter. Children and day care providers get sick. Subway trains go out of service. Electricity goes off and freezes alarm clocks in the distant past.

That's when it pays to have a backup plan. You can find someone to care for your children when the babysitter gets the flu. You can plan an alternative way to get to work. You can set the alarm on your watch as well as the one on your nightstand. Giving such items five minutes of careful thought today can save you hours in the future.

Strategies for long-term planning

Long-term planning is the process of creating descriptions of what you want in 10, 20, or even 50 years from now. Plans that extend beyond our lives are especially powerful. A plan may even include goals to be accomplished several centuries from now. Such plans allow you to contribute to a project that extends well beyond your years.

Use the following suggestions for long-term planning. These suggestions can work for planning anything in your life, from getting an education or managing money to finding a job or developing new relationships.

Keep in mind that there's really no "right" way to do long-term planning. The main thing is to immerse yourself in the process of planning. Then you can see for yourself the benefits it brings. Begin by planning to plan—setting aside time to put goals in writing. From there you can launch your future.

State your goals effectively

Goals are specific changes you'd like to make in yourself or your environment. To help make your goals happen, state them as results you can measure or see. Think in detail about how things would be different if your goal were attained. List the specific changes in what you'd see, feel, touch, taste, hear, or do.

Say that your goal is to become a better student by studying harder. You're headed in a powerful direction; now go for the specifics. Translate that goal into a concrete action, such as "I will study two hours for every hour I'm in class." Measurable goals make clear what actions are needed and what results are expected.

Remember the difference between measurements and values

In planning, it's possible to get the intended results and still miss our purpose. Say that you want to learn to speak Spanish. One way to state that purpose in measurable terms is to write, "I will sign up for a Spanish course and attend at least 98 percent of the class meetings." However, merely showing up for class every day does not guarantee completing the assigned work—or enjoying Spanish.

Ideals, values, emotions, and other sources of non-measurable goals are the "fuel" behind our plans. Often they're what inspired us in the first place. "I want to be a better student," "I want to become a more loving person," or "I want to enjoy music"—none of these is stated as a measurable goal. Yet it's useful to keep such values in mind. They help us remember what our planning is all about.

Work backward, from the future to the present

When you plan, consider working from the general to the specific. Short-range goals are often easier to plan when they grow naturally from long-range goals.

To apply this idea, start planning as far in the future as you can and work backward. The specific length of time doesn't matter. For some people, long-range might mean starting out at 10, 20, or even 50 years from now. For others, imagining three years ahead may feel like reaching into the distant future. Any of these alternatives is fine.

Once you have long-range goals, work backward until you get to a one-day plan. Suppose your 30-year goal is to retire and maintain your present standard of living. Ask yourself, "In order to accomplish that, what needs to be in place in 20 years? To get to that point, what is needed in 10 years? In one year? In one month? One week?" With the answers to such questions, you can make an informed choice about what step to take today.

Write out your plan

Writing uncovers any holes in a plan—gaps in logic, hidden assumptions, contradictions, and other forms of fuzzy thinking. Writing the plan down keeps it specific and powerful.

You can also use other media to shape your plans. For example, make a drawing that represents where you want to be in 20 years. Draw yourself, the people you want to have in your life, and the things you want to have and do. Capturing your plans in a painting, a sculpture, or a collage can do much the same thing

Be willing to act—
even if the plan is not complete

Many careers, successful businesses, and enduring social changes began with the most simple intention or sketchy image. One black woman, Rosa Parks, sparked the civil rights movement by refusing to sit at the back of a bus. Albert Schweitzer first considered doing medical relief work in Africa after he saw a magazine article about the needs of people in the Belgian Congo.

Complete, detailed plans are powerful. At the same time, taking action on an incomplete plan is one way to fill in the gaps. An unfinished plan is no excuse for missing a rewarding experience or ignoring a worthy idea.

Just open your mouth and talk planning

Conversations about planning can bring our intentions into focus. We can even start talking about a plan before we really have one.

In planning, you don't have to go it alone. You can talk to others about your dreams, wishes, fantasies, and goals. You can speak your desire to take charge of your learning, your life, and your career. The more you speak about your goals, the more real they become. Your plan may start out as a hazy ideal. That's fine. By speaking about it with others, you can fill in the details.

Remember to remember

A key part of making any plan work is simply remembering the plan. Yet this can be a challenge. In the midst of an active life, we can easily lose sight of our goals.

To get around this, include your goals on a monthly calendar or daily to-do list. Post notes on your refrigerator. Put your goals on 3x5 cards and tape them to your desk or bathroom mirror. Pin them to a wall. Write them on the back of your hand. Engrave them on a gold plaque. Do whatever it takes to keep the plan alive.

**PRACTICING
CRITICAL THINKING #4**

Working with a group of three to five people, choose an issue on which at least one of you is undecided. State one viewpoint on this issue. Ask those who agree with this viewpoint to go to one side of the room. Ask those who disagree to go to another side. The people who are undecided can stay in the center of the room.

Next, discuss the issue as a group. Based on the reasoning and evidence presented, ask people to re-evaluate their position on the issue—and their position in the room. As people who were undecided come to either agree or disagree with the stated viewpoint, ask them to move to the appropriate side of the room and to explain their reasons for doing so. Remember that people who formerly agreed or disagreed can choose to go to the center of the room if further discussion leaves them undecided.

By doing this exercise, you can also demonstrate how often during a discussion people do see a topic from another point of view. You can also gain insight into the kind of reasoning and evidence that persuades people to change their viewpoint.

Changing your mind based on sound reasoning is a sign of wisdom. When you're finished with this exercise, talk as a group about why some people regard changing your mind as a sign of weakness.

GEARING UP:
Using a long-term planner

Planning a day or a week at a time is a powerful practice. Seeing how your days and weeks fit into a larger picture can yield even more benefits. One way to begin long-term planning is to get an overview of your quarter or semester. Using a quarter, semester, or yearly calendar helps you remember upcoming goals and commitments. On this calendar you can enter test dates, lab sessions, due dates for assignments, days classes will be canceled, and other items that extend beyond the next week or two. Also list interim due dates, such as when you plan to complete the first draft of a term paper. Then, when planning your day or week, scan this calendar to refresh your memory.

Many office supply stores carry academic planners that cover an entire school year. You can also be creative and make your own. A big roll of newsprint pinned to a bulletin board or taped to a wall may do nicely.

Use your academic or yearly planner to mark other significant events, such as:

- birthdays, anniversaries, and other special occasions. Include a "tickler" note well ahead of time to remind you to pick up cards or gifts.
- medical and dental checkups, car maintenance schedules, meetings, luncheons, and other appointments.
- concerts, plays, television and radio programs you want to enjoy.
- due dates for major bills—insurance, taxes, car registration, credit card and installment loan payments, medical expenses, taxes, interest charges, and charitable contributions. Use your calendar to keep track of the amounts you paid.
- trips, vacations, and holidays.

Consider keeping your yearly calendar for years to come. It can be as revealing and as fun to read as a personal journal. This calendar is a snapshot of your life. It says a lot about who you were and who you can be.

Week of	Monday	Tuesday	Wednesday	Thursday	Friday	Saturday	Sunday
9/5							
9/12		English quiz					
9/19			English paper due		Speech #1		
9/26	Chemistry test					Skiing at the lake	
10/3		English quiz			Speech #2		
10/10				Geography project due			
10/17				---No classes---			

LONG-TERM PLANNER: ___/___/___ to ___/___/___

Week of	Monday	Tuesday	Wednesday	Thursday	Friday	Saturday	Sunday
__/__							
__/__							
__/__							
__/__							
__/__							
__/__							
__/__							
__/__							
__/__							
__/__							
__/__							
__/							
__/__							
__/__							
__/__							
__/__							
__/__							
__/__							
__/__							
__/__							
__/__							
__/__							
__/__							
__/__							
__/__							
__/__							
__/__							
__/__							

LONG-TERM PLANNER: ___/___/___ to ___/___/___

Week of	Monday	Tuesday	Wednesday	Thursday	Friday	Saturday	Sunday
__/__							
__/__							
__/__							
__/__							
__/__							
__/__							
__/__							
__/__							
__/__							
__/__							
__/__							
__/__							
__/__							
__/__							
__/__							
__/__							
__/__							
__/__							
__/__							
__/__							
__/__							
__/__							
__/__							
__/__							
__/__							
__/__							
__/__							
__/__							
__/__							
__/__							

THE SEVEN-DAY
antiprocrastination plan

Many students—and their instructors—mention procrastination as a consistent obstacle to meeting their goals. Listed here are seven strategies you can use to eliminate procrastination. Begin with them and then read the following article on motivation for more ideas. Also see "Ways to Change a Habit" in Chapter One.

The suggestions below are tied to the days of the week to help you remember them. Use this list to remind yourself that each day of your life presents an opportunity to stop the cycle of procrastination.

Monday, *Make it meaningful.* What is important about the job you've been putting off? List all the benefits of completing it. Look at it in relation to your goals. Be specific about the rewards for getting it done, including how you will feel when the task is complete.

While you're at it, look for self-defeating beliefs that fuel procrastination and keep you from experiencing the rewards you deserve. Psychologists Jane Burka and Lenora Yuen[2] suggest releasing beliefs such as these: "I must be perfect." "It's safer to do nothing than to take a risk and fail." "There is a right answer, and I'll wait until I find it."

Tuesday, *Take it apart.* Break big jobs into a series of small ones you can do in 15 minutes or less. If a long reading assignment intimidates you, divide it into two-page or three-page sections. Make a list of the sections and cross them off as you complete them so you can see your progress.

Wednesday, *Write an Intention Statement.* Write an Intention Statement on a 3x5 card. For example, if you can't get started on a term paper, you might write, "I intend to write a list of at least 10 possible topics by 9 p.m. I will reward myself with an hour of guilt-free recreational reading." Carry the 3x5 card with you or post it in your study area where you can see it often.

Thursday, *Tell everyone.* Announce publicly your intention to get it done. Tell a friend you intend to learn 10 irregular French verbs by Saturday. Tell your spouse, roommate, parents, and children. Include anyone who will ask whether you've completed it or who will suggest ways to get it done. Make the world your support group.

Friday, *Find a reward.* Construct rewards carefully. Be willing to withhold them if you do not complete the task. Don't pick a movie as a reward for studying biology if you plan to go to the movie anyway. And when you legitimately reap your reward, notice how it feels.

Saturday, *Settle it now.* Do it now. The minute you notice yourself procrastinating, plunge into the task. Imagine yourself at a mountain lake, poised to dive. Gradual immersion would be slow torture. It's often less painful to leap. Then be sure to savor the feeling of having the task behind you.

Sunday, *Say no.* When you keep pushing a task into the low-priority category, re-examine the purpose for doing it at all. If you realize you really don't intend to do something, quit telling yourself that you will. That's procrastinating. Just say NO! Then you're not procrastinating, and you don't have to carry around the baggage of an undone task.

P.S. In some cases, procrastination is positive. Consider the following possibilities.

1. Procrastinate deliberately. You might discover that if you can choose to procrastinate, you can also choose not to procrastinate.

2. Observe your procrastination. Instead of doing something about it, look carefully at the process and its consequences. Avoid judgments. Be a scientist and record the facts. See if procrastination keeps you from getting what you want. Seeing clearly the cost of procrastination may help you kick the habit.

3. Ask yourself whether it's a problem. As one writer put it, "I don't do my best work on deadline. I do my only work on deadline." Some people thrive under pressure, and maybe that style works for you.

Motivation
or "I'm just not in the mood"

The terms *self-discipline, willpower,* and *motivation* are often used to describe something missing in ourselves. Often we invoke these words to explain another's success: "If I were more motivated, I'd get more involved in school." "Of course she got an A. She has self-discipline." "If I had more willpower, I'd lose weight."

However, we can stop looking outside ourselves for these mysterious qualities. Instead, we can say that we're already motivated and disciplined, lacking only certain skills that come from practice. Perhaps what we call motivation is just a habit. The following suggestions offer ways to develop the habit of motivation.

Promise it

Motivation can come simply from being clear about our goals and acting on them. Say that you want to start a study group. Then commit yourself to inviting people and setting a time and place to meet. Promise your classmates that you'll do this, and ask them to hold you accountable. Self-discipline, willpower, motivation—none of those mysterious characteristics needs to get in your way. Just make a promise and keep your word.

Befriend your discomfort

Sometimes keeping your word means doing a task you'd rather put off. The mere thought of doing laundry, reading a chapter in a statistics book, or proofreading a paper can lead to discomfort. In the face of such discomfort, we can procrastinate. Or we can use this barrier as a means to get the task done.

Begin by investigating the discomfort. Notice the thoughts running through your head and speak them out loud, "I'd rather walk on a bed of coals than do this." "This is the last thing I want to do right now."

Also observe what's happening with your body. For example, are you breathing faster or slower than usual? Is your breathing shallow or deep? Are your shoulders tight? Do you feel any tension in your stomach?

Once you're in contact with your mind and body, stay with the discomfort a few minutes. Don't judge it as good or bad. Accepting the thoughts and body sensations robs them of their power. They still may be present, but in time they will stop being a barrier for you.

Discomfort can be a gift—an opportunity to do valuable work on yourself. On the other side of discomfort lies mastery.

Change your mind— and your body

You can also get past discomfort by planting new thoughts in your mind or changing your physical stance. For example, instead of slumping in a chair, sit up straight—or stand up. You can also get physically active by taking a short walk. Notice what happens to your discomfort.

Work with thoughts also. Replace "I can't stand this" with "I'll feel great when this is done" or "Doing this will help me get something I want."

Sweeten the task

Sometimes it's just one aspect of a task that holds us back. That means we could stop procrastinating by merely changing that aspect. If distaste for your physical environment keeps you from studying, then change the environment. Reading about social psychology might seem like a yawner when you're alone in a dark corner of the house. Moving to a cheery, well-lit library could sweeten the task.

Talk about how bad it is

One way to get past negative attitudes is to take them to an extreme. When faced with an unpleasant task, launch into a no-holds-barred gripe session. Pull out all the stops: "There's no way I can start my income taxes now. This is a catastrophe of global proportions, an absolute disaster. This is terrible beyond words . . . ."

Griping taken this far can introduce its own perspective. It shows how self-talk can turn inconveniences into crises.

Turn up the pressure

Sometimes motivation is a luxury. For example, pretend that the due date for your project has been moved up one month. Raising the stress level slightly can move you into action. Then the question of motivation seems beside the point, and meeting the due date moves to the forefront.

Turn down the pressure

The mere thought of starting a huge task can induce anxiety. To get past this feeling, turn down the pressure by taking "baby steps." Divide a large project into small tasks. In 30 minutes or less you could preview a book, create a rough outline for a paper, or solve some math problems. Careful planning can help you discover many such tasks.

Ask for support

Other people can become your allies in overcoming procrastination. For example, form a study group and declare what you intend to accomplish before each meeting. Then ask members to hold you accountable. If you want to begin exercising regularly, ask another person to walk with you three times weekly. People in support groups ranging from Alcoholics Anonymous to Weight Watchers know the power of this strategy.

Adopt a model

One strategy for succeeding at any task is to hang around the masters. Find someone you consider successful and spend time with her. Observe this person and use her as a model for your own behavior. You can "try on" this person's actions and attitudes, looking for tools that feel right for you.

Compare the payoffs to the costs

Cramming for tests, eating poorly, forgetting to exercise—each of these behaviors has a payoff. Cramming might give people more time that's free of commitments. Neglecting exercise can give people more time to sleep.

One way to let go of such behaviors is to first celebrate them—even embrace them. We can openly acknowledge their payoffs.

This can be especially powerful when we follow it up with the next step—determining the costs. For example, skipping a reading assignment gives you time to go to the movies. However, you won't be prepared for your class and you'll have twice as much to read next week.

Maybe there is another way to get the payoff (going to the movies) without paying the cost (skipping the reading assignment). You might choose to give up a few hours of television and read instead.

Comparing the costs and benefits of any behavior can fuel our motivation. We can choose new behaviors because they align with what we want most.

Do it later

At times, it's effective to save a task for later. For example, writing a résumé can wait until you've taken the time to analyze your job skills and write career goals. This is not a lack of motivation—it's planning.

When you do choose "do it later," turn this decision into a promise. Estimate how long the task will take and schedule a specific date and time for it on your calendar.

Heed the message

Sometimes not being motivated—not feeling like it—carries a message that's worth heeding. An example is the student who majors in accounting but seizes every chance to be with children. His chronic reluctance to read accounting textbooks may not be a problem. Instead, it may reveal his desire to major in elementary education. His original career choice might have come from the belief that "real men don't teach kindergarten." In this case not being motivated signals a deeper wisdom trying to get through.

Save time with your
computer

You can use computers to save time and succeed in school. Computers can make it easier for you to revise papers, produce visual aids for speeches, manipulate numbers, manage a mailing list, and track your personal finances. Computers can help you create calendars, store to-do lists, send faxes, and dial phones. One day, perhaps, computers will even take out the garbage and read you the morning paper.

Used with care, a personal computer can help you manage time so well that you'll have more opportunities to relax and get away from the keyboard. Consider the following options.

Stay in contact

With a computer and modem, you can send electronic mail (e-mail) to anyone who's also connected to the same computer network. Using e-mail, you can blast your message down the information highway at digital speed—no trip to the post office necessary.

When you're crunched for time and don't want to mail a long letter, no problem. Just send a paragraph or two via e-mail, much as you would a postcard. E-mail is so fast, you can send shorter notes, send them often, and stay in closer touch with relatives, friends, and job contacts.

Stay informed

Computers offer an efficient way to keep abreast of the news. Choose the level of detail you want. With a computer news service (many are offered on the Internet) you can merely scan the headlines, read the lead paragraph of each article, or display the full text. You can choose from a vast selection of on-line newsletters, newspapers, magazines, and journals.

Crunch numbers quickly

Just about everybody can benefit by crunching numbers with spreadsheets. This type of computer software allows you to create and alter budgets of any size. By plugging in different numbers and assumptions for the future, you can quickly create many scenarios for future income and expenses.

Research efficiently

If you're researching a paper or want to complete a literature review in minimum time, welcome to the computer. With an Internet connection, you can cruise the libraries of the world from your computer—with no travel expenses and often no long-distance phone charges. Even if you don't have an Internet connection, you can search databases, CD-ROMs, and other computer-based resources. By typing in a key word or phrase, you can comb thousands of documents in seconds for a specific fact, reference, or quotation.

Write speedily and edit instantly

Computers can spell r-e-l-i-e-f when you're faced with a writing task. Start with the physical aspects of the craft. Most people find it faster and easier to type on a computer keyboard than on a typewriter.

If you currently take notes for a research paper by using 3x5 cards, consider using a computer instead. A single floppy can store hundreds of pages of text, perhaps the equivalent of a thousand cards.

And when your notes are stored in computer files, you can reduce, rearrange, and rewrite your "cards" with ease.

Save more time by outlining before you write. Many word processing programs allow you to create outlines in a variety of formats. No matter what format you choose, remember that creating outlines can save you hours of writing time. An outline lays bare the structure of your thinking, helping you spot gaps in logic or holes in a plot in advance—before you've drafted hundreds or even thousands of words. You can often do more efficient troubleshooting when you outline in complete sentences rather than words or phrases.

Many writers report the greatest time savings at the revision stage. Computers are tailor-made for this purpose. When you revise with a computer, you don't have to retype an entire page every time when you want to rewrite a word, sentence, or paragraph. Just zero in on the particular passage you want to change and fix it.

Find jobs

When you're looking for work, use a computer to reduce the time you spend on paperwork. Write, edit, and store your résumé and cover letters on disk. Use software to track responses from potential employers. Also use computer-based sources to research businesses, schools, nonprofit organizations, and government agencies.

In the future you might go on-line to circulate résumés and find customers for your products or clients for your services. Some people are already doing this via the Internet.

Avoid the time wasters

To enjoy the full time-saving benefits of a computer, take a few precautions. Stay alert for the following computer-based time wasters.

Trial and error learning. Sometimes flying by the seat of your pants as you learn the computer works well. In other cases, you can save hours by spending a few minutes reading the instructions or by taking a computer class.

Hours that evaporate while you play. When cruising the Internet or playing video games, you might find that a whole morning, afternoon, or evening disappears into the digital void. When you choose to play, set a time limit in advance.

Endless revising. In addition, it can be tempting to keep fiddling with a paper to the point that you miss your deadline. Some writers who use word processors report a tendency to stop and revise every sentence as they write their first draft. This can inhibit the free flow of ideas and slow you down. If something like this happens to you, experiment with dictating your first drafts or writing them the old-fashioned way, with pencil and paper.

Losing data. It's been said that the two most important words in using a computer are *backup* and *save*. This refers to the fact that power surges and loss of electricity can destroy data. New computer users tell stories about losing hours' worth of work in a few seconds.

To prevent this fate, take two simple but powerful steps. First, use spare disks to make backup copies of your work. Then make a backup of your backup disk. Also "save" your work every few minutes. (Your computer manual will explain how.) Doing so can keep your most important creations from evaporating.

Aches and pains. To prevent eye strain from staring too long at a computer screen, take breaks. Rest your eyes from time to time or look out a window. Set up your computer away from windows; that way you can avoid squinting as you look at the screen.

You can avoid lower back problems by paying attention to your posture as you sit at the computer. Adjust your chair so that you can sit comfortably, with your back relaxed and your spine erect. You might wish to place a pillow or small cushion behind your lower back. Type with the keyboard in your lap. This allows your hands to be lower than your elbows and minimizes the tension in your shoulders.

Hardware and software that don't perform up to speed. If you buy a computer, go for the most speed and memory you can afford. Buying a faster modem will save you time and possibly money if you connect to computer networks. Also realize that computer hardware is changing fast. The computer you buy today might be technically outdated in six months. Most users just accept this fact or upgrade their equipment occasionally.

One more caution: Don't expect your grades to soar right after you start using a computer. Computers can perform many tasks with dizzying speed. What they don't do is write papers, create ideas, read textbooks, or attend classes. For those tasks, human beings are unbeatable.

Studying with children underfoot

It is possible to combine effective study time and quality time with children. The following suggestions come largely from students who are also parents. The specific strategies you use will depend on your schedule and the age of your child.

Plan tasks for your child

Silly Putty, Play Doh, Etch-a-Sketch, blocks, coloring books, and other toys can lead your child to creative play. They can also free up study time for you. Gather the toys your child enjoys and keep them on hand. Consider allowing such activities only while you study. This might make the activity even more attractive to your children.

You can set up a desk for the child, just like yours, and even offer rewards for getting his "assignment" done. While he colors, plays with stickers, or flips through a children's book, you can review your notes.

Childproof a room to study in and fill it with toys

Set aside one room or area in your home for children. Remove from it all objects that are unsafe for children and fill it with your child's favorite toys. The goal is a childproof area, one where children can roam freely and play with minimal supervision. Again, consider allowing the child in this room only while you study. Study time then becomes a reward.

Allow for interruptions

It's possible that you'll be interrupted even if you set up child activities in advance. If so, schedule the kind of studying that can be interrupted. You could, for instance, write out or review flash cards with key terms and definitions. Save the tasks that require sustained attention for other times, such as after children go to bed or before they wake up.

Build study time into your school schedule

See if you can arrange for time to study at school before you come home. If you can arrive at school 15 minutes earlier and stay 15 minutes later, you'll squeeze in an extra half-hour of study time that day. Also look for study times between classes.

Use television creatively

Another option is to use television as a babysitter when you can control the programming. Rent a videotape for your child to watch as you study. If you're concerned about your child's becoming a "couch potato," select educational programs that keep your child active.

See if your child can use headphones while watching television. That way, the house stays quiet while you study.

Make it a game

Studying chemistry with a 3-year-old is not as preposterous as it sounds. The secret is to choose the kind of studying that the child can participate in. For instance, use this time to recite. While studying chemistry, make funny faces as you say the properties of the transition elements in the periodic table. Talk in a weird voice as you repeat Faraday's laws. Draw pictures and make up an exciting story about the process of titration.

Use kids as an audience for a speech. If you have invented rhymes, poems, or songs to help you remember formulas or dates, teach them to your children. Be playful. Kids are attracted to energy and enthusiasm.

Sometimes children can even act as private tutors. Ask them to hold flash cards for you. Play "school" with your children as teachers and give them questions to ask you.

Ask for cooperation

Tell the child how important studying is to you and how you appreciate his cooperation. Reward him with attention and praise when he is quiet. When they are included in the process, children are less likely to resent schoolwork as something that takes you away from them. Rather, it becomes something you do together.

When you can't do everything, just do something

One objection to studying with children is "I just can't concentrate. There's no way I can get it all done while children are around." That's OK. Even if you can't comprehend an entire chapter while the kids are running past your desk, you can skim the chapter. Or you could just read the introduction and summary. When you can't get it all done, just get something done.

Caution: If you always study this way, your education may be compromised. Supplement this strategy with others so you can complete crucial tasks.

Attend to your child first

Keep the books out of sight when you first come home. Take 10 minutes to hug your child before you settle in to study. Ask about the child's day. Then explain that you have some work to do. Your child may reward you with 30 minutes of quiet time.

A short time of full, focused attention from an adult is often more satisfying to children than longer periods of partial attention.

Plan study breaks with children

Another option is to take 10 minutes each hour that you study to be with your children. View this not as an interruption but as a study break.

Or schedule time to be with your children when you've finished studying. Let your children in on the plan: "I'll be done reading at 7:30. That gives us a whole hour to play before you go to bed."

Many children love visible reminders that "their time" is approaching. An oven timer works well for this purpose. Set it for 15 minutes of quiet time. Follow that with five minutes of show-and-tell, storybooks, or another activity for your child. Then set the timer for another 15 minutes of studying, another break, and so on.

Develop a routine

Many young children are lovers of routine. They often feel more comfortable when they know what to expect. You can use this to your benefit. One option is to develop a regular time for studying: "From 4 p.m. to 5 p.m. each afternoon is time for me to do my homework." Let your child know this schedule; then enforce it.

Bargain with children. Reward them for keeping the schedule. In return for quiet time, give your child an extra allowance or special treat. Children may enjoy gaining "credits" for this purpose. Each time they give you an hour of quiet time for studying, make an entry on a chart, put a star on their bulletin board, or give them a "coupon." Let children know that after they've accumulated a certain number of entries, stars, or coupons, they can cash in for a big reward—a movie or trip to the zoo.

Ask other adults for help

This suggestion for studying with children is a message repeated throughout the book: Enlist other people in your success.

This can be as simple as asking your spouse, partner, neighbor, or a fellow student to take care of the children while you study. Offer to trade child care with a neighbor: You will take his kids and yours for two hours on Thursday night if he'll take them for two hours on Saturday morning. Some parents start blockwide baby-sitting co-ops based on the same idea.

Find community activities and services

Ask if your school provides a day care service. In some cases, these services are available to students at a reduced cost. Community agencies such as the YMCA may offer similar programs.

You can also find special events that appeal to children. Storytelling hours at the library are one example. While your child is being entertained or supervised, you can stay close by. Use the time to read a chapter or review class notes.

Find a playmate

Another strategy is to find a regular playmate for your child. Some children can pair off with close friends and safely retreat to their rooms for hours of private play. You can check on them occasionally and still get lots of work done.

The ABC daily to-do's
(or working your A's off)

One of the most effective ways to stay on track and actually get things done is to use a daily to-do list. While the Time Monitor/Time Plan is a general picture of the week, your daily to-do list is a specific list of things you want to get done within 24 hours. Keep the list with you, cross out items when you complete them, and add new items when you think of them.

The advantage of keeping a daily list is that you don't have to remember what to do next. It's on the list. A typical day in the life of a student is full of separate, often unrelated tasks—reading, attending lectures, reviewing notes, working at a job, writing papers, doing special projects, research, errands. It's easy to forget an important job on a busy day. When that job is written down, you don't have to trust your memory.

Keep a to-do list every day. It's best to write out the daily to-do list the night before. That way, when your day begins, so will you. Write everything you want to accomplish on one sheet of paper, a daily planning calendar, a special notebook, or a 3x5 card. Cards work well because you can slip them into your pocket.

Rate each task by priority. One way to do this comes from an excellent book, *Take Control of Your Time and Life* by Alan Lakein[3]: Simply label each task A, B, or C.

A's on your list are those things that are most important. These are assignments that are due or jobs that need to be done immediately. These also include activities that lead directly to your long-, mid-, or short-term goals.

The B tasks on your list are important, but less so than your A's. B's might become A's someday. These tasks are important, but not as urgent. They can be postponed if necessary.

C's do not require immediate attention. C items include things like "shop for a new blender" and "get brochures for next year's vacation." C priorities are often small, easy jobs.

Once you've labeled all the tasks on your list, schedule time for all of the A's. The B's and C's can be done in odd moments during the day when you are between tasks and don't have time to start the next A.

When you use the ABC priority method, you might discover a condition common to students: C fever. This is the uncontrollable urge to drop that A task and begin crossing C's off the list. If your history paper is due tomorrow, you might feel compelled to vacuum the rug, call your third cousin in Tulsa, and make a trip to the store for shoelaces. The reasons C fever is so common are that A tasks may be difficult or lengthy and that the risk of failure is higher. Because they are the most important to us, A's can be threatening.

If you notice symptoms of C fever, ask: "Does this job really need to be done now?" "Do I really need to alphabetize my tape collection, or might I better use this time to study for tomorrow's data processing exam?"

Use your to-do list to keep yourself on task, working on your A's. Don't panic or berate yourself when you realize that in the last six hours, you have completed 11 C's and not a single A. Calmly return to the A's.

As you complete tasks, cross them off the list. Crossing off things can be fun, a visible reward for your diligence.

Another option is to put each to-do on its own 3x5 card. This allows for easy sorting of jobs by priority or time.

At the end of the day, evaluate your performance. Look for A's you didn't complete. Look for tasks that repeatedly appear as B's or C's on your list and never seem to get done. Consider changing these to A priority or dropping them altogether. Similarly, you might consider changing an A that didn't get done to a B or C priority.

Develop your own style. You might find that grouping tasks by categories like "errands" or "reading assignments" works best. Be creative.

And accept mistakes. You might assign an A priority to some items that turn out to be true C's. Some of the C's that lurk at the bottom of your list day after day might really be A's. When you keep a list every day, you can discover these errors before they become problems.

Note: The ABC system is not the only way to rank items on your to-do list. Some people prefer the "80-20" system. This is based on the idea that 80 percent of the value from any to-do list comes from only 20 percent of the tasks on that list. So on a to-do list of 10 items, find the two items that will contribute most to your life. Complete those tasks without fail.

Another option is to rank items as "yes," "no," or "maybe." Do all of the tasks marked "yes." Ignore those marked "no." And put all the "maybes" on the shelf for later. You can come back to the "maybes" and mark them "yes" or "no."

Keep in mind the power of planning a whole week or even two weeks at a time in addition to the daily to-do list. Planning in this way can make it easier to put activities in context—to see how your daily goals relate to long-term goals. Weekly planning can also free you from feeling that you have to polish off your whole to-do list in one day. Instead, you can spread tasks over the whole week.

In any case, make starting a to-do list an A priority.

EXERCISE #11
ARE YOU GETTING THERE?

The purpose of this exercise is to let you see how well you are focusing on long-term goals. It's easy to choose long-term goals, commit to them, then forget about them because they seem so far in the future. Yet big goals, like owning a farm, completing a degree, or learning a profession, can be achieved only by stringing together hundreds of small daily goals. This exercise also gives you a chance to look for what barriers are in your way.

Use your completed Time Monitor/Time Plan from pages 42-44 for this exercise. Pick three of your most important long-term goals. You can use the goals you generated in your goal-setting exercise or you can use others. The first step of this exercise is to write those three long-term goals in the space provided below.

Next, go through the completed Time Monitor/Time Plan and circle everything you did that will eventually lead to the accomplishment of the long-term goals you chose.

Then, write down the activities and the time you spent on them under the appropriate goal.

The final step is your assessment of this data. Write this in the form of a Discovery/Intention Statement. What have you learned about yourself by doing this exercise?

Goal:

Time Spent   *Activities*

Goal:

Time Spent   *Activities*

Goal:

Time Spent   *Activities*

By reviewing my Time Monitor/Time Plan and my long-term goals, I learned that . . .

_____

_____

Knowing this, I intend to . . .

_____

_____

Be here now

This Power Process belongs in one of those late-night television ads—the ones in which hyperactive voices, shouting every sentence, describe "amazing," "fantastic," "revolutionary" new tools that chop, slice, dice, catch trout, and fit in your pocket.

The ad might sound like this:

BE HERE NOW!

```
    Yes, that's right
friends!!! BE HERE NOW is a
revolutionary tool for
students. Carry it anywhere.
Use it any time. Get more
out of textbooks. Solve
problems faster. Take tests
better. Can't stay awake in
biology class? No problem
for BE HERE NOW. Millions
sold in Europe! Order today!
Send $39.99 to Power Process
#2, Box 8396 . . .
```

If this Power Process were sold on late-night television, some people might even buy it. Being right here, right now is such a simple idea. It sounds obvious. Where else can you be but where you are? When else can you be there but when you are there? The answer is, you can be somewhere else at any time—in your head. It's common for us to live in our heads, but when we do, we often miss what's happening in the rest of the world.

To "be here now" means to do what you're doing when you're doing it and to be where you are when you're there. Focus your attention on the here and now.

Leaving the here and now

We all have a voice in our head that hardly ever shuts up. If you don't believe it, conduct this experiment: Close your eyes for 10 seconds and pay attention to what is going on in your head. Please do this right now.

Notice something? Perhaps your voice was saying, "Forget it. I'm in a hurry." Another might have said, "I wonder when 10 seconds is up." Another could have been saying, "What little voice? I don't hear any little voice."

That's the voice.

This voice can take you anywhere, any time, especially when you are studying. When the voice takes you away, you might appear to be studying, but your brain is at the beach. According to researchers Claudio Naranjo and Robert Ornstein[4], this is a fundamental property of human consciousness—the ability to function on several different planes at once.

All of us have experienced the voice, as well as the absence of it. When the voice is silent, time seems to no longer exist. We forget worries, aches, pains, reasons, excuses, and justifications. We fully experience the here and now. Life is magic.

There are many benefits of such a state of consciousness. It is easier to discover the world around us when we are not chattering away to ourselves about how we think it ought to be, has been, or will be. Letting go of inner voices and pictures—being totally in the moment—is a powerful tool for students, and there are techniques you can use to keep yourself closer to the here and now.

Do not expect to be rid of daydreams entirely. That is neither possible nor desirable. Inner voices serve a purpose. They enable us to analyze, predict, classify, and understand events out there in the "real" world. Your stream of consciousness serves a purpose. When you are working on a term paper, your inner voices might suggest ideas. When you are listening to your sociology instructor, your inner voices can alert you to possible test questions. When you're about to jump out of an airplane, they could remind you to take a parachute.

Returning to the here and now

A powerful step toward returning to the here and now is to notice when you leave it. Our mind has a mind of its own, and it seems to fight back when we try to control it too much. The thoughts in our mind seem to want to live. If you doubt this, for the next 10 seconds do not, under any circumstance, think of a pink elephant. Please begin not thinking about one now.

Persistent image, isn't it? Most ideas are this insistent when you try to deny them or force them out of your consciousness.

For example, during class you might notice yourself thinking about a test you took the previous day, or a party planned for the weekend, or the CD player you want.

Instead of trying to force a stray thought out of your head—a futile enterprise—simply notice it. Accept it. Tell yourself, "There's that thought again." Then gently return your attention to the task at hand. That thought, or another, will come back. Your mind will drift. Simply notice again where your thoughts take you and gently bring yourself back to the here and now.

Another way to return to the here and now is to notice physical sensations associated with your surroundings. Notice the way the room looks or smells. Notice how the chair feels. Notice the temperature in the room. And bring yourself back to the here and now. Do this as often as necessary, calmly, without irritation.

We can often immediately improve our effectiveness—and our enjoyment—by fully entering into each of our activities, doing one thing at a time. With this idea in mind, remember that no suggestion is absolute. Sometimes choosing to do two or more things at once is useful—even necessary. For example, you might study while doing laundry. You might ask your children to quiz you with flash cards while you fix dinner. The key word is *choose*. When you choose, you're still in charge of your attention.

Experiment with noticing your inner voices. Let go of the ones that prevent you from focusing on learning. Practice the process. Be here now. And now. And now.

The here and now in your future

You also can use Power Process #2 to keep yourself pointed toward your goals. In fact, one of the best ways to get what you want in the future is to realize that you do not have a future. The only time you have is right now. The problem with this idea is that some students will think, "No future, huh? Terrific! Party time!" Being in the here and now, however, is not the same as living for today and forgetting about tomorrow.

Nor is the "be here now" idea a call to abandon goals. Examine this idea closely: Goals exist only in the present.

Goals are merely tools we create to direct our actions right now. Goals, like our ideas of past and future, are useful creations of our minds. They are real only in the here and now.

The power of this idea lies in a simple but frequently overlooked fact: The only time to do anything is now. You can think about doing something next Wednesday. You can write about doing something next Wednesday. You can daydream, discuss, ruminate, speculate, and fantasize about what you will do next Wednesday.

But you can't do anything on Wednesday until it is Wednesday.

Sometimes students think of goals as things that exist in the misty future. And it's easy to postpone action on things in the misty future, especially when everyone else is going to a not-so-misty party.

However, the word *goal* comes from the Anglo-Saxon *gaelan*, which means "to hinder or impede," as in the case of a boundary. That's what a goal does. It restricts, in a positive way, our activity in the here and now. It channels our energy into actions that are more likely to get us what we really want. That's what goals are for. And they are useful only when they are directing action in the here and now.

The process of time management works the same way. You can use the Time Monitor/Time Plan on page 42 to look at your past and plan your future. And the purpose of doing that is to give you more power in the here and now.

The idea behind Power Process #2 is simple. When you plan for the future, plan for the future. When you listen to a lecture, listen to a lecture. When you read this book, read this book. And when you choose to daydream, daydream.

Do what you're doing when you're doing it. Be where you are when you're there. Be here now . . . and now . . . and now.

Time is Money . . .

You might think it strange to find an article about money in this chapter. If so, think about the old saying "Time is money." This cliché points to a profound concept.

According to authors Joe Dominguez and Vicki Robin[5], money is what we accept in exchange for our life energy—our time, passion, and effort. As individuals, Dominguez, Robin, and many others they have taught manage to live on less than $10,000 a year in investment income, freeing up plenty of their life energy for the volunteer work they love.

Managing money is as important to success in school as managing time. The most frequent reason students give for dropping out of school is "I can't afford it." For most students that statement is inaccurate. Before deciding whether the statement is accurate for you, please read the rest of this article. Also read "Education's worth it—and you can pay for it" in Chapter One.

Money management in one sentence

Money produces more unnecessary conflict and worry than almost anything else. Money problems result from spending more than is available. It's that simple. We do everything we can to make the problem complicated.

The solution is also simple: *Don't spend more than you have.* If you are spending more than you have, then increase your income, decrease your spending, or do both. This idea has never won a Nobel Prize in economics, but applying it could end your money worries.

There is a big payoff in making money management seem more complicated than it really is. If we don't understand money, we don't have to be responsible for it. That no longer works when you admit the truth about money: It doesn't work to spend more than you have.

Telling the truth about money is a First Step to an even bigger payoff—the end of your money worries. Here's how it works. First, tell the truth about how much money you have and how much you spend. Then commit to following this simple suggestion: Spend no more than you have. Doing these two things can put an end to many money worries.

This principle does not require that you live like a miser, pinch pennies, and save used dental floss. On the contrary, mastering money is more likely to bring prosperity. The basics of this system can be mastered by anyone.

Start with a budget

Budgeting is really a type of planning. And, like other forms of planning, it creates freedom. When you have a budget and stick to it, you can relax. You are confident. You don't have to worry about whether you can pay your bills. Budgeting is easy because it is mechanical once you get started. The idea is to project how much money is coming in and how much is going out.

Budgets are most useful when you have one for the next month and one for the long run—a year or more.

A monthly budget usually includes the recurring income and expense items—such as paychecks, food costs, and housing—that vary little from one month to the next. It also lists unusual income and expenses, such as loans for school, tuition, and trips.

The long-term budget shows the big picture. It helps you make realistic choices about ways to make or spend money now so you have what you need in the future.

If you discover that the money coming in is less than the money going out, you have three options. You can increase money in, decrease money out, or do both. Generally, it is easier to do both. Soon you can be controlling money, instead of having money control you.

Decrease money out

For many people, the most appealing way to fix a broken budget is to increase income. This approach has a potential problem. When their income increases, many people continue to spend more than they make. You can avoid this dilemma by cutting your expenses, no matter how much money you make.

There are many ways to decrease spending. Experiment with the ideas listed below and create more strategies of your own.

- Look to the big ticket items. When you look for places to cut expenses, go to the items that cost the most. Examples are housing and transportation. Often you can reduce such expenses by living with roommates and taking the bus or a cab.

- Look to the small ticket items. It's amazing how much you can save by cutting back on a snack that costs $1.87 per day or learning how to change the oil on your car.

- Comparison shop. Prices vary. On big items, like cars, the differences can be significant.

- Be aware of quality. The cheapest product is not always the least expensive over the long run.

- Cook for yourself. Many students would be shocked to learn how much money they spent at fast-food restaurants in a year.

- Plan your wardrobe in advance. Stick to one or two color schemes. Find items that you can mix and match with other items.

- Fix things yourself. Many repair or service jobs are easy when you take the time to learn them.

- Pay cash. To avoid interest charges, leave checkbooks and credit cards at home. If you do use a credit card, then pay off the entire credit card balance each month.

- Have free fun. Many libraries loan tapes, CDs, and videotapes. Instead of meeting at a bar, meet at a friend's house, where there is no cover charge.

- Postpone purchases. When you are ready to buy something, wait a week. What seems like a necessity today may not even cross your mind the day after tomorrow.

- Track your money in and money out, down to the penny. You might find that your spending decreases naturally as you learn the details about how much money you really earn and where it actually goes.

If you're in trouble

You can handle money problems in a way that protects a good credit rating. If you get in over your financial head, get specific data. Find out exactly how much money you earn and spend each month. Then be honest with creditors if you can't pay your bills in full. Many will let you pay off a debt in small installments. Also consider credit counseling. Most cities have agencies with professional advisers who can help you straighten out your financial problems. If you're divorced and having serious trouble collecting child support, contact the Association for Children for Enforcement of Support at 1-800-537-7072.

Save for the future

Even if you are in debt, living in an efficiency apartment on a diet of macaroni, you can start saving today. One guideline for economic survival is to build a nest egg equal to three to six months of living expenses. Do this first; then save for major purchases, such as a house, car, your child's education, retirement, or an expensive vacation.

Aim to save at least 10 percent of your take-home pay for as long as you work. Doing so is a big step toward financial peace of mind.

. . . and Money is Time

master student

m a l c o l m x

martyred militant, emerged from the heart of the black ghetto to fight against racial segregation and oppression. At the peak of his power in 1965, his fears of assassination came true.

Many who today hear me somewhere in person, or on television, or those who read something I've said, will think I went to school far beyond the eighth grade. This impression is due entirely to my prison studies.

It had really begun back in the Charlestown Prison, when Bimbi first made me feel envy of his stock of knowledge. Bimbi had always taken charge of any conversation he was in, and I had tried to emulate him. But every book I picked up had few sentences which didn't contain anywhere from one to nearly all of the words that might as well have been in Chinese. When I just skipped those words, of course, I really ended up with little idea of what the book said. So I had come to the Norfolk Prison Colony still going through only book-reading motions . . . .

I saw that the best thing I could do was to get hold of a dictionary—to study, to learn some words. I was lucky enough to reason also that I should try to improve my penmanship. It was sad. I couldn't even write in a straight line. It was both ideas together that moved me to request a dictionary along with some tablets and pencils from the Norfolk Prison Colony school.

I spent two days just riffling uncertainly through the dictionary's pages. I'd never realized so many words existed! I didn't know which words I needed to learn. Finally, just to start some kind of action, I began copying.

In my slow, painstaking, ragged handwriting, I copied into my tablet everything printed on that first page, down to the punctuation marks.

I believe it took me a day. Then, aloud, I read, back to myself, everything I'd written on the tablet. Over and over, aloud, to myself, I read my own handwriting.

I woke up the next morning thinking about those words—immensely proud to realize that not only had I written so much at one time, but I'd written words that I never knew were in the world. Moreover, with a little effort I also could remember what many of these words meant. . . .

I was so fascinated that I went on—I copied the dictionary's next page. And the same experience came when I studied that. With every succeeding page, I also learned of people and places and events from history. Actually the dictionary is like a miniature encyclopedia. Finally the dictionary's A section had filled a whole tablet—and I went on into the B's. That was the way I started copying what eventually became the entire dictionary. . . .

I suppose it was inevitable that as my word base broadened, I could for the first time pick up a book and read and now begin to understand what the book was saying. Anyone who has read a great deal can imagine the new world that opened. Let me tell you something: From then until I left that prison, in every free moment I had, if I was not reading in the library, I was reading on my bunk. You couldn't have gotten me out of books with a wedge. Between Mr. Muhammad's teachings, my correspondence, my visitors—usually Ella and Reginald—and my reading of books, months passed without my even thinking about being imprisoned. In fact, up to then, I never had been so truly free in my life. . . .

Not long ago, an English writer telephoned me from London, asking questions. One was, "What's your alma mater?" I told him, "Books."

From The Autobiography of Malcolm X
by Malcolm X with Alex Haley
Copyright © 1964 by Alex Haley and Malcolm X
Copyright © 1965 by Alex Haley and Betty Shabazz
Reprinted by permission of Random House, Inc.

1 What are at least three ways you can control interruptions when you study?

2 It is effective to leave "holes" in your schedule to allow for the unexpected. True or False. Explain your answer.

3 Suppose that after you choose where to focus your attention, your mind wanders. Power Process #2 suggests that one of the most effective ways to bring your focus back to the here and now is to:

    (A) Slap your cheek and shout "Attention" as loudly as you can.
    (B) Notice that your thoughts have wandered and gently bring them back.
    (C) Sleep.
    (D) Concentrate fully and resist the temptation to be distracted.
    (E) Indulge your distracting thoughts until they disappear.

4 What are at least five of the 25 ways to get the most out of now?

5 In time management terms, what is meant by "This ain't no piano"?

6 Define C fever as it applies to the ABC priority method.

7 Scheduling marathon study sessions once in a while is generally an effective strategy. True or False. Explain your answer.

8 *Describe at least three of the seven strategies for dealing with procrastination.*

9 *What two ideas, taken together, led Malcolm X to request a dictionary along with some tablets and pencils from the Norfolk Prison Colony school?*

10 *"Working your A's off" refers to:*

(A) A strategy for organizing your study area.
(B) Referring to a dictionary when reading unfamiliar material.
(C) The importance of your physical exercise program.
(D) Accomplishing the top-priority items on your to-do list.
(E) A strategy for studying with children underfoot.

JOURNAL ENTRY #14
DISCOVERY/INTENTION STATEMENT

While reading this chapter, what did you discover about the way you manage time?

   I discovered that I . . .

_____

_____

   Pick two strategies for working with time and write a one-sentence Intention Statement about how you plan to use each one in the next 72 hours.

   In regard to strategy one, I intend to . . .

_____

_____

   In regard to strategy two, I intend to . . .

_____

_____

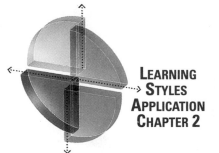

**LEARNING
STYLES
APPLICATION
CHAPTER 2**

Style 1

List five benefits that you could experience by mastering Power Process #2: "Be here now." Think of specific ways that applying this Power Process to your course work could promote your success in school.

Style 2

Review the article "Twenty-five ways to get the most out of now." On a separate sheet of paper, list each of those strategies and rank them using the ABC priority method. Assign an A to those strategies you're most likely to use.

Style 3

Choose one of the strategies mentioned in this chapter for planning your time. Experiment with it for the next week. Then describe how well it worked for you.

Style 4

Think again about the planning strategy you used. Is there any way you could modify this strategy to make it work better for you? Describe what specific changes you would make in applying this technique.

Bibliography

◼ Endnotes

[1] Stephen R. Covey, *The Seven Habits of Highly Effective People: Restoring the Character Ethic* (New York: Simon & Schuster, 1989).

[2] Jane B. Burka and Lenora R. Yuen, *Procrastination: Why You Do It, What To Do About It* (Reading, MA: Addison-Wesley, 1983).

[3] Alan Lakein, *Take Control of Your Time and Life* (New York: New American Library, 1973).

[4] Claudio Naranjo and Robert E. Ornstein, *On the Psychology of Meditation* (New York: Viking, 1971).

[5] Joe Dominguez and Vicki Robin, *Your Money or Your Life: Transforming Your Relationship with Money and Achieving Financial Independence* (New York: Viking, 1992).

◼ Additional Reading

Covey, Stephen R. *First Things First*, New York: Simon & Schuster, 1994.

Ellis, David B. *Creating Your Future*, Rapid City, SD: Breakthrough Enterprises, 1996.

Keyes, Ralph. *Timelock: How Life Got So Hectic and What You Can Do About It*, New York: HarperCollins, 1991.

Scharf-Hunt, Diana, and Pam Hait. *Studying Smart: Time Management for College Students*, New York: HarperPerennial, 1990.

Winston, Stephanie. *Getting Organized*, New York: Warner, 1978.

memory

In this chapter...

■ experience your memory in a new way. Move from "I always forget" to "I will remember." Discover 20 memory techniques, strategies for remembering names, and tools for tapping into your "secret brain." Also learn about loving your problems, and read about successful people who experienced notable failures.

JOURNAL ENTRY #15
DISCOVERY STATEMENT

Describe three situations in which you could be more effective by improving your memory skills.

_____
_____
_____
_____
_____
_____
_____
_____
_____
_____
_____

Now preview this chapter and list five useful memory strategies you can use immediately. Also note the page numbers where these strategies are explained.

Strategy   *Page Number*

_____
_____
_____
_____
_____
_____
_____
_____

THE KEY TO USING YOUR MEMORY more effectively is to realize that—short of injury, disease, or death—your brain never loses anything. Once a thought or perception has been input to your memory it stays there for the rest of your life. What we call forgetting is either the inability to recall stored information or the failure to store information in the first place. For example, during certain kinds of brain surgery, the patient remains conscious. Surgeon Wilbur Penfield[1] found that when sections of the brain are stimulated with a mild electrical current, the patient will often remember events of her childhood with absolute clarity. She can recall details she thought were long forgotten—like the smell of her father's starched shirts or the feel of sunlight warming her face through the window of her first-grade classroom.

You never forget

People under hypnosis have reported similar experiences. Some people have been able to recall events that took place shortly after their birth. Working with police, hypnotists have helped witnesses of crimes remember vital information, such as license plate numbers.

Once information is stored in memory, it is never forgotten. Sometimes, however, we do have difficulty recalling a piece of information from our memory. The data is still in our heads. We simply can't find it.

Just as often, when we think we have forgotten something, the truth is that we never stored it in our memory in the first place.

> **" "**
> *The art of true memory is the art of attention.*
> –SAMUEL JOHNSON

> **" "**
> *Memory is the mother of imagination, reason and skill. . . . This is the companion, this is the tutor, the poet, the library with which you travel.*
> –MARK VAN DOREN

The memory jungle

Think of your memory as a vast, overgrown jungle. This memory jungle is thick with wild plants, exotic shrubs, twisted trees, and creeping vines. It spreads over thousands of square miles—dense, tangled, forbidding. Imagine that the jungle is bounded on all sides by impassable mountains. There is only one entrance to the jungle, a narrow pass through the mountains that opens into a small meadow.

In the jungle there are animals, millions of them. The animals represent all the information in your memory. Imagine that every thought, picture, or perception you ever had is represented by an animal in this jungle. Every single event ever perceived by any of your five senses—sight, touch, hearing, smell, or taste—is also in the jungle. Some of the thought animals, like your picture of the color of your seventh-grade teacher's eyes, are well hidden. Other thoughts, like your telephone number or the position of the reverse gear in your car, are easier to find.

There are two rules of the jungle. Each thought animal must pass through the meadow at the entrance to the memory jungle; and once an animal enters the jungle, it never leaves.

The meadow represents short-term memory. It's the kind of memory that you use when you look up a telephone number. You can look at seven digits and hold them in your short-term memory long enough to dial them.

Short-term memory appears to have a limited capacity (the meadow is small), and short-term memory disappears fast (animals pass through the meadow quickly).

The jungle itself represents long-term memory. This is the kind of memory that allows us to recall information from day to day, week to week, and year to year. Remember that animals never leave the long-term memory jungle.

The following visualizations can help you recall useful concepts about memory.

Visualization #1: A well-worn path

Imagine what happens as a thought, in this case we'll call it a deer, bounds across short-term memory and into the jungle. The deer leaves a trail of broken twigs and hoof prints that you can follow. Brain research suggests that thoughts could wear paths in the memory.[2] These paths are called *neural traces*. The more well-worn the neural trace, the easier it is to retrieve (find) the thought. In other words, the more often the deer retraces the path, the clearer the path becomes. The more often you recall information, and the more often you put the same information into your memory, the easier it is to find.

When you buy a new car, for example, the first few times you try to find reverse you have to think for a moment. After you have found reverse gear every day for a week, the path is worn into your memory. After a year, the path is so well-worn that when you dream about driving your car backward, you even dream the correct motion for finding reverse.

Visualization #2: A herd of thoughts

The second picture you can use to your advantage is the picture of many animals gathering at a clearing—like thoughts gathering at a central location in the memory. It is easier to retrieve thoughts that are grouped together, just as it is easier to find a herd of animals gathered in a clearing than it is to find one deer.

Pieces of information are easier to recall if you can associate them with similar information. For example, it is easier to remember a particular player's batting average if you associate it with other baseball statistics.

Visualization #3: Turning your back

Imagine releasing the deer into the jungle, turning your back on it, and counting to 10. When you turn around, the deer is gone. This is exactly what happens to most of the information we receive.

Generally, people cannot remember 50 percent of the material they have just read. Within 24 hours, most people can recall only about 20 percent. That means that 80 percent of the material is wandering around, lost in the memory jungle.

The remedy is simple: Review quickly. Do not take your eyes off the animal as it crosses the short-term memory meadow, and review it soon after it enters the long-term memory jungle. Wear a path in your memory immediately.

Visualization #4: You are directing the animal traffic

The fourth picture is one with you in it. You are standing at the entrance to the short-term memory meadow, directing herds of animals as they file through the pass, across the meadow, and into your long-term memory. You are taking an active role in the learning process. You are paying attention. You are doing more than sitting on a rock and watching the animal traffic file into your brain. You become part of the process, and as you do, you take control of your memory.

20 memory techniques

Experiment with these techniques to make a flexible, custom-made memory system that fits your style of learning. The 20 techniques are divided into four categories, each of which represents a general principle for improving memory.

Briefly, the categories are:

1) Organize it. Organized information is easier to find.
2) Use your body. Learning is an active process; get all your senses involved.
3) Use your brain. Work with your memory, not against it.
4) Recall it. This is easier when you use the other principles to store information.

The first three categories, which include techniques #1 through #16, are about storing information effectively. Most memory battles are won or lost here. To get the most out of this article, survey the following techniques by reading each title. Then read the techniques. Next, skim them again, looking for the ones you like best.

Mark those and use them.

Organize it.

1. Learn from the general to the specific. Imagine looking at a new painting this way: Blindfold yourself, put a magnifying glass up to your eye, move your face to within inches of the painting; now yank the blindfold off and begin studying the painting; one square inch at a time. Chances are, even after you finish looking at the painting this way, you won't know what it is.

Unfortunately, many students approach new courses and textbooks just this way. They feel driven to jump right in and tackle the details before they get the big picture.

Here is a different approach: Before you begin your next reading assignment, skim it for the general idea. You can use the same techniques you learned in Exercise #1: "Textbook reconnaissance" on page vi.

You can also use this technique at the beginning of a course. Ask someone who has taken it to quickly review it with you. Do a textbook reconnaissance of the reading assignments for the entire course. This technique works best at the beginning of a term, but it's never too late to use it.

If you're lost, step back and look at the big picture. The details might make more sense.

2. Make it meaningful. A skydiver will not become bored learning how to pack her parachute. Her reward for learning the skill is too important. Know what you want from your education; then look for connections between what you want and what you are studying. If you're bogged down in quadratic equations, stand back for a minute. Think about how that math course relates to your goal of becoming an electrical engineer.

When information helps you get something you want, it's easier to remember. That is one reason why it pays to be specific about what you want.

3. Create associations. The data already stored in your memory is arranged according to a scheme that makes sense to you. When you introduce new data, you can recall it more effectively if you store it near similar or related data.

Say you are introduced to someone named Greg. One way to remember his name would be to visualize another person you know named Greg. When you see the new Greg again, your mind is more likely to associate him with a Greg you already know.

Use your body.

4. Learn it once, actively. According to an old saying, people remember 90 percent of what they do, 75 percent of what they see, and 20 percent of what they hear.

These percentages might not be scientifically provable, but the idea behind them is sound. Action is a great memory enhancer. You can test this theory for yourself by studying with the same energy you might bring to the dance floor or the basketball court.

When you sit at your desk, sit up. Sit on the edge of your chair, as if you were about to spring out of it and sprint across the room.

Also experiment with standing up when you study. It's harder to fall asleep in this position. Some people insist their brains work better when they stand.

Pace back and forth and gesture as you recite material out loud. Use your hands. Get your whole body involved in studying.

These techniques are also great ways to battle boredom. Boredom puts memory to sleep. Wake it up by using your arms and legs as well as your eyes, ears, and voice.

Learning can be deceptive. Most learning, especially in higher education, takes place in a passive setting. Students are sitting down, quiet and subdued.

Don't be fooled. Learning takes energy. When you learn effectively, you are burning calories, even if you are sitting at a desk reading a textbook.

5. Relax. When we're relaxed, we absorb new information quicker and recall it with greater accuracy. Some courses in accelerated and "whole mind" learning teach relaxation techniques.

Part of this is common sense. Students who can't recall information during a final exam, when they are nervous, often can recite the same facts later, when they are relaxed.

This idea might seem to contradict technique #4, but it doesn't. Being relaxed is not the same as being drowsy, zoned out, or asleep. Relaxation is a state of alertness, free of tension, during which our minds can play with new information, roll it around, create associations with it, and apply many of the other memory techniques. We can be active and relaxed.

Many books, tapes, and seminars are available to teach you ways to relax. In addition, relaxation exercises are included in this book. Experiment with these exercises and apply them as you study. "Mellowing out" might do more than lower your blood pressure; it might help you succeed in school.

6. Create pictures. Draw diagrams. Make cartoons. Use them to connect facts and illustrate relationships. Relationships within and among abstract concepts can be "seen" and recalled easily when they are visualized. The key is to use your imagination.

For example, in physics, Boyle's law states that the pressure of a quantity of gas is inversely proportional to the volume the gas occupies. That is, if you cut the volume in half, you double the pressure. To remember this concept, you might picture someone "doubled over" using a bicycle pump. As she increases the pressure in the pump by decreasing the volume in the pump cylinder, she seems to be getting angrier. By the time she has doubled the pressure (and halved the volume) she is "boiling" (Boyle-ing) mad.

Another reason to create pictures is that visual information is associated with a different part of the brain than verbal information. When you create a picture of a concept, you are anchoring the information in two parts of your brain. This increases your chances of recalling that information.

To visualize relationships effectively, create action, such as the person using the pump. Make the picture vivid too. The person's face could be bright red. Make her ready to "boil." And involve all your senses. Imagine how the cold metal of the pump would feel and how she would sound as she struggled and grunted with it. (She'd have to struggle. It would take incredible strength to double the pressure in a bicycle pump, not to mention a darn sturdy pump.)

7. Recite and repeat. When you repeat something out loud, you anchor the concept in two different senses. First, you get the physical sensation in your throat, tongue, and lips when voicing the concept. Second, you hear it. The combined result is synergistic, just as it is when you draw pictures. That is, the effect of using two different senses is greater than the sum of their individual effects.

The "out loud" part is important. Reciting silently, in your head, can be useful—in the library, for example—but it is not as effective as making noise. Your mind can trick itself into thinking it knows something when it doesn't. Your ears are harder to fool.

The repetition part is important too. Repetition is the most common memory device because it works. Repetition blazes a trail through the pathways of your brain, making the information easier to find. Repeat a concept out loud until you know it, then say it five more times.

Recitation works best when you recite concepts in your own words. For example, if you want to remember that the "acceleration of a falling body due to gravity at sea level equals 32 feet per second per second," you might say, "Gravity makes an object accelerate 32 feet per second faster for each second that it's in the air at sea level." Putting it in your own words forces you to think about it.

Have some fun with this technique. Recite by writing a song about what you're learning. Sing it in the shower. Use any style you want ("Country, jazz, rock, or rap, when you sing out loud, learning's a snap!").

Or imitate someone. Imagine your textbook being read by Bill Cosby, Madonna, or Clint Eastwood. ("Go ahead, punk. Make my density equal mass over volume.")

Recite and repeat.

It's a technique you can use anywhere.

8. Write it down. This technique is obvious, yet easy to forget. Writing a note to yourself helps you remember an idea, even if you never look at the note again.

You can extend this technique by writing it down not just once, but many times. Let go of the old images of being in elementary school and being forced to write, "I will not throw paper wads" 100 times on the chalkboard after school. Used with items that you choose to remember, repetitive writing is a powerful technique. Writing engages a different kind of memory than speaking. Writing prompts us to be more logical, coherent, and complete. Written reviews reveal gaps in knowledge that oral reviews miss, just as oral reviews reveal gaps that mental reviews miss.

Another advantage of written reviews is that they more closely match the way we're asked to remember materials in school. During your academic career, you'll probably take far more written exams than oral exams. Writing can be an effective way to prepare for tests.

Finally, writing is physical. Your arm, your hand, and your fingers join in. Remember, you remember what you do.

Use your brain.

9. Reduce interference. Turn off the stereo when you study. Find a quiet place that is free from distraction. If there's a party at your house, go to the library. If you have a strong attraction to food, don't torture yourself by studying next to your refrigerator.

Two hours of studying in front of the television might be worth 10 minutes of studying where it is quiet. If you have two hours and want to study and watch television, it's probably better to study for an hour and watch television for an hour. Doing one at a time increases your ability to remember.

10. Overlearn. One way to fight mental fuzziness is to learn more than you intended. Students often stop studying when they think they know the material well enough to pass a test. Another option is to pick a subject apart, examine it, add to it, and go over it until it becomes second nature.

This technique is especially effective for problem solving. Do the assigned problems, then do more problems. Find another text and work similar problems. Make up your own problems and work those. When you pretest yourself in this way, the potential rewards are speed, accuracy, and greater confidence at exam time.

11. Escape the short-term memory trap. Short-term memory is different from the kind of memory you'll need during exam week. For example, most of us can look at an unfamiliar seven-digit phone number once and remember it long enough to dial it. See if you can recall that number the next day.

Short-term memory can fade after a few minutes, and it rarely lasts more than several hours. A short review within minutes or hours of a study session can move material from short-term memory into long-term memory. That quick mini-review can save you hours of study time when exams roll around.

12. Use daylight. Study your most difficult subjects during daylight hours. Many people can concentrate more effectively during the day. The early morning hours can be especially productive, even for people who hate to get up with the sun.

13. Distribute learning. Psychological research suggests that marathon study sessions are not effective.[3] You can get far more done in three two-hour sessions than in one six-hour session.

For example, when you are studying for your American history exam, study for an hour or two; then wash the dishes. While you are washing the dishes, part of your mind reviews what you studied.

Return to American history for a while, then call a friend. Even while you are deep in conversation, part of your mind will be reviewing history.

You can get more done if you take regular breaks, and you can even use them as mini-rewards. After a productive study session, give yourself permission to make a short phone call, listen to a song, or play 10 minutes of hide-and-seek with your kids.

There is an exception to this idea. When you are engrossed in a textbook and cannot put it down, when you are consumed by an idea for a term paper and cannot think of anything else—keep going. The master student within you has taken over. Enjoy the ride.

14. Be aware of attitudes. People who think history is boring tend to have difficulty remembering history. People who believe math is difficult tend to have difficulty recalling mathematical formulas. All of us can forget information that contradicts our opinions.

This is not the same as fighting your attitudes or struggling to give them up. Simply acknowledge them. Notice them. Your awareness can deflate an attitude that is blocking your memory.

One way to befriend a self-defeating attitude about a subject is to relate it to something you are interested in. For example, consider a person who is fanatical about cars. She can rebuild a motor in a weekend and considers that a good time.

From this apparently specialized interest, she can explore a wide realm of knowledge. She can relate the workings of an engine to principles of physics, math, and chemistry. Computerized parts in newer cars lead her to data processing. She can now study how cars have changed our cities and helped create suburbs, a topic that includes urban planning, sociology, business, economics, psychology, and history.

We remember what we find interesting. If you think a subject is boring, remember, everything is related to everything else. Look for connections.

15. Choose what not to store in memory. We can adopt an "information diet." Just as we choose to avoid certain foods, we can choose not to retain certain kinds of information.

Decide what's essential to remember from a reading assignment or lecture. Extract the core concepts. Ask what you'll be tested on, as well as what you want to remember. Then apply memory techniques to those ideas.

16. Combine memory techniques. All of these memory techniques work even better in combination. Choose two or three techniques to use on a particular assignment. Experiment for yourself.

For example, after you take a few minutes to get an overview of a reading assignment (#1), you could draw a quick picture to represent the main point (#6). Or you could overlearn that math formula (#11) by singing a jingle about it (#7) all the way to work. If you have an attitude that math is difficult, you could acknowledge that (#14); then you could distribute your study time in short, easy-to-handle sessions (#13). Combining memory techniques is combining sight, sound, and touch when you study. The effect is synergistic.

Recall it.

17. Remember something else. When you are stuck and can't remember something you know you know, remember something else that is related to it.

If you can't remember your great-aunt's name, remember your great-uncle's name. During an economics exam, if you can't remember anything about the aggregate demand curve, recall what you know about the aggregate supply curve. If you cannot recall specific facts, remember the example the instructor used during her lecture. Information is stored in the same area of the brain as similar information. You can unblock your recall by stimulating that area of your memory.

A brainstorm is a good memory jog. When you are stumped in a test, start writing down lots of answers to related questions and—pop!—the answer you need is likely to appear.

18. Notice when you do remember. Everyone has a different memory style. Some people are best at recalling information they've read. Others remember best what they've heard, seen, or done.

To develop your memory, notice when you recall information easily and ask yourself what memory techniques you're using naturally. Also notice when it's difficult to recall information. Let go of the temptation to judge yourself. Instead, be a reporter. Get the facts, and adjust your learning techniques. And remember to congratulate yourself when you remember.

19. Use it before you lose it. Even information stored in long-term memory becomes difficult to recall if we don't use it regularly. The pathways to the information in our brains become faint with disuse. For example, you can probably remember your current phone number. What was your phone number 10 years ago?

This points to a powerful memory technique. To remember something, access it a lot. Read it, write it, speak it, listen to it, apply it—find some way to make contact with the material regularly. Each time you do so, you widen the neural pathway to the material and make it easier to recall the next time.

Another way to contact the material is to teach it. Teaching demands mastery. When you explain the function of the pancreas to a fellow student, you discover quickly whether you really understand the pancreas.

Study groups are especially effective because they put you on stage. The friendly pressure of knowing you'll teach the group helps to focus your attention.

20. And remember, you never forget. You might not believe that an idea or thought never leaves your memory. That's OK. In fact, it doesn't matter whether you agree with the idea or not. It can work for you anyway.

Test the concept. Adopt an attitude that says, "I never forget anything. I may have difficulty recalling something from my memory, but I never really forget it. All I have to do is find where I stored it."

Many people use the flip side of this technique and get the opposite results. "I never remember anything," they say over and over again. "I've always had a poor memory. I'm such a scatterbrain." That kind of negative self-talk is self-fulfilling.

An alternative is to speak more positively, or at least more accurately. Instead of saying "I don't remember," you can say "It will come to me." The latter statement implies that the information you want is stored in your mind and that you can retrieve it . . . just not right now.

We can also use affirmations that support us as we develop our memories. Possibilities include "I recall information easily and accurately" and "My memory serves me well." Or even "I never forget!"

EXERCISE #12
REMEMBERING YOUR CAR KEYS . . . OR ANYTHING ELSE

Pick something you frequently forget. Some people are chronic car key losers or forget to write down checks in their check register. Others forget anniversaries and birthdays.

Pick your forgettable item or task. Then design a strategy for remembering it. You are on your own, and you are your own best expert. Use any of the techniques in this chapter, research other techniques, and design your own from scratch. Describe your technique and the results on a separate sheet of paper. In this exercise, as in most of the exercises in this book, a failure is also a success. Don't be concerned with whether your technique will work. Design it; then find out. If it doesn't work, use another method.

Give your "secret brain" a chance

Sometimes the way you combine studying with other activities can affect how well you remember information. For example, memory technique #12, "Escape the short-term memory trap," suggested reviewing or reflecting on material shortly after you learn it. This is one way to avoid what psychologists call *retroactive inhibition*[4], something that can happen when a new, unrelated activity interferes with previous learning. Reviewing prevents such a conflict and allows your brain to store information more effectively in your long-term memory. This kind of learning takes place at a level below your awareness. Consider the following scenarios.

Scenario #1

You've just left your evening psychology class after a fascinating lecture on Sigmund Freud's theory of dreams. You want to make it home in time to tuck your children in bed, so you hurry out of class. In five minutes you're cruising down the highway. You decide to flip on the radio as you drive. Doesn't matter what station, just something to help you unwind. After all, it's been a long day—nine hours at the office and three in class. You deserve a break. Later, just before going to sleep, you decide to sneak in a few pages of that mystery novel you've wanted to finish. After you find out who poisoned the butler, you settle in for a well-deserved rest.

Scenario #2

Instead of driving yourself home after your "session with Sigmund," you have arranged to car pool with a classmate. On the way home, you talk about the lecture. The discussion ignites into a debate as you and your friend take opposite stands on a key point of Freud's theory. After you arrive home, you take some time to check in with your children and talk about the day. Later, just before going to sleep, you mull over the conversation and make a mental note to write down your dreams in the morning. You decide to let the mystery novel wait until tomorrow night.

In the morning, you not only write down your dreams, you remember enough about last night's lecture to explain it to your children at breakfast. While you slept, your brain was not only manufacturing dreams but also storing the key points of Freud's theory—something that will come in handy for the midterm exam. In short, you expended the same amount of energy, had the same amount of fun, and saved yourself hours of review time later in the term. Nice work.

NOTABLE FAILURES

"Humbling Cases for Career Counselors" by Dr. Milton E. Larson from Phi Delta Kappan, *February 1973 issue, Volume LIV, No. 6, p. 374, © 1973.*

Creative and imaginative people are often not recognized by their contemporaries. Even more often, they are not recognized in school by their teachers. History is full of examples.

Einstein was four years old before he could speak and seven before he could read. Isaac Newton did poorly in grade school, and Beethoven's music teacher once said of him, "As a composer he is hopeless." When Thomas Edison was a boy, his teachers told him he was too stupid to learn anything. F. W. Woolworth got a job in a dry goods store when he was 21, but his employers would not let him wait on a customer because he "didn't have enough sense." A newspaper editor fired Walt Disney because he had "no good ideas." Caruso's music teacher told him, "You can't sing. You have no voice at all." The director of the Imperial Opera in Vienna told Madame Schumann-Heink that she would never be a singer and advised her to buy a sewing machine. Leo Tolstoy flunked out of college; Wernher von Braun flunked ninth-grade algebra. Admiral Richard E. Byrd had been retired from the Navy as "unfit for service" until he flew over both Poles. Louis Pasteur was rated as "mediocre" in chemistry when he attended the Royal College. Abraham Lincoln entered the Black Hawk War as a captain and came out as a private. Louisa May Alcott was told by an editor that she could never write anything that would have popular appeal. Fred Waring was once rejected for high school chorus. Winston Churchill failed the sixth grade.

Set a trap for your memory

When you want to remind yourself to do something, link that activity to another event that you know will take place.

Say you're walking to class and suddenly you realize that your accounting assignment is due tomorrow. Switch your watch from your left to your right wrist. Every time you look at your watch it becomes a reminder that you were supposed to remember something. (You can do the same with a ring.)

If you empty your pockets every night, put an unusual item in your pocket to remind yourself to do something before you go to bed. To remember to call your sister for her birthday, pick an object from the diaper bag—a teething toy, perhaps—and put it in your pocket. That evening, when you empty your pocket and find the teething toy, you're more likely to call your sister.

The key is to pick events that are certain to occur. Rituals like looking at your watch, reaching for car keys, and untying shoes are seldom forgotten. Tie a triple knot in your shoelace to remind you to set the alarm for your early morning study group meeting.

You can even use imaginary cues. To remember to write a check for the phone bill, picture your phone hanging on the front door. In your mind, create the feeling of reaching for the door knob and grabbing the phone cord instead. When you get home and reach to open the front door, the image is apt to return to you. Link two activities together, and make the association unusual.

Another way to remember something is to tell yourself you will remember it. Relax and say, "At any time I choose, I will be able to recall . . . ." The intention to remember can be more powerful than any memory technique.

PRACTICING CRITICAL THINKING #5

One key to memory is focused attention and observation. Apply this idea by carefully observing a building on your campus or classroom in your school. From your observation, infer the educational philosophy of the person who designed this physical space.

For example, consider the layout of a large classroom with a podium in front for one speaker and seats for several hundred members of an audience. This design could flow from these assumptions:

- *Lectures are an ideal way to convey information and ideas.*
- *Large class sizes can be just as effective as small class sizes.*
- *One person at a time should do most of the speaking, and most of the other people should be listening.*
- *Students should listen primarily to the speaker at the front of the room, not to other students.*

Writing in the space below, describe the classroom or educational building you've chosen to observe, along with your inferences. What did the person who designed this structure think about how education is supposed to happen?

Remembering names

One powerful way to immediately practice memory techniques is to use them to remember names. This skill may not seem as important to a future surgeon as memorizing the names of the major arteries. Even so, remembering names is an important social skill. Here are some ways to master it.

Recite and repeat in conversation.

When you hear a person's name, repeat it. Immediately say it to yourself several times without moving your lips. You could also repeat the name in a way that does not sound forced or artificial: "I'm pleased to meet you, Maria."

Ask the other person to recite and repeat.

You can let other people help you remember their names. After you've been introduced to someone, ask that person to spell the name and pronounce it correctly for you. Most people will be flattered by the effort you're making to learn their names.

Visualize.

After the conversation, construct a brief visual image of the person. For a memorable image, make it unusual. Imagine the name painted in hot pink fluorescent letters on the person's forehead.

Admit you don't know.

Admitting that you can't remember someone's name can actually put people at ease. Most of them will sympathize if you say, "I'm working to remember names better. Yours is right on the tip of my tongue. What is it again?" (By the way, that's exactly what psychologists call that feeling—the "tip of the tongue phenomenon."[5])

Introduce yourself again.

Most of the time we assume introductions are one-shot affairs. If we miss the name the first time, our hopes for remembering are dashed. Instead of giving up, introduce yourself again: "Hello, again. We met earlier. I'm Jesse, and please tell me your name again."

Use associations.

Link each person you meet with one characteristic you find interesting or unusual. For example, you could make a mental note: "Vicki Cheng—tall, black hair" or "James Washington—horn-rimmed glasses." To reinforce your associations, write them on a 3x5 card as soon as you can.

Limit the number of new names you learn at one time.

Occasionally we find ourselves in situations where we're introduced to many people at the same time: "Dad, these are all the people in my Boy Scout troop." "Let's take a tour so you can meet all 32 people in this department."

When meeting a group of people, concentrate on remembering just two or three names. Free yourself of any obligation to remember every one. Few of the people in mass introductions expect you to remember their names. Another way to avoid memory overload is to limit yourself to learning just first names. Last names can come later.

Ask for photos or lists.

In some cases, you may be able to get photos of all the people you meet. For example, a small business where you apply for a job may have a brochure with pictures of all the employees. Ask for individual or group photos and write in the names if they're not included. You can use these photos as "flash cards" as you drill yourself on names.

Go early.

Consider going early to conventions, parties, and classes. Sometimes just a few people show up at these occasions on time. That's fewer names for you to remember. And as more people arrive, you can overhear them being introduced to others—an automatic review for you.

Make it a game.

In situations where many people are new to one another, consider pairing up with another person and staging a contest. Challenge each other to remember as many new names as possible. Then choose an "award"— such as a movie ticket or meal—for the person who wins.

Mnemonic devices

It's pronounced *ne-man'-ik*. It's a trick that can increase your ability to recall everything from speeches to grocery lists. Some entertainers use mnemonics to perform "impossible" feats of memory, such as recalling the names of everyone in a large audience after hearing them just once. Waiters use them to take orders without the aid of pad and pencil, then serve food correctly without asking. Using mnemonic devices, speakers can go for hours without looking at their notes. The possibilities for students are endless.

There is a catch. Mnemonic devices have four serious limitations. First, they don't always help you understand or digest material. Instead of encouraging critical thinking skills, mnemonics assist only rote memorization. Second, the mnemonic device itself is sometimes complicated to learn and time-consuming to develop. It may take more energy to create a mnemonic than to memorize something by using a more traditional memory technique such as repetition. Third, they can be forgotten. Recalling the mnemonic device might be as hard as recalling the material itself. And finally, you may find that mnemonics don't work as well for remembering technical terms in math and science.

In spite of the limitations, mnemonic devices are powerful. There are four general categories: new words, creative sentences, rhymes and songs, and special systems, including the loci system and the peg system.

If you experiment with each, you just might impress your mother-in-law by remembering her birthday and favorite color.

New words

Acronyms are words created by the letters of a series of words. Examples include NASA (**N**ational **A**eronautics and **S**pace **A**dministration), radar (**ra**dio **d**etecting **a**nd **r**anging), scuba (**s**elf-**c**ontained **u**nderwater **b**reathing **a**pparatus), and laser (**l**ight **a**mplification by **s**timulated **e**mission of **r**adiation). You can make up your own words to recall series of facts. A common mnemonic acronym is Roy G. Biv, which has helped thousands of students remember the colors of the visible spectrum (**r**ed, **o**range, **y**ellow, **g**reen, **b**lue, **i**ndigo, and **v**iolet). IPMAT helps biology students remember the stages of cell division (**i**nterphase, **p**rophase, **m**etaphase, **a**naphase, and **t**elephase.)

Creative sentences

Acrostics are sentences that help you remember a series of letters that stand for something. For example, the first letters of the words in the sentence "Every good boy does fine" (E, G, B, D, and F) are the music notes of the lines of the treble clef staff.

Rhymes and songs

Madison Avenue advertising executives spend billions of dollars a year on commercials designed to burn their messages in your memory. Coca-Cola's song, "It's the Real Thing," practically stands for Coca-Cola, despite the fact that it contains artificial ingredients.

Rhymes have been used for centuries to teach children basic facts: "In fourteen hundred and ninety-two, Columbus sailed the ocean blue" or "Thirty days hath September . . . . "

Systems—loci and peg

Use the loci system to create visual associations with familiar locations. It also helps you to remember things in a particular order.

The loci system is an old one. Ancient Greek orators used it to remember long speeches. Say that the orator's position was that road taxes must be raised to pay for school equipment. His loci visualizations might have looked like these:

First, as he walked in the door of his house, he imagined a large porpoise jumping through a hoop. This reminded him to begin by telling the audience the purpose of his speech. Next, he visualized his living room floor covered with paving stones, forming a road leading into the kitchen. In the kitchen, he pictured dozens of school children sitting on the floor because they have no desks.

Now the day of the big speech. The Greek politician is nervous. He is perspiring; his toga sticks to his body. He has cold feet (no socks). He stands up to give his speech and his mind goes blank. "No problem," he thinks to himself. "I am so nervous that I can hardly remember my name. But I can remember the rooms in my house. Let's see, I'm walking in the front door and wow! I see the porpoise. Oh, yeah, that reminds me to talk about the purpose of my speech . . . ."

Unusual associations are the easiest to remember. This system can also be adapted to locations in your body. You visually link things you want to remember with places inside your skin. The shopping list is remembered when you recall the visualization of a loaf of bread stuck in your brain cavity, a large can of frozen orange juice in your larynx, a bunch of broccoli tucked under your collar bone . . . .

The peg system employs key words represented by numbers. For example, 1=bun, 2=shoe, 3=tree, 4=door, 5=hive, 6=sticks, 7=heaven, 8=gate, 9=wine, and 10=hen. In order for this system to be effective, these peg words need to be learned well.

You might use the peg system to remember that the speed of light is 186,000 miles per second. Imagine a hotdog bun (1) entering a gate (8) made of sticks (6). Since we tend to remember pictures longer than we do words, it may be easier to recall this weird scene than the numbers one, eight, and six in order.

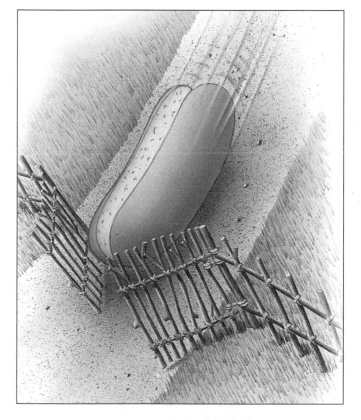

EXERCISE #13
BE A POET

Construct your own mnemonic device for remembering some of the memory techniques in this chapter. Make up a poem, jingle, acronym, or acrostic, or use another mnemonic system. Describe your mnemonic device in the space below.

_____
_____
_____
_____
_____
_____
_____
_____
_____

JOURNAL ENTRY #16
DISCOVERY STATEMENT

Take a minute to reflect on the memory techniques. You already use some of these techniques without being conscious of them. In the space below, list at least three techniques you have used most in the past and describe how you used them.

_____
_____
_____
_____
_____
_____
_____
_____
_____

Love your problems
(and experience your barriers)

We all have problems and barriers that block our progress or prevent us from moving into new areas. We put boundaries on our experiences. We limit what we allow ourselves to be, do, and have.

Problems often work like barriers. When we bump up against one of our problems, we usually turn around and start walking along a different path. And all of a sudden—bump!—we've struck another barrier. And we turn away again.

Our problems might include fear of speaking in front of a group, anxiety about math problems, or reluctance to sound silly trying to speak a foreign language. We might have a barrier about looking silly when trying anything new. Some of us even have anxiety about being successful.

Three ways to handle a barrier

It's natural to have barriers, but sometimes they limit our experience so much that we get bored with life. When this happens, consider the following three ways of dealing with a barrier.

One way is to pretend it doesn't exist. Avoid it, deny it, lie about it. It's like turning your head the other way, putting on a fake grin, and saying, "See, there's really no problem at all. Everything is fine. Oh, that problem. That's not a problem, it's not really there."

In addition to looking foolish, this approach leaves the barrier intact, and we keep bumping into it. We deny the barrier and might not even be aware that we're bumping into it. For example, a student who has a barrier about math might subconsciously avoid enriching experiences that include math.

A second approach is to fight the barrier, to struggle against it. This usually makes the barrier grow. It increases the barrier's magnitude. A person who is obsessed with weight might constantly worry about being fat. He might struggle with it every day, trying diet after diet. And the more he struggles, the bigger the problem gets.

The third alternative is to love the barrier. Accept it. Totally experience it. Tell the truth about it. Describe it in detail. When you do this, the barrier loses its power. You can literally love it to death.

The word *love* might sound like an overstatement. In this Power Process, the word means to accept your problems, to allow and permit them. When we fight a problem it grows bigger. When we accept a problem, we are more likely to deal with it.

Suppose one of your barriers is being afraid of speaking in front of a group. You can use any of these three approaches.

First, you can get up in front of the group and pretend you're not afraid. You can fake a smile, not admitting to yourself or the group that you have any concerns about speaking—even though your legs have turned to rubber bands and your mind is jelly. The problem is, everyone in the room will know you're scared, including you, when your hands start shaking and your voice cracks and you forget what you were going to say.

The second way to approach this barrier is to fight it. You could tell yourself, "I'm not going to be scared," and then try to keep your knees from knocking. Generally, this doesn't work. In fact, your knee-knocking might get worse.

The third approach is to go to the front of the room, look out into the audience, and say to yourself, "I am scared. I notice that my knees are shaking, my mouth feels dry, and I'm having a rush of thoughts about what might happen if I say the wrong thing. Yup, I'm scared and that's OK. As a matter of fact, it's just part of me, so I accept it and I'm not going to try to fight it. I'm going to give this speech even though I'm scared."

You might not actually eliminate the fear; however, your barrier about the fear—which is what stops you—could well disappear. And you might discover that if you examine the fear, love it, accept it, and totally experience it, the fear itself also disappears.

Applying this process

Applying this process is easier if you remember three ideas. First, loving a problem is not necessarily the same as enjoying it. Love in this sense means total and unconditional acceptance.

Second, unconditional acceptance is not the same as unconditional surrender. Accepting a problem is different from giving up or escaping from it. Rather, this process involves escaping *into* the problem—diving into it headfirst and getting to know it in detail.

Third, loving a problem does not need to keep us stuck in the problem. When people first hear about this Power Process, they often think it means to be resigned to the problem. Actually, loving a problem does not stop us from acting. Loving a problem does not keep us mired in it. In fact, fully accepting and admitting the problem usually assists us in taking effective action—and perhaps in freeing ourselves of the problem once and for all.

At times loving our problems helps us love them to death. When we totally experience pain, it often diminishes and sometimes it disappears. This strategy can work with emotions, past traumas, and even physical pain.

Make it your aim to love the pain—that is, to fully accept the pain and know all the details about it. Far from being solid, most pain has a wavelike quality. It rises, reaches a peak of intensity, and then subsides for a moment. See if you can watch the waves come and go.

When you are willing to love your problems, you drain them of much of their energy.

JOURNAL ENTRY #17
DISCOVERY STATEMENT

On a separate sheet of paper, describe one or two barriers that keep you from getting what you want in school. First read about barriers as discussed in Power Process #3: "Love your problems." If you have trouble identifying a barrier, review the Discovery Wheel you completed in Chapter One.

JOURNAL ENTRY #18
INTENTION STATEMENT

Complete the following Intention Statement on a separate sheet of paper. It is in three parts.

1. Describe how you could set up circumstances that would allow you to experience the barrier you discovered. What could you do to put yourself right up against the barrier?

To experience the barrier, I could . . .

Also, I could . . .

2. Brainstorm a list of possible benefits or rewards you would enjoy if you let yourself experience away the barrier (love to death). Do this on 3x5 cards or a separate sheet of paper.

3. This is for the courageous. Pick just one circumstance that you intend to set up in order to experience the barrier you have written about. This can be your opportunity to love it to death. Choose a circumstance that you can arrange within the next three days. For example, if your barrier is fear of speaking in front of a group, the circumstance you arrange could be to ask a question in class or giving a speech.

I intend to . . .

PRACTICING
CRITICAL THINKING #6

Videotape a television debate or discussion that involves a panel of experts on a given topic. When you play back the program, stop the tape after a question to one of the experts and predict how that person will respond to the question. Also describe what you think would be an effective response from the expert. Then start the tape again so that you can observe the expert's actual response and evaluate that response. As you do this exercise, stay alert for errors in reasoning, claims that are presented without evidence, unsystematic thinking, bias, jumping to conclusions, or stereotypes. Write your observations on a separate sheet of paper.

master student

helen keller

author and lecturer, illness left her blind,
deaf, and mute at the age of 19 months

The morning after my teacher came she led me into her room and gave me a doll. The little blind children at the Perkins Institution had sent it and Laura Bridgman had dressed it; but I did not know this until afterward. When I had played with it a little while, Miss Sullivan slowly spelled into my hand the word "d-o-l-l." I was at once interested in this finger play and tried to imitate it. When I finally succeeded in making the letters correctly I was flushed with childish pleasure and pride. Running downstairs to my mother I held up my hand and made the letters for doll. I did not know that I was spelling a word or even that words existed; I was simply making my fingers go in monkey-like imitation. In the days that followed I learned to spell in this uncomprehending way a great many words, among them *pin*, *hat*, *cup*, and a few verbs like *sit*, *stand*, and *walk*. But my teacher had been with me several weeks before I understood that everything has a name.

One day, while I was playing with my new doll, Miss Sullivan put my big rag doll into my lap also, spelled "d-o-l-l" and tried to make me understand that "d-o-l-l" applied to both. Earlier in the day we had had a tussle over the words "m-u-g" and "w-a-t-e-r." Miss Sullivan had tried to impress it upon me that "m-u-g" is mug and that "w-a-t-e-r" is water, but I persisted in confounding the two. In despair she had dropped the subject for the time, only to renew it at the first opportunity. I became impatient at her repeated attempts and, seizing the new doll, I dashed it upon the floor. I was keenly delighted when I felt the fragments of the broken doll at my feet. Neither sorrow nor regret followed my passionate outburst. I had not loved the doll. In the still, dark world in which I lived there was no strong sentiment or tenderness. I felt my teacher sweep the fragments to one side of the hearth, and I had a sense of satisfaction that the cause of my discomfort was removed. She brought me my hat, and I knew I was going out into the warm sunshine. This thought, if a wordless sensation may be called a thought, made me hop and skip with pleasure.

We walked down the path to the well house, attracted by the fragrance of honeysuckle with which it was covered. Someone was drawing water and my teacher placed my hand under the spout. As the cool stream gushed over one hand she spelled into the other the word *water*, first slowly, then rapidly. I stood still, my whole attention fixed upon the motions of her fingers. Suddenly I felt a misty consciousness as of something forgotten— a thrill of returning to thought; and somehow the mystery of language was revealed to me. I knew then that "w-a-t-e-r" meant the wonderful cool something that was flowing over my hand. That living word awakened my soul, it gave it light, hope, joy, set it free! There were barriers still, it is true but barriers that could in time be swept away.

I left the well house eager to learn. Everything had a name, and each name gave birth to a new thought. As we returned to the house, every object which I touched seemed to quiver with life. That was because I saw everything with the strange, new sight that had come to me.

From The Story of My Life
by Helen Keller
pp. 22–24, 1905

1 *Explain how the "recite and repeat" memory technique leads to synergy.*

2 *Give a specific example of setting a "trap" for your memory.*

3 *What is a visualization that can help you remember Boyle's law?*

4 *Define* acronym *and give an example.*

5 *Memorization on a deep level can take place if you:*

      (A) Repeat the idea.
      (B) Repeat the idea.
      (C) Repeat the idea.
      (D) All of the above.

6 *Mnemonic devices are tricks that can increase your ability to:*

      (A) Distribute your learning.
      (B) Manage your time.
      (C) Check your tire pressure.
      (D) Understand or digest material.
      (E) Recall information.

7 *Briefly describe at least three memory techniques.*

8 There are four general categories for mnemonics given in the text. Explain two of them.

9 Once you unconditionally accept any problem, you will be able to enjoy it. True or False. Explain your answer.

10 Combining studying with related activities can allow your brain to store information more effectively in your long-term memory. True or False. Explain your answer.

JOURNAL ENTRY #19
DISCOVERY/INTENTION STATEMENT

After reading and doing this chapter, write about what you learned about your current memory skills.

I discovered that I . . .

_____

_____

Pick three memory techniques and write a short Intention Statement about how you will use them in the next week.

I intend to . . .

_____

_____

_____

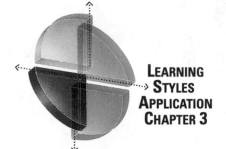

**LEARNING
STYLES
APPLICATION
CHAPTER 3**

Style 1

Write a short paragraph describing the way you feel when you want to remember something but have trouble doing so. Think of three specific incidents in which you experienced this problem. Examples are trying to remember someone's name or a fact you needed in order to answer a test question.

Style 2

List and explain the five most useful memory techniques you gained from this chapter. Choose the techniques that are likely to work best for you.

Style 3

For each of the five techniques you just listed, describe a specific way you could apply that technique while attending class or studying.

Style 4

Return once more to your top five memory techniques. Now describe how you could apply each technique in an area of your life other than school.

Bibliography

■ Endnotes

[1]Wilbur Penfield, "Consciousness, Memory and Man's Conditioned Reflexes," in Karl Pribram (ed.), *On the Biology of Learning* (New York: Harcourt Brace Jovanovich, 1969).

[2]H. Hyden, "Biochemical Aspects of Learning and Memory," in Karl Pribram (ed.), *On the Biology of Learning* (New York: Harcourt Brace Jovanovich, 1969).

[3]Ernest R. Hilgard et al, *Introduction to Psychology* (New York: Harcourt Brace Jovanovich, 1974), 261. Hilgard et al, 1974, 234.

[4]R.W. Brown and D. MacNeil, "The tip of the tongue phenomenon," *Journal of Verbal Learning and Verbal Behavior*, 5: 327-37, 1966.

[5]Ibid.

■ Additional Reading

Brown, Alan C. *Maximizing Memory Power*, New York: Wiley, 1986.

Higbee, Kenneth L. *Your Memory: How It Works and How to Improve It*, Englewood Cliffs, NJ: Prentice-Hall, 1977.

Lucas, Jerry, and Harry Lorayne. *The Memory Book*, New York: Ballantine Books, 1975.

reading

In this chapter...

■ are suggestions for students who say "I can read well" and for those who feel drowsy the minute they spot a textbook. One key is **Muscle Reading**—another term for staying alert, active, and aware as you read. Use the techniques in this chapter to **read faster** while increasing comprehension and to **learn new words.** You can do this even when reading tough material or when learning a second language. Also **notice your mental pictures,** and choose pictures that promote your success.

JOURNAL ENTRY #20
DISCOVERY STATEMENT

Think about how reading skills relate to your educational goals. Preview this chapter and review your Discovery Wheel, especially the section on reading. Then list below what you want to learn from this chapter.

I want to learn . . .

_____
_____
_____
_____
_____
_____
_____

JOURNAL ENTRY #21
DISCOVERY STATEMENT

Take 10 minutes to read as much as you can of the article titled "Muscle Reading" starting on page 103. Then close this book and on a separate sheet of paper, write a summary of what you read.

Next, compare your summary to the original text. Was your summary complete and accurate? Did you encounter any problems in reading this material—such as words you didn't understand or paragraphs you paused to reread? Sum up your reading experience by completing this statement: I discovered that I . . .

Now list some specific reading skills you want to gain by working through this chapter.

PICTURE YOURSELF SITTING AT A DESK, an open book in your hands. Your eyes are open too, and it looks as if you're reading. Suddenly your head jerks up. You blink. You realize your eyes have been scanning the page for 10 minutes, and you can't remember a single thing you have read.

Or picture this: You've had a hard day. You were up at 6 a.m. to get the kids ready for school. A co-worker called in sick and you missed your lunch trying to do your job and his. You picked up the kids, then had to shop for dinner. Dinner was late, of course, and the kids were grumpy. Finally, you got to your books at 8 p.m., and you began plodding through something called "the equity method of accounting for common stock investments." You tell yourself, "I am preparing for the future," as you claw your way through two paragraphs and begin the third.

Suddenly everything in the room looks different. Your head is resting on your elbow, which is resting on the equity method of accounting. The clock reads 11:30 p.m. Say good-bye to three hours.

Sometimes, the only difference between a sleeping pill and a textbook is that the textbook doesn't have a warning on the label about operating heavy machinery.

"Muscle Reading" is a technique you can use to avoid mental mini-vacations and reduce the number of unscheduled naps during study time, even after a hard day. More than that, Muscle Reading is a way to decrease effort and struggle by increasing energy and skill. Once you learn this technique, you can actually spend less time on your reading and get more out of it.

This is not to say you can avoid all work and still challenge yourself in your education. Muscle Reading might even look like more work at first. Effective textbook reading is an active, energy-consuming, sit-on-the-edge-of-your-seat business. That's why this strategy is called Muscle Reading.

Muscle Reading

> *Reading furnishes our mind only with materials of knowledge; it is thinking that makes what we read ours.*
> —JOHN LOCKE

> *There would seem to be almost no limit to what people can and will misunderstand when they are not doing their utmost to get at a writer's meaning.*
> —EZRA POUND

HOW
Muscle Reading
WORKS

The key idea behind Muscle Reading is that your textbooks have something you want. They offer knowledge and valuable information. Sometimes the value is so buried that extracting it requires skill and energy.

Muscle Reading is a three-phase technique you can use to accomplish that extraction. Each of the three phases has three steps. To assist your recall of all nine steps, memorize three short sentences:

> **Pry out questions.**
> **Root up answers.**
> **Recite, review, and**
> **review again.**

Take a moment to invent images for each of those sentences. First, visualize or feel yourself prying questions out of a text. These are questions you want answered based on your brief survey of the assignment. Make a mental picture of yourself scanning the territory, spotting a question, and reaching into the text to pry it out. Hear yourself saying, "I've got it. Here's my question."

Then root up the answers to your questions. Get your muscles involved. Flex. Feel the ends of your fingers digging into the text to root up the answers to your questions.

Finally, hear your voice reciting what you have learned. Hear yourself making a speech about the material. Hear yourself singing it.

These sentences are an acrostic. The first letter of each word stands for one Muscle Reading process.

Thus:

Pry	**O**ut	**Q**uestions.	**R**oot	**U**p	**A**nswers.
r	r	u		e	n
e	u	e		n	s
v	t	s		d	w
i	l	t		e	e
e	i	i		r	r
w	n	o		l	
	e	n		i	
				n	
				e	

Recite,	**R**eview, and	**R**eview again.
e	e	e
c	v	v
i	i	i
t	e	e
e	w	w

Configured another way, the three phases and nine steps look like this:

Before you read: Pry out questions.
Step 1: Preview
Step 2: Outline
Step 3: Question

While you read: Root up answers.
Step 4: Read
Step 5: Underline
Step 6: Answer

After you read: Recite, review, and review again.
Step 7: Recite
Step 8: Review
Step 9: Review again

A nine-step reading strategy might seem cumbersome and unnecessary for a two-page reading assignment. It is. Keep in mind that Muscle Reading is not an all-or-nothing package. Use it appropriately. You can choose what steps to apply as you read. The main point is to preview, read, and review. The nine steps are just strategies for accomplishing those three tasks.

Muscle Reading takes a little time to learn. At first you might feel it's slowing you down. That's natural. Mastery comes with time and practice. If you're still concerned about time, give yourself some options. For example, apply the following techniques to just one article or part of a chapter.

Before you read

Step 1: Preview

Before you begin, survey the entire assignment. You did a survey of this book for Exercise #1: "Textbook reconnaissance." Research indicates that this technique, called previewing, can significantly increase your comprehension of reading material.

If you are starting a new book, look over the table of contents and flip through the text page by page. Even if your assignment is merely a few pages in a book, you can benefit from a brief preview of the table of contents.

Keep the preview short. If the entire reading assignment will take less than an hour, your preview might take five minutes. Previewing is also a way to get yourself started when an assignment looks too big to handle. It is an easy way to step into the material.

When previewing, look for familiar concepts, facts, or ideas. These items can help link new information to previously learned material. Look for ideas that spark your imagination or curiosity. Ask yourself how the material can relate to your long-term goals. Inspect drawings, diagrams, charts, tables, graphs, and photographs.

Keep an eye out for summary statements. If the assignment is long or complex, read the summary first. Many textbooks have summaries in the introductions or at the end of each chapter.

Read all chapter headlines, section titles, and paragraph headlines. These are often brief summaries in themselves.

If you expect to use a book extensively, read the preface. The author often includes a personal perspective in a preface. A picture of the person behind the words can remove barriers to understanding. Look for lists of recommended books and articles. If you have difficulty with a concept, sometimes another viewpoint can nail it down for you.

Before you begin reading, take a few moments to reflect on what you already know about this subject, even if you think you know nothing. This technique prepares your brain to accept the information that follows.

Finally, determine your reading strategy. Skimming might be enough for some assignments. For others, all nine steps of Muscle Reading might be appropriate. Ask yourself these questions: "How will I be tested on this material?", "How useful will this knowledge be later?", "How much time can I afford to spend on this assignment?"

To clarify your reading strategy, you might write the first letters of the Muscle Reading acrostic in a margin or at the top of your notes and check off the steps you intend to follow. Or write the Muscle Reading steps on 3x5 cards and then use them for bookmarks.

You don't have to memorize what you preview to get value from this step. Previewing sets the stage for incoming information by warming up a space in your mental storage area.

EXERCISE #14
IT'S HARD TO KNOW WHAT'S GOING ON . . . UNTIL YOU HAVE THE BIG PICTURE

Read the following paragraph and then summarize it in one sentence.

"With hocked gems financing him, he defied all scornful laughter that tried to prevent his scheme. 'Your eyes deceive,' they said. 'It is like a table, not an egg.' Now three sturdy sisters sought truth. As they forged along, sometimes through calm vastness, yet more often over turbulent peaks and valleys, their days became weeks as many doubters spread fearful rumors about the edge. At last, from nowhere winged creatures appeared, signifying the journey's end."

Summarize this paragraph.

_____
_____
_____
_____
_____
_____
_____
_____

Most people have difficulty knowing what in the world the previous paragraph is about. If it were part of a reading assignment you had previewed and you had noticed it is about Christopher Columbus, then it would have made more sense. Read it again while thinking about the famous world traveler.

Step 2: Outline

The amount of time you spend on this step will vary. For some assignments, fiction and poetry for example, skip it. For other assignments, a 10-second mental outline is all you need.

With complex material, take time to understand the structure of what you are about to read. If your textbook provides chapter outlines, spend some time studying them.

If a text does not provide an outline, sketch a brief one in the margin of your book or at the beginning of your notes. Then, as you read and take notes, you can fill in your outline.

Section titles and paragraph headlines can serve as major and minor topics for your outline. If assigned reading does not contain section titles or headlines, you can outline the material as you read. In this case, outlining actively organizes your thoughts about the assignment.

Use whatever outline style works best for you. Some readers prefer traditional Roman numeral outlines. Others prefer mind maps or notes in the Cornell format. (These methods are explained in Chapter Five.) If your text includes headings in bold or italic print, you can also outline right in the text. Assign numbers or letters to each heading, just as you would for a traditional outline.

Outlining can make complex information easier to understand.

Step 3: Question

Ask yourself what you want from an assignment before you begin reading. Your preview might suggest some questions. Imagine the author is in the room with you. What would you ask him? How can he help you get what you want from your education? Create a dialogue. Begin your active participation in the book before you start to read.

Write down a list of questions. Be tough. Demand your money's worth from your textbook. If you do not understand a concept, write specific questions about it. The more detailed your questions, the more powerful this technique becomes. Knowledge is born of questions.

If a reading assignment seems irrelevant, sit back for a minute and think about what it is you want from your time in school. Check to see if your education will be complete without this piece of the puzzle. Even if a particular assignment doesn't have personal meaning for you at the moment, it may be tied to a broader goal like getting a certain grade in the class.

Another useful technique is to turn chapter headings and section titles into questions. For example, if a subtitle is "Transference and Suggestion," you can ask yourself, "What are transference and suggestion?", "How does transference relate to suggestion?" Make up a quiz as if you were teaching this subject to your classmates.

Make the questions playful or creative. Have fun with this technique. You don't need to get an answer to every question you ask. The purpose of making up questions is to get your brain involved in the assignment. Take your unanswered questions to class, where they can be springboards for class discussion.

Learning to ask effective questions takes practice, and you can discover rewards for developing this skill. The questions you formulate help you stay alert through complicated reading.

Boredom and fatigue tend to disappear when you're busy finding answers. In fact, when you find one, expect to feel a burst of energy. It might be a small burst, if it was a small question. Or it might bring you right out of your chair if the question was important to you. If you find a series of answers in a reading assignment, you might finish the assignment feeling more energetic than when you began.

For some assignments, you might spend considerable time previewing, outlining, and asking questions before you

The Universal Law of Reading

FIRST COROLLARY:
To read effectively, always sit in a canoe and wear a face mask, snorkel, and flippers.

SECOND COROLLARY:
Don't believe everything you read.

start reading. The potential rewards are understanding and remembering more of what you read and saving time.

While you read

Step 4: Read

At last! You have previewed the assignment, organized it in your mind, and formulated questions. Now you are ready to begin reading.

As you read, be conscious of where you are and what you are doing. Practice Power Process #2: "Be here now." When you notice your attention wandering, gently bring it back to the present.

One way to stay in the here and now is to make tick marks on scrap paper whenever you notice your attention flagging.

You might make many tick marks at first. That's OK. The marks signify your attentiveness, so don't be discouraged by lots of them. Most students notice that as they pay attention to their attention, the number of tick marks decreases.

If a personal problem or some other concern is interfering with your concentration, experiment with this idea. Write down the problem along with a commitment to a future course of action. Getting the problem down on paper, with a commitment to take action, can free your mind for the present task.

Another way to stay focused is to avoid marathon reading sessions. Schedule breaks and set a reasonable goal for the entire session. Then reward yourself with an enjoyable activity for five or 10 minutes

every hour or two. With practice, some students find they can stay focused up to three hours without a break.

For difficult reading, set shorter goals. Read for a half hour, then break. Most students find that shorter periods of reading distributed throughout the day and week can be more effective than long sessions.

You can use the following three techniques to stay focused as you read.

First, visualize the material. Form mental pictures of the concepts as they are presented. If you read that a voucher system can help control cash disbursements, picture a voucher handing out dollar bills.

Second, read it out loud—especially complicated material. Some of us remember better and understand more quickly when we hear an idea.

Third, get a feel for the subject, literally. For example, let's say you are reading about a microorganism, a paramecium, in your biology text. Imagine what it would feel like to run your finger around the long, cigar-shaped body of the organism. Imagine feeling the large fold of its gullet on one side, and feel the hairy little cilia as they wiggle in your hand.

A final note: It's easy to fool yourself about reading. Just having an open book in your hand and moving your eyes across a page doesn't mean you are reading effectively. Reading textbooks takes energy, even if you do it sitting down. One study revealed that corporation presidents usually wear out the front of their chairs first. Approach your reading assignment like the company president. Sit up. Keep your spine straight. Use the edge of your chair.

And avoid reading in bed, except for fun.

Step 5: Underline

Deface your books. Use them up. Have fun writing and coloring in them. Indulge yourself as you never could with your grade-school texts. Keeping textbooks clean and neat might not help you get what you want from them.

The purpose of making marks in a text is to create signals for reviewing. Underlining or highlighting can save lots of time when you study for tests.

A secondary benefit of marking is that when you read with a pen in your hand, you are involving another mode of perception, your kinesthetic sense—that is, your sense of touch and motion. Being physical with your books can help build strong neural pathways in your memory.

Avoid underlining or highlighting too soon. Wait until you have completed a section or concept to make sure you know what is important. Then mark up the text. Sometimes stopping after each paragraph works best. For some assignments, you might want to read a larger section before deciding what to mark.

Some people prefer colored highlighters to pens for marking up a text. Pens can make underlined sections—in other words, the important parts—harder to read than the rest of the book. You can still use a pen for making notes in the margins and circling important sections.

Underline or highlight sparingly, usually less than 10 percent of the text. If you mark up too much on a page, you defeat the purpose, which is to flag the most important material for review.

Write in the margins of your texts. Write summary statements and questions. Mark passages that you don't understand. If you find a list or series of elements in a paragraph, you can circle and number them.

It's true that marking up your textbooks can lower their resale value. The money you lose by doing it is ridiculously small compared to the value of your education. Writing in your textbooks helps you wring every ounce of value out of them.

Step 6: Answer

As you read, get the answers to your questions and write them down. Fill in your outline. Write down new questions and note when you don't get the answers you wanted to find. Use these notes to ask questions in class, or see your instructor personally.

When you read, create an image of yourself as a person in search of the answers. You are a detective, watching for every clue, sitting erect in your straight-back chair, as alert as a Zen master, curious as Sherlock Holmes or Nancy Drew, demanding that your textbook give you what you want—the answers.

After you read

Step 7: Recite

Talk to yourself about what you have read. Or talk to someone else. When you finish reading an assignment, make a speech about it. One classic study indicates that you profitably devote up to 80 percent of your study time to active reciting.[1]

One way to get yourself to recite is to look at each underlined point. Note what you marked, then put the book down and start talking out loud. Explain as much as you can about that particular point.

To make this technique more effective, do it in front of a mirror. It may seem silly, but the benefits can be enormous. You can reap them at exam time.

Friends are even better than mirrors. Form a group and practice teaching each other what you have read. One of the best ways to learn anything is to teach someone else.

There is a secret buried in this suggestion. That secret is, have someone else do the work. Your instructors might not appreciate this suggestion, but it can be a salvation when you're pressed for time. Find a friend you trust and split up the reading assignment. Each of you can teach half the assignment to the other. (Warning: You might be far better versed in the part you read and teach. And if your friend misses an important part, you could miss it too.)

Talk about your reading whenever you can.

Step 8: Review

Plan to do your first complete review within 24 hours of reading the material. Sound the trumpets, this is critical: A review within 24 hours moves information from your short-term memory to your long-term memory. It can save you hours later on. Review within one day. If you read it on Wednesday, review it on Thursday.

During this review, look over your notes and clear up anything you don't understand. Recite some of the main points again.

At first, you might be discouraged by how much you think you forgot from the previous day. Don't worry. Notice how quickly you pick up the material the second time. One of the characteristics of memory is that even when you cannot recall something immediately, you can relearn it more easily if you have already learned it once. And relearning wears a deeper path into your memory.

This review can be short. You might spend as little as 15 minutes reviewing a two-hour reading assignment. Investing that time now can later save you hours when studying for exams.

Also remember that you can stop to review and check your comprehension at any point, even before you complete a whole reading assignment.

Step 9: Review again

The final step in Muscle Reading is the weekly or monthly review. This step can be very short—perhaps only four or five minutes per assignment. Simply go over your notes. Read the highlighted parts of your text. Recite one or two of the more complicated points.

The purpose of these reviews is to keep the neural pathways to the information open and to make them more distinct. That way, the information can be easier to recall. You can accomplish these short reviews anytime, anywhere, if you are prepared. Take your text to the dentist's office, and if you don't have time to read a whole assignment, review last week's assignment or the previous week's assignment. Conduct a five-minute review while you are waiting for a bus, for your socks to dry, or for the water to boil. Three-by-five cards are a handy review tool. Write ideas, formulas, concepts, and facts on cards and carry them with you. These short review periods can be effortless and fun.

Sometimes longer review periods are appropriate. For example, if you found an assignment difficult, consider rereading it. Start over, as if you had never seen the material. Sometimes a second reading will provide you with surprising insights. Your previous experience acts as a platform from which you can see aspects that didn't appear during the first reading.

Schedule some review periods well in advance. You might set aside one hour on a Saturday or a Sunday to review several subjects. Keep your reviews short and do them often.

Finally, take some time to reflect on what you read. As you walk to and from class, in your discussions with other students, or before you go to bed at night, turn over new ideas in your mind. Take time to play with them. Develop a habit of regular review.

Psychologists speak of the primacy-recency effect[2], which suggests that we most easily remember the first and last items in any presentation. Previewing and reviewing your reading is a powerful way to put this theory to work for you.

JOURNAL ENTRY #22
DISCOVERY STATEMENT

Now that you have read about Muscle Reading, review your assessment of your reading skills in the Discovery Wheel on page 17. Do you still think your evaluation was accurate? What new insights do you have about the way you read textbooks? Are you a more effective reader than you thought? Less effective? Record your observations below.

_____
_____
_____
_____
_____
_____
_____
_____
_____
_____
_____
_____
_____
_____
_____
_____
_____

Name ______________________ Date ____/____/____

Journal Entry #23
Discovery Statement

Check off the Muscle Reading techniques you already use.

	Preview	Outline	Question	Read	Underline	Answer	Recite	Review	Review again
Always									
Often									
Sometimes									
Seldom									
Never									

Exercise #15
Make it a habit

Changing our reading style is as complicated as changing how we tie our shoes. We've been doing both since we started school.

This chapter suggests a significant change in how you read. This exercise can help that change become automatic. During the next week fill out the assignment section of this page, listing pages and book titles that you intend to read within a week or two. As you read each of those assignments, check off the Muscle Reading techniques as you apply them. By the time you have used this technique 10 times, you could have a new habit.

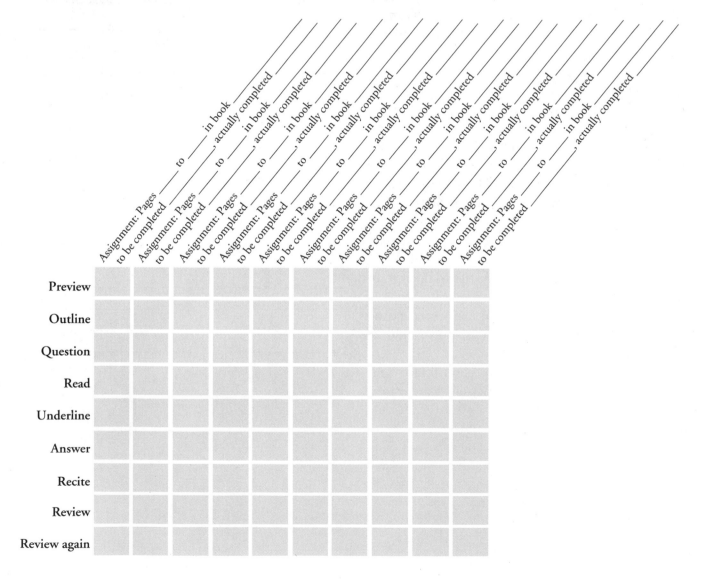

	Assignment: Pages ___ to ___ in book ___ to be completed ___, actually completed ___	Assignment: Pages ___ to ___ in book ___ to be completed ___, actually completed ___	Assignment: Pages ___ to ___ in book ___ to be completed ___, actually completed ___	Assignment: Pages ___ to ___ in book ___ to be completed ___, actually completed ___	Assignment: Pages ___ to ___ in book ___ to be completed ___, actually completed ___	Assignment: Pages ___ to ___ in book ___ to be completed ___, actually completed ___	Assignment: Pages ___ to ___ in book ___ to be completed ___, actually completed ___	Assignment: Pages ___ to ___ in book ___ to be completed ___, actually completed ___	Assignment: Pages ___ to ___ in book ___ to be completed ___, actually completed ___	Assignment: Pages ___ to ___ in book ___ to be completed ___, actually completed ___
Preview										
Outline										
Question										
Read										
Underline										
Answer										
Recite										
Review										
Review again										

Reading fast

One way to read faster is to read faster. This may sound like double talk, but it is a serious suggestion. The fact is, most people can read faster simply by making a conscious effort to do so. In fact, you probably can read faster without any loss in comprehension. Your comprehension might even improve.

Here are some guidelines from the "just do it" school of speed reading.

First, get your body ready. Get off the couch. Sit at a desk or table and sit up, on the edge of your chair, with your feet flat on the floor. If you're feeling adventurous, read standing up.

Next, set a time limit. Use a clock or a digital watch with a built-in stopwatch to time yourself. The objective is not to set speed records, so be realistic. For example, set a goal to read a chapter in an hour. If that works, set a goal of 50 minutes to read a similar chapter. Test your limits. The idea is to give yourself a gentle push, increasing your reading speed without sacrificing comprehension.

Another hint from the "just do it" school is relax. It's not only possible to read fast when you're relaxed, it's easier. Relaxation promotes concentration. (And remember, relaxation is not the same thing as sleep.)

Experiment with the "just do it" method right now. Read the rest of this article as fast as you can. After you finish, come back and reread the same paragraphs at your usual rate. Notice how much you remembered from your first sprint through. Many people are surprised to find how well they comprehend material even at dramatically increased speeds.

You also can read faster by moving your eyes faster. When we read, our eyes leap across the page in short bursts called *saccades* (pronounced sa-käds). A saccade is also a sharp jerk on the reins of a horse—a violent pull to stop the animal quickly. Our eyes stop like that too, in pauses called *fixations*.

Although we experience the illusion of continuously scanning each line, our eyes really take in groups of words, usually about three at a time. For more than 90 percent of reading time, our eyes are at a dead stop, in those fixations.

Your eyes can move faster if they take in more words with each burst—six instead of three, for example. You can do this by following your finger as you read. The faster your finger moves, the faster your eyes move. You also can use a pen, pencil, or 3x5 card as a guide.

Our eyes also make *regressions*. That is, they back up and reread words. Ineffective readers and beginning readers make many regressions.

You can reduce regressions by paying attention to them. Use the handy 3x5 card to cover words and lines you have read. This can reveal how often you stop and move the card back. Don't be discouraged if you stop often at first. Being aware of it helps you naturally begin to regress less frequently.

When you're in a hurry, scan the assignment and read the headings, subheadings, lists, charts, graphs, and summary paragraphs. The summaries are especially important. They are usually at the beginning or end of a reading assignment.

Another way to read faster is to avoid vocalizing. Obviously, you're more likely to read faster if you don't read aloud or move your lips. You can also increase your speed if you don't subvocalize—that is, if you don't mentally "hear" the words as you read them. To stop doing it, just be aware of it.

Practice reading faster with simpler material at first. That way, you can pay closer attention.

A cautionary note about these techniques: Speed isn't everything. Skillful readers vary their reading rate according to their purpose and the nature of the material. An advanced text in analytic geometry, for example, usually calls for a different reading rate than the Sunday comics.

You also can use different reading rates on the same material. For example, you might sprint through an assignment for the key words and ideas, then return to the difficult parts for a more thorough reading.

And finally, remember the first rule of reading fast: Just say go!

When reading is tough

Sometimes ordinary reading methods are not enough. Every student gets bogged down in a murky reading assignment sooner or later. You can use the following techniques to drain the swamp when you are up to your neck in textbook alligators.

1. Read it again, Sam. Difficult material—such as the technical writing in science courses—is often easier the second time around. If you read an assignment and are completely lost, do not despair. Admit your confusion. Sleep on it. When you return to the assignment, regard it with fresh eyes.

2. Look for essential words. If you are stuck on a paragraph, mentally cross out all the adjectives and adverbs and read the sentence without them. Find the important words. These will usually be verbs and nouns.

3. Hold a mini-review. Pause briefly to summarize what you've read so far, verbally or in writing. Stop at the end of a paragraph and recite, in your own words, what you have read. Jot down some notes or create a short outline or summary.

4. Read it aloud. Make noise. Read a passage aloud several times, each time using a different inflection, emphasizing a different part of the sentence. Be creative. Imagine that you are the author talking.

5. Use your instructor. Admit when you are absolutely stuck and make an appointment with your instructor. Most teachers welcome the opportunity to work individually with students. Be specific about your confusion. Point out the paragraph that you found toughest to understand.

6. Stand up. Changing positions periodically can combat fatigue. Play with standing as you read, especially if you get stuck on a tough passage and decide to read it aloud.

7. Find a tutor. Many schools provide free tutoring services. If tutoring services are not provided by your school, other students who have completed the course can assist you.

8. Use another text. Find one in the library. Sometimes a concept is easier to understand if it is expressed another way. Children's books, especially children's encyclopedias, can provide useful overviews of baffling subjects.

9. Pretend you understand, then explain it. We often understand more than we think we do. Pretend it's clear as a bell and explain it to another person or even yourself. Write your explanation down. You might be amazed by what you know.

10. Ask: What's going on here? When you feel stuck, stop reading for a moment and diagnose what's happening. At these stop points, mark your place in the margin of the page with a penciled *S*. Seeing a pattern to your marks over several pages might indicate a question you want to answer before reading further. Or you might discover a reading habit you'd like to change.

**PRACTICING
CRITICAL THINKING #7**

One of the suggested strategies for understanding difficult reading material is to read another book on the same subject. This is one example of critical thinking skills—explaining and assessing alternative views on an issue.

Apply this strategy now. Find and read a newspaper or magazine article that's relevant to one of your current reading assignments. Now summarize and compare the viewpoints on the subject presented by the authors you've read. List the major question addressed by both authors along with the answers they offer. Look for points of disagreement and agreement. Also consider the methods the authors used to reach their conclusions and the evidence they presented. Determine if one author's viewpoint is more reasonable than the other's, given all the suitable evidence. On a separate sheet of paper, write a paragraph to state and support your conclusion.

Read with a dictionary in your lap

Malcolm X demonstrated one way to improve vocabulary. While in prison, he read and copied the entire dictionary. Few of us have such a single-minded sense of purpose with regard to vocabulary building. Yet we all share the ability and desire to learn. You can use that natural ability to strengthen your vocabulary by concentrating on words that interest you.

Look up unfamiliar words. Pay special attention to words that arouse your curiosity.

You can regularly use two kinds of dictionaries: the desk dictionary and the unabridged dictionary. A desk dictionary is the one you use several times a day, the one you own. Keep this book within reach (maybe in your lap) so you can look up unfamiliar words. You can find a large, unabridged dictionary in the library. It provides more complete information about words and definitions not included in your desk dictionary and a history of each word.

Construct a word stack

When you find an unfamiliar word, write it down on a 3x5 card. Copy the sentence in which it occurred below the word. You can look up each word immediately or accumulate a stack of these cards and look them up later. Write the definition on the back of the 3x5 card and add the diacritical marks that tell you how to pronounce it.

To expand your definitions and find the history behind the word, you can take your stack of cards to an unabridged dictionary. As you find related words in the dictionary, add them to your stack. These cards become another portable study aid that you can review in your spare moments.

Learn—even when your dictionary is across town

When you are listening to a lecture and hear an unfamiliar word or when you are reading on the bus and run across a word you don't know, you can still build your word stack. Pull out a 3x5 card and write down the word and its sentence. Later, you can look up the word and put the definition on the back of the card.

Use more options for learning words

There are other strategies for dealing with new words. One is to guess the meaning of the words from context. To do this, reread the sentences that surround the new word and see if they point to a logical meaning. Or simply circle or highlight the word and continue reading. When you're done, you can look up all unfamiliar words at one time.

Another suggestion is to divide the word into syllables and look for familiar parts. This works well if you make it a point to learn common prefixes (beginning syllables) and suffixes (ending syllables). For example, the suffix *-tude* usually refers to a condition or state of being. Knowing this makes it easier to conclude that *habitude* refers to a usual way of doing something and that *similitude* means "being similar or having a quality of resemblance."

**EXERCISE #16
RELAX**

Eye strain can be the result of continuous stress. You can use this exercise to take a break from your reading.

1. Sit on a chair or lie down and take a few moments to breathe deeply.

2. Close your eyes, place your palms over your eyes, and visualize a perfect field of black.

3. Continue to be aware of the blackness for two or three minutes while you breathe deeply.

4. Now remove your hands from your eyes and open your eyes slowly.

5. Relax for a minute more, then continue reading.

Englisch lesen als zweite Sprache

English as a second language

En lisant l'anglais comme une deuxieme langue

Читать по-английски как иностранный язык

『第二外国語としての英語講読』

Leer el inglés como segunda lengua

The English language is full of exceptions to the rules. It is probably one of the more difficult languages to learn. Contrary to the rules of phonetics, for example, words are often not spelled the way they sound. Even trying to spell the word *phonetics* using phonetics can get you into trouble.

No matter what your native language is, consider using the following suggestions as you master English. Also note that many of these suggestions can apply to learning any language.

Give it time. Reading English slowly can aid comprehension. So can reading at different rates by intentionally varying your reading speed. Accept how fast you read right now, even as you seek to increase your speed. As you practice, both your reading speed and comprehension can improve. There are no instant pills to take. Learning English takes time.

Use Muscle Reading. Many of the Muscle Reading techniques apply to reading English as a second language. For example, it is effective to read some assignments more than once. The first time through, look for major ideas and be aware of the general content. When you read it the second time, fill in more of the details.

Get at word meanings. Have a dictionary handy. Before looking up any unknown word, see if you can figure out its meaning from the context. If someone says, "It will probably be cold at the football game so be sure to bring a warm XXXXX," you would probably not show up with a calculator or a fishing pole.

Practice speaking English. Look for times when you can practice speaking English. Asking questions or making comments in class is an effective way to practice. It allows you to be more involved and can increase your understanding of the course content. Another way to practice is to repeat aloud what you have just read.

The more you practice English, the faster you can learn. Relying on translations or spending much of your time speaking your native language could slow your progress.

Practice writing in English. Writing in English, which involves spelling and a more precise use of grammar, may be more difficult than either reading or speaking. Grocery lists, to-do lists, notes to friends, appointments on calendars, and personal journal entries are opportunities to practice writing.

Think in English. Thinking in English is a variation of speaking it. The next time you want to explore some future project or remember the trip you took last summer, think about it in English. Some students are pleasantly surprised to note that they even start dreaming in English.

Learn academic English. Formal, academic English might vary greatly from your own English dialect. Consider approaching academic English as a foreign language, even if English is your native tongue. The techniques that help you learn French or Spanish can also help you master the English you use in school.

Celebrate your gains. Acknowledge yourself and celebrate when you make small gains. It is probably not possible to improve your English skills 100 percent, all at once. One hundred small gains of 1 percent each are likely to accomplish the same things. Lots of little learnings can amount to major shifts in your English proficiency.

Use school services. Many schools have ESL (English as a Second Language) programs that offer a variety of services. Examples are tutoring services, as well as courses and workshops on learning English. Your adviser or counseling office can direct you to these programs.

We live like royalty

Reading allows us to go beyond the limits of time and space.

Using our imagination, we can travel anywhere on the planet or enter scenes from the future or our distant past. Reading can change our perspective and open our eyes to how lucky we are.

For example, reading can reveal our wealth. Through reading, we can change our point of view from thinking that we don't have enough money to discovering that we live like royalty.

Step back in time a few hundred years and imagine how a king or queen might have lived. These ruling monarchs would have enough to eat. Several times a year, they would have a feast. In their food would be spices from the four corners of the earth. These people would eat until they were stuffed. And after a meal, they could summon entertainment with the snap of a finger. If they wanted music, a clap of the hands would bring forth dozens of songs. If they wanted humor, they could summon a court jester. If they wanted variety or drama, they could watch the actors of the court.

Transportation was no problem. Horses were always ready, and a driver would chauffeur the king or queen from kingdom to kingdom in a matter of days or weeks.

Dress was lavish. Monarchs wore the finest clothes—smooth, colorful, clean. Unlike the clothes of lesser mortals, the royal wardrobe kept its owners dry and warm. The king and queen got new clothes at least once a year and never had to wear anything that was full of holes.

Their house was a castle. It was clean, dry, and had warm fireplaces in many rooms. The inhabitants were safe from nature and most intruders.

In short, these people lived a royal existence. And they didn't have it nearly as good as most people in North America today!

Notice your pictures and let them go

The brain's job is to manufacture images. We use mental pictures to make predictions about the world, and we base much of our behavior on those predictions. When a cook adds chopped onions, mushrooms, and garlic to a spaghetti sauce, he has a picture of how the sauce will taste and measures each ingredient according to that picture.

Just about any time we feel a need, we conjure up a picture of what will satisfy that need. A baby feels hunger pangs and starts to cry. Within seconds, the mother appears and the baby is satisfied. What's more, the baby stores a mental picture of her mother feeding her. She connects that picture with stopping the hunger pangs. Voilà! She knows how to solve the hunger problem, and the picture goes on file.

According to psychologist William Glasser[3], our minds function like a huge photo album. Its pages include pictures of all the ways we've satisfied needs in the past. Whenever we feel dissatisfied, we mentally search the album for a picture of how to make the dissatisfaction go away. With that picture firmly in mind, we behave to make the world outside our heads match the pictures inside.

Pictures are not strictly visual images. They can involve any of the senses. When you buy a CD, you have a picture of how it will sound. When you buy a sweater, you have a picture of how it will feel.

A problem with pictures

The pictures we make in our heads are survival mechanisms. Without them, we couldn't get from one end of town to the other. We couldn't feed or clothe ourselves. Without a picture of a socket, we couldn't screw in a light bulb.

Pictures can also get in our way. For example, take the case of a student who plans to attend a college he hasn't visited. He chose this school for its strong curriculum and good academic standing, but his brain didn't stop there. In his mind, the campus has historic buildings with ivy-covered walls and tree-lined avenues. The professors, he imagines, will be combinations of Oprah Winfrey and Phil Donahue. His roommate will be his best friend. The cafeteria will be a cozy nook serving delicate quiche and fragrant teas. He will gather there with fellow students for hours of stimulating intellectual conversation. The library will have every book; the computer lab, every new piece of technology.

The school turns out to be four gray buildings downtown, next to the bus station. The first class he attends is taught by an overweight, balding professor, wearing a purple and orange bird of paradise tie. He has a bad case of the sniffles. The cafeteria is a nondescript hall with machine food, and the student's apartment is barely large enough to accommodate his roommate's tuba.

This hypothetical student gets depressed. He begins to think about dropping out of school.

The problem with pictures is that they sometimes prevent us from seeing what is really there. That happened to the student in this story. His pictures prevented him from noticing that the school is in the heart of a culturally vital city—close to theaters, museums, government offices, clubs, and all kinds of stores. The professor with the weird tie is not only an expert in his field, he is also a superior teacher. The school cafeteria is skimpy because it can't compete with the variety of inexpensive restaurants in the area. There may even be hope for a tuba-playing roommate.

Anger and disappointment are often the results of our pictures. We set up expectations of events before they occur. These can then lead to disappointment. Sometimes we don't even realize that we have the expectation.

Racism flourishes when people hold inaccurate pictures about each other and refuse to let them go. These pictures can lead to shallow stereotypes. They work against the foreign exchange student in your English class or the visiting lecturer from Mexico.

The next time you discover you are angry, disappointed, or frustrated, look to see which of your pictures aren't being fulfilled.

Often there is disappointment even if the event that you pictured turns out to be better than you imagined. For instance, you might have expected the Philosophy of Logic class you're taking as a graduation requirement to be hopelessly boring. You get to class and discover that the professor has a great sense of humor and relates logic processes to practical examples. Disappointment occurs when you maintain a position that philosophy is boring while being aware of your experience that it's interesting and practical.

What to do

Having pictures is unavoidable. Letting these pictures run your life is avoidable. Awareness is the key. The technique for dealing with pictures is so simple and so effortless, it might seem silly.

One way to deal with pictures is to notice them. Be aware of them. Just open up your mental photo album and notice how the pictures there influence your thoughts, feelings, and actions. Just becoming aware of what your pictures are and how they affect you can be a huge step toward decreasing their power.

Then, in the most gentle manner possible, let your pictures go. Let them drift away as if they were wisps of smoke picked up by the gentle wind.

Pictures are persistent. They come back over and over. Notice them again and let them go again. At first, a picture might return repeatedly and insistently. Pictures are like independent beings. They want to live.

If you can see the picture as a thought independent from you, you will likely find it easier to let it go. You are more than your thoughts. Many images and words will pop into your head in the course of a lifetime; you do not have to identify with them all. You can let pictures go without giving up yourself.

If your pictures are interfering with your education, visualize them scurrying around inside your head. See yourself tying them to a brightly colored helium balloon and letting them go. Let them float away again and again.

Sometimes we can let go of old pictures and replace them with new ones. We stored all those pictures in the first place. We can replace them. Our student's new picture of a great education can include the skimpy cafeteria, the professor with the weird tie, and the roommate with the tuba.

We can take charge of the images that float through our minds. We don't have to be ruled by an album of antique pictures. Instead, we can stay aware of our pictures and keep looking for new ones. And when those new pictures no longer serve us, we can also let them go.

PRACTICING CRITICAL THINKING #8

Read an editorial in a newspaper or magazine. Analyze this editorial by taking notes in a three-column format on a separate sheet of paper. Use the first column for listing major points; the second for minor, supporting points; and the third for key facts or statistics that support the major or minor points. For example:

MAJOR POINT
The "female condom" is not yet an effective method of birth control.

SUPPORTING POINT
Few studies exist on this method.

KEY FACT
One of the few studies showed a 26 percent failure rate for the female condom.

Ask another person to do this exercise with you. Then compare and discuss your notes. In the space below, describe how your opinions on this issue were modified in light of the reasons and evidence presented.

_____

_____

_____

_____

_____

_____

_____

master student

b a r b a r a   j o r d a n

*black congresswoman and lawyer, was
named one of the 10 most influential
women in Texas*

So I was at Boston University in this new
and strange and different world, and it
occurred to me that if I was going to succeed at this
strange new adventure, I would have to read longer and
more thoroughly than my colleagues at law school had to
read. I felt that in order to compensate for what I had
missed in earlier years, I would have to work harder, and
study longer, than anybody else . . . . I did my reading not
in the law library, but in a library at my graduate dorm,
upstairs where it was very quiet, because apparently
nobody else studied there. So I would go there at night
after dinner. I would load my books under my arm and
go to the library, and I would read until the wee hours of
the morning and then go to bed . . . .

I was always delighted when I would get called
upon to recite in class. But the professors did not call
on the "ladies" very much. There were certain favored
people who always got called on, and then on some rare

occasions a professor would come in and would
announce: "We're going to have Ladies Day today."
And he would call on the ladies. We were just tolerated.
We weren't considered really top drawer when it came to
the study of law.

At some time in the spring, Bill Gibson, who was
dating my new roommate, Norma Walker, organized a
black study group, as we blacks had to form our own.
This was because we were not invited into any of the
other study groups. There were six or seven in our
group—Bill, and Issie, and I think Maynard Jackson—
and we would just gather and talk it out and hear
ourselves do that. One thing I learned was that you had
to talk out the issues, the facts, the cases, the decisions,
the process. You couldn't just read the cases and study
alone in your library as I had been doing; and you
couldn't get it all in the classroom. But once you had
talked it out in the study group, it flowed more easily
and made a lot more sense. . . .

Finally I felt I was really learning things, really going
to school. I felt that I was getting educated, whatever that
was. I became familiar with the process of thinking. I
learned to think things out and reach conclusions and
defend what I had said.

In the past I had got along by spouting off.
Whether you talked about debates or oratory, you dealt
with speechifying. But I could no longer orate and let that
pass for reasoning because there was not any demand for
an orator in Boston University Law School. You had to
think and read and understand and reason. I had learned
at twenty-one that you couldn't just say a thing is so
because it might not be so, and somebody brighter,
smarter, and more thoughtful would come out and tell
you it wasn't so. Then, if you still thought it was, you had
to prove it. Well, that was a new thing for me. I cannot, I
really cannot describe what that did to my insides and to
my head. I thought: I'm being educated finally.

1 What is an acrostic that can help you remember the nine steps of Muscle Reading?

2 You must complete all nine steps of Muscle Reading to get the most out of any reading assignment. True or False. Explain your answer.

3 Describe at least four strategies you can use to preview a reading assignment.

4 What is a benefit of outlining a reading assignment?

5 Define the terms prefix and suffix and explain how they can assist you in learning the meanings of new words.

6 To get the most benefit from marking a book, underline at least 20 percent of the text. True or False. Explain your answer.

7 Explain at least three techniques you can use when reading is tough.

8 *Mental pictures are strictly visual images. True or False. Explain your answer.*

9 *After talking with her classmates about issues, facts, cases, decisions, and process, Barbara Jordan:*

    (A) Learned that others were brighter, smarter, and more thoughtful than she was.
    (B) Discovered that the material flowed more easily and made a lot more sense.
    (C) Realized that she could work by herself, challenging her own ideas and thinking independently.
    (D) Decided to work harder and study longer than anybody else.
    (E) All of the above.

10 *List at least three hints for increasing your reading speed.*

JOURNAL ENTRY #24
DISCOVERY/INTENTION STATEMENT

Review what you learned about your reading habits in this chapter and complete the following sentence:

    I discovered that . . .

_____

_____

    Quickly review this chapter and choose three techniques that you will put into practice.

    I intend to . . .

_____

_____

_____

_____

_____

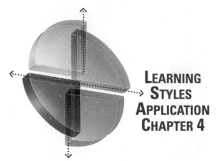

**LEARNING
> STYLES
APPLICATION
CHAPTER 4**

Style 1

Brainstorm a list of current reading assignments you could use to practice the nine steps of Muscle Reading.

Style 2

List 10 new ideas or suggestions for reading you learned from this chapter.

Style 3

Take the list you made for Style 2 and rank each idea's potential usefulness to you. Assign a 1 to the most useful idea and a 10 to the least useful one. Then describe how you will practice the top three ideas on your list.

Style 4

Create your own procedure for effective reading. Consider how you would adapt or modify the steps of Muscle Reading. List and describe each step of your procedure.

Bibliography

◼ Endnotes

[1]G.S. Gates, "Recitation as a factor in memorizing," *Archives of Psychology*, No. 40, 1917.

[2]R. Rosnow and E. Robinson (ed.), *Experiments in Persuasion* (New York: Academic Press, 1967).

[3]William Glasser, *Take Effective Control of Your Life* (New York: Harper & Row, 1984).

◼ Additional Reading

Adler, Mortimer, and Charles Van Doren. *How to Read a Book*, New York: Touchstone, 1972.

Barzun, Jacques, and Henry F. Graff. *The Modern Researcher*, New York: Harcourt Brace Jovanovich, 1977.

Gilbart, Helen W. *Pathways: A Guide to Reading and Study Skills*, Boston: Houghton Mifflin, 1982.

Pauk, Walter. *How to Study in College*, Boston: Houghton Mifflin, 1974.

Rial, Arlyne F. *Speed Reading Made Easy*, Garden City, NY: Doubleday, 1985.

Soukhanov, Anne H., ed. *The American Heritage Dictionary of the English Language*, Boston: Houghton Mifflin, 1992.

Wurman, Richard Saul. *Information Anxiety*, New York: Doubleday, 1989.

notes

In this chapter...

■ **experiment with three broad paths to taking more powerful notes—observe, record, and review. Learn ways to take effective notes on reading, improve your handwriting, and catch up with instructors who talk fast. Also see how concept maps can give your notes new life. In addition, discover "I create it all"—a way to flourish even if you find your classes boring, your friends irritating, or your circumstances difficult.**

JOURNAL ENTRY #25
DISCOVERY STATEMENT

Recall a recent incident in which you had difficulty taking notes. Perhaps you were listening to an instructor who talked fast, or you got confused and stopped taking notes altogether. Describe the incident here.

_____
_____
_____
_____
_____
_____

Now preview this chapter for five suggestions that you can use right away to take better notes. Sum up each of those suggestions in a few words and note page numbers where you can find out more about each suggestion.

I discovered that I could . . .

_____
_____
_____
_____
_____
_____

ONE WAY TO UNDERSTAND NOTE TAKING is to realize that taking notes is the least important part of the process.

Effective note taking consists of three parts: observing, recording, and reviewing. First, you observe an event—most often a statement by the instructor. Then you record your observations of that event—that is, you "take notes." Finally, you review what you have recorded.

Each part of the process is essential, and each depends on the others. Your observations determine what you record. What you record determines what you review. Less obviously, how well you review can determine how effective your next observations will be. For example, if you review your notes on the Sino-Japanese War of 1894, the next day's lecture on the Boxer Rebellion of 1900 will make more sense.

Certainly, legible and speedy handwriting is also useful in taking notes. A knowledge of outlining is handy too. A nifty pen, a new notebook, even a fancy tape recorder are all great note-taking devices.

And they're all worthless, unless you participate as an energetic observer in class and regularly review your notes after class. If you take those two steps, you can turn even the most disorganized chicken scratches into a powerful tool.

The note-taking process flows

> " "
> I write to understand as much as to be understood.
> —ELIE WIESEL

> " "
> This is what learning is. You suddenly understand something you've understood all your life, but in a new way.
> —DORIS LESSING

> " "
> Rather than try to gauge your note-taking skill by quantity, think in this way: am I simply doing clerk's work or am I assimilating new knowledge and putting down my own thoughts? To put down your own thoughts you must put down your own words. . . . If the note taken shows signs of having passed through a mind, it is a good test of its relevance and adequacy.
> —JACQUES BARZUN & HENRY GRAFF

Observe

The note-taking process flows

Sherlock Holmes, a fictional master detective and student of the obvious, could track down a villain by observing the wrinkles in his hat and the mud on his shoes. In real life, a doctor can save a life by observing a mole—one a patient has always had—that suddenly deserves medical attention. An accountant can save a client thousands of dollars by observing the details of a spreadsheet. A student can save hours of study time by observing that she gets twice as much done at a particular time of day.

Keen observers see facts and relationships. They know ways to focus their attention on the details, then tap their creative energy to discover patterns.

To sharpen your classroom observation skills, experiment with the following techniques and continue to use those that you find most valuable.

Set the stage

1. Complete outside assignments.
Nothing is more discouraging (or boring) than sitting through a lecture about the relationship of the Le Chatelier principle to the principle of kinetics if you have never heard of Le Chatelier or kinetics.

Instructors usually assume that students complete assignments, and they construct their lectures accordingly. The more familiar you are with a subject, the easier it will be to understand in class.

2. Bring the right materials.
A good pen does not make you a good observer, but the lack of a pen or a notebook can be distracting enough to take the fine edge off your concentration. Make sure you have a pen, pencil, notebook, and any other materials you will need. Consider bringing your textbook to class, especially if the lectures relate closely to the text.

If you are consistently unprepared for class, that might be a message about your intentions concerning the course. Find out if it is. The next time you're in a frantic scramble to borrow pen and paper 37 seconds before class begins, notice the cost. Use the borrowed pen and paper to write yourself a Discovery Statement about your lack of preparation. Consider whether you intend to be successful in the class.

3. Sit front and center.
Students who get as close as possible to the front and center of the classroom often do better on tests for several reasons. The closer you sit to the lecturer, the harder it is to fall asleep. The closer you sit to the front, the fewer interesting, or distracting, heads there are to watch between you and the instructor. Material on the board is easier to read from up front. Also, the instructor can see you more easily when you have a question.

Instructors are usually not trained as actors or performers. Some instructors can project their energy to a large audience; many cannot. A professor who sounds boring from the back of the room might sound more interesting if you're closer. Get close to the energy.

And finally, sitting up front is a way to commit yourself to getting what you want out of school. One reason students gravitate to the back of the classroom is that they think the instructor is less likely to call on them. Sitting in back can signal a lack of commitment. When you sit in front you are declaring your willingness to take a risk and participate.

4. Conduct a short preclass review. Arrive early, then put your brain in gear by reviewing your notes from the previous class. Scan your reading assignment. Look at the sections you have underlined. Review assigned problems and exercises. Note questions you intend to ask.

5. Clarify your intentions. Write a short Intention Statement about what you plan to get from the class. Describe your intended level of participation or the quality of attention you will bring to the subject. Be specific. If you found previous class notes to be inadequate, write down things you intend to do to make your notes from this class session more useful.

"Be here now" in class

6. Accept your wandering mind. The techniques in Power Process #2: "Be here now" can be especially useful when your head soars into the clouds. Don't fight daydreaming. When you notice your mind wandering, look at it as an opportunity to refocus your attention. If you notice that your attention is wandering from thermodynamics to beach parties, let go of the beach.

7. Notice your writing. When you discover yourself slipping into a fantasyland, notice how your pen feels in your hand. Notice how your notes look. Paying attention to the act of writing can bring you back to the here and now.

You also can use writing more directly to clear your mind of distracting thoughts. Pause for a few seconds and write those thoughts down. If you're distracted by thoughts of errands you want to run after class, list them on a 3x5 card and stick it in your pocket. Or simply put a symbol, such as an arrow or asterisk, in your notes to mark the places where your mind started to wander. Once your distractions are out of your mind and safely stored on paper, you can gently return your attention to taking notes.

8. Be with the instructor. In your mind, put yourself right up front with the instructor. Imagine that you and the instructor are the only ones in the room and the lecture is a personal talk with you. Pay attention to the instructor's body language and facial expressions. Look the instructor in the eye.

9. Notice your environment. When you become aware of yourself daydreaming, bring yourself back to class by paying attention to the temperature in the room, the feel of your chair, or the quality of light in the room. Run your hand along the surface of your desk. Listen to the fan running or the sound of the teacher's voice. Be in that environment.

10. Postpone debate. When you hear something you disagree with, note your disagreement and let it go. Don't allow your internal dialogue to drown out subsequent material. If your disagreement is persistent and strong, make note of this and then move on. Internal debate can prevent you from absorbing new information. It is OK to absorb information you don't agree with. Just absorb it with the mental tag "I don't agree with this and my instructor says . . . ."

11. Let go of judgments about lecture styles. Human beings are judgment machines. We evaluate everything, especially other people. If another person's eyebrows are too close together (or too far apart), if she walks a certain way or combs her hair a certain way, we instantly make up a story about her. We do this so quickly that the process is usually not a conscious one.

Don't let your attitude about an instructor's lecture style, habits, or appearance get in the way of your education. You can decrease the power of your judgments if you pay attention to them and let them go.

You can even let go of judgments about rambling, unorganized lectures. Turn them to your advantage. Take the initiative and organize the material yourself. While taking notes, separate the key points from the examples and supporting evidence. Note the places where you got confused and make a list of questions to ask.

12. Participate in class activities. Ask questions. Volunteer for demonstrations. Join in class discussions. Be willing to take a risk or look foolish if that's what it takes for you to learn. Chances are, the question you think is "dumb" also is on the minds of several of your classmates.

13. Relate the class to your goals. If you have trouble staying awake in a particular class, write at the top of your notes how that class relates to a specific goal. Note the reward or payoff for reaching that goal.

14. Think critically about what you hear. This might seem contrary to #10: "Postpone debate." It's not. You may choose not to think critically about the instructor's ideas during the lecture. That's fine. Do it later, as you review and edit your notes. This is a time to list questions or write your agreements and disagreements.

Watch for clues

15. Be alert to repetition. When an instructor repeats a phrase or idea, make a note of it. Repetition is a signal that the instructor thinks the information is important.

16. Listen for introductory, concluding, and transition words and phrases. These include phrases like *the following three factors, in conclusion, the most important consideration, in addition to, on the other hand.* These phrases and others signal relationships, definitions, new subjects, conclusions, cause and effect, and examples. In other words, they reveal the structure of the lecture. You can use these phrases to organize your notes.

17. Watch the board or overhead projector. If an instructor takes time to write something down, consider that another signal that the material is important. Copy all diagrams and drawings, equations, names, places, dates, statistics, and definitions.

18. Watch the instructor's eyes. If an instructor glances at her notes and then makes a point, it is probably a signal that the information is especially important. Anything she reads from her notes is a potential test question.

19. Highlight the obvious clues. Instructors will often tell students point-blank that certain information is likely to appear on an exam. Make stars in your notes beside this kind of information. Instructors are not trying to hide what's important.

20. Notice the instructor's interest level. If the instructor is excited about something, it is more likely to appear on an exam. Pay attention if she seems more animated than usual.

JOURNAL ENTRY #26
DISCOVERY STATEMENT

Think back on the last few lectures you have attended and also recall some of the lecture classes you attended years ago. How do you currently observe (listen to) lectures? What specific behaviors do you have as you sit and listen? How are those behaviors different from those long ago?

_____

_____

_____

_____

_____

_____

_____

_____

_____

_____

_____

_____

_____

_____

_____

_____

_____

Record

The note-taking process flows

The format and structure of your notes arc more important than how fast you write or how pretty your handwriting is. The following techniques can improve the effectiveness of your notes.

1. Use the Cornell format of note taking.

In his writing on student success, Walter Pauk[1] suggests a note-taking system he calls the Cornell format. It works like this: On each page of your notes, draw a vertical line, top to bottom, 1 1/2 inches from the left edge of the paper. Write your notes to the right of the line. Reserve the area to the left of the line for key word clues and sample questions. Fill in the left-hand column when you review your notes.

2. Create mind maps.

This system, developed by Tony Buzan[2], can be used in conjunction with the Cornell system, although in some circumstances you might want to use mind maps exclusively.

To understand mind maps, first review the features of traditional note taking. Roman numeral/capital letter outlines contain main topics that are followed by minor topics which, in turn, are subdivided further. They organize a subject in a sequential, linear way.

Such organization, however, doesn't reflect some other aspects of brain function. This point has been made in the discussions about "left brain" and "right brain" activities. Some people use the term *right brain* when referring to creative, pattern-making, visual, intuitive brain activity. They use the term *left brain* when talking about the orderly, logical, step-by-step characteristics of thought. Writing teacher Gabrielle Rico[3] uses another metaphor. She refers to the left-brain mode as our "sign mind" (concerned with words) and the right-brain mode as our "design mind" (concerned with visuals).

A mind map uses both kinds of brain functions. Mind maps can contain lists and sequences and show causes. They also provide a picture of a subject. Mind maps are visual patterns that can provide a framework for recall. They work on both verbal and nonverbal levels.

One benefit of mind maps is that they quickly, vividly, and accurately show the relationships between ideas is a visual way. Further, mind mapping helps you think from general to specific. By choosing a main topic, you focus first on the big picture, then zero in on subordinate ideas. And by using only key words, you can condense a large subject into a small area on a mind map. You review more quickly

Metal Conductive	Hard, shiny, malleable (roll into sheets), ductile (pulled into wires). Conducts electric current & heat. 3 or fewer electrons in outer level so good conductors because electrons can move thru.
Metallic Bond	Outer electrons distributed as common electric cloud. Electrons shared equally by all ions which explains properties (conductive, malleable, ductile) → ions slide by each other & can be displaced w/o shattering.
Alkali Metals	Soft metals. Most reactive — kept under oil so won't react directly w/oxygen or H_2O. Forms compound by ionic bonding. Can identify alkalis by flame test. Electrons gain energy when heated. When cooling, lose energy as light. Ex:

by looking at the key words on a mind map than by reading notes word for word. The sample mind map on page 133 illustrates these points.

As you build a mind map on paper, you are also constructing a map in your mind. When you are finished, the picture of the map enters your memory. You could throw away your paper mind map and still retain most of the benefits of making it.

The following guidelines can assist you in creating mind maps.

- Give yourself plenty of room. Use blank paper that measures at least 11 by 17 inches. If that's not available, turn regular notebook paper on its side so that you take notes in a horizontal (instead of vertical) format. Another option is to find software that allows you to draw flow charts or diagrams. Then you can generate mind maps on a computer.
- Determine the main concept of the lecture. Write that concept in the center of the page and circle it.
- Record concepts related to the main concept on lines radiating from the center.
- Use key words only. Aim for one word per line. Though this may seem awkward at first, it prompts you to summarize and reduce ideas to their essence. That's fewer words for you to write now and fewer to review when it comes time to review for tests. Key words are usually nouns and verbs that carry the bulk of the speaker's ideas. Choose words that are rich in associations and those that can help you re-create the lecture.
- Use shorthand symbols and abbreviations.
- Use color to organize your mind map. If there are three main subjects covered in the lecture, you can record each subject in a different color.
- Add images and symbols.

One mind map does not have to include all the ideas in a book or article. Instead, you can link mind maps. For example, draw a mind map that sums up the five key points in a chapter; then make a separate, more detailed mind map for each of those key points. Within each mind map, include references to the other mind maps. This helps in seeing the relationships among many ideas.

Some students pin several mind maps next to each other on a bulletin board or tape them to a wall. That gives a dramatic and effective look at the big picture.

Mind maps can be used along with Cornell-format notes in a number of ways. You can divide your note paper in half, reserving one half for mind maps and the other for information more suited to the traditional paragraph method: equations, long explanations, and word-for-word definitions. You also can incorporate a mind map into your paragraph-style notes wherever you feel one is appropriate. Mind maps are also useful for summarizing notes taken in Cornell format.

Another way to use mind maps is to abandon the Cornell format, draw a line down the center of the page, and use the left-hand side for mind mapping and the right-hand side for more linear information, such as lists, graphs, and paragraphs.

3. Write notes in outline form. You can use a standard Roman numeral outline or a free-form, indented outline to organize the information in a lecture.

The outline form illustrates major points and supporting ideas. The main advantage to taking notes in outline form is that it can totally occupy your attention. You are not only recording ideas but also organizing them. That can be an advantage if material is presented in a disorganized way.

I. Bones - living organs, 206 in body, 18% of weight
A. Marrow - in center of bones. Contains nerves & blood vessels
  1. Red
    a. in flat bones (ribs) & ends of long bones
    b. produces red blood cells in adults
  2. Yellow - mostly flat tissue
    a. in center of long bones
    b. might make red blood cells if great blood loss or w/ certain blood diseases
B. Haversian canals - carry blood thru bones (for oxygen, food & waste)
C. Periostium - protective membrane covers bone
D. Composed of:
  1. Minerals, organic matter, H_2O
    a. Calcium & phosphorus present as calcium phosphate ($Ca_3 (PO_4)_3$) &

4. Write notes in paragraphs. When it is difficult to follow the organization of a lecture or to put information into outline form, create a series of informal paragraphs. These paragraphs will contain few complete sentences. Reserve complete sentences for precise definitions, direct quotes, and important points that the instructor emphasizes by repetition or other signals, like the phrase *This is an important point*. For other material, apply the suggestions in technique #5: "Use key words."

Write related thoughts in a paragraph and leave a space when the lecturer moves to another point. That way, you can go back and add information the instructor offers later. When you review your notes, you can reorganize them and create an outline.

5. Use key words. An easy way to sort the extraneous material from the important points is to take notes using key words.

Key words or phrases contain the essence of communication. They include technical terms, names, numbers, equations, and words of degree: *most, least, faster*, etc.

Key words are laden with associations. They evoke images and associations with other words and ideas. They trigger your memory. That makes them powerful review tools.

One key word can initiate the recall of a whole cluster of ideas. A few key words can form a chain from which you can reconstruct an entire lecture.

To see how key words work, take yourself to an imaginary classroom. You are now in the middle of an anatomy lecture. Picture what the room looks like, what it feels like, how it smells. You hear the instructor say:

OK, what happens when we look directly over our heads and see a piano falling out of the sky? How do we take that signal and translate it into the action of getting out of the way? The first thing that happens is that a stimulus is generated in the neurons—receptor neurons—of the eye. Light reflected from the piano reaches our eyes. In other words, we see the piano. The receptor neurons in the eye transmit that sensory signal, the sight of the piano, to the body's nervous system. That's all they can do, pass on information. So, we've got a sensory signal coming into the nervous system. But the neurons that initiate movement in our legs are effector neurons. The information from the sensory neurons must be transmitted to effector neurons or we will get squashed by the piano. There must be some kind of interconnection between receptor and effector neurons. What happens between the two? What is the connection?

Key words you might note in this example include *stimulus, generated, receptor neurons, transmit, sensory signals, nervous system, effector neurons,* and *connection*. You could reduce the instructor's 148 words to these 12 key words. With a few transitional words, your notes might look like this:

> Stimulus (piano) generated in receptor neurons (eye).
> Sensory signals transmitted by nervous system to effector neurons (legs).
> What connects receptor to effector?

Note the last key word, *connection*. This word is part of the instructor's question, which leads to the next point in the lecture. Be alert for questions like this. They can help you organize your notes, and they are often clues for test questions.

6. Use pictures and diagrams. Make relationships visual. Copy all diagrams from the board and invent your own.  This technique can be used anytime, with or without mind mapping.

A drawing of a piano falling on someone who is looking up, for example, might be used to demonstrate the relationship of receptor neurons to effector neurons. Label the eyes "receptor" and the feet "effector."

That picture implies that the sight of the piano must be translated into a motor response. By connecting the explanation of the process with the unusual picture of the piano falling, you can link the elements of the process together.

7. Copy material from the board. Record all formulas, diagrams, and problems. Copy dates, numbers, names, places, and other facts. If it's on the board, put it in your notes. You can even use your own signal or code to flag that material. If it appears on the board, it can appear on a test.

8. Use a three-ring binder. Three-ring binders have several advantages over other kinds of notebooks.

First, pages can be removed and spread out when you review. This way, you can get the whole picture of a lecture.

Second, the three-ring binder format will allow you to insert handouts right into your notes easily.

Third, you can insert your own out-of-class notes in the correct order. You can easily make additions, corrections, and revisions.

9. Use only one side of a piece of paper. When you use one side of a page, you can review and organize all your notes by spreading them out side by side. Most students find the benefit well worth the cost of the paper.

10. Use 3x5 cards. As an alternative to using notebook paper, use 3x5 cards to take lecture notes. Copy each new concept on a separate 3x5 card. Later, these cards can be organized in an outline form, and they can be used as pocket flash cards.

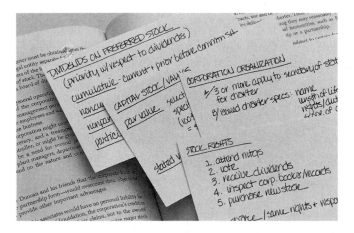

11. Keep your own thoughts separate. For the most part, avoid making editorial comments in your lecture notes. The danger is that when you return to your notes, you may mistake your own idea for that of the instructor. If you want to make a comment—either a question to be asked later or a strong disagreement—clearly label it as your own. Pick a symbol or code and use it in every class.

12. Use an "I'm lost" signal. No matter how attentive and alert you are, you might get lost and confused in a lecture. If it is inappropriate to ask a question, record in your notes that you were lost. Invent your own signal—for example, a circled question mark. When you write down

your code for "I'm lost," leave space for the explanation or clarification that you will get later. The space will also be a signal that you missed something. Later, you can call your instructor or ask to see a fellow student's notes. As long as you are honest with yourself when you don't understand, you can stay on top of the course.

13. Label, number, and date all notes. Develop the habit of labeling and dating your notes at the beginning of each class. Number the page too. Sometimes the sequence of material in a lecture is important. Write your name and phone number in each notebook. Class notes become more and more valuable as a term proceeds.

14. Use standard abbreviations. Be consistent with your abbreviations. If you make up your own abbreviations or symbols, write a key explaining them in your notes.

Avoid vague abbreviations. When you use an abbreviation like *comm.* for *committee*, you run the risk of not being able to remember whether you meant *committee, commission, common, commit, community, communicate,* or *communist.*

One way to abbreviate is to leave out vowels. For example, *talk* becomes *tlk, said* becomes *sd, American* becomes *Amrcn.*

WARNING: Abbreviations can be hazardous to your academic health. If you are inconsistent or if you use vague abbreviations, there will be a price to pay in confusion later on. One way to avoid that is to write out abbreviated terms during pauses in a lecture, when the meaning of your shorthand is still fresh in your short-term memory.

15. Use blank space. Notes tightly crammed into every corner of the page are hard to read and difficult to use for review. Give your eyes a break by leaving plenty of space.

Later, when you review, you can use the blank space in your notes to clarify points, write questions, or add other material. Often instructors return to material covered earlier in the lecture. If you leave adequate space, you can add information.

16. Use tape recorders effectively. There are persuasive arguments for not using a tape recorder. Here are the main ones.

When you tape a lecture, there is a strong temptation to daydream. After all, you can always listen to the lecture again. Unfortunately, if you let the recorder do all the work, you are skipping a valuable part of the learning process. Your active participation in class can turn a lecture into a valuable study session.

There are more potential problems. Listening to tape-recorded lectures can take a lot of time—more time than reviewing written notes. Tape recorders can't answer the questions you didn't ask in class. Also, tape recorders malfunction. In fact, the unscientific Hypothesis of Recording Glitches states that the tendency of tape recorders to malfunction is directly proportional to the importance of the material.

With those warnings in mind, some students can use a tape recorder effectively. For example, you can use recordings as backups to written notes. Turn the recorder on, then take notes as if it weren't there. Recordings can be especially useful if an instructor speaks fast. (Check with your instructor first. Some prefer not to be taped.)

You also could record yourself after class, reading your written notes. Teaching the class to yourself is a powerful review tool. Instead of taping all your notes, for example, you might record only the key facts or concepts.

You can have fun too. As you tape, speak in funny voices. Do imitations of your teachers or favorite actors. Add background music. Make these tapes enjoyable for listening. You can use the recordings you make or the backup recordings from class to review while you drive, wash dishes, or exercise.

Some tape recorders have a feature called compressed speech. This speeds up the voice on the tape, which can save you listening time.

Knowing the pitfalls of tape recorders, experiment for yourself. Then adopt a strategy that works for you.

17. Use complete sentences when material is important. Sometimes key words aren't enough. When an instructor repeats a sentence word for word, she might be sending you a signal. Technical definitions are often worded precisely because even a slightly different wording will render the definitions useless or incorrect.

18. Take notes in different colors. You can use colors as highly visible organizers. For example, you can signal important points with red. Or use one color ink for notes about the text and another color for lecture notes. Notes that are visually pleasing can be easier to review.

19. Use graphic signals. The following ideas can be used with any note-taking format, including mind maps.

Use brackets, parentheses, circles, and squares to group information that belongs together.

Use stars, arrows, and underlining to indicate important points. Flag the most important points with double stars, double arrows, or double underlines.

Use arrows and connecting lines to link related groups, to show causation, and to replace words like *leads to*, *becomes*, and *produces*.

Use equal signs and greater- and less-than signs to indicate compared quantities.

Use question marks for their obvious purpose. Use double question marks to signal tough questions or especially confusing points.

To avoid creating confusion with graphic symbols, use them carefully and consistently. Write a "dictionary" of the symbols you use in the front of your notebooks, like the one shown above.

Review

The note-taking process flows

Think of reviewing as an integral part of note taking rather than as an added task. In order for information to be useful, it needs to be available to your recall.

1. Review within 24 hours. In the last chapter, when you read the suggestion to review what you've read within 24 hours, you were asked to sound the trumpet. Well, if you have one, get it out and sound it again. This might be the most powerful note-taking technique you can use. It can save you hours of review time later in the term.

Many students are surprised by how much they can remember of a lecture in the minutes and hours after class. They are even more surprised by how well they can read even the sloppiest notes.

Unfortunately, short-term memory deteriorates quickly. The good news: If you get back to your notes for a quick review soon enough, you can move that information from short-term to long-term memory. And you can do it in just a few minutes—often 10 minutes or less.

The sooner you review your notes the better, especially if the class was difficult. In fact, you can start reviewing during class. When your instructor pauses to set up the overhead projector or erase the board, scan your notes. Dot the *i*s, cross the *t*s, and write out unclear abbreviations. Another way to use this technique is to get to your next class as quickly as you can. Then use the four or five minutes before the lecture to review the notes you just took in the previous class.

If you do not get to your notes immediately after class, you can still benefit by reviewing later in the day. A review right before you go to sleep can also be valuable.

Think of the day's unreviewed notes as leaky faucets, constantly dripping, losing precious information until you shut them off with a quick review. Remember, it's possible to forget up to 80 percent of the material within 24 hours—unless you review.

2. Edit notes. During your first review, fix words that are illegible. Write out abbreviated words that might be unclear to you later. Make sure you can read everything. If you can't read something or don't understand something you can read, mark it and make a note to ask your instructor or another student. Check to see that your notes are labeled with the date and class and that the pages are numbered. You can edit with a different colored pen or pencil if you want to distinguish between what you wrote in class and what you filled in later.

3. Fill in key words in the left-hand column. This task is important if you are to get the full benefit of using the Cornell format. Using the key word principles described earlier in this chapter, go through your notes and write key words or phrases in the left-hand column.

These key words will speed the review process later. As you read your notes and focus on extracting key concepts, your understanding of the lecture is further reinforced.

4. Conduct short weekly review periods. Once a week, review all your notes again. The review sessions don't need to take a lot of time. Even a 20-minute weekly review period is valuable. Some students find that a weekend review, say on Sunday afternoon, helps them stay in continuous touch with the material. Scheduling regular review sessions on your calendar helps develop the habit.

As you review, step back for the larger picture. In addition to reciting or repeating the material to yourself, ask questions about it: "Does this relate to my goals?", "How does this relate to information I already know, in this field or another?", "Will I be tested on this material?", "What will I do with this material?", "How can I relate it to something that deeply interests me?", "Am I unclear on any points?", "If so, what exactly is the question I want to ask?"

5. Use your key words as cues to recite. With a blank sheet of paper, cover your notes, leaving only the key words in the left-hand margin showing. Take each key word in order and recite as much as you can about the point. Then uncover your notes and look for important points you missed.

6. Consider typing up your notes. Some students type clean copies of their handwritten notes, on either a typewriter or a computer. The argument for doing it is twofold. First, typed notes are easier to read and take up less space. In addition, the process of typing them forces you to review the material.

Yet another alternative is to bypass handwriting altogether and take notes on a small laptop computer. Some newspaper reporters do this. Possible drawbacks: Laptops cost money, and computer errors can wipe out your notes.

In any case, experiment with typing notes and see what works for you. For example, you might type up only portions of notes—summaries or outlines.

7. Create mind map summaries. Mind mapping is an excellent way to make summary sheets. After making your map, look at your original notes and fill in anything you missed. This system is fun to use. It's quick, and it gives your brain a hook on which to fasten the material.

EXERCISE #17
TELEVISION NOTE-TAKING PRACTICE

You can use evening news broadcasts to practice listening for key words, writing quickly, focusing your attention, and reviewing.

The next time you watch the news, do it with pen and paper. During the commercials, review and revise your notes. At the end of the broadcast, spend five minutes reviewing your notes. Create a mind map of a few news stories, then re-create the news of the day for a friend.

This exercise will help you develop an ear for key words. Since you can't ask questions or ask the speaker to slow down, you train yourself to stay totally in the moment. If you get behind, you learn not to panic, but to leave a space and return to the broadcast.

Don't be discouraged if you miss a lot the first time around. Do this exercise several times and observe how your mind works.

You can also ask a friend to do the same exercise and then compare notes the next day.

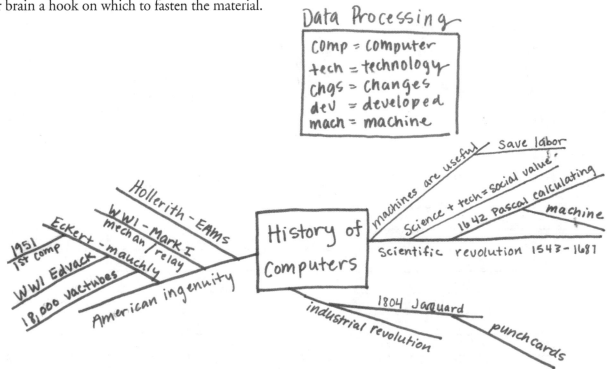

JOURNAL ENTRY #27
DISCOVERY STATEMENT

Think about the way you have conducted reviews of your notes in the past. Respond to the following statements by checking "always," "often," "sometimes," "seldom," or "never" after each.

I review my notes immediately after class.
_____Always_____Often_____Sometimes_____Seldom_____Never

I conduct weekly reviews of my notes.
_____Always_____Often_____Sometimes_____Seldom_____Never

I make summary sheets of my notes.
_____Always_____Often_____Sometimes_____Seldom_____Never

I edit my notes within 24 hours.
_____Always_____Often_____Sometimes_____Seldom_____Never

Before class I conduct a brief review of the notes I took in the previous class.

_____Always_____Often_____Sometimes_____Seldom_____Never

EXERCISE #18
APPLY A PROCESS

"Love your problems" was the Power Process presented in Chapter Three. Write how you can apply the idea of loving your problem to the task of note taking.

_____
_____
_____
_____
_____
_____
_____
_____
_____
_____

JOURNAL ENTRY #28
DISCOVERY STATEMENT

For this journal entry, you will need a few pages of your old notes—the older, the better. If possible, use notes from last year. If you have some notes you took several years ago, they will work perfectly.

Look over those notes as if you were to be tested on them tomorrow. Then, in the space provided here, write down a one-paragraph summary of what those notes tell you today.

_____
_____
_____
_____
_____
_____
_____
_____
_____
_____
_____
_____
_____

Next, engage an editor's eye and evaluate your notes. And remember, editors look for the positive as well as the negative. Write down what is effective about your notes and what is ineffective. Be specific about strengths and weaknesses of your current note-taking techniques.

_____
_____
_____
_____
_____
_____
_____
_____
_____

Improving your handwriting

Many people are resigned to writing illegibly for the rest of their lives. They feel they have no control over handwriting.

Yet everyone's handwriting does change. Your signature when you're on top of the world is not the same as when you are down in the dumps. Handwriting also changes as we mature.

If you unconsciously change your handwriting, you can change it consciously. The prerequisite for improving your handwriting is simply a desire to do so.

If you want to write more legibly, however, here are some possibilities.

Use the First Step technique. Take a First Step by telling the truth about the problem. Admit it and acknowledge your desire to improve.

The problem, by the way, is not bad handwriting; it's the impact of the writing. The problem is "I can't read my notes and therefore I have difficulty studying," or "The people I work with are always getting upset because they can't read what I write."

Use creative visualizations. Find a quiet spot to sit, relax your whole body, close your eyes, and see yourself writing clearly. Feel the pen as it moves over the page, and picture neat, legible letters as you write them.

Keep your eye on the ballpoint. Watch the way you write. Don't "try" to change. Focus all your attention on the tip of the pen, right where it meets the paper. When you do this, let go of judgments or evaluations about how you write. By focusing your attention on the tip of your pen, you are giving your brain something to do, thereby letting your body do the writing.

Demonstrate your excellence. At least once a day, write something as clearly as you can. Write it as if it were going to appear on the front page of the *New York Times*. You will program your body to write clearly.

Revise sloppy writing immediately. Use an erasable pen or pencil. When you write something sloppily, fix it immediately. At first, you might find yourself rewriting almost everything. Using this technique helps you naturally learn to write legibly the first time.

Practice with the best materials. When you put a quality pen to fancy paper, there is incentive to produce clean, crisp, pleasing lines. Practice with these fine materials by writing letters to people you care about.

Take a calligraphy course. Improve your eye-hand coordination with calligraphy. The practice you get working with a calligraphy pen may improve your overall writing.

Dot all *i*'s and cross all *t*'s. The time you spend dotting and crossing will eliminate time spent scratching your head.

Ensure that holes exist. Leave holes in your *a*'s, *e*'s, and *o*'s. If you don't, they can easily be mistaken for *i*'s.

Notice problem letters. Go through your notes and circle letters you have difficulty deciphering. Practice writing these letters.

When understanding is critical, print. When an important idea must be letter-perfect, print it. Printing will stand out from your other notes. And you can read printing faster when you review.

Appreciate the value of legible writing. Notice how you feel when your own handwriting works well for you. Write a Discovery Statement when you become aware that you have improved your handwriting, and list the benefits of the improvement.

I create it all

This is a powerful tool in times of trouble. When things go wrong, Power Process #5 can lead the way to solutions. "I create it all" means treating all the experiences, events, and circumstances in your life as if you created them.

For example, when your dog tracks fresh tar on the white carpet, when your political science teacher is a crushing bore, when your spouse dents the car, when your test on Latin American literature focuses on an author you've never read—it's time for Power Process #5. Tell yourself, "I created it all."

"Baloney!" you shout. "I didn't let the dog in, that guy really is a bore, I wasn't even in the car, and nobody told me to read Gabriel Garcia Marquez. I didn't create these disasters."

Good points. Obviously, "I create it all" is one of the most unusual and bizarre suggestions in this book. It certainly is not an idea to be believed. In fact, believing it can get you in trouble. "I create it all" is strictly a practical idea. When it works, use it. When it doesn't, don't.

Keeping that caution in mind, consider how powerful Power Process #5 can be.

This is really about the difference between two distinct positions in life: being a victim or being self-responsible (self-generating= a victor).

A victim of circumstances is controlled by outside forces. We've all felt like victims at one time or another. When tar-footed dogs tromped on the white carpets of our lives, we felt helpless.

In contrast, we can take responsibility. *Responsibility* is the important word. It does not mean "blame." Far from it. Responsibility is "response-ability." It is the ability to choose a response.

Applying this process

Many students approach grades from the position of being victims. When the student who sees the world this way gets an F, she reacts something like this:

"Oh, no!" (Slaps forehead.)

"Rats!" (Slaps forehead again.)

(Students who get lots of F's often have flat foreheads.)

"Another F! That teacher couldn't teach her way out of a wet paper bag. She can't teach English for nothing. And that textbook—what a bore! How could I read that with a houseful of kids making noise all the time? And then the gang came over and wanted to party and . . . ."

The problem with this viewpoint is that while the student is justifying herself, she's robbing herself of the power to get anything but an F. She's giving all her power to a "boring teacher," a "bad textbook," "noisy children," and "the gang."

There is another way, called "choosing your response." You can say that you choose your grades by choosing your actions. Then you are the source, rather than the result, of the grades you get. The student who got an F could react like this:

"Another F. Oh, shoot, well, hmmm . . . . How did I choose this F? What did I do to create it?"

Now, that's power. By asking "How did I contribute to this outcome?" you give yourself a measure of control. You are no longer the victim.

This student might continue by saying, "Well, let's see. I didn't review my notes after class. That might have done it" or "I studied in the same room with my children while they watched TV. Then I went out with my friends the night before the test. Well, that probably helped me fulfill some of the requirements for getting an F."

The point is this: When the F is the result of your kids, your roommate, the book, or the teacher, you probably can't do anything about it. However, if you chose the F, you can choose differently next time. You are in charge.

Choosing our thoughts

There are times when you don't create it all. You do not "create" earthquakes, floods, avalanches, or monsoons. However, if we look closely, we discover that we do create a larger part of our circumstances than most of us are willing to admit.

For example, we can choose our thoughts. And thoughts can control our perceptions by screening information from our senses.

We are never conscious of everything in our environment. If we were, we'd go crazy from sensory overload. Instead, our brains filter out most sensory inputs, and this filtering colors the way we think about the world.

Imagine for a moment that the universe is whole and complete. It is filled with everything you would ever want, including happiness, love, and material wealth. When you adopt this position, your brain will look for sensory input that supports this idea.

Now take the opposite view. Imagine that happiness, love, and wealth are scarce. Now your brain has a different mission. You will tend to see the stories about poverty, hate, suicide, drug addiction, or unemployment. You could easily miss the stories of people who recovered from addiction, rose out of poverty, or resolved conflict.

Many people have no experience of abundance or happiness. Maybe it is because their thoughts limit what they see. By choosing new thoughts, we can see the same circumstances in new ways.

Choosing our behaviors

Moment by moment we make choices about what we will do and where we will go. The results of these choices are where we are in life. A whole school of psychology called control theory is based on this point, and psychiatrist William Glasser[4] has written extensively about it.

All those choices help create our current circumstances—even those circumstances that are not "our fault." After a car accident we tell ourselves: "It just happened. That car came out of nowhere and hit me." We forget that driving five miles per hour slower and paying closer attention might have allowed us to miss the driver who was "to blame."

Some cautions

The presence of blame is a warning that "I create it all" is being misused. Power Process #5 is not about blaming yourself or others.

And it is not to be applied to other people. For example, if someone tells you about an aspect of your behavior that she finds annoying, this is not the time to reply, "Get off my back; *you* create it all." Remember, the power in this idea is seeing how *you* create it, not how she did.

Similarly, feeling guilty is another warning signal. If you are feeling guilty, you have actually just shifted the blame from another person to yourself.

Another caution is that Power Process #5 is not a religion. Acting as if you "create it all" does not mean denying God. It is simply a way to expand the choices you already have.

Power Process #5 is easy to deny. Tell your friends about it, and they're likely to say, "What about world hunger? I didn't cause that. What about people who get cancer? Did they create that?"

These are good arguments, and they miss the point. There are victims of rape, abuse, incest, and other violence. These people can still use "I create it all" to choose their response to the people and events that violated them.

Some people approach world hunger, imprisonment, and even cancer with this attitude: "Pretend for a moment that I am responsible for this. What will I do about it?" These people see problems in a new way, and they find choices that other people miss.

Power Process #5 is not always about disaster. It also works when life is going great. Often we give credit to others for our good fortune when, in fact, it's time to pat ourselves on the back. By choosing our behavior and thoughts, we can create A's, interesting classes, enjoyable relationships, material wealth, and contributions to a better world.

How people use this process

Throughout history, people have used Power Process #5, even if they didn't call it by the same name. Viktor Frankl[5], a famous psychiatrist and a survivor of Nazi concentration camps, created courage and dignity out of horror and humiliation. Reflecting on his experiences at Auschwitz and other camps, he wrote, "Everything can be taken from a man but one thing: the last of the human freedoms—to choose one's own attitude in any given set of circumstances, to choose one's own way."

Writer William E. B. DuBois created an enduring book—*The Souls of Black Folk*—out of the experience of racial discrimination in America.

Thousands of people are living productive lives and creating positive experiences out of a circumstance called cancer.

Whenever tar-footed dogs are getting in the way of your education, remember Power Process #5. You instantly open yourself to a world of choices. You give yourself power.

EXERCISE #19
THEY MADE ME DO IT

Write down some of the activities you have completed in the last 24 hours, from making the bed to going to class. List these activities in one of the following columns: the activities you chose to do or the activities that other people required you to do. If there was a particular person requiring you to do something, write that person's name after the activity.

Activities I chose	Activities others chose for me
_____	_____
_____	_____
_____	_____
_____	_____
_____	_____

Of the activities others chose for you, which ones were truly consistent with your values and purposes? If you discover you did some things that you didn't want to do, consider not doing them in the future. On a separate sheet of paper, write how you feel about the activity and why you don't want to do it. Consider sending this communication to the person who "made" you do the activity.

JOURNAL ENTRY #29
DISCOVERY/INTENTION STATEMENT

Of the classes in which you are presently enrolled, pick the one you find least interesting. In this space, write all the ways you make the class uninteresting (or less interesting than other classes).

_____
_____
_____
_____
_____

Now write down three ways you can re-create this class as interesting.

_____
_____
_____
_____
_____
_____

When Instructors talk *fast*

1. Take more time to prepare for class. Familiarity with a subject increases your ability to pick out key points. If an instructor lectures quickly or is difficult to understand, conduct a thorough preview of material to be covered.

2. Be willing to make choices. When an instructor talks fast, focus your attention on key points. Instead of trying to write everything down, choose what you think is important. Occasionally you will make a wrong choice and neglect an important point. Worse things could happen. Stay with the lecture, write down key words, and revise your notes immediately after class.

3. Exchange photocopies of notes with classmates. Your fellow students might write down something you missed. At the same time, your notes might help them.

4. Leave large empty spaces in your notes. Leave plenty of room for filling in information you missed. Use a symbol that signals you've missed something, so you can remember to come back to it.

5. See the instructor after class. Take your class notes with you and show the instructor what you missed.

6. Use a tape recorder. Taping a lecture gives you a chance to hear it again whenever you choose. Some tape recorders will allow you to vary the speed of the tape. With this feature, you can perform magic and actually slow down the instructor's speech.

7. Before class, take notes on your reading. You can take detailed notes on the text before class. Leave plenty of blank space. Take these notes with you to class and simply add your lecture notes to them.

8. Go to the lecture again. Many classes are taught in multiple sections. That gives you the chance to hear a lecture at least twice—once at your regular class time and again in another section of the class.

9. Learn shorthand. Some note-taking systems, known as shorthand, are specifically designed for getting ideas down fast. Books and courses are available to help you learn these systems. You can also devise your own shorthand. Invent one- or two-letter symbols for common words and phrases.

10. Ask questions—even if you're totally lost. Most instructors allow time for questions. This is a time to ask about the points you missed.

There may be times when you feel so lost that you can't formulate a question. That's OK. One option is to just report this fact to the instructor. The instructor can often guide you to a clear question. Another option is to just ask any question. Often this will lead you to the question you really want to ask.

11. Ask the instructor to slow down. This is the most obvious solution. If asking her to slow down doesn't work, ask her to repeat what you missed.

EXERCISE #20
THE IN-CLASS OXYGENATOR

When you become sleepy in class, the problem might be lack of oxygen. You can run through the following process in 30 seconds.

1. Straighten your spine. Put both feet on the floor, uncross your arms and legs, sit up straight, and hold your head up straight.

2. Take a deep breath and while you're holding it, tense the muscles in your body. Start with the muscles in your feet, then the legs, thighs, stomach, chest, shoulders, neck, jaw, forehead, arms, and hands. Hold these muscles tense for the count of five and then relax and exhale.

3. Breathe deeply three times. Inhale slowly and deeply, breathing into your belly as well as your chest. Pause momentarily at the top of the breath and then exhale completely. When you have exhaled as much as you can, force out more air by contracting the muscles of your stomach. Do this breathing three times.

4. Repeat step #2. You've now activated all of your muscles and filled your body with oxygen. You are ready to return your attention to the task at hand.

Practice this exercise now by completing it twice. Then make a mental note so that the next time you're sleepy in class or while you're studying, you can use this exercise. With a little practice, you can make it subtle. Your instructor and classmates won't even notice you're doing it.

TAKING NOTES ON READING

Taking notes on reading requires the same skills that apply to class notes: observation, recording, and review. Just remember that there are two kinds of notes on reading: review notes and research notes.

Review notes

Review notes will look like the notes you take in class. Sometimes you will want more extensive notes than you can write in a margin of your text. You can't underline or make notes in library books' margins, so make separate notes when you use these sources.

Mind map summaries of textbook material are particularly useful for review. You can also outline the material in the text or take notes in paragraph form. Single out a particularly difficult section of a text and make separate notes. Or make mind map summaries of overlapping lecture and text material.

Use the left-hand column for key words and questions, just as you do in your class notes.

Research notes

Research notes—those you make for papers and speeches—follow a different format. Creating papers and speeches is a special challenge, and the way you take notes can help you face those challenges.

Use the mighty 3x5 card. There are two kinds of research cards: source cards and information cards. Source cards identify where information is found. For example, a source card on a book will show the title, author, publisher, date, and place of publication. Source cards are written for magazine articles, interviews, tapes, or any other research material.

When you write source cards, give each one a code—either the initials of the author, a number, or a combination of numbers and letters.

The beauty of using source cards is that you are creating your bibliography as you do the research. When you are done, simply alphabetize the cards by author and—voilà!—instant bibliography.

Write the actual notes on information cards. At the top of each information card, write the code for the source from which you got the information. Also include the page number your notes are based on.

The most important point to remember about information cards: Write only one piece of information on each card. You can use your information cards to construct an outline of the paper by sorting the cards. Placing more than one fact on each card creates a barrier to organizing your outline.

Thinking about notes

Whether you are making review notes or research notes, use your own words as much as possible. When you do so, you are thinking about what you are reading. If you do quote your source word for word, put that material in quotation marks.

Many students like to close the book after reading an assignment and quickly write down a summary of the material. This writing can be loose, without any structure or format. The important thing is to do it right away, while the material is fresh in your mind.

Special cases

The style of your notes can vary according to the material. If you are assigned a short story or poem, read the entire work once without taking any notes. On your first reading, enjoy the piece. When you finish, write down your immediate impressions. Then go over the piece and make brief notes on characters, images, symbols, settings, plot, point of view, or other aspects of the work.

Normally, you would ask yourself questions before you read an assignment. When you read fiction or poetry, however, ask yourself questions after you have read the piece. Then reread (or skim it if it's long) to get answers. Your notes can reflect this question-and-answer process.

When you read scientific or other technical material, copy important formulas, and write down data that might appear on an exam. Re-create important diagrams and draw your own visual representations of concepts.

GET TO THE BONES OF YOUR BOOK WITH
Concept maps

PRACTICING CRITICAL THINKING #9

oncept mapping, a tool pioneered by Joseph Novak and D. Bob Gowin[6], is a way to make the main ideas in a book leap off the page. Making a concept map forces you to reduce an author's message to its essence—its bare bones. This visual device helps in discovering how a text is organized. Concept maps also promote critical thinking by helping you uncover gaps in logic.

Like mind maps (which are explained in this chapter), concept maps let you form multiple connections between ideas. People who find mind maps too unstructured or messy may find concept maps more appealing.

To create a concept map, follow four steps:

1. List the key concepts in the text. Aim to express each concept in three words or less. Most concept words are nouns, including terms and proper names.

At this point, you can list the concepts in any order. For ease in ranking the concepts later, you might wish to write each one on a single 3x5 card.

2. Rank the concepts so that they flow from general to specific. On a large sheet of paper, write the main concept at the top of the page. Include the most specific concepts near the bottom. Arrange the remaining concepts in appropriate places throughout the middle of the page. Circle each concept.

3. Draw lines that connect the concepts. On these connecting lines, add words that describe the relationship between the concepts. Again, limit yourself to the fewest words needed to make an accurate link. Linking words are often verbs, verb phrases, or prepositions.

4. Finally, review your map. Look for any concepts that are repeated in several places on the map. Eliminate these repetitions by adding more links between concepts. Also look for accurate linking words and missing concepts.

To the right is a sample concept map.

Use a concept map as a tool to interpret and assess a piece of writing. First, list the key concepts from a chapter (or section of a chapter) in a textbook you're reading. Then connect these concepts with linking words, using the format described in the article on this page.

Now take a few minutes to evaluate the author's presentation. Pay special attention to the links between concepts. Are they accurate? Do they reflect false assumptions or logical fallacies? Write your evaluation in the space that follows.

_____

_____

_____

_____

_____

_____

_____

_____

_____

_____

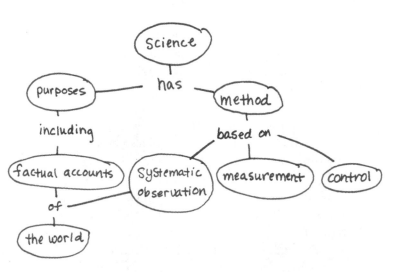

master student

rudolfo anaya

Chicano novelist, short-story writer, playwright, and scriptwriter, uses religion, dreams, and Spanish-American legends and folklore in his critically acclaimed trilogy of novels about growing up in New Mexico

I read a great deal when I was a child, in grade school. I not only ran in a gang and did everything that normal, red-blooded Chicano boys do as they grow up, but I also used to spend a lot of time reading. I was the only one in the gang that used to go to the library on Saturday mornings. It was a decrepit, old building, run by one of the teachers, who volunteered to open it on Saturdays. Many Saturday mornings she and I were the only ones at the library. I sat there and read and leafed through books, and took some home. I read a lot of comic books and saw a lot of movies. I think all of that was important, in some respect, to the question of what influenced me when I was young. I also heard stories. Any time that people gathered, family or friends, they told stories, *cuentos* (tales), *anecdotes*, *dichos* (sayings), *adivinanzas* (riddles). So I was always in a milieu of words, whether they were printed or in that oral tradition . . . .

Through formal education, I was exposed to many writers, not only to American literature and contemporary writers, but world literature. I think it's very important for Chicano students, whether or not they're going to be writers, to engage in some kind of educational process. We cannot hide our heads in the sand and pretend that everything that is important and good and of value will come only out of our culture. We live in a small world where many other cultures have a great deal to offer us.

Both my father and my mother spoke Spanish, and I was raised speaking Spanish in an almost completely Spanish background. I did not learn English until I started first grade. Now I speak more fluently in English . . . .

There are some of us who have had, at one time, a great disadvantage. We came from poor families, poor in the sense that we had no money, but we were rich with love and culture and a sense of sharing and imagination. We had to face a school system that very often told us we couldn't write. It did not teach us our own works, and we had nothing to emulate, to read of our own. So of course we were very disadvantaged in that way . . . . But I kept at it. You can call it what you want; it's something you know you have to do, and eventually you find the rhythm and you keep practicing the skills and the elements. I don't think they become any easier, to tell you the truth. After ten or fifteen years now, I'm still in the process of learning about writing; a process that never finishes. That's exciting!

Even today Chicano children are being told they are at a disadvantage because they don't have command of the English language. The sooner you begin to tell children that, the more they begin to believe it; you build in a self-fulfilling prophecy. That is not right! We have, as I have stated before, a rich culture, rich tradition, a rich oral tradition, and we have, through part of our roots, a rich literary tradition. So we have to change that around *y en vez de decir que no tenemos el talento* [and instead of saying that we don't have the talent], say, "You can write! You do have talent! You can produce literature that is valuable!" We have to go out and tell the kids in high school and grade school, *cuando estan chiquitos* [when they are little], "You can write, you can write about what you know, your experience is valuable, who you are is valuable, and how you view the world and society and the cosmos is valuable. Put it down on paper, paint a picture, make a drawing, write music!"

From Chicano Authors: Inquiry by Interview
by Juan D. Bruce-Novoa
Copyright © 1980
Reprinted by permission of University of Texas Press

1 What are the three major steps in effective note taking as explained in this chapter?

2 Techniques you can use to "set the stage" for note taking do not include:

   (A) Completing outside assignments.
   (B) Bringing the right materials.
   (C) Setting aside questions in order to concentrate.
   (D) Conducting a short preclass review.
   (E) Sitting front and center.

3 What is an advantage of sitting to the front and center of the classroom?

4 Sometimes instructors behave in ways that indicate the material they are presenting is important. Describe at least three.

5 An effective way to postpone debate during a lecture is to ignore your own opinions and passively record the instructor's words. True or False. Explain your answer.

6 When using the Cornell method of note taking:

   (A) Write the main point on a line or in a box, circle, or any other shape.
   (B) Use only Roman numeral outline form.
   (C) Copy each new concept on a separate 3x5 card.
   (D) Remember that it doesn't work when used along with a mind map format.
   (E) Draw a vertical line about 1 1/2 inches from the left edge of the paper.

7 Explain how key words can be used. Then select and write down at least five key words from this chapter.

8 *Reviewing within 24 hours assists short-term memory only. Long-term memory requires reviews over a longer period of time. True or False. Explain your answer.*

9 *Compare and contrast source cards and information cards. (How are they alike and how are they different?)*

10 *Briefly discuss one of the cautions given regarding the use of Power Process #5: "I create it all."*

JOURNAL ENTRY #30
DISCOVERY/INTENTION STATEMENT

Quickly review this chapter and summarize what you learned about your note-taking skills.

I discovered that I . . .

_____

_____

Write an Intention Statement declaring how you will use two techniques from this chapter.

I intend to . . .

_____

_____

_____

_____

Name _____ Date _____/_____/_____

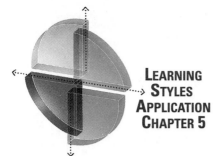

**LEARNING
STYLES
APPLICATION
CHAPTER 5**

Style 1
Imagine that you've just been invited to give a 20-minute talk about overcoming test anxiety. You have only 24 hours to prepare your presentation. Review the options for taking notes explained in this chapter and choose those you think would be most effective to use in this situation.

Style 2
Compare and contrast the various methods of note taking mentioned in this chapter, including mind maps, the Cornell system, and 3x5 cards. List the distinctive benefits and features of each method. How are the methods alike? How do they differ?

Style 3
Keep in mind that you do not have to use one style of taking notes for all your classes. List possible situations in which you could use each of the major note-taking methods described in this chapter.

Style 4
Create an original technique for taking notes. Think about how you could modify or combine several of the methods mentioned in this chapter.

Bibliography

Endnotes

[1]Walter Pauk, *How to Study in College* (Boston: Houghton Mifflin, 1974).

[2]Tony Buzan, *Use Both Sides of Your Brain* (New York: Dutton, 1974).

[3]Gabrielle Rico, *Writing the Natural Way* (Los Angeles: J.P. Tarcher, 1983).

[4]William Glasser, *Take Effective Control of Your Life* (New York: Harper & Row, 1984).

[5]Frankl, Viktor, *Man's Search for Meaning* (New York: Simon & Schuster, 1970).

[6]Joseph Novak and D. Bob Gowin, *Learning How to Learn* (New York: Cambridge University Press, 1984).

Additional Reading

Buzan, Tony. *Make the Most of Your Mind*, New York: Simon & Schuster, 1977.

Corey, Gerald. *I Never Knew I Had a Choice*, Monterey, CA: Brooks-Cole, 1982.

Glasser, William. *Schools Without Failure*, New York: Harper & Row, 1968.

tests

In this chapter...

■ see tests as performances—opportunities to demonstrate your mastery. You can prepare for tests in the way a musician prepares for a concert—through focused attention and rehearsal. Disarm tests and even celebrate mistakes. Learn ways to predict test questions, spot key words, and solve math and science problems. While you're at it, harness the power of cooperative learning by studying with other people. Also discover ways to release anxiety—techniques that can help you manage tests or any other form of stress. Along the way, you can even have some fun.

JOURNAL ENTRY #31
DISCOVERY STATEMENT

Mentally re-create a time when you had difficulty taking a test. Do anything that helps you re-experience this event. You could draw a picture of yourself in this situation, list some of the questions you had difficulty answering, or describe the feelings you had after finding out your score on the test.

Describe that experience in detail here.

_____
_____
_____
_____
_____
_____
_____
_____
_____
_____

Now preview this chapter, looking for three strategies that could prevent such incidents from happening again. List those strategies here.

I discovered that I could . . .

_____
_____
_____
_____
_____
_____

N THE SURFACE, TESTS DON'T LOOK DANGEROUS, but we treat them as if they were land mines. Suppose a man walks up to you on the street and asks, "Does a finite abelian P-group have a basis?" Will you break out in a cold sweat? Will your muscles tense up? Will your breathing become shallow?

Probably not. Even if you have never heard of a finite abelian P-group, you are likely to remain coolly detached.

Disarm tests

However, if you find the same question on a test and if you have never heard of a finite abelian P-group, then your hands might get clammy.

Grades (A to F) are what we use to give power to tests. And there are lots of misconceptions about what grades are. Grades are not a measure of intelligence. Grades don't measure creativity. They are not an indication of your ability to contribute to society. Grades are simply a measure of how well you do on tests.

Some people think that a test score measures what a student accomplished in a course. This is false. A test score is a measure of what a student scored on a test. If you are anxious about a test and blank out, then the grade cannot measure what you learned. The reverse is also true: If you are good at taking tests and a lucky guesser, the score won't be an accurate reflection of what you've learned.

Grades are not a measure of self-worth. Yet we tend to give test scores the power to determine how we feel about ourselves. Common thoughts are "If I fail a test, I am a failure" or "If I do badly on a test, I am a bad person." The truth is that if you do badly on a test, you are a person who did badly on a test. That's all.

Carrying around misconceptions about tests and grades can put undue pressure on your performance. It's like balancing on a railroad track. Many people can walk along the rail and stay balanced for several seconds. Yet the task seems entirely different if the rail is placed between two buildings, 52 stories up.

It is easier to do well on exams if you don't exaggerate the pressure on yourself. Don't give the test some magical power over your worth as a human being. Academic tests are not a matter of life or death. Even scoring low on important tests—entrance tests for college or medical school, law boards, CPA exams—usually mean only a delay.

Whether a risk is real or imaginary, it can reach the point where it is paralyzing. The way to deal with tests is to keep the risk in perspective. Keep the railroad track on the ground.

> **" "**
>
> *Learn from the mistakes of others—you can never live long enough to make them all yourself.*
> –JOHN LUTHER

> **" "**
>
> *When we begin to take our failures non-seriously, it means we are ceasing to be afraid of them. It is of immense importance to learn to laugh at ourselves.*
>
> –KATHERINE MANSFIELD

What to do before the test

Manage review time

A key to successful test preparation is managing review time. The biggest benefit of early review is that facts have time to roam around in your head. A lot of learning takes place when you are not "studying." Your brain has time to create relationships that can show up when you need them—like during a test. Use short daily review sessions to prepare the way for major review sessions. Reviewing with a group often generates new insights and questions.

Daily reviews

Daily reviews include the short pre- and postclass reviews of lecture notes. Research indicates that this is an effective tool for moving ideas from short-term to long-term memory. You can also conduct brief daily reviews when you read. Before you begin a new reading assignment, scan your notes and the sections you underlined in the previous assignment. Use the time you spend waiting for the bus or doing the laundry to conduct short reviews.

Concentrate daily reviews on two kinds of material: material you have just learned, either in class or in your reading, and material that involves simple memorization (equations, formulas, dates, definitions).

Conduct short daily reviews several times throughout the day. To make sure you do, include them on your daily to-do list. Write down, "5 min. review of biology" or "10 min. review of economics," and give yourself the satisfaction of crossing them off.

Begin to review the first day of class. The first day, in fact, is important for review. Most instructors outline the whole course at that time. You can start reviewing within seconds after learning. During a lull in class, go over the notes you just took. And immediately after class, review your notes again.

Weekly reviews

Weekly reviews are longer—about an hour per subject. These review periods are also more structured than short daily reviews. When a subject is complex, the brain requires time to dig into the material. Avoid skipping from subject to subject too quickly. Review each subject at least once a week.

These weekly sessions include reviews of assigned reading and lecture notes. Look over any mind map summaries or flash cards you have created. You can also practice answering questions.

Major reviews

Major reviews are usually conducted the week before finals or other major exams. They integrate concepts and deepen understanding of the material presented throughout the term. These are longer review periods, two to five hours at a stretch, punctuated by sufficient breaks. Remember that the effectiveness of your review begins to drop after an hour or so unless you give yourself a short rest.

After a certain point, short breaks every hour might not be enough to refresh you. That's when it's time to quit.

Learn what your limits are by being conscious of the quality of your concentration. During long sessions, study the most difficult subjects when you are the most alert: at the beginning of the session.

Your commitment to review is your most powerful ally. Create a system of rewards for time spent reviewing. Use the Intention Statements in this chapter or invent your own to draw detailed plans for review time.

Create review tools

Checklists, mind map summaries, and flash cards take the guesswork and much of the worry out of studying. When you use these tools, you divide a big job into smaller parts. Your confidence could increase and you will probably sleep better at night.

Study checklists

Study checklists are used the way a pilot uses a preflight checklist. Pilots go through a standard routine before they take off. They physically mark off each item: test flaps, check magnetos, check fuel tanks, adjust instruments, check rudder. They use a written list to be absolutely certain they don't miss anything. Once they are in the air, it's too late, and the consequences of failing to check the fuel tanks could be drastic.

Taking an exam is like flying a plane. Once the test begins, it's too late to memorize that one equation you forgot.

Make a list for each subject. List reading assignments by chapters or page numbers. List dates of lecture notes. Write down various types of problems you will need to solve. Write down other skills you must master. Include major ideas, definitions, theories, formulas, and equations. For math and science tests, choose some problems and do them over again as a way to review for the test.

A study checklist is not a review sheet; it is a kind of to-do list. Checklists contain the briefest possible description of each item to study.

Begin keeping a study checklist the very first day of class. Add to it as the term progresses. When you conduct your final review sessions, check items off the list as you review them.

Mind map summary sheets

There are several ways to make a mind map as you study for tests. You can start by creating a map totally from memory. When you use this technique, you might be surprised by how much you already know. Mind maps release floods of information from the brain because the mind works by association. Each idea is linked to many other ideas. When you think of one, other associations come to mind. An advantage of mind mapping is that you don't have to stifle any of these associations just because they don't come next in a sequential outline.

Everything fits in a mind map. Let the associations flow, and if one seems to go someplace else, simply start another branch on your map. After you have gone as far as you can using recall alone, go over your notes and text and fill in the rest of the map.

Another way to create a mind map summary is to go through your notes and pick out key words. Then, without looking at your notes, create a mind map of everything you can recall about each key word. Finally, go back to your notes and fill in material you left out. You can also start a mind map with underlined sections from your text.

Make mind maps for small, detailed subjects as well as for large ones. You can mind map a whole course or a single lecture or a single point from a lecture.

Flash cards

Three-by-five flash cards are like portable test questions. You can take them with you anywhere and use them anytime. On one side of the cards, write the questions. On the other, write the answers. It's that simple.

Use flash cards for formulas, definitions, theories, key words from your notes, axioms, dates, foreign language phrases, hypotheses, and sample problems.

Create flash cards regularly as the term progresses. You can buy an inexpensive card file to keep your flash cards arranged by subject.

Carry a pack of flash cards with you whenever you think you might have a spare minute to review them. Keep a few blank cards with you too. That way, you can make new flash cards whenever you recall new information to study.

Plan a strategy

Knowing what is going to be on your test does not require using highly sophisticated technology or breaking intricately coded messages. Before a test, some instructors hand out lists of questions to be used as study guides. Even if they don't, the following strategies can help you predict most of the test questions.

Do a dry run

One of the most effective ways to prepare for a test is to practice the tasks you'll actually do on the test. Write up your own exam questions and take this "test" several times before the actual test. Say that the test will include mainly true/false or short-answer questions. Brainstorm a list of such questions—a mock test—and do a dry run.

Also predict the level of questions. Some are likely to call for rote memorization; others might require application or analysis.

You might even type up this "test" so it looks like the real thing. You could write out your answers in the room where the test will actually take place. When you walk in for the real test, you'll be in familiar territory.

Ask the instructor what to expect

One great source of information about the test is the person who will create it—your instructor. Ask him what to expect. What topics will be emphasized? What kinds of questions will it contain? How can you best allocate your review time? The instructor may decline to give you any of this information. Even so, you've lost nothing by asking. More often, though, instructors will answer some or all of your questions about the test.

Get copies of old exams

Copies of previous exams for the class may be available from the instructor, other students, the instructor's department, the library, or the counseling office. Old tests can help you plan a review strategy.

One caution: If you rely on old tests exclusively, you may gloss over material the instructor has added since the last test. Also check your school's policy about making past tests available to students. Some may not allow it, or may allow it on only a limited basis.

As you begin

Prepare yourself for the test by arriving early. That often leaves time to do a relaxation exercise.

While you're waiting for the test to begin and talking with classmates, avoid the question "How much did you study for this test?" This question may only fuel the anxiety that you didn't study enough.

Pay particular attention to verbal directions given as the test is distributed. Then scan the whole test immediately. Evaluate the importance of each section. Notice how many points each part of the test is worth and estimate how much time you will need for each section; use its point value as your guide. For example, don't budget 20 percent of your time for a section that is worth only 10 percent of the points.

Read the directions slowly. Then reread them. Nothing is more agonizing than discovering that you lost points on a test only because you failed to follow the directions. If the directions call for short answers, give short answers. Sometimes you will be asked to answer two out of three questions. It's frustrating to find that out as you finish your third answer. When the directions are confusing, ask about them.

Jot down memory aids, formulas, equations, facts, or other material you know you'll need and might forget. Do this in the margins. If you use a separate sheet of paper, you may appear to be cheating.

Now you are ready to begin.

What to do during the test

In general

It's time to begin. If necessary, allow yourself a minute or two of "panic" time. This is time to notice any tension you feel and apply one of the techniques explained in "Let go of test anxiety" later in this chapter.

Answer the easiest, shortest questions first. This gives you the experience of success. It also stimulates associations and prepares you for more difficult questions.

Next answer multiple choice, true/false, and fill-in-the-blank questions. Then proceed to short-answer and essay questions. Use memory techniques when you're stuck.

Pace yourself. Watch the time; if you are stuck, move on. Follow your time plan.

Leave plenty of space between answers. The space makes it easier on the person who grades your test. You can use the extra space, if there's time, to add information.

Look for answers in other test questions. A term, name, date, or other fact that escapes you might appear in the test itself. You can also use other questions to stimulate your memory.

In quick-answer questions (multiple choice, true/false), your first instinct is usually best. If you think your first answer is wrong because you misread the question, do change your answer.

Multiple choice questions

Check the directions to see if the questions call for more than one answer.

Answer each question in your head before you look at the possible answers. If you can come up with the answer before you look at the choices, you eliminate the possibility of being confused by those choices.

Be sure to read all answers to multiple choice questions before selecting one. Sometimes two answers will be similar and only one will be correct.

If you have no clue as to what the answer is and if incorrect answers are not deducted from your score, use the following guidelines to guess.

1. If two answers are similar, except for one or two words, choose one of these answers.
2. If two answers have similar-sounding or similar-looking words (intermediate, intermittent), choose one of these answers.
3. If the answer calls for a sentence completion, eliminate the answers that would not form grammatically correct sentences.
4. If two quantities are almost the same, choose one.
5. If answers cover a wide range (4.5, 66.7, 88.7, 90.1, 5000.11), choose one in the middle of the range.
6. If there is no penalty for guessing and none of the above techniques works, close your eyes and go for it.

Note: None of these suggestions for guessing is meant to take the place of studying for the test.

True/false questions

Answer true/false questions quickly. Often these questions are not worth many points individually.

Read carefully. Sometimes one word can make a statement inaccurate. If any part of the true/false statement is false, the statement is false.

Look for qualifiers, like *all, most, sometimes, never,* or *rarely.* These are the key words upon which the question depends. Absolute qualifiers such as *always* or *never* generally indicate a false statement.

Machine-graded tests

To do well on these tests, make sure the answer you mark corresponds to the question you are answering. Check the test booklet against the answer sheet whenever you switch sections and whenever you come to the top of a column. Watch for stray marks; they can look like answers.

Open-book tests

When studying for the test, write down any formulas you will need on a separate sheet. Place Post-It notes on important pages of the book (tables, for instance) so you don't have to waste time flipping through the pages. You could also use paper clips. If you plan to use your notes, number them and write a short table of contents.

Prepare thoroughly for open-book exams. They are usually the most difficult tests.

f is for feedback, not failure

Feedback is one of the fundamental facts of life and ideas of science, yet only in the last 50 years have we recognized its all-pervasive presence. The idea is simple: A feedback mechanism registers the actual state of a system, compares it to the desired state, then uses the comparison to correct the state of the system.

Feedback is goal-oriented, definite. A feedback process tells living cells when to manufacture proteins and when to stop. Sometimes the goal is something as dynamic as an equilibrium. An explosion of the rabbit population is followed by a growth in the lynx population is followed by a collapse of the rabbit population is followed by a collapse of the lynx population—a feedback loop that maintains the balance of nature.

In modern technology, feedback is the essence of automation. It runs lathes, lands airplanes, steers rockets. The economy is a huge, slow-moving, multiple feedback system. So is democracy. Fast or slow, movement is the essence of feedback. It implies purpose and progress. Like a walker on a high wire, it continually achieves and re-achieves balance in order to achieve something beyond balance. It can never rest.

Excerpt, "Feedback is one of the functional facts . . . It can never rest" from The Search for Solutions *by Horace Freeland Judson, Copyright © 1980 by Playback Associates. Reprinted by permission of Henry Holt and Company, Inc.*

Short-answer / fill-in-the-blank tests

These questions often ask for definitions or short descriptions. Concentrate on key words and facts. Be brief.

Research going back over 60 years indicates that overlearning material can really pay off.[1] When you know a subject backward and forward, you can answer this type of question almost as fast as you can write.

Essay questions

When you set out to answer an essay question, your first task is to find out what the question is asking—precisely. If a question asks that you *compare* Gestalt and Reichian therapies, no matter how eloquently you *explain* them, you are on a one-way trip to No Credit City.

Standard essay questions are defined in the next article. Knowing them can make all the difference on an essay test.

Before you write, make a quick outline. There are three reasons for doing this. First, you might be able to write faster. Second, you're less likely to leave out important facts. Third, if you don't have time to finish your answer, your outline could win you some points.

When you start to write, get to the point. Forget introductions. Sentences such as "There are many interesting facets to this difficult question" cause acute pain for teachers grading tests.

One way to get to the point is to include part of the question in your answer. Suppose the question is "Discuss how increasing the city police budget may or may not contribute to a decrease in street crime." Your first sentence might be "An increase in police expenditures will not have a significant effect on street crime for the following reasons." Your position is clear. You are on your way to the answer.

When you expand your answer with supporting ideas and facts, start out with the most solid points. Don't try for drama by saving the best for last.

Some final points in regard to style:

1. Write legibly. Grading essay questions is in large part a subjective process. Sloppy, difficult-to-read handwriting might actually lower your grade.

2. Be brief. Avoid filler sentences that say nothing. ("The question certainly bears careful deliberation in order to take into account all the many interesting facts pertaining to this important period in the history of our great nation.") Write as if you expect the person grading your test to be tired, bored, and overworked. Even a well-rested instructor doesn't like to wade through a swamp of murky writing in order to spot an occasional lonely insight.

3. Use a pen. Many instructors will require this because pencil is difficult to read.

4. Write on one side of the page only. If you write on both sides of the page, writing will show through and obscure the writing on the other side. If necessary, use the blank side to add points you missed. Leave a generous left-hand margin and plenty of space between your answers in case you want to add to them later.

Finally, if you have time, review your answers for grammar and spelling errors, clarity, and legibility.

Words to watch for in essay questions

The following words are commonly found in essay test questions. Understanding them is essential to success on such questions. If you want to do well on essay tests, then study this page thoroughly. Know these words backward and forward. To heighten your awareness of them, underline the words when you see them in a test question.

Analyze: Break into separate parts and discuss, examine, or interpret each part.

Compare: Examine two or more things. Identify similarities and differences.

Contrast: Show differences. Set in opposition.

Criticize: Make judgments. Evaluate comparative worth. Criticism often involves analysis.

Define: Give the meaning; usually a meaning specific to the course or subject. Explain the exact meaning. Definitions are usually short.

Describe: Give a detailed account. Make a picture with words. List characteristics, qualities, and parts.

Discuss: Consider and debate or argue the pros and cons of an issue. Write about any conflict. Compare and contrast.

Enumerate: List several ideas, aspects, events, things, qualities, reasons, etc.

Evaluate: Give your opinion or cite the opinion of an expert. Include evidence to support the evaluation.

Explain: Make an idea clear. Show logically how a concept is developed. Give the reasons for an event.

Illustrate: Give concrete examples. Explain clearly by using comparisons or examples.

Interpret: Comment upon, give examples, describe relationships. Explain the meaning. Describe, then evaluate.

Outline: Describe main ideas, characteristics, or events. (Does not necessarily mean "write a Roman numeral/letter outline.")

Prove: Support with facts (especially facts presented in class or in the text).

Relate: Show the connections between ideas or events. Provide a larger context.

State: Explain precisely.

Summarize: Give a brief, condensed account. Include conclusions. Avoid unnecessary details.

Trace: Show the order of events or progress of a subject or event.

If any of these terms are still unclear to you, go to your unabridged dictionary. Thorough knowledge of these words helps you give the teacher what he is requesting.

**PRACTICING
CRITICAL THINKING #10**

Read a short published essay. Imagine that you are an English teacher who's going to grade this essay. Give the essay a letter grade or numerical score, as you wish. On a separate sheet of paper, state your criteria—your bases for assigning the grade—and justify the grade you gave.

Now reflect on the criteria you just used. A grade could measure achievement toward an absolute standard. Or, it could measure a student's development from the point where he or she started. Write about which of these criteria you would use (or any others) and when you would apply them.

CONTRARY TO POPULAR BELIEF, FINALS WEEK DOES NOT HAVE TO BE A DRAG.

In fact, if you have used techniques in this chapter, exam week can be fun. By planning ahead, you will have done most of your studying long before finals arrive. You could feel confident and relaxed.

When you are well prepared for tests, you can even use fun as a technique to enhance your performance. The day before a final, go for a run or play a game of basketball. Take in a movie or a concert. Watch television. A relaxed brain is a more effective brain. If you have studied for a test, your mind will continue to prepare itself even while you're at the movies.

Get plenty of rest too. There's no need to stay up until 3 a.m. cramming if you have used the techniques in this chapter.

On the day of the big test you can wake up refreshed, have a good breakfast, and walk into the exam room with a smile on your face.

You can also leave with a smile on your face, knowing that you are going to have a fun week. It's your reward for studying regularly throughout the term.

If this kind of exam week sounds inviting, you can begin preparing for it right now.

Ways to predict test questions

Predicting test questions can do more than get you a better grade on a test. It can keep you focused on the purpose of the course and help you design your learning strategy. It can be fun too.

First, get organized. Have a separate section in your notebook labeled "Test Questions." Add several questions to this section after every lecture and assignment.

You also can create your own code or graphic signal—maybe a *T!* in a circle—to flag possible test questions in your notes.

The format of a test can help you predict questions. Ask your instructor to describe the test—how long it will be and what kind of questions to expect (essay, multiple choice). Do this early in the term so you can be alert for possible test questions from the very beginning.

During lectures you can watch for test questions by observing not only what the instructor says but also how he says it. Instructors give clues. For example: Instructors might repeat important points several times, write them on the board, or return to them in subsequent classes.

They might use certain gestures when making critical points. They might pause, look at notes, or read passages word for word.

Also pay attention to questions the instructor poses to students, and note questions other students ask.

When material from reading assignments also is covered extensively in class, it is likely to be on the test.

Use the essay question words on page 153 as a guide to turn the key words in your notes into questions.

Put yourself in your instructor's head. What kind of questions would you ask? Make practice test questions.

Save all quizzes, papers, lab sheets, and graded material of any kind. Quiz questions have a way of appearing, in slightly altered form, on final exams. If copies of previous exams are available, use them to predict test questions.

For science courses and other courses involving problem solving, practice working problems using different variables.

You can also brainstorm test questions with other students. This is a great activity for study groups.

Finally, be on the lookout for these words: *This material will be on the test.*

EXERCISE #21
MASTER REVIEW SCHEDULE

Schedule review time on the one-month calendar on page 155. Mark the appropriate dates of the month in the upper left-hand corner of every square, then schedule weekly review periods for each subject. Write down the name of the subject and block out time to review it. If you already use a monthly or weekly planner, use it to schedule your review time.

Also schedule at least two major review periods. The length of these review periods could range from two to five hours, depending on your needs.

The more difficult it is for you to find time for review, the greater the benefit of this exercise. Use your imagination and skill to create extra time to review.

This exercise will give you an opportunity to step back and look at your overall review habits. For a longer view, photocopy this calendar and make a review plan for two or three months.

Monday	Tuesday	Wednesday	Thursday	Friday	Saturday	Sunday

Name_____

Month_____

Name _____

Month _____

Monday	Tuesday	Wednesday	Thursday	Friday	Saturday	Sunday

Notable Failures

PART TWO—*People often fail, or at least are told they are failures, many times before they reach their goals. Consider the following examples.*

Einstein's parents thought he was retarded. He spoke haltingly until age 9 and after that he answered questions only after laboring in thought about them. He was advised by a teacher to drop out of high school: "You'll never amount to anything, Einstein."

Charles Darwin's father said to his son, "You will be a disgrace to yourself and all your family." (Darwin did poorly in school.)

Henry Ford barely made it through high school.

Sir Isaac Newton did poorly in school and was allowed to continue only because he failed at running the family farm.

Pablo Picasso was pulled out of school at age 10 because he was doing so poorly. A tutor hired by Pablo's father gave up on Pablo.

Giacomo Puccini's first music teacher said that Puccini had no talent for music. Later Puccini composed some of the world's greatest operas.

The machines of the world's greatest inventor, **Leonardo da Vinci**, were never built, and many wouldn't have worked anyway.

Clarence Darrow became a legend in the courtroom as he lost case after case.

Edwin Land's attempts at instant movies (Polarvision) absolutely failed. He described his attempts as trying to use an impossible chemistry and a nonexistent technology to make an unmanufacturable product for which there was no discernible demand.

After the success of the show *South Pacific,* composer **Oscar Hammerstein** put an ad in *Variety* that listed over a dozen of his failures. At the bottom of the ad, he repeated the credo of show business, "I did it before, and I can do it again."

Asked once about how he felt when his team lost a game, **Joe Paterno**, coach of the Penn State University football team, replied that losing was probably good for them since that was how the players learned what they were doing wrong.

R. Buckminster Fuller built his geodesic domes by starting with a deliberately failed dome and making it "a little stronger and a little stronger . . . a little piece of wood here and a little piece of wood there, and suddenly it stood up."

Igor Stravinsky said, "I have learned throughout my life as a composer chiefly through my mistakes and pursuits of false assumptions, not by my exposure to the founts of wisdom and knowledge."

Charles Goodyear bungled an experiment and discovered vulcanized rubber.

Before gaining an international reputation as a painter, **Paul Gauguin** was a failed stockbroker.

The game MONOPOLY® was developed by **Charles Darrow**, an unemployed heating engineer. Darrow presented his first version of the game to a toy company in 1935. That company originally rejected the game for containing 52 "fundamental errors." Today the game is so successful that its publisher, Parker Brothers, prints more than $40 billion of MONOPOLY® money each year. That's twice the amount of real money printed annually by the U.S. mint.

Reprinted with permission by Stillpoint Publishing, Walpole, NH (USA) 03608 from the book *Diet For A New America* by John Robbins and excerpt(s) from *Information Anxiety* by Richard Saul Wurman, copyright © 1989 by Richard Saul Wurman, used by permission of Doubleday, a division of Bantam Doubleday, Dell Publishing Group, Inc.

Let go of test anxiety

If you freeze during tests and flub questions when you know the answers, you might be suffering from test anxiety. A little tension before a test is good. That tingly, butterflies-in-the-stomach feeling you get from extra adrenaline can sharpen your awareness and keep you alert. Sometimes, however, tension is persistent and extreme. It causes loss of sleep, appetite, and sometimes even hair. That kind of tension is damaging. It is a symptom of test anxiety, and it can prevent you from doing your best on exams.

Other symptoms include nervousness, fear, dread, irritability, and a sense of hopelessness.

Boredom also can be a symptom of test anxiety. Frequent yawning immediately before a test is a common reaction. Yawning looks like boredom, and it is often a sign of tension. It means oxygen is not getting to the brain because the body is tense. A yawn is one way the body increases its supply of oxygen.

You might experience headaches, an inability to concentrate, or a craving for food. For some people, test anxiety makes asthma or high blood pressure worse.

During an exam, symptoms can include confusion, panic, mental blocks, fainting, sweaty palms, or nausea.

Symptoms after a test include:

Mock indifference: "I answered all the multiple choice questions as 'none of the above' because I was bored."

Guilt: "Why didn't I study more?"

Anger: "The teacher never wanted me to pass this stupid course anyway."

Blame: "If only the textbook weren't so dull."

Depression: "After that test, I don't see any point in staying in school."

Test anxiety can be serious. Students have committed suicide over test scores. It can also be managed.

Test anxiety has two components, mental and physical. The mental component of stress includes all your thoughts and worries about tests. The physical component includes feelings, sensations, and tension.

The following techniques deal with the mental and physical components of stress in any situation, whether it be test anxiety or stage fright.

Dealing with thoughts

1. Yell "Stop!" When you notice that your thoughts are racing, that your mind is cluttered with worries and fears, that your thoughts are spinning out of control, mentally yell "Stop!" If you're in a situation that allows it, yell it out loud.

This action is likely to momentarily break the cycle of worry. Once you've stopped it for a moment, you can use any one of the following techniques.

2. Daydream. When you fill your mind with pleasant thoughts, there is no room left for anxiety. When you notice yourself worrying about an upcoming test, substitute your thoughts of doom with visions of something you like to do. Daydream about being with a special friend or walking alone in a special place.

3. Visualize success. Most of us live up to our own expectations, good or bad. If you spend a lot of time mentally rehearsing how it will be to fail, you increase your chances for failure.

Once you've stopped the cycle of worry, take time to rehearse what it will be like when you succeed. Be specific. Create detailed pictures, actions, and even sounds as part of your visualization.

4. Focus. Focus your attention on a specific object. Examine details of a painting, study the branches on a tree, or observe the face of your watch (right down to the tiny scratches in the glass). During an exam, take a few seconds to listen to the sound of the lights in the room. Touch the surface of your desk and notice the texture. Concentrate all your attention on one point. Don't leave room in your mind for anxiety-related thoughts.

5. Praise yourself. Talk to yourself in a positive way. Many of us take the first opportunity to say, "Way to go, dummy! You don't even know the answer to the first question on the test." Most of us wouldn't dream of treating a friend that way, yet we do this to ourselves.

An alternative is to give yourself some encouragement. Treat yourself as well as you would treat your best friend. Consider telling yourself, "I am very relaxed. I am doing a great job on this test."

6. Consider the worst. Rather than trying to stop worrying, consider the very worst thing that could happen. Take the fear to the limit of absurdity.

Imagine the catastrophic problems that might occur if you fail the test. You might say to yourself, "Well, if I fail this test, I might fail the course, lose my financial aid, and get kicked out of school. Then I won't be able to get a job, so the bank would repossess my car, and I'd start drinking. Pretty soon I'd be a bum on skid row . . . ."

Keep going until you see the absurdity of your predictions. After you stop chuckling, you can backtrack to discover a reasonable level of concern.

Your worry about failing the entire course if you fail the test might be justified. At that point ask yourself, "Can I live with that?" Unless you are taking a test in parachute packing and the final question involves demonstrating jumping out of a plane, the answer will almost always be yes. (If the answer is no, use another technique. In fact, use several other techniques.)

The cold facts are hardly ever as bad as our worst fears. Shine a light on your fears and they become more manageable.

Dealing with feelings

1. Breathe. You can calm physical sensations within your body by focusing your attention on your breathing. Concentrate on the air going in and out of your lungs. Experience it as it passes through your nose and mouth.

Do this for two to five minutes. If you notice that you are taking short, shallow breaths, begin to take longer and deeper breaths. Fill your lungs so that your abdomen rises, then release all the air. Imagine yourself standing on the tip of your nose. Watch the breath pass in and out as if your nose were a huge ventilation shaft for an underground mine.

2. Scan your body. Simple awareness is an effective technique to reduce the tension in your body.

Sit comfortably and close your eyes. Focus your attention on the muscles in your feet and notice if they are relaxed. Tell the muscles in your feet that they can relax.

Move up to your ankles and repeat the procedure. Next go to your calves and thighs and buttocks, telling each group of muscles to relax.

Do the same for your lower back, diaphragm, chest, upper back, neck, shoulders, jaw, face, upper arms, lower arms, fingers, and scalp.

3. Tense and relax. If you are aware of a particularly tense part of your body or if you discover tension when you're scanning your body, you can release this with the tense-relax method.

**EXERCISE #22
TWENTY THINGS
I LIKE TO DO**

One way to relieve tension is to mentally yell "Stop!" and substitute a pleasant image (day-dream) for the stressful thoughts and emotions you are experiencing.

In order to create a supply of pleasant images to recall during times of stress, conduct an eight-minute brain-storm about things you like to do. Your goal is to generate at least 20 ideas. Time yourself and write as fast as you can on a separate sheet of paper.

When you have completed your list, study it. Pick out two activities that seem especially pleasant, and elaborate on them by creating a mind map. Write down all the memories you have about that activity.

You can use these images to calm yourself in stressful situations.

To do this, find a muscle that is tense and make it even more tense. If your shoulders are tense, pull them back, arch your back, and tense your shoulder muscles even more tightly, then relax. The net result is that you can be aware of the relaxation and allow yourself to relax more.

You can use the same process with your legs, arms, abdomen, chest, face, and neck. Clench your fists, tighten your jaw, straighten your legs, and tense your abdomen all at once. Then relax.

4. Use guided imagery. Relax completely and take a quick fantasy trip. Close your eyes, relax your body, and imagine yourself in a beautiful, peaceful, natural setting. Create as much of the scene as you can. Be specific. Use all your senses.

For example, you might imagine yourself at a beach. Hear the surf rolling in and the sea gulls calling to each other. Feel the sun on your face and the cool sand between your toes. Smell the sea breeze. Feel the mist from the surf on your face. Notice the ships on the horizon and the rolling sand dunes.

Some people find that a mountain scene or a lush meadow scene works well. You can take yourself to a place you've never been or re-create an experience out of your past. Find a place that works for you and practice getting there. When you become proficient you can return to it quickly for trips that may last only a few seconds.

With practice you can even use this technique while you are taking a test.

5. Describe it. Focus your attention on your anxiety. If you are feeling nauseated or if you have a headache, then concentrate on that feeling. Describe it to yourself. Tell yourself how large it is, where it is located in your body, what color it is, what shape it is, what texture it is, how much water it might hold if it had volume, and how heavy it is.

6. Be with it. Describe it in detail and don't resist it. If you can completely experience a physical sensation, it will often disappear. People suffering from severe and untreatable pain have used this technique successfully.

7. Exercise aerobically. This is one technique that won't work in the classroom or while you're taking a test. Yet it is an excellent way to reduce body tension.

Do some kind of exercise that will get your heart beating at twice your normal rate and keep it beating at that rate for 15 or 20 minutes. Aerobic exercises include rapid walking, jogging, swimming, bicycling, basketball, or anything that elevates your heart rate and keeps it elevated.

8. Get help. When these techniques don't work, when anxiety is serious, get help. If you become withdrawn, have frequent thoughts about death, get depressed and stay depressed for more than a few days, or have prolonged feelings of hopelessness, see a counselor.

Depression and anxiety are common among students. Suicide is the second leading cause of death among young adults between the ages of 15 and 25. This is tragic and unnecessary. Many schools have counselors available. If not, the student health service or another office can refer you to community agencies where inexpensive counseling is available.

PEANUTS

JOURNAL ENTRY #32
DISCOVERY STATEMENT

On a separate sheet of paper, do a timed, four-minute brainstorm of all the reasons, rationalizations, justifications, and excuses you have used to avoid studying. Be creative. Then review your list, pick the three you use most, and write them in the space below.

_____

_____

_____

_____

_____

_____

EXERCISE #23
REHEARSE FOR SUCCESS

Sit up in a chair, legs and arms uncrossed. Close your eyes, let go of all thoughts, and focus on your breathing for a minute or two.

Then relax various parts of your body, beginning with your feet. Relax your toes, your ankles. Move up to your calves and thighs. Relax your buttocks. Relax the muscles of your lower back, abdomen, and chest. Relax your hands, arms, and shoulders. Relax your neck, jaw, eyelids, and scalp.

When you are completely relaxed, imagine yourself in an exam room. It's the day of the test. Visualize taking the test successfully. The key is detail. See the test being handed out. Notice your surroundings. Hear the other students shuffle in their seats. Feel the desk, the pen in your hand, and the exam in front of you. See yourself looking over the exam calmly and confidently. You discover that you know all the answers.

Stay with this image for a few minutes. Next, imagine yourself writing quickly. Watch yourself turn in the test with confidence. Finally, imagine receiving the test grade. It is an A. Savor the feeling.

As soon as you realize you are feeling anxious about an upcoming test, begin using this technique. The more you do this visualization, the better it can work.

JOURNAL ENTRY #33
INTENTION STATEMENT

Pick one of the reasons for avoiding studying that you listed in Journal Entry #32. Write an Intention Statement about what you will do to begin eliminating that excuse. Make this Intention Statement keepable with a time line and a reward.

I intend to . . .

_____

_____

_____

_____

_____

PEANUTS reprinted by permission of UFS, Inc.

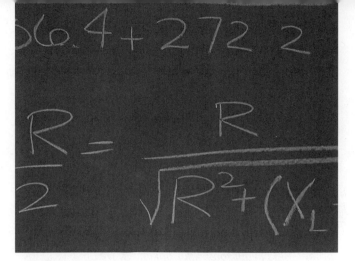

Overcoming math and science anxiety

When they open books about math or science, some capable students break out in a cold sweat. This is a symptom of two conditions sweeping over students across the world—math and science anxiety.

If you want to improve your math or science skills, you're in distinguished company. Albert Einstein felt he needed to learn more math to work out his general theory of relativity. So he asked a friend, mathematician Marcel Grossman, to teach him. It took several years. You won't need that long.

Think of the benefits of overcoming math and science anxiety. Many more courses, majors, jobs, and careers could open up for you. Knowing these subjects can also put you at ease in everyday situations: calculating the tip for a waitperson, planning your finances, working with a spreadsheet on a computer. Speaking the languages of math and science can also help you feel at home in a world driven by technology.

Many schools offer courses in overcoming math and science anxiety. It pays to check them out. The following suggestions can start you on the road to enjoying science and mathematics.

Notice your pictures about math and science

Sometimes what keeps people from succeeding at math and science is their mental picture of scientists and mathematicians. Often that picture includes a man dressed in a faded plaid shirt, baggy pants, and wingtip shoes. He's got a calculator on his belt and six pencils jammed in his shirt pocket.

Such pictures are far from the truth. Succeeding in math and science won't turn you into a nerd. Not only can you enjoy school more, you'll find that your friends and family will still like you.

Our mental pictures about math and science can be funny. At the same time, they have serious effects. For many years, science and math were viewed as fields for white males. That excluded women and people of color. Promoting success in these subjects for all students is a key step in overcoming racism and sexism.

Look out for shaky assumptions

Sheila Tobias[2], author of several books on overcoming math anxiety, points out that people often make faulty assumptions about how math and science are learned. They can include:

- Math calls only for logic, not imagination.
- There's only one right way to do a science experiment or solve a math problem.
- There is a magic secret to doing well in math or science.

These ideas can be easily refuted. To begin, mathematicians and scientists regularly talk about the importance of creativity and imagination in their work. At times they find it hard to explain how they arrive at a particular hypothesis or conclusion. Few of them boast about exceptional memories. And as far as we know, the only secret they count on is hard work.

Get your self-talk out in the open and change it

When students fear math and science, they often say negative things to themselves about their abilities in these subjects. Many times this self-talk includes statements such as:

- "I'll never be fast enough at solving math problems."
- "I'm one of those people who can't function in a science lab."
- "I'm good with words, so I can't be good with numbers."

Faced with this kind of self-talk, you can take three steps:

1. **Get a clear picture of such statements.** When they come up, speak them out loud or write them down. When you get the little voice out in the open, it's easier to refute it.

2. **Next, do some critical thinking about these statements.** Look for the hidden assumptions they contain. Separate what's accurate about them from what's false.

   Negative self-statements are usually based on scant evidence. They can often be reduced to two simple ideas: "Everybody else is better at math and science than I am" and "Since I don't understand it right now, I'll never understand it." Both of these are illogical. Many people lack confidence in their math and science skills. To verify this, just ask other students.

3. **Start some new self-talk.** Use statements that affirm your ability to succeed in math and science:
   - "When learning about math or science, I proceed with patience and confidence."
   - "Any confusion I feel now will be resolved."
   - "I learn math and science without comparing myself to others."
   - "I ask whatever questions are needed to aid my understanding."
   - "I am fundamentally OK as a person, even if I make errors in math and science."

Notice your body sensations

Math or science anxiety is seldom just a "head trip." It registers in our bodies too. Examples are a tight feeling in the chest, sweaty palms, drowsiness, or a mild headache.

Let those sensations come to the surface. Instead of repressing them, open up to them. Doing so often decreases their urgency.

Make your text an A priority

In a history, English, or economics class, the teacher may refer to some of the required readings only in passing. In contrast, math and science courses are often text-driven. That is, class activities follow the format of the book closely. This makes it doubly important to master your reading assignments. It's crucial to master one concept before going to the next and to stay current with your reading.

Read slowly when appropriate

It's ineffective to breeze through a math or science book as you would the newspaper. To get the most out of your text, be willing to read each sentence slowly and reread it as needed. A single paragraph may merit 15 or 20 minutes of sustained attention.

Read chapters and sections in order, as they're laid out in the text. To strengthen your understanding of the main ideas, study all tables, charts, graphs, case studies, and sample problems. From time to time, stop. Close your book and mentally reconstruct the steps of an experiment or a mathematical proof.

Read actively

Science is not only a body of knowledge, it is an activity. To get the most out of your math and science texts, read with paper and pencil in hand. Work out examples and copy diagrams, formulas, or equations. Study diagrams, charts, and other illustrations carefully. Understand each step used in solving a problem or testing a hypothesis.

Examples are particularly important. When reading texts in other courses, you might skim over examples to focus on major concepts. Math and science call for close attention to detail. In some cases, examples included in the text are the main points.

Participate actively in class

Success in math and science depends on your active involvement. Attending class regularly, coming to class with homework finished, speaking up when you have a question, and seeking extra help can be crucial. Some students assume that they'll never be any good in math and science and then behave in a way that confirms that belief. Get around this mental trap by giving at least the same amount of time to math and science that you give to other courses. If you want to succeed, make daily contact with these subjects.

Learn from specific to general

A powerful way to learn many subjects is to get an overview of the main topics before you focus on details. You may want to use the opposite strategy when studying math and science. Learning these subjects often means comprehending one limited concept before going on to the next one. Through this kind of work, you gradually get the big picture. Jumping to general conclusions too soon might be confusing or inaccurate.

Don't be surprised if you feel you're going backward once in a while—as if something you used to understand well seems like gibberish now. This can result from the way math and science concepts are presented: The rules and general principles often come first, followed by the exceptions and conflicting evidence.

Remind yourself of the big picture

Pause occasionally to get the big picture of the branch of science or math you're studying. What's it all about? What basic problems is the discipline trying to solve? How is this knowledge applied in daily life?

For example, much of calculus has to do with finding the areas of "funny shapes"—shapes, other than circles, that have curves. Physics studies how matter and energy interact. Physics and calculus are used by many people, including architects, engineers, and space scientists.

Ask questions fearlessly

In any subject, learning comes when we ask questions. And there are no dumb questions. To master math and science, ask whatever questions will aid your understanding. Students come to higher education with widely varying backgrounds in these subjects. What you need to ask may not be the same as for the other people in your class. Go ahead and ask.

One barrier to asking questions is the thought "Will the teacher think I'm stupid or ill-prepared if I ask this? What if he laughs or rolls his eyes?" With competent instructors this will usually not happen. If it does remember your reasons for going to school. Your purpose is not to impress the teacher but to learn. And sometimes learning means admitting ignorance.

Take a First Step about your current knowledge

Math and science are cumulative. That is, concepts tend to build upon each other in sequential order. If you struggled with algebra, for example, you could have trouble with trigonometry or calculus.

To ensure that you have an adequate base of knowledge, tell the truth about your current level of knowledge and skill. Before you register for a math or science course, seek out the assigned texts for the class. Look at the kind of material that's covered in early chapters. If that material seems new or difficult for you, see the instructor and express any concerns you have. Ask for suggestions on ways to prepare for the course.

Remember that it's OK to continue your study of math and science from your current level of ability—whatever that level might be.

Use lab sessions to your advantage

Laboratory work is crucial to many science classes. To get the most out of these sessions, prepare. Know in advance what procedures you'll be doing and what materials you'll need. If possible, visit the lab before your assigned time and get to know the territory. Find out where materials are stored and where to dispose of chemicals or specimens. Bring your lab notebook and worksheets to record and summarize your findings.

If you're not planning to become a scientist, the main point is to understand the process of science—how scientists observe, collect data, and arrive at conclusions. This is more important than the result of any one experiment.

Use cooperative learning

Math and science are often seen as solitary endeavors where students either sink or swim on their own. This does not have to be your experience. Instead of going it alone, harness the power of cooperative learning. Study math and science with others. That way you can learn about different approaches to reaching solutions.

By studying with others and creating an environment where it's OK to make mistakes, you can overcome a variety of fears. From the first day of a math or science course, be on the lookout for potential study group members. You can start to associate math and science with the fun of group interaction.

JOURNAL ENTRY #34
DISCOVERY STATEMENT

Most of us can recall a time when learning became associated with anxiety. For many people, this happened early with math and science.

One step to getting past this anxiety is to write a math or science autobiography. Recall specific experiences where you first felt stress over these subjects. Where were you? How old were you? What were you thinking and feeling? Who else was with you? What did those people say or do?

Describe one of these experiences in the space below.

_____

_____

_____

_____

_____

Now recall any incidents in your life that gave you positive feelings about math or science. Again, describe one of these incidents in detail. Use the space below.

_____

_____

_____

Now sum up the significant discoveries you made while describing these two sets of experiences.

I discovered that my biggest barrier in math or science is . . .

_____

_____

I discovered that the most satisfying part of doing math and science is . . .

_____

_____

_____

_____

JOURNAL ENTRY #35
INTENTION STATEMENT

List three actions you will take to overcome any anxiety you feel about math or science. Then schedule a specific time for taking each action.

Action 1: I intend to . . .

_____

_____

_____

_____

_____

_____

_____

_____

Action 2: I intend to . . .

_____

_____

_____

_____

_____

_____

Action 3: I intend to . . .

_____

_____

_____

_____

_____

_____

_____

_____

Special techniques for math and science tests

1. Translate problems into English. Putting problems into words aids your understanding. When you study equations and formulas, put those into words too. The words help you see a variety of applications for each formula. For example, $c^2 = a^2 + b^2$ can be translated as "the square of the hypotenuse of a right triangle is equal to the sum of the squares of the other two sides."

2. Perform opposite operations. If a problem involves multiplication, check your work by dividing; add, then subtract; factor, multiply; square root, square; differentiate, integrate.

3. Use time drills. Practice working problems fast. Time yourself. Exchange problems with a friend and time each other. You can also do this in a study group.

4. Analyze before you compute. Set up the problem before you begin to solve it. When a problem is worth a lot of points, read it twice, slowly. Analyze it carefully. When you take time to analyze a problem, you can often see ways to take computational shortcuts.

5. Make a picture. Draw an elaborate, colored picture or a diagram if you are stuck. Sometimes a visual representation will clear a blocked mind.

6. Estimate first. Estimation is a good way to double-check your work. Doing this first can help you notice if your computations go awry, and then you can correct the error quickly.

7. Check your work systematically. When you check your work, ask yourself, "Did I read the problem correctly?", "Did I use the correct formula or equation?", "Is my arithmetic correct?", "Is my answer in the proper form?"

Avoid the temptation to change an answer in the last few minutes—unless you're sure the answer is wrong. In a last-minute rush to finish the test, it's easier to choose the wrong answer.

8. Review formulas. Right before the test, review any formulas you'll need to use. Then write them on the margin of the test or on the back of the test paper.

**JOURNAL ENTRY #36
DISCOVERY STATEMENT**

Explore your feelings about tests. Complete the following sentences.

As exam time gets closer, one thing I notice I do is . . .

_____

_____

When it comes to taking tests, I have trouble . . .

_____

_____

The night before a test I usually feel . . .

_____

_____

The morning of a test I usually feel . . .

_____

_____

During a test I usually feel . . .

_____

After the test I usually feel . . .

_____

_____

When I get my score I usually feel . . .

_____

_____

H O W   T O
CRAM
(even though you shouldn't)

First, know the limitations of cramming and be aware of the costs. Cramming won't work if you neglected all the reading assignments or if you skipped all the lectures except the ones you daydreamed through.

The more courses you have to cram for, the less effective cramming will be.

Cramming is not the same as learning. When you rely on cramming, you cheat yourself of true education. You won't remember what you cram.

This point is especially important to recognize if you cram for midterm exams. Some students think they are actually learning the material they cram into their heads during midterm tests. They will be unpleasantly surprised during finals.

Cramming is also more work. It takes longer to learn material when you do it under pressure. You can't save time by cramming.

The purpose of cramming, therefore, is only to make the best of the situation. Cram to get by in a course so that you can do better next time. It might help raise a grade, if you have been reasonably attentive in class, have taken fair notes, and have read or skimmed most of the material for the course.

Those are the limitations and costs of cramming. Here is a six-step cramming process.

1. Make choices. Don't try to learn it all when you cram. You can't. Instead, pick out a few of the most important elements of the course and learn those backward, forward, and upside down.

For example, you can devote most of your attention to the topic sentences, tables, and charts in a long reading assignment instead of reading the whole assignment. A useful guideline is to spend 25 percent of cramming time learning new material and 75 percent of cramming time drilling yourself on that material.

2. Make a plan. Cramming is always done when time is short. That is all the more reason to take a few minutes to create a plan. Choose what you want to study (suggestion #1), determine how much time you have, and set deadlines for yourself. It's easy to panic and jump right in. Making a plan can save you time and allow you to work faster.

3. Use mind map review sheets and flash cards. Condense the material you have chosen to learn into mind maps. Choose several elements of the mind maps to put on 3x5 flash cards. Practice re-creating the mind maps, complete with illustrations. Drill yourself with the flash cards.

4. Recite ad nauseam. The key to cramming is repetitive recitation. Recitation can burn facts into your brain like no other study method. Go over your material again and again and again. One option is to tape-record yourself while you recite. Then play the tape as you fall asleep and as you wake up in the morning.

5. Relax. Because you do not learn material well when you cram, you are more likely to freeze and forget it under the pressure of an exam. Relaxation techniques can be used to reduce test anxiety, both before and during the test.

6. Don't "should" on yourself. The title of this article uses a word you should avoid: *should*. For example, you could start your cramming session by telling yourself you should have studied earlier, you should have read the assignments, and you should have been more conscientious. By the time you open your book you might feel too guilty and depressed to continue.

Consider this approach. Tell yourself it would have been more effective to study earlier and more often. Remind yourself you will have an opportunity to do that next time. Give yourself permission to be the fallible human being you are.

In short, lighten up. Our brains work better when we aren't criticizing ourselves.

And one more thing. Don't say "don't," either.

8 REASONS TO CELEBRATE mistakes

Many people are haunted by the fear of failure. Most of us fear making mistakes or being held responsible for a major breakdown. We fear that mistakes could cost us grades, careers, money, or even relationships.

It's possible to take an entirely different attitude toward mistakes. Rather than fearing them, we could actually celebrate them. We could revel in our redundancies, frolic in our failures, and glory in our goof-ups. We could marvel at our mistakes and bark with loud laughter when we blow it.

A creative environment is one in which failure is not fatal. Businesses, striving to be on the cutting edge of competition, desperately seek innovative changes. Yet innovation requires risk-taking—and along with it, the chance of failing.

This is not idle talk. There are real places where people celebrate mistakes. Management consultant Tom Peters gives these examples in an issue of the *Executive Excellence* newsletter:

• *One marketing director at Pizza Hut ended up with $5 million in unused sunglasses when a sales promotion scheme backfired. (The sunglasses were specifically designed for viewing the movie* Back to the Future, Part 2.) *He was promoted soon afterward, and the company's profits still increased 36 percent that year.*

• *The chief executive officer of Temps & Co., a temporary services firm, opens some meetings by asking managers to describe their biggest mistakes. The person with the "best" mistake gets a $100 prize. One of the winning mistakes was typing a social security number in the place of the dollar amount and cutting a multimillion-dollar paycheck.*

• *At its First Annual Doobie Awards, the Public Broadcasting System honored prominent mistakes made by its members. Nominees included an executive whose "improved" time sheets required three sign-offs instead of one. "It's a way of not taking ourselves too seriously," said one recipient of the award. "It gets a message across . . . . That it's okay to try and fail."*

Following are eight solid reasons for celebrating mistakes.

1. Celebration allows us to notice the mistake.
Celebrating mistakes gets them out in the open. Mistakes that are hidden cannot be corrected. It's only when we shine a light on a mistake and examine it that we can fix it.

This is the opposite of covering up mistakes or blaming others for them. Hiding mistakes takes a lot of energy—energy that could be channeled into correcting errors.

2. Mistakes are valuable feedback. A manager of a major corporation once made a mistake that cost his company $100,000. He predicted that he would be fired when his boss found out. Instead, his boss responded, "Fire you? I can't afford to do that. I just spent $100,000 training you." Mistakes are part of the learning process.

Not only are mistakes usually more interesting than most successes—they're often more instructive.

3. Mistakes demonstrate that we're taking risks. People who play it safe make few mistakes. Making mistakes gives evidence that we're stretching to the limit of our abilities, growing, risking, and learning.

Fear of making mistakes can paralyze us. This fear might frighten us into inaction. We could become afraid to do anything for fear of blowing it. Celebrating mistakes helps us move into action and get things done.

4. Celebrating mistakes reminds us that it's OK to make them. When we celebrate, we remind ourselves that the person who made the mistake is not bad—just human.

This is not a recommendation that you set out to make mistakes. Mistakes are not an end in themselves. Rather, their value lies in what we learn from them. When we make a mistake, we can admit it and correct it.

5. Celebrating mistakes includes everyone. It reminds us that the exclusive club named the Perfect Performance Society has no members. All of us make mistakes. When we notice them, we can work together. Blaming others or the system prevents the cooperative efforts that can improve our circumstances.

6. Mistakes occur only when we aim at a clear goal. We can express concern about missing a target only if the target is there in the first place. If there's no target or purpose, then there's no concern about missing. Making a mistake affirms something of great value—that we have a plan.

7. Mistakes happen only when we're committed to making things work. Systems work when people are willing to be held accountable. Openly admitting mistakes promotes accountability.

Imagine a school where there's no concern about quality and effectiveness. Teachers usually come to class late. Residence halls are never cleaned, and scholarship checks are always late. What's more, the administration is in chronic debt, students seldom pay tuition on time, and no one cares.

In this school, the word *mistake* would have little meaning. Mistakes become apparent only when people are committed to improving the quality of an institution. Mistakes go hand in hand with a commitment to quality.

8. Celebrating mistakes cuts the problem down to size. On top of the mistake itself, there is often a layer of regret, worry, and desperation about having made the mistake in the first place. Not only do people have a problem with the mistake, they have a problem with having made the mistake.

When we celebrate mistakes, we eliminate that layer of concern. When our anxiety about making a mistake is behind us, we can get down to the business of correcting the mistake.

EXERCISE #24
MASTER MIND MAP (PART ONE)

On a separate sheet of paper, create a mind map of the first six chapters of this book. Use a large sheet of paper for this purpose. Create your map without reviewing. (Don't even look up chapter titles.) This exercise is for you to demonstrate to yourself how much material you retain. You might be surprised by the results.

After creating your master mind map, go back through the text and review each chapter, spending no more than 10 minutes per chapter. Then, based on this review, revise your mind map to make it more accurate and complete.

Detach

Power Process #6 allows you to release the powerful, natural student within you. It is especially useful whenever negative emotions are getting in the way of your education.

Attachments are addictions. When we are attached to something, we think we cannot live without it, just as a drug addict feels he cannot live without drugs. We believe our well-being depends on fulfilling our attachments.

We can be attached to just about anything—expectations, ideas, objects, self-perceptions, people, results, rewards. The list is endless.

One person, for example, may be so attached to his car that he takes an accident as a personal attack. Pity the poor unfortunate who backs into this person's car. He might as well back into the owner himself.

Another person may be attached to her job. Her identity and sense of well-being depend on it. She could become suicidally depressed if she gets fired.

We can be addicted to our emotions as well as to our thoughts. We can identify with our anger so strongly that we are unwilling to let it go. We can also be addicted to our depression and reluctant to give it up. Rather than perceive these emotions as liabilities, we can see them as indications that it's time to practice detachment.

Most of us are addicted, to some extent, to our identities. We are Americans, veterans, high achievers, Elks, bowlers, loyal friends, Episcopalians, business owners, humanitarians, devoted parents, dancers, hockey fans, or birdwatchers. If we are attached, these are not just roles. Instead, they dictate who we are.

When these identities are threatened, we might fight for them as if we were defending our lives. The more addicted we are to the identity, the harder we fight. It's like a drowning man—the more he resists drowning, the more he literally becomes "attached" to his would-be rescuer, grasping and grabbing, until they both sink.

Ways to recognize an attachment

When we are attached and things don't go our way, we might feel irritated, angry, jealous, confused, fatigued, bored, frightened, or resentful.

Suppose you are attached to getting an A on your physics test. You feel as though your success in life depends on getting an A. It's not just that you want an A. You need an A. During the exam the thought "I must get an A" is in the back of your mind as you begin to work a problem. And the problem is difficult. The first time you read it you have no idea how to solve it. The second time you aren't even sure what it's asking. The more you read it, the more confused you get. To top it all off, this problem is worth 40 percent of your score.

The harder you work, the more stuck you get and the louder the thought in the back of your head: "I must get an A; I Must Get An A; I MUST GET AN A!"

At this point your hands begin to sweat and shake. Your knees feel weak. You feel nauseated. You can't concentrate. You flail about for the answer as if you were drowning. You look up at the clock, sickened by the inexorable sweep of the second hand. You are doomed.

Now is a time to reach for Power Process #6: "Detach."

Ways to use this process

Practice a variety of strategies to move toward detachment:

- Practice observer consciousness. This is the quiet state above and beyond your usual thoughts, the place where you can be aware of being aware. It's a tranquil place, apart from your emotions. From here, you observe yourself objectively, as if you were someone else. Pay attention to your emotions and physical sensations. If you are confused and feeling stuck, tell yourself, "Here I am, confused and stuck." If your palms are sweaty and your stomach is one big knot, admit it.

- Practice perspective. Put current circumstances into a larger perspective. View your personal issues within the larger context of your community, your nation, or your planet. You will likely see them from a different point of view. Imagine the impact your current problems will have 20 or even 100 years from now.

- Take a moment to consider the worst that could happen. During that physics exam, notice your attachment to getting an A. Even flunking the test will not ruin your life. Seeing this helps you put the test in perspective.

- Practice breathing. Calm your mind and body with breathing or relaxation techniques.

It might be easier to practice these techniques when you're not feeling strong emotions. Notice your thoughts, behaviors, and feelings while watching television or discussing ideas. The skill you gain at these times can make it easier to detach in more difficult circumstances.

Practice detaching. The key is to let go of automatic emotional reactions whenever you don't get what you want.

Rewrite the equation

To further understand this notion of detaching, borrow an idea from mathematics. When you're upset, look for the hidden equation.

An equation is any set of words joined by an equal sign (=) that forms a true statement. Examples are $2 \times 2 = 4$ and $a + b = c$.

Equations also work with words. In fact, our self-image can be thought of as a collection of equations. For example, the thought "I am capable" can be written as the equation $I = capable$. "My happiness depends on my car" can be written as $happiness = car$. The statement "My well-being depends on my job" becomes $well\text{-}being = job$.

Each equation is a tip-off to an attachment. Often, when we're upset, a closer look reveals that one of our attachments is threatened. The person who believes that his happiness is equal to his current job will probably be devastated if his company downsizes and he's laid off.

Once we discover a equation, we can rewrite it. In the process, we can watch our upsets disappear. The person who gets laid off can change his equation to $my\ happiness = my\ happiness$. In other words, his happiness does not have to depend on any particular job. If he's skilled at learning, he can get a new job that he loves. He can even change careers if that makes sense.

Some cautions

Giving up an addiction to being an A student does not mean giving up being an A student. And giving up an addiction to a job doesn't mean getting rid of the job. Rather, it means not investing your well-being in the grade or the job. Keep your desires and goals alive and healthy while detaching from the compulsion to reach them.

Notice also that detachment is different from denial. Denial implies running from whatever you find unpleasant. In contrast, detachment includes accepting your emotions and knowing the details of them—down to the very thoughts and physical sensations involved. It's OK to be angry or sad. Once you accept and fully experience your emotions, you can more easily move beyond them. The more you deny them, the more they persist.

Being detached is not the same as being apathetic. We can be 100 percent detached and 100 percent involved at the same time. In fact, our commitment to achieving a particular result is usually enhanced by being detached from it.

Detach and succeed

When we are detached, we perform better. When we think everything is at stake, results might suffer. Without anxiety and the need to get an A on the physics test, we are more likely to recognize the problem and remember the solution.

Power Process #6 is useful when you notice that attachments are keeping you from getting what you want. Behind your attachments is a master student. By detaching, you release that master student. Detach.

Cooperative learning—
STUDY WITH PEOPLE

Education often looks like competition. We compete for entrance to school, for grades when we're in school, and for jobs when we leave school. In that climate, it's easy to overlook the power of cooperation.

Consider the idea that competition is not necessary for success in school. In some cases, competition actually works against your success. It is often stressful. It can strain relationships. According to staff members at the Institute for Cooperative Learning at the University of Minnesota, people can often get more done by sharing their skills and resources than by working alone.[3]

We are social animals, and we draw strength from groups. Study groups feed you energy. Aside from offering camaraderie, fellowship, and fun, study groups elevate your spirit on days when you just don't want to work at your education. You are more likely to keep an appointment to study with a group than to study by yourself. If you skip a solo study session, no one may know. If you declare your intention to study with others who are depending on you, your intention gains strength. In addition to drawing strength from the group when you're down, you can support others.

Almost every job is accomplished by the combined efforts of many people. For example, manufacturing a single car calls for the contribution of designers, marketing executives, electricians, welders, painters, office workers, computer programmers, and many others. Jobs in today's economy call for teamwork—the ability to function well in groups. That's a skill you can start developing by studying with others.

Study groups are especially important if going to school has thrown you into a new culture. Joining a study group with people you already know, as well as with people from other cultures, can ease the transition. Promote your success in school by refusing to go it alone.

Forming a study group

When you form a support group, look for dedicated students. Find people you are comfortable with and who share some of your academic goals.

You can include people who face academic or personal challenges similar to your own. For example, if you are divorced and have two toddlers at home, you might look for other single parents who have returned to school.

To get the benefit of other perspectives, also include people who face challenges different from yours. Studying with friends is fine, but if your common interest is beer and jokes, beware of getting together to work.

Look for people who pay attention, ask questions, and take notes during class. Ask them to join your group. Choose people with similar educational goals but different backgrounds and methods of learning. You can gain from seeing the material from a new perspective.

Ask two or three people to get together for a snack and talk about group goals, meeting times, and other logistics. You don't have to make an immediate commitment.

Limit groups to five or six people. Larger groups are unwieldy. Test the group first by planning a one-time session. If that session works, plan another. After several successful sessions, you can schedule regular meetings.

Another way to get into a group is to post a note on a bulletin board asking interested students to contact you. Or pass around a sign-up sheet before class. The advantage of these methods is that you don't have to face rejection. The disadvantages are that this method takes more time and you don't get to choose who applies.

Conducting a study group

There are many ways to conduct a study group. Begin with the following suggestions and see what works.

Test each other by asking questions. Each group member can agree to bring four or five sample test questions to each meeting; then you can all take the test made from these questions.

Practice teaching each other. Teaching is a great way to learn something. Turn the material you're studying into a list of topics. Then assign specific topics for each person to teach the group. When you teach something, you naturally assume a teacher's attitude—"I know this"—as opposed to a student's attitude—"I still have to learn this." Also, the vocalization involved in teaching further reinforces your memory.

Compare notes. Make sure you all heard the same thing in class and that you all recorded the important information. Ask other students about material in your notes that is confusing to you.

Brainstorm test questions. Set aside five or 10 minutes each study session to use the brainstorming techniques described in Chapter Eight. You can add these to the "Test Questions" section of your notebook.

Set an agenda for each meeting. Select activities from this article, or create other activities to do as a group. Set approximate time limits for each agenda item and determine a quitting time. Finally, end each meeting with assignments for each member.

Work in groups of three at a computer to review a course. Choose one person to operate the keyboard. Another person can dictate summaries of lectures and assigned readings. The third person can act as fact checker, consulting textbooks, lecture notes, and class handouts as needed.

Create wall-sized mind maps or concept maps to summarize a textbook or series of lectures. Work on large sheets of butcher paper, or tape together pieces of construction paper. When doing a mind map, assign one "branch" of the mind map to each member of the study group. Use a different colored pen or marker for each branch. (For more information on concept maps and mind maps, see Chapter Five.)

Pair off to do "book reports." One person can summarize an assigned reading. The other person can act as an interviewer on a talk show, posing questions and asking for further clarification.

Ask members of your group to prepare and deliver full-length lectures on different topics of a course. Volunteer to lecture on a topic that you know least about, and come prepared to answer questions from other group members.

Take advantage of group support in personal areas too. Other people might have insight into your problems involving transportation, childcare, finances, time scheduling, and a host of other subjects. Use groups as a tool for getting what you want from school.

**PRACTICING
CRITICAL THINKING #11**

Create a short multiple-choice "exam" on a topic in a course you're taking right now. Ask several people from this course to take this exam. Then, as a group, discuss the answers to each question. Ask people to reveal the answer they chose for each question and their reasons for choosing the answer. After this discussion, ask what choices people would now make and what led them to revise their thinking.

**JOURNAL ENTRY #37
INTENTION STATEMENT**

I intend to form a study group. I intend to take steps to get the group organized.

I will set up the first group meeting by . . . (date)

_____

My reward for fulfilling this intention will be . . .

_____

_____

_____

master student

f r e d　s m i t h

*a graduate of Yale, is the founder and
CEO of Federal Express Corporation*

Frederick W. Smith may have a common last
name, but he is a most uncommon man.
What other American business leader of today had a
revolutionary idea and converted it into a company that,
starting from scratch and with heavy early losses, passed
the $500 million revenue mark and had a 10 percent net
profit margin in a few years?

What other American business leader with so
brilliant an idea first wrote it out in a college paper that
was graded C? Or says that the people with the greatest
impact on him have been a poorly educated sergeant
whom he led in combat and a science professor who liked
to buzz a university stadium in a fighter plane?

Fred Smith is chairman and chief executive officer of
Memphis-based Federal Express Corporation, an air cargo
firm that specializes in overnight delivery door-to-door,
using its own planes.

To put it another way, Fred Smith is Federal Express.

Smith got his revolutionary idea in the 60's while
majoring in economics and political science at Yale.

Technological change had opened a radically new
transportation market, he decided . . . .

"Steamboats and trains were the logistics arm of the
Industrial Revolution's first stage," he says. "Trucks
became a good logistics arm later—and still are because
of their flexibility. But moving the parts and pieces to
support the Electronics Age requires very fast transportation over long distances. I became convinced that a
different type of system was going to be a major part of
the national economy. . . ."

Smith spelled it out in an overdue economics paper.
To cut cost and time, packages from all over the country
would be flown to a central point, there to be distributed
and flown out again to their destinations—a hub-and-
spokes pattern, his company calls it today. The flying
would be late at night when air lanes were empty.
Equipment and documents from anywhere in the U.S.
could be delivered anywhere in the U.S. the next day . . . .

For the benefit of business history, it would be nice
to have that college paper today. But who saves college
papers, particularly those done in one night and
branded mediocre?

He says one reason he was no scholastic superstar
was that many courses he had to take didn't interest him.
Other things did. He and two faculty members resurrect-
ed a long-dormant flying club at Yale. One of his cohorts
was Professor Norwood Russell Hansen.

"Russ taught the psychology of science—how
science was developed," Smith says. "I was a friend of his,
not one of his students. He had a big impact on me
because of his outlook on life. He was a great singer and a
pianist of virtual concert talent. He rode a motorcycle,
and he had a World War II fighter plane that he flew all
over the place. He buzzed Yale Bowl from time to time.
He marched to the beat of a different drummer. . . ."

Will Smith be successful in future undertakings?
Says Arthur C. Bass, vice chairman: "A few years ago,
some of us used to let off steam in the afternoon playing
basketball on a court behind an apartment house. It was
amazing—no matter who had the ball and no matter
where Fred was on the court, if Fred's side needed to score
to win, he would get the ball and make the winning
basket. That's the way he is in the business world."

*A Business Visionary Who Really Delivered by Fred Smith,
from* Nation's Business, *November 1981
Reprinted by permission,* Nation's Business,
Copyright ©1981, U.S. Chamber of Commerce

1 *Preparing for tests can include creating review tools. What are at least two of these tools?*

2 *When answering multiple choice questions, it is best to read all the possible answers before answering the question in your head. True or False. Explain your answer.*

3 *The presence of absolute qualifiers, such as* always *or* never, *generally indicates a false statement. True or False. Explain your answer.*

4 *When answering essay questions, which of the following techniques is least effective?*

    (A) Before you write, make a quick outline.
    (B) Try for drama by saving the best points for last.
    (C) Find out precisely what the question is asking by knowing standard essay question words.
    (D) Include part of the question in your answer.
    (E) Avoid filler sentences that say nothing.

5 *Grades are:*

    (A) A measure of creativity.
    (B) An indication of your ability to contribute to society.
    (C) A measure of intelligence.
    (D) A measure of test performance.
    (E) C and D.

6 *How is detachment different from denial?*

QUIZ
C O N T I N U E D

7 *Choose one technique for taking math and science tests and explain how it, or some variation of it, could apply to taking a test in another subject.*

8 *What are at least three benefits of participating in a study group?*

9 *Describe at least three techniques for dealing with the thoughts connected to test anxiety.*

10 *Describe at least three techniques for dealing with the physical feelings connected to test anxiety.*

JOURNAL ENTRY #38
DISCOVERY/INTENTION STATEMENT

Review what you learned in this chapter and complete the following sentence.

In reading and doing this chapter, I discovered that . . .

_____

_____

Write about your intention to use one of the stress management techniques and test-taking hints from this chapter. I intend to . . .

_____

_____

Name _____ Date _____/_____/_____

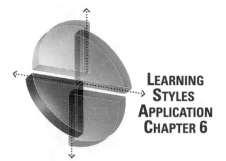

**LEARNING
STYLES
APPLICATION
CHAPTER 6**

Style 1
Write a short paragraph explaining ways you are already effectively using any of the techniques in this chapter.

Style 2
List 10 new suggestions for reviewing course material or taking tests that you gained from reading this chapter.

Style 3
Of the 10 new suggestions you just listed, choose five that you will actually use. Describe when or where you could use each technique.

Style 4
Explain how the suggestions given in this chapter for managing test anxiety could help you manage any stress you're currently experiencing. Think about ways to use these suggestions outside your schoolwork.

Bibliography

Endnotes

[1] W.C.F. Krueger, "The effect of overlearning on retention," *Journal of Experimental Psychology*, 12:71-78, 1929.

[2] Sheila Tobias, *Succeed with Math: Every Student's Guide to Conquering Math Anxiety* (New York: College Board, 1987).

[3] David Johnson et al., *Cooperation in the Classroom* (Edina, MN: Interaction Books, 1988).

Additional Reading

Kogelman, Stanley, and Joseph Warren. *Mind Over Math*, New York: Dial Press, 1978.

Mallow, Jeffry V. *Science Anxiety: Fear of Science and How to Overcome It*, New York: Thomond, 1981.

McCarthy, Michael J. *Mastering the Information Age*, Los Angeles: J.P. Tarcher, 1991.

Pauk, Walter. *How to Study in College*, Boston: Houghton Mifflin, 1974.

diversity

In this chapter...

■ explore ways that people differ and discover strategies for succeeding in a diverse society. Begin by seeing value in diversity and by gaining skills in communicating across cultures. Also adapt to the culture of higher education, deal with sexism and sexual harassment, and master the art of returning to school at any age. What's more, experiment with choosing your conversations as a tool for immediately raising the quality of your life.

JOURNAL ENTRY #39
DISCOVERY STATEMENT

Brainstorm some possible benefits you could gain by being able to get along more effectively with people of other races or ethnic groups. Write your ideas on a separate sheet of paper.

Next, preview this chapter for any ideas or techniques that could help you attain these benefits. Briefly sum up those ideas on your sheet of paper.

JOURNAL ENTRY #40
DISCOVERY STATEMENT

On a separate sheet of paper, describe an incident where you were discriminated against because you differed in some way from the other people involved. This could result from any kind of difference, such as your hair length, style of dressing, political affiliation, religion, skin color, age, or accent. How would you have liked the other people to have responded to you?

Now describe an incident where someone you know experienced a similar kind of discrimination based on a similar difference. Scan this chapter for ideas that could help you respond more effectively to such discrimination and list those ideas on your paper.

THOSE OF US WHO CAN study, work, and live with people from other cultures, economic classes, and races will enjoy more success in school, on the job, and in our neighborhoods. This means learning new ways to think, speak, and act. Learning about diversity opens up a myriad of possibilities—an education in itself. This can be frightening, frustrating, or even painful at first. It can also be exciting, enriching, and affirming.

Our classrooms, offices, and factories will become a "rainbow coalition" of people from many different cultures, socioeconomic backgrounds, and races. Already the people we call "minorities" are a numerical majority across the world. By the year 2056, the "average" United States resident will list his or her ancestry as African, Asian, Hispanic, or Arabic—not white European. In many city school systems, Caucasian students are already a minority in numbers. This is not the result of government policy or pressure from special-interest groups. It simply is a fact—one for which many people feel ill-prepared.

The cultures of the world meet daily. Several forces are shrinking our globe. One is the growth of a world economy. Another is the "electronic village" forged across nations by newspapers, radios, televisions, telephones, fax machines, and computers.

We have an opportunity to benefit from this change instead of merely reacting to it. At one time, only sociologists and futurists talked about the meeting of cultures. Now all of us can enter this conversation. We can value cultural diversity and learn how to thrive with it.

Diversity is a fact—and a value

> " "
> I'll walk where my own nature would be leading. It vexes me to choose another guide.
> –EMILY BRONTË

> " "
> We don't see things as they are, we see things as we are.
> –ANAÏS NIN

> " "
> Acceptance, goodwill and respect are the cornerstones of successful communication and exchange–ones that cross all barriers of class, gender, race, and ability.
> –BOB ABRAMMS-MEZOFF
> DIANE JOHNS

Diversity is a reality

We have always lived with people of different races and cultures. Many of us come from families who immigrated to the United States or Canada just two or three generations ago. What's more, the things we eat, the tools we use, and the words we speak are a cultural tapestry woven by many different peoples.

Think about a common daily routine. A typical American citizen awakens in a bed (an invention from the Near East). After dressing in clothes (often designed in Italy), he eats breakfast on plates (made in China), eats a banana (grown in Honduras), and brews coffee (shipped from Nicaragua). And after breakfast he reads the morning newspaper (printed by a process invented in Germany and on paper originally made in China). Then he flips on a tape player (made in Japan) and listens to music (possibly performed by a band from Cuba).

Multiculturalism refers to racial and ethnic diversity—and many other kinds of diversity as well. As anthropologist Dorothy Lee[1] reminds us, culture is simply one society's solutions to perennial human problems, such as how to dress, eat, worship, celebrate holidays, resolve conflict, work, think, and learn.

From this standpoint, we can speak of the culture of large corporations or the culture of the fine arts. There are the cultures of men and women, heterosexual and homosexual people, rich and poor, and older and younger people. Also included are differences between urban and rural dwellers, people who are able-bodied and those with disabilities, and people from two-parent families and people from single-parent families. Diversity in religion is a fact too. This can be especially difficult to accept, since many of us identify strongly with our religious faith.

This chapter explores only some of the ways people differ, including differences in race, gender, and ethnic group. Yet the suggestions offered here can help you respond effectively to

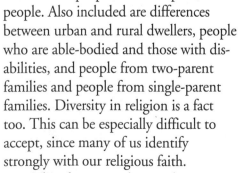

the many kinds of diversity you'll encounter. Higher education could be your chance to develop the attitudes of tolerance, open-mindedness, and respect for individual differences.

Discrimination is also real

The ability to live with diversity is now more critical than ever. Racism and other forms of discrimination still exist, even on campus. Consider the following situations.

- Members of a sociology class are debating the merits of reforming the state's welfare system. The instructor calls on a student from a reservation and says, "Tell us. What's the Native American perspective on this issue anyway?" Here the student is being typecast as a spokesperson for her entire ethnic group.
- Students in a mass media communications class are learning to think critically about television programs. They're talking about a situation comedy set in an urban high-rise apartment building with mostly African American residents. "Man, they really whitewashed that show," says one student. "It's mostly about inner-city black people, but they didn't show anybody getting welfare, doing drugs, or joining gangs." The student's comment perpetuates common racial stereotypes.
- On the first day of the term, students of English composition enter a class taught by a professor from Puerto Rico. One of the students asks the professor, "Am I in the right class? Maybe there's been a mistake. I thought this was supposed to be an English class, not a Spanish class." The student assumed that only Caucasian people can be qualified to teach English courses.

Forrest Toms of Training Research and Development defines racism as "prejudice plus power"—the power to define reality, to enshrine one set of biases. The operating assumption behind racism is that differences mean deficits.

When racism lives, we all lose—even those groups with social and political power. We lose the ability to make friends and to function effectively on teams. We crush human potential. People without the skills to bridge cultures are already at a disadvantage.

Higher education offers a chance to change this. Academic environments can become cultural laboratories—places for you to meet people of other races and cultures in an atmosphere of tolerance. People who create alliances outside their group are preparing to succeed in both school and work.

Diversity is valuable

It takes no more energy to believe that differences enrich us than it does to believe that differences deplete us. Diversity in a society offers one case of synergy, the idea that the whole is more than the sum of its parts. Consider some examples: A symphony orchestra consists of many different instruments, and when played together their effect is multiplied many times. A football team has members with different specialities, but together they can win a league championship.

Diversity offers another example of synergy. Embracing diversity adds value to any organization and can be far more exciting than just meeting the minimum requirements for affirmative action.

Today we are waking up not only to the fact of diversity but also to the value of diversity. Biologists tell us that diversity of animal species benefits our ecology.

The same idea applies to the human species. Through education our goal can be to see that we are part of a complex world—that our culture is different from, not better than, others. Knowing this, we can stop saying, "This is the way to work, learn, relate to others, and view the world." Instead, we can say, "Here is the way I have been doing it. I would also like to see your way."

Learning to live with diversity is a process of returning to "beginner's mind"—a place where we question our biases and assumptions. This is a magical place, a place of new beginnings and options. It takes courage to dwell in beginner's mind—courage to go outside the confines of your own culture and world view. It can feel uncomfortable at first. Yet there are lasting rewards to gain.

As you read the following articles, look at yourself. This chapter aims to help you meet your own biases. With knowledge about your prejudices you can go beyond them. You can discover ways to communicate across cultures.

Each idea in this chapter is merely a starting point. When it comes to overcoming the long history of prejudice and discrimination, there are no quick, easy answers. Continue to experiment and see what works for you. As you read, constantly ask, "How can I use this material to live and work more effectively in a multicultural world?" The answers could change your life.

EXERCISE #25
CLARIFY YOUR VALUES

On a separate sheet of paper, list four of your key values. Sum up each value in one or two words, such as love, contribution, wealth, *or* creativity.

Next, for each value, list three or four statements that describe specifically what you would do, say, or have when you behave consistently with that value. For example, if your value is financial security, you could write, "I save at least 10 percent of my take-home pay each month" or "I have enough money to live comfortably for three months even if I lose my job."

etting started communicating with people of other cultures is a learned skill—a habit. According to management consultant Stephen R. Covey[2], a habit is the point where desire, knowledge, and skill meet. Desire is about wanting to do something. Knowledge is seeing what to do. And skill is understanding how to do it.

These three factors are equally important for bridging gaps in cultural understanding. This article speaks to the first two factors—knowledge and desire—and also provides suggestions for gaining skills.

Desire to communicate

When our actions are truly grounded in the desire to understand others, we can be much more effective. Knowing techniques for communicating across cultures is valuable, yet these cannot take the place of the sincere desire and commitment to create understanding. If you truly see the value of cultural diversity, you can discover and create ways to build bridges to other people.

James Anderson[3], dean of the Division of Undergraduate Studies at North Carolina State University, speaks of the relationship between analytic and relational styles. Most of our schools favor students with an analytical style. These students learn abstract concepts easily and are adept at reading, writing, and discussing ideas. They can learn parts of a subject even if they don't have a view of the whole. Often these students are self-directed, and their performance is not affected by the opinions of others.

A bias toward the analytical style tends to exclude students with a relational style. Students with a relational style learn by getting the big picture of a subject before the details. They learn better initially by speaking, listening, and doing, rather than by reading or writing. These students prefer to learn about subjects that relate to their concerns or about subjects presented in a lively, humorous way. In addition, they are influenced by the opinions of people they value and respect. All these things point to a unique learning style.

Differing styles exist in every aspect of life—family structure, religion,

Know about other cultures

Back up your desire with knowledge. People from different cultures read differently, write differently, think differently, eat differently, and learn differently than you. Knowing this, you can be more effective with your classmates, coworkers, and neighbors.

Cultures differ in many dimensions. One of the most important dimensions is style. We can also speak of learning styles, communication styles, relationship styles, and other styles.

relationships with authority, and more. Native Americans might avoid confrontation and seek mediators to resolve conflict. People from certain Asian cultures might feel it's rude to ask questions. Knowing about such differences can help you avoid misunderstandings.

Today there is a wealth of material about cultural diversity. Begin with an intention to increase your sensitivity to other cultures. The greater our knowledge of other cultures, the easier we can find it to be tolerant. The more we explore our differences, the more we can discover our similarities.

Be willing to ask questions and share ideas with all kinds of people. In short, just get the conversation started.

You can learn something valuable from anyone when you reach out.

Gain skills

With the desire to communicate and gain knowledge of other cultures, you can work on specific skills. Some possibilities follow.

Respond to these ideas on three levels. The first is personal—becoming aware of your own biases. The second is interpersonal—forming alliances with people of other races and cultures. The third is institutional. Here you can point out the racism and discrimination that you see in organizations. Be an advocate for change.

Be active

Learning implies activity. Learning ways to communicate across cultures is no exception. It's ineffective to assume that this skill will come to you merely by your

being in the same classrooms with people from other races and ethnic groups. It's not their responsibility to raise your cultural awareness. That job is yours, and it calls for energy.

Think critically

Communicating across cultures is closely linked to critical thinking. To embrace diversity, we can learn to avoid errors of perception, judgment, and premature reaction. (Many of these are explained further by Vincent Ryan Ruggiero in the book *Becoming a Critical Thinker*.)

Stereotypes offer examples of poor critical thinking. When we hear statements such as "Black people depend on welfare," we can shift our thinking skills into high gear. We can ask for evidence and insist on accurate information—for example, the fact is that many people on welfare are Caucasian.

Within stereotypes we can sometimes find a kernel of truth. An example is the statement "Women are highly emotional." In fact, some women focus on emotional responses as they learn. But then, so do some men. When we make statements about a whole group of people based on observation of a few members, we put on the blinders of prejudice. One path of escape is critical thinking.

Look for common ground

Some goals cross culture lines. Most people want health, physical safety, economic security, and education.

Most students want to succeed in school and prepare for a career. They share the same teachers. They have access to many of the same resources at school. They meet in the classroom, on the athletic field, and at cultural events. To promote cultural understanding, we can become aware of and celebrate our

differences. We can also return to our common ground.

Practice looking for common ground. You can cultivate friends from other cultures. Do this through volunteering, serving on committees, or joining study groups—any activity where people from other cultures are also involved. In this way, your understanding of other people unfolds in a natural, spontaneous way.

The trick is to keep a balance, to honor the differences among people while remembering what they have in common.

Assume differences in meaning

Each day, we can make an intention to act and speak with the awareness that cultures differ. To do so, we can look for other possible meanings of our words and actions.

Assume that differences in meanings exist, even if you don't know what they are. After first speaking to someone from another culture, don't assume that you've been understood—or that you fully understand the other person. The same action can have different meanings at different times, even for members of the same culture. Check it out. Verify what you think you have heard. Listen to see if what you spoke is what the other person received.

If you're speaking to someone who doesn't understand English well, keep the following ideas in mind.

- Speak slowly and distinctly.
- To clarify your statement, don't repeat the same words over and over again. Restate your message in simple, direct language. Avoid slang.
- Use gestures to accompany your words.
- Since English courses for non-native speakers often emphasize written English, write down what you're saying. Print your message in block letters, all caps.
- Stay calm and avoid nonverbal messages that you're frustrated.

Look for individuals, not group representatives

Sometimes the way we speak glosses over differences among individuals and reinforces stereotypes. For example, a student worried about his grade in math expresses concern over "all those Asian students who are skewing the class curve." Or a Caucasian music major assumes that his African American classmate knows a lot about jazz. We can avoid such errors by seeing people as individuals—not spokespersons for an entire group.

Get inside another culture

You may find yourself fascinated by one particular culture. Consider learning as much about it as possible. Immerse yourself in that culture. Read novels, see plays, go to concerts, listen to music, look at art, take courses, learn the language. Seek out opportunities to speak with members of that culture. Your knowledge will be an opening to new conversations.

Celebrate your own culture

Learning about other cultures does not mean abandoning your own. You could gain new appreciation for it. You may even find out that members of your group have suffered discrimination—for example, that Irish people once lived in ghettos in the United Kingdom. In the process, you gain new insight into the experiences of other people.

Find a translator, mediator, or model

People who move with ease in two or more cultures can help us greatly. Diane de Anda[4], a professor at the University of California, Los Angeles, speaks of three kinds of people who can communicate across cultures. She calls them *translators*, *mediators*, and *models*.

A *translator* is someone who is truly bicultural—a person who relates skillfully to people in a mainstream culture and people from a contrasting culture. This person can share his own experiences in overcoming discrimination, learning another language or dialect, and coping with stress. He can point out differences in meaning between cultures and help resolve conflict.

Mediators are people who belong to the dominant or mainstream culture. Unlike translators, they may not be bicultural. However, mediators value diversity and are committed to cultural understanding. Often they are teachers, counselors, tutors, mentors, or social workers.

Models are members of a culture who are positive examples. They are students from any racial or cultural group who participate in class and demonstrate effective study habits. Models can also include entertainers, athletes, and community leaders.

Your school may have people who serve these functions, even if they're not labeled translators, mediators, or models. Some schools have mentor or "bridge" programs that pair new students with teachers of the same race or culture. Students in these programs get coaching in study skills and life skills; they also develop friendships with a possible role model. Ask your student counseling service about such programs.

Develop support systems

Many students find that their social adjustment affects their academic performance. Students with strong support systems—such as families, friends, churches, self-help groups, and mentors—are using a powerful strategy for success in school. As an exercise, list the support systems that you rely on right now. Also list new support systems you could develop.

Support systems can help you bridge culture gaps. With a strong base of support in your own group, you can feel more confident in meeting people outside that group.

Ask for help

If you're unsure about how well you're communicating, ask questions: "I don't know how to make this idea clear for you. How might I communicate better?", "When you look away from me during our conversation, I feel uneasy. Is there something else we need to talk about?", "When you don't ask questions, I wonder if I am being clear. Do you want any more explanation?" Questions like these can get cultural differences out in the open in a constructive way.

Change the institution

None of us are individuals living in isolation. We live in systems that can be racist. As a student, you might see people from another culture ignored in class, passed over in job hiring, underrepresented in school organizations, or ridiculed. The only way to stop these actions is to point them out.

Federal civil rights laws, as well as the written policies of most schools, ban discrimination on racial and ethnic grounds. If your school receives federal aid, it must set up procedures that protect students against such discrimination. Find out what those procedures are and use them if necessary.

Throughout recent history, much social change has been fueled by students. When it comes to ending discrimination, you are in an environment where you can make a difference. Run for student government. Write for school publications. Speak at rallies. Express your viewpoint. Engage in debate. This is training for citizenship in a multicultural world.

Reap the rewards

The price we pay for failure to understand other cultures is fear and bigotry. These presume that one group has the right to define all others. Such attitudes cannot withstand the light of knowledge, compassion, and common values.

**PRACTICING
CRITICAL THINKING #12**

Choose one article from this book and summarize its main ideas in three ways: visually (using a chart, diagram, or mind map), in outline form, and in paragraph form. Now assess how well each method worked for you. Was one note-taking method more efficient for you than another? Do you see any options for adopting a new method of note taking? Can any methods be combined in useful ways? How? Write your answers in the space below.

_____
_____
_____
_____
_____
_____
_____
_____
_____
_____
_____
_____
_____
_____
_____
_____
_____
_____

Adapting to the culture of HIGHER EDUCATION

You share one thing in common with other students at your school, college, or university: Entering higher education represents a change in your life. You've joined a new culture with its own set of rules, both spoken and unspoken. The skills you practice in making this transition can apply to making any transition in life—whether it's a new job, new relationship, or new community.

Begin by taking a First Step about your reactions to entering higher education. It's OK to feel anxious, isolated, homesick, or worried about doing well academically. Such emotions are common among students.

One of the few constants in life is the fact of change. All the cells in your body will regenerate several times during your life. The thoughts, feelings, and behaviors that make up your sense of self are in flux too. That's especially true as you enter a new environment.

This fact of change can work in your favor. Chances are that any initial discomfort you feel about academic life will wane over time. For other ideas about making the transition, consider the following.

Understand how higher education differs from high school

Even if you attended high school many years ago, you can find it useful to review some basic differences between secondary and postsecondary education. Unlike attendance at high school, attendance at a college or university is optional. And if you've gone to public schools all your life, you've probably never had tuition payments to worry about. With higher education that changes too.

Higher education also presents you with more choices—where to attend school, how to structure your time, where to live, and with whom to associate.

You might experience new academic standards as well. Often there are fewer tests in college than in high school, and the grading may be tougher. You'll probably find that teachers expect you to study more than you did in high school. At the same time, your instructors may give you less guidance about what or how to study.

Watch for differences in teaching styles. Often college and university professors are steeped in their subject matter. Many did not take courses in how to teach. They may not be as engaging as some of your high school teachers. And some professors are more interested in research than in teaching. Once you understand such differences, you can begin to work with them.

Balance work and school schedules

Full-time students can find that working too many hours outside of class compromises their success in school. This is especially true during their first year of higher education. As you coordinate your work and study schedules, consider the limits on your energy and time. Also create "buffer zones" in your schedule—pockets of unplanned time that you can use for unforeseen events.

Decrease the unknowns

Before classes begin, get a map of the campus and walk through your first day's schedule. Do this with a classmate or friend. Visit your instructors in their offices and introduce yourself. Anything you do to familiarize yourself with the new routine can help.

Seek stability zones

Not all the facets of our lives have to change at the same time. Balance change in one area of your life with stability in another. When attending school, keep in contact with family members and old friends. Maintain long-term relationships. This includes relationships with key places, such as your childhood home. Postpone other major changes for now.

Form support systems

With higher education may come a kind of culture shock and the thought "I don't know who I am anymore." To deal with this, build support systems into your life. Cultivate new friendships, including those with members of other races and cultures. Campus activities, student services, and study groups are ways to do so. Other student services include career planning and placement, counseling services, financial aid, student ombudspersons, language clubs, and programs for minority students.

Seek out teachers and students whom you admire and who can become mentors for you. Cultivate a relationship with a role model who in effect says, "I did it, and so can you." Some schools offer formal mentoring programs for this purpose.

Remember earlier transitions

Recall times in the past when you coped with major change. Write Discovery Statements describing those experiences in detail. List any strategies you used to effectively make those transitions. You've weathered major change before, and you can make it again.

Work with your academic adviser

Meet with your academic adviser regularly. This person has a big picture of all the resources available on campus and how they can benefit you. Your school may offer peer advisory programs as well. Keep in mind that even when you work with an adviser, you're still in charge of your education. And don't be afraid to change advisers when that seems appropriate.

Take the initiative in meeting new people

Promise yourself to meet one new person each week, and write an Intention Statement describing specific ways to do so. Introduce yourself to classmates. Prime times to do that are just before and after class. Realize that most of the people in this new world of higher education are waiting to be welcomed. You can do that job.

Learn the language of higher education

Higher education often presents students with a baffling set of new words. Some terms you might hear for the first time are these:

Academic freedom—The right of instructors to study controversial issues and express unpopular points of view without the threat of job loss—as long as students' safety and civil rights are maintained.

Accreditation—A process used in judging the merit of the programs offered by a school. An accredited school is recognized as meeting standards set by a professional organization, such as the American Bar Association.

Attrition—A general term referring to the number of students who drop out of a school or a program offered by that school.

CLEP—An acronym for College Level Examination Program. Passing a CLEP test may allow you to earn college credit for skills and knowledge you already possess.

GPA—An abbreviation for grade point average, a snapshot of your overall academic performance. In most schools, an A equals four points, a B is three points, a C two points, a D one point, and an F equals no points.

Major—A related group of courses that reflects the dominant focus of your higher education. Academic majors often form the basis for later career choices or programs in graduate school.

Matriculated—A term describing a student who has been accepted for a degree program and has begun taking courses for that program.

Minor—A group of courses often related to but different from a student's major field of study. Not all schools require a minor, even if they require students to choose a major.

Practicum—A course or program that covers a specialized topic in depth. In some cases, this word refers to work-study arrangements that earn college credit.

Prerequisite—A preparatory course that students are usually required to complete before they can register for another course.

Probation—A formal notice that a student's grade point average or conduct is not acceptable to the school's administration. Probation usually amounts to a warning—and a request that students raise their academic performance. Students who fail to do so may eventually be suspended or dismissed from school.

Quarter—A term that describes a common length of courses offered by a school. Quarters usually last about 10 weeks. In these schools, courses are offered four times a year, including summer session.

Semester—Another term for a school's typical course length. Semesters often last about 14 weeks.

Syllabus—A document students usually receive on the first day of a class, offering an overview of the course. Often included in a syllabus is an outline of topics, assignments, grading requirements, and related course details.

Tenure—Usually refers to lifetime employment for a professor, unless that person is shown to be incompetent or immoral. Even tenured professors can lose their jobs if a college or university cuts budgets or reduces staff.

These are just a few examples. Many more such terms are explained in a book that's usually free for the taking—your school catalog. Check it out. Consider it a secondary text for your student success course, and keep it next to *Becoming a Master Student* on your bookshelf.

The art of reentry—
Going back to school as an older student

If you're returning to school after a long break from the classroom, there's no reason to feel out of place. Returning adults and other nontraditional students are already a majority in some schools.

Being an older student puts you on strong footing. With a rich store of life experience, you can ask questions and make connections between course work and daily life. Many instructors will especially enjoy working with you.

Following are some suggestions for returning adult students. Even if you don't fit in this category, you can look for ways to apply these ideas.

Ease into it

If you're new to higher education, consider easing into it. Go to school part-time before making a full-time commitment.

Plan your week

Many older students report that their number one problem is time. One solution is to plan your week. By planning a week at a time instead of just one day, you get a bigger picture of your roles as student, employee, and family member. For many more suggestions on managing time, see Chapter Two.

Delegate tasks

Consider hiring others to do some of your household work or errands. Yes, this costs money. It's also an investment in your education and future earning power.

If you have children, delegate some of the chores to them. Or start a meal co-op in your neighborhood. Cook dinner for yourself and someone else one night each week. In return, ask that person to furnish you with a meal on another night. A similar strategy can apply to childcare and other household tasks.

Add 15 minutes to your day

If you're pressed for time, get up 15 minutes earlier or stay up 15 minutes later. Chances are, the lost sleep won't affect your alertness during the day. Meanwhile, you can use the extra time to scan a reading assignment or outline a paper. Stretching each day by just 15 minutes yields 91 extra hours in a year. That's time you can use to promote your success in school.

Get to know younger students

You share a central concern with younger students: succeeding in school. It's easier to get past the generation gap when you remember this. Consider pooling resources with younger students. Share notes, form study groups, or edit each other's term papers.

Get to know other returning students

Introduce yourself to other older students. Being in the same classroom gives you an immediate bond. You can exchange work and home phone numbers with these people. Build a network of mutual support. Some students even adopt a buddy system, pairing up with another student in each class to complete assignments and prepare for tests.

Find common ground with instructors

Many of the people who teach your classes may be juggling academics, work, and family lives too. That gives you one more way to break the ice with instructors.

Enlist your employer's support

Employers often promote continuing education. Further education can increase your skills either in a specific subject or in working with people. That makes you a more valuable employee or consultant.

Let your employer in on the plan. Point out how the skills you gain in class will help you meet work objectives. Or offer informal "seminars" to share what you're learning in school.

Get extra mileage out of your current tasks

You can look for specific ways to merge your work and school lives. Some schools will offer academic credit for work and life experience. Likewise, your company may reimburse employees for some tuition costs or even grant time off to attend classes.

Experiment with combining tasks. For example, when you're assigned a research paper, choose a topic that relates to your current job tasks.

Look for child care

For some students, returning to class means looking for child care outside the home. Many schools offer child care at school for reduced rates for students.

Review your subjects before you start classes

Say that you're registered for trigonometry and you haven't taken a math class since high school. Then consider brushing up on the subject before classes begin. Also talk to future instructors about ways to prepare for their classes.

Prepare for an academic environment

If you're used to an efficient corporate setting, school life may present some frustrations. A lack of advanced computer systems may slow down your class registration. Faculty members may take a little longer to return your calls or respond to letters, especially during holiday and summer breaks. Knowing the rhythm of academic life can help you plan around these events.

Be willing to let go of old images about how to study

Many older students find it effective to view their school assignments exactly as they would view a project at work. They use the same tactics in the library as on the job, which often helps them learn more actively.

"Publish" your schedule

After you plan your study and class sessions for the week, post your schedule in a place where others will see it. You can treat this as a game. Make your schedule look like an "official" document. Designate open slots in your schedule where others can sign up for "appointments" to see you.

Share your educational plans

The fact that you're in school will affect the key relationships in your life. Committing to classes and studying may prompt feelings of guilt about taking time away from others. You can prevent problems by discussing these issues ahead of time.

Another strategy is to actively involve your spouse, partner, or close friends in your schooling. Offer to give them a tour of the school and introduce them to your instructors.

Take this a step further and ask the key people in your life for help. Ask them to think of ways they can support your success in school and to commit to those actions. Make education a joint mission that benefits you all.

Stay tuned to these

School can be a frightening place for new students. People of diverse cultures, older students, commuters, and people with disabilities can feel excluded. Some people attend classes for years and still feel they're standing on the outside, looking in.

You don't have to be a stranger to school life. Networking is one way to break through the barriers that keep students isolated.

The *American Heritage Dictionary* defines *networking* as "an informal system whereby persons having common interests assist each other." The term most often is applied to business, but education can be a social enterprise too. In fact, it works better that way. Students who overcome feelings of isolation increase their chances of staying in school and succeeding. Networks also prepare students for the work world, where most projects involve teamwork. You can begin networking immediately. Here are some techniques you can use.

1. Introduce yourself to classmates. Get to class early and break the ice by discussing the previous assignment, or stay late and talk about the lecture.

2. Plan to meet people. Write an Intention Statement promising to meet three new people each week. Plan who these people will be and how and when you intend to meet them.

3. See your instructor. If you feel lost in a class, make an appointment to see your instructor outside class. You might discover a human being who wants you to succeed.

4. Form a study group. Peer pressure can be positive. Study with students who excel, and also look for partners from different racial, ethnic, religious, or socioeconomic backgrounds. Diversity will add depth to your group and stimulate everyone's thinking.

5. Join a support group. People with common problems can share solutions. Many schools have support groups for everything from dealing with prejudice to overcoming addictions to learning computer software.

6. Join a club. Your membership in the Spanish club can support your success in Spanish class. A computer users group, a chess club, a Bible study group, or an Islamic student association can put you in touch with potential friends.

7. Join a professional society. Many professional societies have student chapters. Examples include the International Association of Business Communicators, Sigma Delta Chi (for journalists), and the American Society for Training and Development. You can meet people and get career guidance too.

8. Perform! Try out for a play or join a band. These can be good ways for nontraditional students to get involved in school activities. Members of the Bagpipe Club will be so glad to see a fellow piper, they won't care how old you are.

9. Join a political organization. Both major political parties and many minor ones have student organizations.

10. Play ball! You don't have to be a world-class athlete to play sports. As a matter of fact, keeping fit is one of the marks of a master student. Most schools have intramural leagues. Many have clubs for runners, bicyclists, hikers, rock climbers, wheelchair basketball players, and other athletes. Instruction is often available too.

11. Find a mentor. A mentor is an adviser or coach. She can be anyone you trust—another student, a graduate student, a teacher, or a person in the community. Mentors can coach you in study skills or career skills. They also can teach by example, which is one of the most powerful and

persuasive ways to teach. Be clear about your reasons for choosing a mentor. Avoid selecting someone just because that person is like you in age, race, or social class. Choose someone who can make a difference in your life.

When you meet people whom you consider to be excellent learners, observe them. Isolate specific things they do and say to promote their mastery. Then imitate one of these behaviors. See if it works for you. Also observe any self-defeating habits you see in other students, and see if you can draw lessons from them.

Sometimes you can be your own mentor. Observe yourself during the times you're "on" as a student— times when learning is effortless and joyful. Notice the attitudes and actions that are promoting your success in those moments.

12. Use school media. School newspapers can alert you to interesting activities and people. Radio stations and bulletin boards can be sources of information about clubs, support groups, political organizations, and social activities. Also, check the school catalog and directory.

13. Hang out at the student union. The student union or activities center often is a hub for social activities, special programs, and free entertainment. Clubs and organizations often meet there too.

14. Study at the library. It's quiet, it's comfortable, and it's a place to meet other serious students.

15. Use student services. These include career planning and placement centers, counseling services, financial aid offices, student health services, and student advocates. Many of these services are free to students. Going to school puts you in contact with an extraordinary network of services. All that remains is for you to use them.

**PRACTICING
CRITICAL THINKING #13**

Read an editorial in your local newspaper. Then form the strongest possible arguments for at least two points of view on this issue. Include a point of view that's different from your current one. Write them in the space below.

_____
_____
_____
_____
_____
_____
_____
_____
_____

Afterward examine your sets of arguments. What impact did this exercise have on your thinking on this issue?

_____
_____
_____
_____
_____
_____
_____
_____
_____
_____

Dealing with sexism . . .

Sexism and sexual harassment are real. They are terms for events that occur at schools, colleges, and universities across the world. Nearly all of these incidents are illegal or against school policies.

In the United States, women make up the majority of first-year students in higher education. Yet until the early nineteenth century, they were banned from colleges and universities. Today women in higher education still encounter bias based on gender.

This bias can take many forms. For example, instructors might gloss over the contributions of women. Students in philosophy class may never hear of Hypatia, the ancient Greek philosopher. Those majoring in computer science may never learn about Grace Hopper, who developed a computer language named COBOL. And your art history textbook may not mention the Mexican painter Frida Kahlo or the American artist Georgia O'Keeffe.

Though men can be subjects of sexism and sexual harassment, women are more likely to experience this form of discrimination. Even the most well-intentioned people may behave in ways that hurt or discount women. Sexism takes place when:

- instructors use only masculine pronouns—*he, his,* and *him*—to refer to both men and women.

- career counselors hint that careers in mathematics and science are not appropriate for women.

- students pay more attention to feedback from a male teacher than from a female teacher.

- women are not called on in class, their comments are ignored, or they are overly praised for answering the simplest questions.

- examples given in a textbook or lecture assign women to only traditionally "female" roles— wife, mother, daycare provider, elementary school teacher, nurse, and the like.

- people assume that middle-aged women who return to school have too many family commitments to study adequately or do well in their classes.

Many kinds of behavior—both verbal and physical—fall under the title of sexual harassment. *Sexual Harassment: It's Not Academic,* a pamphlet from the U.S. Department of Education, quotes women who experienced harassment in higher education:

- *I was discussing my work in a public setting when a professor cut me off and asked if I had freckles all over my body.*

- *The professor made a fool of himself pursuing me . . . and then blurted, "You know I want to sleep with you; I have a great deal of influence. Now, of course I don't want to force you into anything, but I'm sure you're going to be sensible about this."*

- *The financial officer made it clear that I could get the money I needed if I slept with him.*

- Playboy *centerfolds were used as Anatomy teaching slides. . . . In slides, lectures, teaching aids, and even our own student note service, we found that nurses were presented as sexy, bitchy, or bossy but never as professional health care workers.*

The feminist movement has raised our awareness about discrimination against women. We can now respond to sexism and sexual harassment in the places we live, work, and go to school. Specific strategies follow.

Point out sexist language and behavior

When you see examples of sexism, point them out. Your message can be more effective if you use "I" messages instead of personal attacks, as explained in Chapter Ten. Point out the specific statements and actions that you consider sexist. You could rephrase a sexist comment so that it targets another group, such as

African Americans or Jews. People may spot anti-Semitism or racism more readily than sexism.

Keep in mind that men can also be subjects of sexism, ranging from antagonistic humor to exclusion from jobs that have traditionally been done by women.

Observe your own language and behavior

Looking for sexist behavior in others is effective. Detecting it in yourself can be just as powerful. Write a Discovery Statement about specific comments that could be heard as sexist. Then notice if you say these things. Also ask people you know to point out such statements. Follow up with an Intention Statement that describes how you plan to change your speaking or behavior.

Encourage support for women

Through networks, women can work to overcome the effects of sexism. Strategies include study groups for women, women's job networks, and professional organizations, such as Women in Communications. Other examples are counseling services and health centers for women, family planning agencies, and rape prevention centers. Check your school catalog and library to see if these are available at your school.

If your school does not have the women's networks you want, form them. Sponsor a one-day or one-week conference on women's issues. Create a discussion or reading group for the women in your class, department, residence hall, union, or neighborhood.

Set limits

Women, value yourselves. Recognize your right to an education without the distraction of inappropriate and invasive behavior. Trust your judgment about when your privacy or your rights are being violated. Decide now what kind of sexual comments and actions you're uncomfortable with—and refuse to put up with them.

If you are sexually harassed, take action

Some key federal legislation protects the rights of women. One is Title VII of the Civil Rights Act of 1964. Guidelines for interpreting this law offer the following definition of harassment.

Unwelcome sexual advances, requests for sexual favors, and other verbal or physical conduct of a sexual nature constitute sexual harassment when:

1) *Submission to this conduct becomes a condition of employment.*

2) *Women's response to such conduct is used as a basis for employment decisions.*

3) *This conduct interferes with work performance or creates an offensive work environment.*

The law also states that schools must take action to prevent sexual harassment.

Another relevant law is Title IX of the Education Amendments of 1972. This act bans discrimination against students and employees on the basis of sex. It applies to any educational program receiving federal funds.

Learn your school's procedures for enforcing these laws and use them when appropriate. Federal government agencies, such as the Office for Civil Rights and the Equal Employment Opportunity Commission, can also help.

Your community and school may also offer resources to protect women against discrimination. Examples are public interest law firms, legal aid societies, and unions that employ lawyers to represent students.

. . . and sexual harassment

Students with disabilities—
ASK FOR WHAT YOU WANT

Equal opportunity for people with disabilities is the law. In the United States, both the Civil Rights Act of 1964 and the Rehabilitation Act of 1973 offer legal protection. The Americans with Disabilities Act of 1990 extends earlier legislation.

It used to be that students with disabilities faced a restricted set of choices in school. For instance, many had trouble majoring in subjects that called for using technical equipment—engineering, science, or medicine. New technology, such as computers and calculators operated with voice commands, can change that. Students with disabilities may now choose from any course or major offered in higher education.

Even the most well-intentioned instructors can forget about promoting learning for people with disabilities. That's when it pays for you to speak up. Begin with the suggestions in Chapter Ten for being assertive, using "I" messages, and listening actively. All of them can help you succeed in school. So can the following.

Use available resources

A wealth of resources already exists to support your success in school. To start, check into services offered by your state. Departments of rehabilitation often provide funds for education or can help you find that money. State commissions on disabilities can guide you to services. In addition, the Job Accommodation Network (1-800-526-7234) offers help in placing employees with learning or physical disabilities.

Also find out about services at your school. Libraries might furnish books in Braille or on audiotapes for the visually impaired. Many counseling and student health centers target certain services to people with disabilities. Some schools offer disability resource centers. Other services to ask about include:

- permits that allow you to park a car closer to classrooms.
- note-taking services.
- lecture transcriptions.
- textbook reading services and textbooks on tape.
- sign language interpreters.

- help in selecting courses and registering for classes.
- assistants for laboratory courses in science.
- shuttle buses for transportation between classes.
- closed captioning for instructional television programs.
- TTY/TDD devices for students with hearing impairments.
- assistance with taking tests.

Speak assertively

Tell instructors when it's appropriate to consider your disability. If you use a wheelchair, for example, ask for appropriate transportation on field trips. If you have a visual disability, request that instructors speak as they write on the chalkboard. Also ask them to use high-contrast colors and to write legibly.

Plan ahead

Meet with your counselor or adviser to design an educational plan—one that takes your disability into account. A key part of this plan is choosing instructors. Ask for recommendations before you register for classes. Interview prospective instructors and sit in on their classes. Express an interest in the class, ask to see a course outline, and discuss any adjustments that could help you successfully complete the course. Some of the services you request may take extra time to deliver. Allow for possible delays as you plan your schedule.

Use empowering words

Changing just a few words can make the difference between asking for what you want and apologizing for it. When people refer to disabilities, you might hear words like *special treatment, accommodation,* and *adaptation.* Experiment with using *adjustment* and *alternative* instead. The difference between these terms is equality. Asking for an adjustment in an assignment is asking for the right to produce equal work—not for special treatment that "waters down" the assignment.

Ask for appropriate treatment

Many instructors are eager to help you. At times they might go overboard. For example, a student who has trouble writing by hand might ask to complete in-class writing assignments on a computer. "OK," the teacher replies, "and take a little extra time. For you there's no rush."

For some students this is a welcome response. For others there is no need for an extended time line. They can say, "Thank you for thinking of me. I'd prefer to finish the assignment in the time frame allotted for the rest of the class."

Take care of yourself

Many students with chronic illnesses or disabilities find that rest breaks are essential. If this is true for you, write such breaks into your daily or weekly plan.

A related suggestion is to treat yourself with respect. If your health changes in a way that you don't like, avoid berating yourself. Even when you do not choose the conditions in your life, you can choose your attitude toward those conditions.

It's important to accept compliments and periodically review your accomplishments in school. Fill yourself with affirmation. As you educate yourself, you are attaining mastery.

EXERCISE #26
EXPLORE STEREOTYPES

Gather with a diverse group of students and on a separate sheet of paper, write your answers to this question: What do you never again want to hear people say about your race, ethnic group, or culture? Share your answers.

JOURNAL ENTRY #41
DISCOVERY/INTENTION STATEMENT

Review your experience with Exercise #26. Describe how you felt doing the exercise, along with any new insights into bias and stereotyping.

I discovered that I . . .

_____

_____

_____

_____

_____

_____

Also list any changes in your speaking or behavior that you want to make after doing this exercise.

I intend to . . .

_____

_____

_____

_____

_____

_____

PRACTICING
CRITICAL THINKING #14

On a separate sheet of paper, write down the first words that come to mind when you hear the following terms: musician, Eskimo, homeless people, mathematicians, football players, Rhodes scholars. Do this now.

Next, exchange lists with a friend. Discuss any evidence of stereotypes or bias in the responses. Write down your conclusions.

What counts as evidence of bias? Why? Write a brief response.

Choose your conversations
and your community

Certain things are real for us because we can see them, touch them, hear them, smell them, or feel them. Books, pencils, tables, chairs, food, other people—all are real in this sense. Much of the time they enter our lives in a straightforward, uncomplicated way.

Many other aspects of our lives, however, do not have this kind of reality. None of us can point to a purpose, for example. Nor would a purpose step up and introduce itself or buy you lunch. The same is true about other abstract concepts, such as quality, intelligence, love, trust, human rights, or student success.

Such ideas are created by our words. They don't really exist until we begin talking about them. According to communication theorist Lee Thayer[5], these concepts come alive for us only to the degree that we define them, discuss them, question them, debate them, read about them, and write about them. In short, we create and sustain these ideas by staying in conversations about them. Through our words, we make them so. And, as S.I. Hayakawa's[6] study of general semantics reminds us, the ideas we create through conversation translate into our actions.

Keep in mind that conversations can exist in many forms. One involves people talking out loud to each other. At other times, the conversation takes place inside our head and we call it thinking. We are even having a conversation when we read a book or magazine, watch television or a movie, or write a letter or a report.

Conversations shape our lives

All this has three implications that wind their way through every aspect of our lives. One is that conversations exercise incredible power over what we think, feel, and do. We become our conversations. They shape our attitudes, our decisions, our opinions, our emotions, and our actions. Each of these results largely from what we say over and over again, to ourselves and others. If you want clues as to what a person will be like tomorrow, listen to what she's talking about today.

Conversation is constant

This leads to a second discovery. Given that conversations are so powerful, it's amazing how few people act on this fact. They swim in a constant sea of conversations, almost none of which they genuinely choose.

Consider how this works. It begins when we pick up the morning paper. The articles on the front page invite us to a conversation about current events. Often the headlines speak of war, famine, unemployment figures, and other species of disaster. The advertisements start up a conversation about fantastic products for us to buy. They talk about hundreds of ways for us to part with our money.

That's not all. If we flip on the radio or television, scores of other conversations await us. Thanks to modern technology, many of these conversations take place in stereo, high-resolution images, and living color 24 hours each day.

Something happens when we tune in to conversation in any of its forms. We give someone else permission to dramatically influence our thoughts—the conversation in our heads. When we watch a movie, that movie becomes the images in our minds. When we read a book, that book becomes the voice in our heads. It's possible to let this happen dozens of times each day without realizing it.

You have a choice

The real power of this process lies in a third discovery: You can choose your conversations. Certain conversations create real value for us. They give us fuel for reaching our goals. Others distract us from what we want. They might even create lasting unhappiness and frustration.

We can choose more of the conversations that exhilarate and sustain us. Sometimes we can't control the outward circumstances of our lives. Yet no matter what happens, we retain the right to choose two empowering conversations: We can talk about where to focus our attention and what to do next.

Suppose that you meet with an instructor to ask for some guidelines for writing a term paper. She launches into a tirade about your writing skills and lack of preparation for higher education. This presents you with several options. One is to talk about what a jerk the instructor is and give up on the idea of learning to write well. Another option is to refocus the conversation on what you can do to improve your writing skills. You can follow up by working with a writing tutor or taking a basic composition class. These two sets of conversations will have vastly different consequences for your success in school.

The conversations we have are dramatically influenced by the people we associate with. If you want to change your attitudes about almost anything—prejudice, politics, religion, humor—then choose your conversation by choosing your community. Spend time with people who speak and live out the attitudes you value. Use conversations to change habits. Use conversations to create new options in your life.

A big part of this Power Process is choosing not to participate in certain conversations. Sometimes we find ourselves in conversations that are not empowering—gripe sessions, gossip, and the like. That's a time for us to switch the conversation channel. It can be as simple as excusing ourselves and walking away. Sometimes we can redirect the conversation by posing a new question or introducing a new topic. At other times we can choose to stop reading certain books or cease watching some television programs. We might choose not to be with certain people. We might leave a job, seek a new place to live, or withdraw from certain projects.

Some conversations are about antagonism. Instead of resolving conflict, they fan the flames of prejudice, half-truths, and misunderstanding. We can begin taking charge of these conversations by noticing where they start and how they continue.

You can take charge of the conversation inside your head too. If that conversation is not consistent with your goals and values, just pick up a pencil. Write a letter to a friend, or to yourself. Write a Discovery Statement about the movie inside your head, and then start writing a new script with dialogue that empowers you.

Conversations promote success

All this gets down to succeeding in school. Excelling in higher education means allowing plenty of time for the conversations that start in class and continue in our textbooks and notes. You can extend those conversations by visiting the instructor during office hours, talking to classmates, and forming study groups. You can read other books and engage in other conversations that support your work in school.

Right now you're holding a conversation about student success. This conversation has a big red cover that features the words *Becoming a Master Student*. Its chapters invite you to 12 sub-conversations that can make a real difference in what you get for your hard-earned tuition money.

When we choose our conversations, we discover a tool of unsurpassed power. This tool has the capacity to remake our thoughts—and thus our lives. It's as simple as choosing the next article you read or the topic you discuss with a friend.

Begin applying this Power Process today. Start choosing your conversations and watch what happens.

JOURNAL ENTRY #42
DISCOVERY STATEMENT

In the space below, list two conversations you've had today and summarize their content. Now reflect on those conversations. Determine whether they were in line with your values and goals. Write down your ideas.

_____

_____

_____

_____

_____

_____

_____

_____

_____

_____

_____

_____

_____

_____

_____

_____

_____

_____

_____

_____

master student

charlayne hunter-gault

one of two students to desegregate the University of Georgia, is a national correspondent for PBS's "NewsHour" with Jim Lehrer

I studied the comic-strip character Brenda Starr as I might have studied a journalism textbook, had there been one. I had been reading the funny papers, as we called them, all my life, and along with Dick Tracy and Dagwood, Brenda Starr was one of my favorite characters. I loved her sense of adventure, and the adventures she was always having as the star reporter on the *New York Daily Flash*. I especially loved the mystery and romance in her life, a lot of which was supplied by Basil St. John, a one-eyed

connoisseur of black orchids. The fact that Brenda Starr was a redheaded, blue-eyed white woman who worked in an all-white newsroom did not even register with me until, one day during my senior year, I had a conversation with my counselor about what I wanted to do after I graduated. "I want to be a reporter." By that time, I had been editor of the paper for two years—the first junior ever to be appointed to the position, thanks to Mrs. Evans.

"You better hang up those pipe dreams and go on over there to Spelman [the black women's college] and become a teacher," she told me in all seriousness. And while she didn't say it in so many words, it was clear to me what she meant: Journalism is a white man's profession; even your precious Brenda Starr is an exception! I later told Mrs. Evans about the conversation; she looked at me the way she usually did when she was about to cut with a verbal knife so sharp it left no visible marks, and said ever so sweetly, "Now, we know what to do with advice like that, don't we?"

Excerpt from In My Place
by Charlayne Hunter-Gault
Copyright © 1992 by Charlayne Hunter-Gault.
Reprinted by permission of Farrar, Straus & Giroux, Inc.
and Sterling Lord Literistic.

1 *Racial, ethnic, and other kinds of diversity have become key factors in our lives only in the last decade or two. True or False. Explain your answer.*

2 *List the strategies for communicating across cultures.*

3 *Give two examples of sexist behavior that could take place in higher education.*

4 *Explain the difference between an adjusted assignment and an alternative assignment as it can apply to a student with a disability.*

5 *Give three examples of the ways that higher education can differ from high school.*

6 *Define the term* academic freedom.

7 *Define the terms* translator, mediator, *and* model *as explained in this chapter and give one example of each term.*

8 *Explain how creating stability zones can help you adapt to the culture of higher education.*

9 *Whether you are a traditional or a nontraditional student, describe at least three suggestions for older students returning to school that you could use.*

10 *Explain four strategies for taking charge of the conversations in your life.*

JOURNAL ENTRY #43
DISCOVERY/INTENTION STATEMENT

After reviewing this chapter, describe what you learned about the way you relate to people from different racial, ethnic, or cultural backgrounds.

> *I discovered that I . . .*

_____

_____

> *Now choose two suggestions for communicating across cultures and describe how you will use them to promote your success in school.*

> *I intend to . . .*

_____

_____

_____

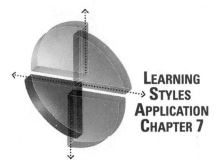

**LEARNING
STYLES
APPLICATION
CHAPTER 7**

Style 1
Brainstorm a list of the most valuable suggestions you gained from this chapter on the following topics.

• Exploring your potential biases and lack of knowledge about other cultures

• Building relationships with people from other cultures

Style 2
Describe any examples of discrimination, sexism, or sexual harassment you've personally witnessed.

Style 3
Create a list of five major goals you'd like to accomplish in your lifetime. For each goal, list three majors that could provide the skills and knowledge needed to accomplish that goal.

Style 4
List three specific actions you can take to begin conversations that promote your success in school. For ideas, review Power Process #7: "Choose your conversations and your community."

Bibliography

■ Endnotes

[1] Dorothy Lee, *Freedom and Culture* (Englewood Cliffs, NJ: Prentice-Hall, 1959).

[2] Steven R. Covey, *The Seven Habits of Highly Effective People: Restoring the Character Ethic* (New York: Simon & Schuster, 1989).

[3] James Anderson, personal communication, 1990.

[4] Diane de Anda, *Bicultural Socialization: Factors Affecting the Minority Experience* (Washington, DC: National Association of Social Workers, 1984).

[5] Lee Thayer, "Communication—Sine Qua Non of the Behavioral Sciences" in David L. Arm (ed.), *Vistas in Science* (Albuquerque, NM: University of New Mexico, 1968).

[6] S. I. Hayakawa, *Language in Thought and Action* (New York: Harcourt Brace Jovanovich, 1939).

■ Additional Reading

Beckham, Barry, ed. *The Black Student's Guide to Colleges*, Hampton, VA: Beckham House, 1984.

Burke, Anna Mae Walsh. *Are You Ready: A Survival Manual for Women Returning to School*, Englewood Cliffs, NJ: Prentice-Hall, 1980.

Condon, John C., and Fathi S. Yousef. *Introduction to Intercultural Communication*, New York: Macmillan, 1975.

Hecht, Miriam, and Lillian Traub. *Dropping Back In: How to Complete Your College Education Quickly and Economically*, New York: E. P. Dutton, 1982.

Katz, Montana, and Veronica Vieland. *Get Smart! A Woman's Guide to Equality on Campus*, New York: Feminist Press, 1988.

thinking

In this chapter...

go deeply into a skill that underlies most of what you do in school—thinking. Learn specific techniques for **creating new ideas,** thinking critically, uncovering assumptions, spotting logical fallacies, solving problems, and making decisions. Also think about math and science with more ease, and use computers to think more powerfully.

JOURNAL ENTRY #44
DISCOVERY STATEMENT

Describe a time when you felt stuck in your thinking, unable to choose among several different solutions to a problem or several stands on a key issue in your life. List the specific time, place, and circumstances involved.

_____
_____
_____
_____
_____
_____
_____
_____

Now scan this chapter for any useful ideas or techniques on decision making and critical thinking. Note below any strategies that look especially promising to you.

I discovered that I might be able to improve my thinking skills by . . .

_____
_____
_____
_____
_____
_____
_____

Critical thinking: A survival skill

SOCIETY DEPENDS ON PERSUASION. Advertisers want you to spend money. Political candidates want you to "buy" their stands on the issues. Teachers want you to agree that their classes are vital to your success. Parents want you to accept their values. Authors want you to read their books. Broadcasters want you to spend your time in front of the radio or television, consuming their programs and not those from the competition. The business of persuasion embraces all of us.

According to one estimate, a typical American sees 30,000 television commercials each year. And that's just one medium of communication. Add to that the writers and speakers who enter your life through radio, magazines, books, brochures, and fund-raising appeals—all with a product, service, cause, or opinion for you to embrace.

This leaves us with hundreds of choices about what to buy, what to do, and who to be. It's easy to lose our heads in the crosscurrent of competing ideas—unless we develop skills in critical thinking. When we think critically, we make choices with open eyes.

Uses of critical thinking

Critical thinking underlies reading, writing, speaking, and listening. These are the basic elements of communication—a process that occupies most of our waking hours.

Critical thinking also plays an important part in social change. Consider that the institutions in any society—courts, governments, schools, businesses—are the products of a certain way of thinking.

> **" "**
> Creativity was in each one of us as a small child. In children it is universal. Among adults it is almost nonexistent. The great question is: What has happened to this enormous and universal human capacity? That is the question of the age.
> –TILLIE OLSEN

> **" "**
> I always wanted to be somebody, but I should've been more specific.
> –LILY TOMLIN

> **" "**
> In most lives insight has been accidental. We wait for it as a primitive man awaited lightning for a fire. But making mental connections is our most crucial learning tool; the essence of human intelligence is to forge links; to go beyond the given; to see pattern, relationships, context.
> –MARILYN FERGUSON

Any organization draws its life from certain assumptions about the way things should be done. Before the institution can change, those assumptions need to be loosened up or reinvented. In many ways, the real location of an institution is inside our heads.

Critical thinking also helps us uncover bias and prejudice. This is a first step toward communicating with people of other races and cultures.

Crises occur when our thinking fails to keep pace with reality. An example is the ecological crisis, which sprang from the assumption that people could pollute the earth, air, and water without long-term consequences. Consider how different our world would be if our leaders had thought like the first woman chief of the Cherokees. Asked about the best advice her elders had given her, she said, "Look forward. Turn what has been done into a better path. If you are a leader, think about the impact of your decision on seven generations into the future."

Novelist Ernest Hemingway once said that anyone who wanted to be a great writer must have a built-in, shockproof crap detector. That inelegant comment points to a perennial truth: As critical thinkers, we can be constantly on the lookout for thinking that's inaccurate, sloppy, or misleading.

This is a skill that will never go out of style. History offers a continuing story of half-truths, faulty assumptions, and other nonsense once commonly accepted as true:

- Bloodsucking leeches can be used to cure disease.

- Illnesses result from an imbalance in the four vital fluids: blood, phlegm, water, and bile.

- Racial integration of the armed forces will lead to the destruction of soldiers' morale.

- Caucasians are inherently more intelligent than people of other races.

- Mixing the blood of the races will lead to genetically inferior offspring.

- Women are incapable of voting intelligently.

- We will never invent anything smaller than a transistor. (That was before the computer chip.)

- Computers will usher in the age of the paperless office.

In response to such ideas rose the critical thinkers of history. These men and women courageously pointed out that—metaphorically speaking—the emperor had no clothes.

Critical thinking is a path to freedom from half-truths and deception. You have the right to question what you see, hear, and read. Acquiring this ability is one of the major goals of a liberal education.

Critical thinking as thorough thinking

For some people, the term *critical thinking* has negative connotations. If you prefer, use the words *thorough thinking* instead. Both terms point to the same array of activities: sorting out conflicting claims, weighing the evidence for them, letting go of personal biases, and arriving at reasonable views. This adds up to an ongoing conversation, a constant practice—a process, not a product.

We live in a society that seems to value quick answers and certainty. This is often at odds with effective thinking. Thorough thinking is the ability to examine and re-examine ideas that may seem obvious. Such thinking takes time and the willingness to say three subversive words: *I don't know.*

Thorough thinking is also the willingness to change our point of view as we continue to examine a problem. This calls for courage and detachment. Just ask anyone who has given up a cherished point of view in light of new evidence.

Skilled students are thorough thinkers. They distinguish between opinion and fact. They ask powerful questions. They make detailed observations. They uncover assumptions and define their terms. They make assertions carefully, basing them on sound logic and solid evidence. Almost everything that we call *knowledge* is a result of these activities. This means that critical thinking and learning are intimately linked.

It's been said that human beings are rational creatures. Yet no one is born a thorough thinker. This is a learned skill. Use the suggestions in this chapter to claim the vast, latent thinking powers that are your birthright.

Finding "aha!"—
Creativity fuels critical thinking

The first half of this book is about the nuts and bolts of education. It offers suggestions for ways to tell the truth about your skills as a student and ways to set goals to improve them. Also included are guidelines for managing your time, making your memory more effective, improving your reading skills, taking useful notes, and prospering during exams. Those techniques are about the business of acquiring knowledge.

The point of all this is not just to have knowledge. The point is to use original thinking to create new knowledge—not in a mechanical way, like a computer, but in imaginative and innovative ways. That's the primary agenda for the second half of this book, beginning with this chapter.

Begin with creative thinking, a powerful starting point for critical thinking. Creativity can expand our awareness and open the door to new points of view. Often it's powerful to generate many points of view on an issue or many answers to a question before we begin thinking critically about them.

Central to all this is something called the "aha!" experience. Nineteenth-century poet Emily Dickinson described the aha! this way: "If I feel physically as if the top of my head were taken off, I know that is poetry." Aha! is the burst of creative energy heralded by the arrival of a new, original idea. It is the sudden emergence of a new pattern, a previously undetected relationship, or an unusual combination of familiar elements. It is an exhilarating experience.

Aha! does not always result in a timeless poem or a Nobel Prize. It can be inspired by anything from playing a new riff on a guitar to discovering why your car's fuel pump doesn't work. A nurse might notice that one of his patients has a symptom everyone else missed. That's an aha! An accountant might discover a tax break for a client. That's an aha! A teacher might invent a way to reach a difficult student. Aha!

School is a natural breeding ground for aha!s. Term papers, speeches, math problems, science projects, even tests—all of these can inspire aha!, especially in the hands of skilled students. These students can be joyful, alive, energetic, and spontaneous. All of these qualities attract aha!

The flip side of aha! is following through. The creative process is both fun *and* work. It is effortless and uncomfortable. It's the result of luck and persistence. It involves spontaneity and step-by-step procedures.

Many people overlook the follow-up to creative thinking—critical thinking. The latter step involves molding and shaping a rough-cut idea into a polished creation. Employers in all fields are desperately seeking those rare people who can find aha! and do something with it. The necessary skills include the ability to spot assumptions, weigh evidence, separate fact from opinion, organize thoughts, and avoid errors in logic. You'll find more details on each of these topics throughout this chapter. All this can be demanding work. Just as often, it can be energizing and fun.

Use this chapter to discover the joy of aha! in creative thinking. Follow it up with skills at critical thinking, and you have a combination that can supercharge your success in school.

Tangram

A tangram is an ancient Chinese game that stimulates the "play instinct" so critical to creative thinking. The cat figure below was created by rearranging the seven sections of a square.

Hundreds of images can be created in this manner. Playing with tangrams allows you to see relationships you didn't see before. Rules of the game are simple: Use these seven pieces to create something that wasn't there before. Be sure to use all seven.

Make your own tangram by cutting pieces like those above out of poster board. When you make a pattern you like, trace around the outside edges of it and see if a friend can discover how you did it.

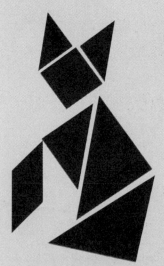

Techniques for creative thinking

You can use the following techniques to generate ideas about everything from term papers and math problems to remodeling a house or rewriting the Constitution. With practice, you can set the stage for creative leaps, jump with style, and land on your feet with brand-new ideas in your hands.

Conduct a brainstorm

Brainstorming is a technique for finding solutions, creating plans, and discovering new ideas. When you are stuck on a problem, brainstorming can break the logjam.

For example, if you run out of money two days before payday every week, you could brainstorm ways to make your money last longer. You can brainstorm ways to pay for your education. You can brainstorm ways to find a job.

The purpose of brainstorming is to generate as many solutions as possible. Sometimes the craziest, most outlandish solutions, while unworkable in themselves, lead to new ways to solve problems. The brainstorming process works like this:

First, formulate the issue or problem precisely by writing it down. For example, you might write, "Methods and techniques I can use to get more information about multinational trade organizations in Central Africa."

Next, set a time limit for your brainstorming session. Use a clock to time it to the minute. Digital sports watches with built-in stopwatches work well. Experiment with various lengths of time. Both short and long brainstorms can be powerful.

Before you begin, sit quietly for a few seconds to collect your thoughts. Then start timing and write as fast as you can.

Write down everything. Accept every idea. If it pops into your head, put it down on paper. Quantity, not quality, is the goal. Avoid making judgments and evaluations during the brainstorming session.

After the session, review, evaluate, and edit. Toss out the truly nutty ideas, but not before you give them a chance.

For example, during your brainstorm on Central African trade organizations you might have written, "Go to Central Africa and ask someone about them." Impossible? Are you certain your school wouldn't give you a semester of independent study to research the subjects? Are you positive a trade organization wouldn't offer a scholarship to pay for the trip?

Brainstorms often produce surprising solutions that look wacky at first and that later produce life-changing results. Stay open to possibilities.

Here are some other tips for brainstorming sessions.

Let go of the need for a particular solution. Brainstorming sessions can reveal new ways of thinking about old problems.

Relax. Creativity is enhanced by a state of relaxed alertness. If you are tense or anxious, use some of the relaxation techniques throughout the text.

Set a quota or goal for the number of solutions you want to generate. Goals give your subconscious mind something to aim for.

Use 3x5 cards for each solution. When you review your session, you can lay the cards out on a table and arrange them in patterns to look for relationships. Or you can arrange them in order of priority.

Brainstorm with others. This is a powerful technique. Group brainstorms take on lives of their own. Assign one member of the group to write down solutions. Feed off the ideas of others, and remember to avoid evaluating or judging anyone's idea during the brainstorm.

Multiply brainstorms. Pick one item from your first brainstorm and conduct another brainstorm about that idea.

Be wild and crazy. If you get stuck, think of an outlandish idea and write it down. One well-placed crazy idea can unleash a flood of other, more workable solutions.

Focus and let go

Focusing and letting go are alternating parts of the same process. Intense focus taps the resources of your conscious mind. Letting go gives your subconscious mind time to work. When you focus for intense periods and then let go for a while, the conscious and subconscious parts of your brain work in harmony. Each brings its own strengths and talents to produce the highest-quality result.

Focusing attention means being in the here and now. To focus your attention on a project, notice when you pay attention and notice when your mind wanders. And involve all your senses.

For example, if you are having difficulty composing at a typewriter or word processor, practice focusing by listening to the sounds as you type. Notice the feel of the keys as you strike them. When you know the sights, sounds, and sensations you associate with being truly in focus, you'll be able to repeat the experience and focus on your composing more easily.

You can use your body to focus your concentration. Some people concentrate better lying down. Others focus more easily if they stand or pace back and forth. Still others need to have something in their hands. Notice what works for you and use it.

Be willing to accept conflict, tension, and discomfort. Notice them and allow them to be, rather than fighting against them. Look for the specific thoughts and body sensations that make up the discomfort. Allow them to come fully into your awareness and let them pass.

You might not be focused all the time. Periods of inspiration may last only seconds. Be gentle with yourself when you notice your concentration has lagged.

In fact, that might be a time to let go. "Letting go" means not forcing yourself to be creative.

Practice focusing for short periods at first, then give yourself a break. Phone a friend. Get up and take a walk around your desk or around your block. Take a few minutes to look out your window. Listen to a couple of tunes on the stereo, or better yet, sing a few songs to yourself.

You also can break up periods of focused concentration with stretches, sit-ups, or pushups. Use relaxation and breathing exercises. Muscle tension and the lack of oxygen can inhibit self-expression.

Movies, music, walks in the park, and other pleasant activities stir the creative soup that's simmering in your brain.

Take a nap when you are tired. Thomas Edison took frequent naps. Then the light bulb clicked on.

Cultivate creative serendipity

The word *serendipity* comes from a story by Horace Walpole: "The Three Princes of Serendip." The princes had a knack for making lucky discoveries. Serendipity is that knack. This is more than luck. It is the ability to see something valuable that you weren't looking for. History is full of serendipitous people.

Edward Jenner noticed "by accident" that milkmaids seldom got smallpox. The result was his discovery that mild cases of cowpox immunized them. Penicillin also was discovered "by accident." Alexander Fleming was growing bacteria in a laboratory petri dish. A spore of *penicillium notatum*, a kind of mold, apparently blew in the window and landed in the dish. It killed the bacteria. Fleming isolated the active ingredient. A few years later, during World War II, it saved thousands of lives. Had Fleming not been alert to the possibility, the discovery might never have been made.

You can train yourself in the art of serendipity.

First, keep your eyes open. You might find a solution to an accounting problem in a Saturday morning cartoon. You might discover a term paper subject at the corner convenience store.

Multiply your contacts with the world. Resolve to meet new people. Join a study or discussion group. Read. Go to plays, concerts, art shows, lectures, and movies. Watch television programs you normally wouldn't watch. Use idea files and play with data, as described below.

Finally, expect discoveries. One secret of "luck" is being prepared to recognize it when you see it.

Keep idea files

We all have ideas. People labeled "creative" are those who treat their ideas with care. That means recognizing, recording, and following up on them.

One way to keep track of ideas is to write them on 3x5 cards. Invent your own categories and number the cards so you can cross-reference them. For example, if you have an idea about making a new kind of bookshelf, you might file it under "Remodeling." The card might also be filed under "Marketable Ideas." On one card, you can write your ideas, and on the other you can write, "See card #321—Remodeling."

Include in your files powerful quotes, random insights, notes on your reading, and useful ideas you encounter in class. Collect jokes too.

Keep a journal. Journals don't have to be exclusively about your thoughts and feelings. You can include your observations of the world around you, quotes from friends, important or offbeat ideas—anything.

To fuel your creativity, read voraciously, including newspapers and magazines. Keep a clip file of interesting articles. Explore beyond mainstream journalism. There are hundreds of small-circulation specialty magazines. They cover almost any subject you can imagine.

Keep letter-sized files of important correspondence, magazine and newspaper articles, and other material. You can also create idea files on a personal computer using word processing, outlining, or database software.

Safeguard your ideas even if you're pressed for time. Jotting down four or five words is enough to capture the essence of an idea. You can write down one quote in a minute or two. And if you carry 3x5 cards in a pocket or purse, you can record ideas while standing in a line or waiting for appointments to begin.

Review your files regularly. Something that was an amusing thought in November might be the perfect solution to a problem the following March.

Collect and play with data

Look from all sides at the data you collect. Switch your attention from one aspect to another. Examine each fact, and avoid getting stuck on one particular part of a problem.

Turn a problem upside down by picking a solution first, before you know it will work, and working backward. Ask other people to look at the data. Solicit opinions.

Living with the problem invites a solution. Write down data, possible solutions, or a formulation of the problem on 3x5 cards and carry them with you. Look at them before you go to bed at night. Review them when you are waiting for the bus. Make them part of your life and think about them frequently.

Look for the obvious solution or the obvious "truths" about the problem, then dump them! Ask yourself, "Well, I know X is true, but if X were not true, what would happen?" Or ask the reverse: "If that were true, what would follow next?"

Put unrelated facts next to each other and invent a relationship, even if it seems absurd at first. In *The Act of Creation*, novelist Arthur Koestler[1] writes that finding a context in which to combine opposites is the essence of creativity.

Make imaginary pictures with the data. Condense it. Categorize it. Put it in chronological order. Put it in alphabetical order. Put it in random order. Order it from most to least complex. Reverse all those orders. Look for opposites.

It has been said that there are no new ideas, only new ways to combine old ideas. Creativity is the ability to discover those new combinations.

Create while you sleep

There's a part of our minds that works as we sleep. You've experienced this directly if you've ever fallen asleep with a problem on your mind and awakened the next morning with a solution. For some people, the solution appears in a dream or in the twilight consciousness just before falling asleep or waking.

You can experiment with this process. Ask yourself a question as you fall asleep. Keep pencil and paper or a tape recorder near your bed. The moment you wake up, begin writing or speaking and see if an answer to your question emerges.

To capture your ideas, keep a notebook by your bed at all times. Many people have awakened from a dream with a great idea, only to fall asleep and lose it. Put the notebook where you can find it easily.

Refine ideas and follow through

Many people ignore this part of the creative process. How many great money-making schemes have we had that we never pursued? How many good ideas have we had for short stories that we never wrote? How many times have we said to ourselves, "You know, what they ought to do is attach two handles to one of those things, paint it orange, and sell it to police departments. They'd make a fortune." And we never realize that we are "they."

Genius resides in the follow-through—the application of perspiration to inspiration. One powerful tool you can use to follow through is the Discovery and Intention Journal Entry System.

Write your idea in a Discovery Statement and then write what you intend to do about it in an Intention Statement. Use the guidelines listed in Chapter One.

You also can use the writing techniques in Chapter Nine as a guide for refining your ideas. Another way to refine an idea is to simplify it. And if that doesn't work, mess it up. Make it more complex.

Finally, keep a separate file in your idea file for your own inspirations. Return to it regularly to see if there is anything you can use. Today's defunct term paper idea could be next year's A in speech class.

Trust the process

Learn to trust your creative process—even when no answers are in sight. Often people are reluctant to look at problems if no immediate solution is in sight. They are impatient. If the answer isn't quickly apparent, they avoid frustration by giving up. Most of us do this to some degree with personal problems. If we are having difficulty with a relationship and don't see an immediate solution, we deny the problem's existence rather than face it.

Trust that a solution will show up. Frustration and a feeling of being stuck are often signals that a solution is imminent.

Sometimes solutions break through in a giant AHA! More often they come in a series of little aha!s. Be aware of what your aha!s look, feel, and sound like. That sets the stage for even more flights of creative thinking.

PRACTICING CRITICAL THINKING #15

Review the master student profiles included throughout this book. Focus on one person and explain how he or she displays qualities of a critical thinker. Summarize your conclusions in the space below.

_____

_____

_____

_____

_____

_____

_____

_____

_____

_____

_____

_____

_____

_____

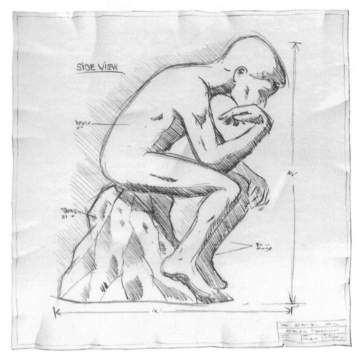

SIDE VIEW

Qualities of a critical thinker

Critical thinking is an approach to the world, a way of life that goes beyond skill or technique. Critical thinkers have hearts as well as heads, and their overall attitudes or habits of mind are at least as important as their arsenal of skills.

Critical thinkers trust their own reasoning, give fair-minded consideration to others' points of view, and even approach serious thinking in the spirit of play. As you read "The master student" in Chapter One and as you read the master student profiles throughout this book, you'll learn about real people who've shown these qualities.

During the late 1980s, the American Philosophical Association explored the qualities of a critical thinker, inviting 46 men and women from throughout the United States and Canada to take part in a research project. These scholars came from the sciences, the humanities, and education. Their task was to agree on answers to two questions: "What is college-level critical thinking?" and "What leads us to conclude that a person is an effective critical thinker?"

After two years of work, this panel emerged with a list of critical thinking dispositions—seven qualities that distinguish effective critical thinkers from other people. More details about each of these qualities follow, based on the writing of Peter Facione[2], dean of the College of Arts and Sciences, Santa Clara University.

1. Truth-seeking. Critical thinkers want to know truth. In their quest, they are willing to consider and even accept ideas that undermine their assumptions or self-interest. These thinkers follow reason and evidence wherever they lead.

"Critical thinkers are honest with themselves," writes Vincent Ryan Ruggiero[3], author of *Becoming a Critical Thinker.* "Through uncritical thinking, people deceive themselves. They pretend that the truth is what they wish it to be. They persuade themselves that they can drive 30 miles per hour over the speed limit without endangering themselves or others. They think drinking a six-pack of beer each day is no signal of a drinking problem, or that missing class has no effect on grades. . . . Critical thinkers avoid such maneuvers."

2. Open-minded. A skilled critical thinker not only recognizes that people disagree—she values this fact. She respects the right of others to express different views.

Beyond seeking out a variety of viewpoints, critical thinkers check their speaking and thinking for signs of bias. This skill, discussed in more detail in Chapter Seven, is crucial for dealing with the diversity of people on campus and on the job.

3. Analytical. The critical thinker recognizes statements that call for evidence. He is alert to potential problems. In addition, the critical thinker foresees possible consequences of adopting a point of view.

4. Systematic. Staying organized and focused are two more qualities of a critical thinker. She's willing to patiently gather evidence, test ideas, and stay with a tough or complex question.

5. Self-confident. This quality of a critical thinker supports the others. Since he trusts his intellectual skills, the critical thinker is willing to seek truth, listen with an open mind, and do the hard and useful work of thinking.

6. Inquisitive. The critical thinker wants to know. She is hungry for facts and concepts. She is willing to explore the universe of ideas even before she knows how to apply the insights she gains.

7. Mature. As a mature person, the critical thinker possesses a wisdom born of experience. He understands that a problem can have several solutions—even solutions that seem to contradict each other. He resists the desire to reach quick, superficial answers, and he is willing to suspend judgment when evidence is incomplete. At the same time, he recognizes that human beings are often called to act before all the facts are in.

Finding a critical thinker in yourself and others

The critical thinker is more than a concept or abstract idea. With some experience, you can learn to recognize the qualities of a critical thinker in yourself and the people around you. You can listen for and generate statements such as these:

"Let's follow this idea and see where it leads, even if we feel uncomfortable with what we find out." (TRUTH-SEEKING)

"I have a point of view on this subject, and I'm anxious to hear yours as well." (OPEN-MINDED)

"Taking this stand on the issue commits me to take some new actions." (ANALYTICAL)

"The speaker made several interesting points, and I'd like to hear some more evidence to support each one." (SYSTEMATIC)

"After reading this book for the first time, I was confused. I'll be able to understand it after studying the book some more." (SELF-CONFIDENT)

"When I saw that painting for the first time, I wanted to know what was going on in the artist's life when she painted it." (INQUISITIVE)

"I'll wait to reach a conclusion on this issue until I gather some more facts." (MATURE)

The critical thinker is one aspect of the master student who lives inside you.

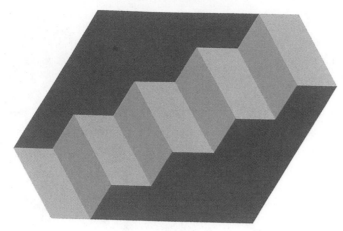

Becoming a critical thinker

Critical thinking is a path to intellectual adventure. Though there are dozens of possible approaches, the process can be boiled down to concrete steps. This article offers some starting points for your journey.

Think of the following suggestions as a toolbox for critical thinking. For other handy implements, see the articles in this chapter about uncovering assumptions and detecting logical fallacies. Also see *Becoming a Critical Thinker* by Vincent Ryan Ruggiero.

Be willing to say "I don't know"

Some of the most profound thinkers of our time have practiced the art of critical thinking by using two magic phrases: *I don't know* and *I'm not sure yet.*

Those are words many people do not like to hear. We live in times when people are criticized for changing their minds. Our society rewards quick answers and quotable "sound bites." We're under considerable pressure to utter the truth in 15 seconds or less.

In such a society, it is a courageous and unusual act to pause, to look, to examine, to be thoughtful, to consider many points of view—and to not know. When a society embraces half-truths in a blind rush for certainty, commitment to uncertainty can move us forward.

This willingness to give up certainty can be hardest to accept when it comes to notions that seem obvious. "Many things are certain," some people say. "For example, it's obvious that two plus two equals four."

Think again. When we use the base-three number system, two plus two equals 11. A child learning to write numerals might insist that two and two makes 22. And a biologist might joke that two plus two adds up to a whole lot more than four when we're talking about the reproductive life of rabbits.

Even scientific knowledge is not certain. At a moment's notice, the world can deviate from what we call "laws" of nature. Those laws exist inside our heads—not in the world. What's more, modern science tells us many things that contradict everyday certainties. For example, physics presents us with a world where solid objects are made of atoms spinning around in empty space, where matter and energy are two forms of the same thing. Even in mathematics and the "hard" sciences, the greatest advances take place when age-old beliefs are re-examined.

Define your terms

Imagine two people arguing about whether an employer should extend family health care benefits to people who live together but are unmarried. To one person, the word *family* means a mother, father, and children. The other person applies the word *family* to any long-term, supportive relationships between people who live together. Chances are, the debate will go nowhere until these people realize they're defining the same word in different ways.

Much opinion conflict can be resolved—or at least clarified—when we define our key terms up front. This is especially true with abstract, emotion-laden terms such as *freedom*, *peace*, *progress*, or *justice*. Blood has been shed over the meaning of these words. It pays for us to define them with care.

Practice tolerance

Having opinions about issues is natural. When you stop having opinions, you're probably not breathing anymore. The problem comes when we hold opinions in a way that leads to defensiveness, putdowns, or putoffs.

Going hand in hand with critical thinking is tolerance for attitudes that differ from yours. Consider that many of the ideas we currently accept—democracy, Christianity, voting rights for women, civil rights for people of color—were once considered the claims of "dangerous" and unpopular minorities. This historical perspective helps us accept a tenet of critical thinking: What seems outlandish today may become widely accepted a century, a decade, or even a year from now.

Understand before criticizing

When encountering any new viewpoint, we're not obligated to agree. Even so, critical thinking demands that we take the time to *understand* an idea before rejecting or modifying it. One mark of skilled debaters is that they can sum up the viewpoints they disagree with—often better than the people who *hold* those viewpoints can.

Strictly speaking, none of us live in the same world. Our habits, preferences, outlooks, and values are as individual as our fingerprints. Each of them is shaped by our culture, our upbringing, our experiences, and our choices. Speeches, books, articles, works of art, television programs, views expressed in conversation—all come from people who inhabit a different world than yours. Until we've lived in another person's world for a while, it's ineffective to dismiss her point of view.

This basic principle is central to many professions. Physicians diagnose before they prescribe. Lawyers brief themselves on the opponent's case. Effective teachers find out what a student already knows before they guide her to new ideas. Skilled salespeople find out what a customer's needs are before they present a product.

Effective understanding calls for listening without judgment. To enter another person's world, sum up her viewpoint in your own words. If you're conversing with that person, keep revising your summary until she agrees you've stated her position accurately. If you're reading an article, write a short summary of it. Then scan the article again, checking to see if your summary is on track.

Many of us find it difficult to fully permit others a point of view that is much different from ours. Instead we can actually celebrate other people's opinions, knowing that diversity leads to valuable new ideas.

Watch for hot spots

Notice any anger or discomfort you feel when conversations shift to certain topics. During a presidential election, for instance, politics often becomes a "hot spot"—an area in which defenses rise, assumptions run rampant, and tempers quickly flare. All these things get in the way of thinking thoroughly.

Most of us have hot spots. For some people they include abortion or handgun control. Other people heat up when they talk about the death penalty or world government.

It pays for each of us to discover our special hot spots. We can also make a clear intention to practice critical thinking when we encounter these topics.

To cool down your hot spots, seek out the whole world of ideas. Avoid intellectual ruts. Read magazines and books that challenge the opinions you currently hold. If you consider yourself liberal, pick up the *National Review*. If you are a socialist, sample the *Wall Street Journal*. Do the same with radio and television programs. Make it a point to talk with people who differ from you in education level, race, ethnic group, or political affiliation. And to hone your thinking skills, practice defending an idea you consider outrageous.

Also remember that your current opinions and your basic identity are not the same. For more details, see Power Process #1: "Ideas are tools" and Power Process #6: "Detach."

Consider the source

Look again at that article on the unfeasibility of cars powered by natural gas; it may have been written by an executive from an oil company. Check out the "authority" who disputes the connection between smoking and lung cancer; that person might be the president of a tobacco company.

This is not to say that we should dismiss the ideas of people who have a vested interest in their opinions. Rather, we can seek out contrasting viewpoints on these issues.

Seek out alternative views

Imagine Karl Marx, Cesar Chavez, and Donald Trump gathered in one room to choose the most desirable economic system. Picture Gandhi, Winnie Mandela, and General George Patton in a seminar on conflict resolution. Visualize Jesse Jackson, Bill Clinton, and Mother Theresa in a discussion about how to balance the national budget. When you seek out alternative points of view, such events can take place in your mind's arena.

Dozens of viewpoints exist on every critical issue—how to reduce crime, end world hunger, prevent war, educate our children, and countless others. In fact, few problems allow for any permanent solution. Each generation produces new answers, based on current conditions. Our search for answers is a conversation that spans centuries. On each question, many voices are waiting to be heard. You can take advantage of this diversity by seeking out alternative viewpoints.

Ask questions

Stripped to its essence, critical thinking means asking and answering questions. If you want to practice this skill, get into the habit of asking powerful questions.

In *How to Read a Book*, Mortimer Adler and Charles Van Doren[4] list four questions that sum up the whole task of thinking about another person's ideas:

1. What is the writing or speech about as a whole? To answer this question, state the basic theme in one sentence. Then list the major and minor topics covered.

2. What is being said in detail, and how? List the main terms, assertions, arguments. Also state what problems the writer or speaker is trying to solve.

3. Is it true? Examine the author's logic and evidence. Look for missing information, faulty information, incomplete analysis, and errors in reasoning. Also determine which problems the writer or speaker truly solved and which remain unsolved.

4. What of it? After answering the first three questions, prepare to change your thinking or behavior as a result of encountering new ideas.

These four questions apply not only to reading but also to any other intellectual activity. They get to the heart of critical thinking.

Look for at least three answers

When asking questions, we can let go of the temptation to settle for just one answer. Once you have come up with an answer, say to yourself, "Yes, that is one answer. Now what's another?" Using this approach can sustain honest inquiry, fuel creativity, and lead to conceptual breakthroughs.

Be prepared: The world is complicated, and critical thinking is a complex business. Some of your answers may contradict each other. Resist the temptation to have all your ideas in a neat, orderly bundle.

Be willing to change your mind

So many discussions generate heat instead of light. Often the people involved come already committed to certain viewpoints—which they have no intention of changing. They might just as well stop talking to each other.

We can avoid this trap by entering discussions with an open mind. When talking to another person, be willing to walk away with a new point of view—even if it's the one you brought to the table. After thinking thoroughly, we can adopt new viewpoints or hold our current viewpoints in a different way.

Lay your cards on the table

Science and uncritical thinking differ in many ways. Uncritical thinkers shield themselves from new information and ideas. In contrast, scientists constantly look for facts that contradict their theories. In fact, science never proves anything once and for all. Scientific theories are tentative and subject to change. Scientists routinely practice critical thinking.

We can follow their example. When talking or writing, we can put all our ideas on the table for examination. We can allow others to fully examine our opinions and beliefs. When doing so, we make room for new ideas that can make a real difference in our lives.

Examine the problem from different points of view

Imagine that two people are standing across from each other. Between them, suspended from the ceiling at eye level, is a ball. One person argues that the ball is red. The other person claims that the ball is green. As they rotate their positions and change their points of view, they see that the ball is actually red on one side and green on the other.

Sometimes new ideas are born when we view the world from a new angle. When early scientists watched the skies, they concluded that the sun revolved around the earth. Later, when we gained the mathematical tools to "stand" in another place, we could clearly see that the earth was revolving around the sun. This change in position not only sparked new thinking—it permanently changed our picture of the universe.

Write about it

Thoughts move randomly at blinding speed. Writing slows that process down. Gaps in logic that slip by us in thought or speech are often exposed when we commit the same ideas to paper. Doing so allows us to see all points of view on an issue more clearly—and therefore to think thoroughly. Writing is an unparalleled way to practice precise, accurate thinking.

Construct a reasonable view

One humorist compared finding the truth to painting a barn door by throwing open cans of paint at it. Few people who throw at the door miss it entirely. Yet no one can really cover the whole door in one toss.

People who express their viewpoints are seeking truth. Yet almost no reasonable person claims to have covered the whole barn door—to have the Whole Truth about anything. Instead, each viewpoint is one approach among many possible approaches. If you don't think that any one viewpoint is complete, then it's up to you to combine the perspectives on the issue. In doing so, you choose an original viewpoint. This, like composing a song or painting a picture, is a creative act and an exhilarating exercise in critical thinking.

Create on your feet

The latest thing around executive offices these days are "stand-up" desks. These desks are raised; you stand at them instead of sit.

Standing has advantages over sitting for long periods. You stay more alert and creative when you're on your feet. A study from the University of California indicates that problem-solving ability improves 20 percent when people stand. Increased heart rate and blood flow to the brain could be key factors.

Standing is great for easing lower-back pain too. Sitting aggravates the spine and supporting muscles.

You can join the ranks of some influential people who spend their days standing rather than sitting on the job. They claim to get more done and are more comfortable doing it.

The list of stand-up creators includes Robert Birk, chairman of Merrill Lynch & Co. George Shinn, chairman and chief executive officer of First Boston Corp., and C. Peter McColough, chairman of Xerox, along with Xerox's president and at least one vice president, have switched to standing-style desks. So did Colin Powell, former chairman of the Joint Chiefs of Staff. Hillary Clinton insisted on a standing desk for Bill Clinton's office.

This is a technique with tradition. Thomas Jefferson used a stand-up desk, upon which he wrote the Declaration of Independence. Donald Rumsfeld, former secretary of defense, used one at the White House and continues to use one in private business. Winston Churchill, Ernest Hemingway, and Virginia Woolf were fond of standing while working.

Experiment with this idea. Consider setting your desk up on blocks or putting a box on top of your desk so you can stand while writing, preparing speeches, or studying.

assumptions

Consider the following argument:

Orca whales mate for life.
Orca whales travel in family groups.
Science has revealed that Orca whales are intelligent.
Therefore, Orca whales should be saved
from extinction.

One idea underlies this line of thought:

Any animal that displays significant human
characteristics deserves special protection.

Whether or not you agree with this argument, consider for a moment the process of making assumptions. Assumptions are assertions that guide our thinking and behavior. Often these assertions are unconscious. People can remain unaware of their most basic and far-reaching assumptions—the very ideas that shape their lives.

Spotting assumptions can be tricky, since they are usually unstated and offered without evidence. What's more, human beings can hold scores of assumptions at the same time. Those assumptions may even contradict each other, making for muddled thinking and confused behavior. This makes uncovering assumptions a feat worthy of the greatest detective.

Letting our assumptions remain subconscious can erect barriers to our success. Take the person who says, "I don't worry about saving money for the future. I think life is meant to be enjoyed today—not later." This statement rests on at least two assumptions: Saving money is not enjoyable, and we can enjoy ourselves only when we're doing something that calls on us to spend money.

It would be no surprise to find out that this person runs out of money near the end of each month and depends on cash advances from high-interest credit cards. He is shielding himself from some ideas that could erase his debt: Saving money can be a source of satisfaction, and many enjoyable activities cost nothing.

When we remain ignorant of our assumptions, we make it easier for people with hidden agendas to do our thinking for us. Demagogues and unethical advertisers know that unchallenged assumptions are potent tools for influencing our attitudes and behavior.

Take this claim from an advertisement: *Successful students have large vocabularies, so sign up today for our seminar on word power!* Embedded in this sentence are several assumptions. One is that a cause-effect relationship exists between a large vocabulary and success in school. Another is that a large vocabulary is the single or most important factor in that success. This claim also assumes that the advertiser's seminar is a good way to develop your vocabulary.

In reality, none of these assumptions may be true. A large vocabulary is only one factor in student success. It's also doubtful that large vocabularies cause student success. Instead, both a large vocabulary and success may be related to other factors, such as the ability to read well. Finally, other methods of developing your vocabulary might be just as effective as the advertiser's seminar.

Assertions and opinions flow from our assumptions. Heated conflict and hard feelings often result when people argue on the level of opinions—forgetting that the real conflict lies at the level of their assumptions.

An example is the question about whether the government should fund public works programs that create jobs during a recession. People who advocate such programs often assume that creating such jobs is an appropriate task for the federal government. On the other hand, people who argue against such programs may assume that the government has no business interfering with the free workings of the economy. There's little hope of resolving this conflict of opinion unless we deal with something more basic: our assumptions about the proper role of government.

You can follow a three-step method for testing the validity of any viewpoint. First, look for the assumptions—the implied assertions. Second, write out these assertions. Finally, see if you can find any exceptions to them. This technique helps detect many errors in logic.

PRACTICING
CRITICAL THINKING #16

Gather several print advertisements or taped television commercials. Identify any techniques that the advertisers are using to persuade you, such as appealing to emotions or playing on fears. In the space below, briefly describe the advertisement and the techniques you noticed.

_____

_____

_____

_____

_____

Do the techniques work as well on you now that you've noticed them? Explain.

_____

_____

_____

_____

_____

EXERCISE #27
WORKING WITH ASSUMPTIONS

Read several issues of any widely circulated magazine. After doing so, note the basic assumptions that flow between the lines. Sum up the editors' values—their basic assumptions about what's important in life. For example, articles in People magazine might be based on the assumption that happiness is being rich and well-known. List the assumptions below.

_____

_____

_____

_____

_____

_____

Computer software
that can help you think

Modern technology offers a potent tool for critical thinking—the computer. While no computer can actually think for you, some software can prompt you as you define problems, brainstorm solutions, represent ideas visually, or even craft the characters for a novel.

Use style and grammar checkers

Many word processing programs offer features to aid you with the mechanics of writing and thinking. For example, *Microsoft Word* and *WordPerfect* include spelling checkers and utilities for compiling indexes, tables of contents, footnotes, and bibliographies. In addition, you can use a computer-based dictionary or thesaurus. Also look for style checkers, such as *Grammatik,* that flag incomplete sentences, passive verbs, and possible errors in grammar.

Some style checkers also estimate the reading level of your writing—for example, from more difficult (twelfth-grade level) to less difficult (fifth-grade level). One mark of a skilled thinker is the ability to explain a complex subject in terms that non-specialists can understand. Revise your paper so it reads at a lower difficulty level. If doing so oversimplifies your writing, you can revise again and reach a compromise.

Outline your ideas

The ability to organize ideas in outline form represents a high degree of thinking skill. Outlining forces you to distinguish major ideas from minor points and supporting facts.

Many word processing programs include an outlining feature. You can use this feature to write headlines at various levels. In this article, for instance, the title "Computer software that can help you think" is a major headline. "Outline your ideas" is a subhead that falls one level under the title. You could also think of the topic sentence of each paragraph in this article as a sub-headline (a headline that falls under a subhead).

Outlining tools make it easy to rearrange headlines, assign them to different levels, and insert paragraphs under each headline. You can use outlining software to organize your notes on textbooks and lectures. Divide a chapter or a lecture into sections, then write a headline to capture the main idea of each section. To save time when you review, just display the headlines and scan them— much like skimming a daily newspaper.

Some outlining software offers advanced features. These programs will convert your outlines into charts, mind maps, and other visuals. An excellent example is *MORE* from Symantec, Inc. *Three by Five* from MacToolKit formats notes and outlines just like conventional 3x5 cards. You can even print out the results on actual cards.

Create new ideas and solve problems

Programs such as *Problem Solver* from Mind Link include a series of writing exercises, sample analogies, and word association games designed to help you see new connections between ideas. *Inspiration*, published by Inspiration Software, helps you create diagrams, flow charts, project schedules, and outlines. Use this program and others like it to express ideas in both verbal and visual forms.

Plan your life

Many computer applications can function as personal information managers. These products generally help you keep track of calendar items, to-do lists, names, addresses, phone numbers, and other notes. Examples are *ClarisOrganizer, Day-Timer,* and *Now Up-to-Date & Contact.*

A reminder

The titles mentioned in this article are just a few examples of software that can help you think. Many more are available from computer dealers, wholesalers, and software catalogs. To keep abreast of the latest developments, check out the software reviews in current computer magazines.

Ways to fool yourself—
Six common mistakes in logic

1. Jump to conclusions. Jumping to conclusions is the only exercise that some lazy thinkers get. This fallacy involves drawing conclusions without sufficient evidence. Take the bank officer who hears about a college student failing to pay back an education loan. After that, the officer turns down all loan applications from students. This person has formed a rigid opinion on the basis of hearsay. Jumping to conclusions—also called *hasty generalization*—is at work here.

2. Attack the person. This mistake is common at election time. An example is the candidate who claims that her opponent has failed to attend church regularly during the campaign. People who indulge in personal attacks are attempting an intellectual sleight of hand—trying to divert our attention from the truly relevant issues.

3. Appeal to an "authority." A professional athlete endorses a brand of breakfast cereal. A soft drink company pays a famous musician to feature its product in a rock video. The promotional brochure for an advertising agency lists all the large companies that have used its services.

In each case, the people involved are trying to win your confidence—and your dollars—by citing authorities. The underlying assumption is usually this: *Famous people and organizations buy our product. Therefore, you should buy it too.* Or: *You should accept this idea merely because someone who's well-known says it's true.*

Appealing to authority is usually a substitute for producing real evidence. It invites sloppy thinking.

When our only evidence for a viewpoint is an appeal to authority, it's time to think more thoroughly.

4. Point to a false cause. Just because one event follows another does not mean that the two events have a cause-effect relationship. All we can really say is that the events may be correlated. As children's vocabularies improve, for example, they can get more cavities. This does not mean that increasing your vocabulary causes cavities! Instead, the increase in cavities is due to other factors, such as physical maturation and changes in diet.

5. Think in "all-or-nothing" terms. Consider these statements: *Doctors are greedy . . . . You can't trust politicians . . . . Students these days are just in school to get high-paying jobs; they lack idealism . . . . Homeless people don't want to work.*

These opinions imply the word *all.* They gloss over individual differences, claiming that all members of a group are exactly alike. They also ignore key facts—for instance, that some doctors volunteer their time at free medical clinics, and that many homeless people are children who are too young to work. All-or-nothing thinking is one of the most common errors in logic.

6. Base arguments on emotion. The politician who ends every campaign speech with flag-waving and slides of his mother eating apple pie is staking his future on appeals to emotion. Get past the fluff and see if you can uncover any ideas.

GAINING SKILL AT
decision making

Our lives are largely a result of the decisions we've made—and the actions that followed from those decisions. By making new decisions, we can create new results in our lives.

A folksy saying sums it up: "If you do what you've always done, you'll get what you've always gotten." To that we can add: If you keep making the same decisions, you'll do what you've always done.

We are making decisions all the time, whether we realize it or not. Even avoiding decisions is a form of decision making. The student who puts off studying for a test until the last minute is really saying, "I've decided this course is not important" or "I've decided not to give this course much time."

When people refuse to make decisions, they leave their lives to chance. Philosopher Walter Kaufman[5] calls this *decidophobia*—fear of making decisions. He defines *autonomy* as "making with open eyes the decisions that give shape to one's life."

Effective decision making banishes excuses. By taking charge of our decisions, we take charge of our lives. Decide right now to apply some of the following suggestions, and you might take your overall decision making to new heights.

Recognize decisions

Decisions are more than wishes or desires. There's a world of difference between "I wish I could be a better student" and "I'm committed to taking more powerful notes, reading with greater retention, and reviewing my class notes daily." Decisions are specific and lead to focused action.

When we decide, we narrow down. We give up actions that are inconsistent with our decision. Deciding to eat fruit instead of ice cream for dessert rules out the next trip to the malt shop.

Clarify your values

When we know specifically what we want from life, making decisions can become easier. This is especially true when we define our values precisely and put them in writing. Saying that you value education is fine. Now give that value some teeth. Note that you value continuous learning as a chance to upgrade your career skills, for instance. That can make registering for next quarter's classes much easier.

Make informed decisions

Powerful decisions flow from the quality of the information we have on hand. Many times failure results from missing the facts needed to make a decision.

Base your decisions on a life plan

The value of having a long-term plan for our lives is that it provides a basis for many of our year-to-year and week-to-week decisions. When we're clear about what we want to accomplish in five years, 10 years, or even 50 years, it's easier to make a meaningful to-do list for today.

Use time as an ally

Sometimes we face dilemmas—situations in which any course of action leads to undesirable consequences. In such cases, consider putting a decision on hold. Wait it out. Do nothing until the circumstances change, making one alternative clearly preferable to another— or until an effective solution announces itself.

Use intuition

Some decisions seem to make themselves. A solution pops into our mind and we gain newfound clarity. Suddenly we realize what we've truly wanted all along.

Using intuition is not the same as forgetting about the decision or refusing to make it. Intuitive decisions usually arrive after we've gathered the relevant facts and struggled with a problem for some time.

Act on your decision

Action is a clue to a true decision. Once we actually make a decision, we usually follow it with action. There comes a time to move from the realm of reflection and possibility to the arena of action. What we gain is valuable feedback about the results of our decisions— and the opportunity to make even more decisions.

The average American is exposed to thousands of advertising messages per day. The United States, with 6 percent of the world's population, receives 57 percent of the world's advertising. Unless you are stranded on a desert island, you are affected by commercial messages. To avoid brainwashing, practice critical thinking.

Advertising serves a useful function. It helps us make choices about spending money. We decide among cars, kitchen appliances, health clubs, books, plants, groceries, home builders, dog groomers, piano tuners, vacation spots, locksmiths, movies, amusement parks—the list is endless.

Advertising space is also expensive, and the messages are carefully crafted. They can play on our emotions and be dangerously manipulative.

For example, consider the messages that advertising conveys about your health. Advertising alcohol, tobacco, and pain relievers is big business. Newspapers, magazines, radio, and television depend on advertising these products for much of their revenue.

Ads for alcohol glorify drinking. One of their aims is to convince heavy drinkers that the amount they drink is normal. Twenty-seven percent of all people who drink consume 93 percent of the alcohol sold. Advertisers imply daily drinking is the norm, pleasant experiences are enhanced by drinking, holidays naturally include alcohol, parties are a flop without it, relationships are more romantic over cocktails, and everybody drinks. Each of these implications is questionable.

Advertising can affect our self-images. A typical advertising message is "You are not OK unless you buy our product." These messages are painstakingly programmed to get you to buy clothes, makeup, and hair products to make you look OK; drugs, alcohol, and food to make you feel OK; perfumes, toothpaste, and deodorant to make you smell OK. Advertising also promotes the idea that buying the right product is essential to having valuable relationships in your life.

Advertising affects what we eat. Multimedia advertisers portray the primary staples of our diets as breakfast cereals, candy bars, and soft drinks. A U.S. Department of Agriculture study revealed that the least nutritious foods receive the most advertising money.

Another problem with advertising is the image it has commonly portrayed of women. The basic message has been that women are inferior to men, lack intelligence, and are sex objects. The woman presented in many ads

WARNING: Advertising can be dangerous to your health

either spends her day discussing floor wax and laundry detergent or sits around looking sexy. Other women handle everything from kitchen to bedroom to boardroom—Superwoman.

These images are demeaning to women and damaging to men. Women lose when they allow their self-images to be influenced by ads. Men lose when they expect real-life women to be as shallow or as beautiful as portrayed. Many men pointlessly search for a woman who looks like the ones they see on television and in magazines. Advertising photography creates illusions. The next time you're in a crowd, notice how few people look like those in the media.

Advertising frequently excludes people of color. If our perceptions were based solely on advertising, we would be hard pressed to know that our society is racially and ethnically diverse.

Know how a multibillion-dollar industry threatens your health and well-being. Use advertising as a continual opportunity to develop the qualities of a critical thinker.

JOURNAL ENTRY #45
DISCOVERY STATEMENT

Think of a time when, after seeing an advertisement or commercial, you craved a certain food or drink or you really wanted to buy something. Describe in detail which part of the advertising influenced you.

_____
_____
_____
_____
_____
_____

Find a bigger problem

Most of the time we view problems as barriers. They are a source of inconvenience and annoyance. They get in our way and prevent us from having happy and productive lives. When we see problems in this way, our goal becomes to eliminate problems.

This point of view might be flawed. It is impossible to live a life without problems. Besides, they serve a purpose.

The word *problem* stems from the ancient Greek word *proballein*, which means "to throw forward." Problems are opportunities to participate in life. Problems stimulate us and pull us forward.

When problems are seen this way, the goal becomes not to eliminate them, but to find problems that are worthy of us. Worthy problems are those that draw on our talents, move us toward our purpose, and increase our skills. The challenge is to tackle those problems that provide the greatest benefits for ourselves and others. Viewed in this way, problems give meaning to our lives.

Problems fill the available space

Problems seem to follow the same law of physics that gases do. They expand to fill whatever space is available. If your only problem for the entire day is to write a follow-up letter to a job interview, you can spend the whole day finding paper and pen, thinking about what you're going to say, writing the letter, finding an envelope and stamp, going to the post office, and thinking about all the things you forgot to say.

If, on that day, you also need to shop for groceries, the problem of the letter shrinks to make room for another problem. If you also want to buy a car, it's amazing how quickly and easily the letter and the grocery shopping are finished. One way to handle little problems is to find bigger ones.

Remember that the smaller problems are still to be solved. The goal is to do this with less time and energy.

Bigger problems are plentiful

Bigger problems are not in short supply. Consider world hunger. Every minute of every day, 24 people die because they don't have enough to eat. Each day, 35,000 people die of hunger or hunger-related diseases. Each year, about 13 million people die because they don't have enough food.

Consider the devastating effects of alcoholism. One of every four people in the United States is directly affected by her own drinking or the alcoholism of someone in her family. Consider nuclear war that threatens to end life on the planet. Child abuse, environmental pollution, human rights violations, drug abuse, street crime, energy shortages, poverty, and wars throughout the world await your attention and involvement. You can make a contribution.

Play full out

Considering bigger problems does not have to be depressing. In fact, it can be energizing—a reason for getting up in the morning. Taking on a huge project is a tool for creating passion and purpose.

Some people spend vast amounts of time in activities they consider boring: their jobs, their hobbies, their relationships. They find themselves going through the motions, doing the same walk-on part day after day without passion or intensity. Writer Henry David Thoreau described their existence as "lives of quiet desperation."

The suggestion to play full out holds another possibility: We can spend much of our time fully focused and involved. We can experience efficiency and enthusiasm as natural parts of our daily routines. Energy and vitality can accompany most of our activities.

When we take on a big problem, we play full out. We do justice to our potentials. We then love what we do, and we do what we love. We're awake, alert, and engaged. Playing full out means living our lives as if our lives depended on it.

You make a difference

Perhaps your little voice is saying, "That's crazy. I can't do anything about these global problems" or "Everyone knows that hunger has always been around and always will be, and there is nothing anyone can do about it." These thoughts prevent you from taking on bigger problems.

Realize that you can make a difference. Your thoughts and actions can change the quality of life on the planet.

This is your life. It's your school, your city, your country, and your world. Own it. Treat it with the same care you would a prized possession.

The surest way to be sure that your problems are worthy of your talents and energies is to take on bigger ones. Take responsibility for problems that are bigger than you are sure you can handle. Then watch your other problems shrink.

One response is to give up—quit. Another is to resign ourselves to drudgery and dive into the work with a deep sigh, always feeling the weight of a monumental job. And after accepting responsibility for it, we may feel obligated to handle the entire job alone. When this happens, we are less effective. Our feelings of being overwhelmed are reinforced.

"Find a smaller problem" is really another way of combining the Power Process "Be here now" with a time management tool known as "divide and conquer." It works this way: Divide a gigantic project into many small jobs. Rather than worrying about the huge problem, ignore it for now. Turn your attention to a specific little job until it is complete, carefully attending to details. Do the same with the next small job, and the next.

The role of planning is critical. Finding a smaller problem is not the same as finding busywork. Without planning, we can end up completing jobs of low priority. That can sabotage the project. If we plan effectively, the small jobs we do are those most critical to the big picture.

Using this procedure, we can string a number of successes together, one after another. Success breeds success. Not only are we accomplishing many important tasks—we're also building a pattern of improving skills. When we look up from our work to see the huge job we were faced with—poof! The job has shrunk. Our problem may have even disappeared. That's the power of finding a smaller problem.

... or a smaller one

This idea appears to conflict with the strategy "Find a bigger problem." Like all the ideas in this book, "Find a smaller problem" is offered in the spirit of "ideas are tools." These ideas are not true or false, good or bad. Keep in mind that different jobs call for different tools.

It's easy to feel overwhelmed when faced with a huge task—writing a thesis, studying for a final, choosing a career, finding a job, or ending hunger on the planet. By telling ourselves how difficult things are, we can feel disempowered.

EXERCISE #28
FIX-THE-WORLD BRAINSTORM

This exercise works best with four to six people. Pick a major world problem like hunger, nuclear proliferation, poverty, totalitarianism, or pollution. Then conduct a 10-minute brainstorm on all the steps an individual could take to contribute to solving the problem. Use the brainstorming techniques beginning on page 206. Remember not to evaluate or judge the solutions during the process. The purpose of a brainstorm is to generate a flow of ideas.

After the brainstorming session, discuss the process and the solutions that it generated. Did you feel any energy from the group? Were any new or exciting ideas created? Are any of the ideas worth pursuing? On a separate sheet of paper, write Discovery and Intention Statements about them.

Solving problems—
Try the four P's

PROBLEM SOLVING and critical thinking hinge on the same processes. When you solve problems, you put thinking skills to work in ways that remove barriers to your success.

More specifically, problem solving is a chance to practice two types of thinking. One type involves opening up alternatives and considering as many options as possible. Here you go for the "aha!" Your creative thinking skills come into play as you generate new definitions of the problem and brainstorm possible solutions.

The other type of thinking involves narrowing down. Out of all the possibilities you generated, you choose one idea for follow-up or one solution to act on.

One name for the opening-up process is *divergent thinking*. The narrowing-down process is *convergent thinking*. In essence, problem solving is a kind of dance between convergent and divergent thinking. The trick is to know what kind of thinking you're doing at any given moment and what kind of thinking is most appropriate at the time.

If you've understood the concepts of this book, you already know a lot about problem solving. Just tie together that knowledge into a simple procedure that you can remember.

Try this one for fun. Think of the four P's of problem solving: Define the *problem*, generate *possibilities*, create a *plan*, and perform your *plan*.

 Define the problem
This step paves the way for the remaining three. Once we define a problem, we're well on the way to no longer having a problem.

Problems are subtle creatures, skilled at hiding themselves. In defining problems, we bring them out in the open. We admit that the problem *exists*, and that's powerful. Many problems feel so thorny that we'd rather deny or forget about them. When we define a problem, we pull the wool from over our eyes.

In addition, a problem that is clearly defined is half solved. With a clear definition of the problem in hand, we may already know what actions are needed to solve it.

To define a problem effectively, understand what a problem is—a mismatch between what you want and what you have. Problem solving is all about reducing the gap between these two factors.

Start with what you have. Tell the truth about what's present in your life right now, without shame or blame. Write down the specifics. Instead of saying that you're lousy at reading textbooks, write, "I often get sleepy while reading my physics assignments, and after closing the book I often cannot remember what I just read."

Next, describe in detail what you want. Again, go for specifics: "I want to remain alert as I read about physics. I also want to accurately summarize each chapter I read."

One more point: When we define a problem in limiting ways, our solutions merely generate new problems. As Einstein said, "The world we have made is a result of the level of thinking we have done thus far. We cannot solve problems at the same level at which we created them."

This idea has many applications to our success in school. An example is the student who struggles with note taking. The problem, he thinks, is that his notes are too sketchy. The logical "solution" is to take more notes, and his new goal is to write down almost everything his instructors say. This only generates new headaches. No matter how fast and furiously he writes, the student cannot capture all the instructors' comments. What's more, his hands ache and his head spins after every class.

Consider what happens when this student defines the problem in a new way. After more thought, he decides that his dilemma is not the quantity of his notes but their quality. He adopts a new format for taking notes, dividing his paper into two columns. In the right-hand column he writes down only the main points of each lecture. And in the left-hand column he notes two or three supporting details for each point.

While doing so, he makes the joyous discovery that there are usually just three or four core ideas to remember from each lecture. He originally thought the solution was to take more notes. What really worked was taking notes in a new way.

Chapter One in this book offers many tools for defining problems. In particular, see "First Step: Truth is a key to mastery," "Seven Discovery Statement guidelines," and the Discovery Wheel exercise, all in Chapter One.

Generate possibilities

So far you've been working hard at convergent thinking—narrowing down to a specific definition of the problem. Now put on your divergent thinking hat. Open up. Brainstorm as many possible solutions to the problem as you can. The article on creativity techniques in this chapter offers many suggestions for doing this.

As strange as it sounds, forgetting about the problem for a while can also work wonders. First, immerse yourself in defining the problem and creating possible solutions. Then consciously let the problem go for a day or two. Don't be surprised if a solution comes to you while you're doing something totally unrelated to the problem— swimming, gardening, doing the dishes, or even sleeping. That's the power of the subconscious mind, which is percolating ideas and generating solutions even when you don't realize it.

Another useful tool is writing. Putting our thoughts on paper forces us to be more accurate and precise when defining a problem. With pen in hand, we can also capture the results of our brainstorms for later review.

Create a plan

It's time to narrow down again. After re-reading your problem definition and list of possibilities, choose the solutions that seem most workable. Think about what specific actions will reduce the gap between what you have and what you want. To make your plan even more powerful, put it in writing. Use the guidelines for Intention Statements in Chapter One.

Perform your plan

Before implementing your plan, take a minute to relish the work you've done so far. You've defined the problem, opened up possible solutions, and created a specific plan.

The final step gets you off your chair and out into the world. Now you actually *do* what you planned. And there are few things as satisfying as checking items off your to-do list—especially when you know they are helping you solve a problem.

Though this step doesn't take long to explain, it's as significant as the others. Ultimately our skill in solving problems lies in what we do. Through the quality of our actions, we become the architect of our success.

EXERCISE #29
TRANSLATING GOALS INTO ACTION

Choose one long-range goal—any basic value, personal project, or social change you'd like to see. Examples are learning to fly, improved health care for chronically ill children, improving your handwriting, eating a more healthy diet, becoming an astronaut, inventing energy-saving technology, improving the effectiveness of American schools, or becoming a better parent. List one of those goals on a separate sheet of paper.

Next, list some actions consistent with this goal. Ask yourself, "What specific actions are needed to meet my goal?" List those actions. Finally, translate any action you just listed into steps you could complete in less than one hour or could start in the next 24 hours.

Solving math and science problems

Solving word problems is a key part of reading textbooks about math and science. Approach math and science problems the way rock climbers approach mountains. The first part is devoted to preparations you make before you get to the rock. The second part is devoted to techniques used on the rock (problem) itself.

To the uninitiated, rock climbing looks dangerous. For the unprepared, it is. A novice might come to a difficult place in a climb and panic. When a climber freezes, he is truly stuck. Experienced climbers figure out strategies in advance for as many situations as possible. With preparation and training, the sport takes on a different cast.

Sometimes students get stuck, panic, and freeze with academic problems. Use the following techniques to avoid that. Experiment with these techniques as you work through textbooks in math and science. You can also use them on tests.

Before you get to the rock

1. Practice. Work lots of problems. Do assigned problems and more. Make up your own. Work with a classmate and make up problems for each other to solve. The more problems you do, the more comfortable you're likely to feel solving new ones. Set clear goals for practice and write Intention Statements about meeting those goals.

Some students memorize the problems and answers discussed in class—without learning the formulas or general principles behind the problems. This kind of rote learning doesn't allow them to practice applying the principles or formulas to new problems. One solution is to understand ways to arrive at those answers.

2. Divide problems by type. Make a list of the different kinds of problems and note the elements of each. By dividing problems into type or category, you can isolate the kinds of problems you have that are difficult for you. Practice those more and get help if you need it.

3. Know your terminology. Mathematicians and scientists often borrow words from plain English and assign new meanings to them. For example, for most of the world, *work* means a "job." For the physicist, *work* is force multiplied by distance. To ensure that you understand the terminology, see if you can restate the problem in your own words. Translate equations into English sentences. Use 3x5 flash cards to study special terms.

4. Understand formulas. You might be asked to memorize some formulas for convenience. If you understand the basic concepts behind these formulas, it is easier to recall them accurately. More important, you will probably be able to re-create the formulas if your recall falters. Understanding is preferable to memorization.

5. Use summary sheets. Groups of terms and formulas can be easier to memorize if you list them on a sheet of paper or put them on 3x5 cards. Mind map summary sheets allow you to see how various kinds of problems relate to one another. You create a structure on which you can hang data, and that helps your recall.

6. Play with possibilities. There's usually not one "right" way to solve a problem. Several approaches or formulas may work, though one may be more efficient than another. Be willing to think about the problem from several angles or to proceed by trial and error.

7. Notice when you're in deep water. It's tempting to shy away from difficult problems. Unfortunately, the more you do this, the more difficult the problems become. Math and science courses present wonderful opportunities to use the First Step technique explained in Chapter One. When you feel that you're beginning to get into trouble, write a precise Discovery Statement about the problem. Then write an Intention Statement about what you will do to solve the problem.

8. When practicing, time yourself. Sometimes speed counts. Notice how fast you can work problems. This gives you an idea of how much time to allot for different types of problems.

9. Use creative visualizations. Before you begin a problem-solving session, take a minute to relax, breathe deeply, and prepare yourself for the task ahead. Then use the techniques described on pages 224 and 225 to see yourself solving problems successfully.

On the rock

1. Survey the territory thoroughly. Read the problem at least twice before you begin. Read slowly. Be certain you understand what is being asked.

Let go of the expectation that you'll find the solution right away. You may make several attempts at solving the problem before you find a solution that works.

2. Sort the facts. Survey the problem for all of the givens. Determine the principles and relationships involved. Look for what is to be proven or what is to be discovered. Write these down.

3. Set up the problem. Before you begin to compute, determine the strategy you will use to arrive at the solution. When solving equations, carry out the algebra as far as you can before plugging in the actual numbers.

Remember that solving a math or science problem is like putting together a puzzle. You may work around the edges for a while and try many pieces before finding one that fits.

4. Cancel and combine. When you set up a problem logically, you can take shortcuts. For example, if the same term appears in both dividend and divisor, they will cancel each other.

5. Draw a picture. Make a diagram. Pictures help keep the facts straight. They show relationships more effectively than words.

To keep on track, record your facts in tables. Consider using three columns labeled "What I already know," "What I want to find out," and "What relates the two." This last column is the place to record a formula that can help you solve the problem.

6. Read the problem aloud. Sometimes the sound of your voice will jar loose the solution to a problem. Talk yourself through the solution. Read equations out loud.

7. Check results. Work problems backward, then forward. Start at both ends and work toward the middle to check your work.

Take a minute to make sure you kept the units of measurement clear. Say that you're calculating the velocity of an object. If you're measuring distance in meters and time in seconds, then the final velocity should be in meters per second.

Another way to check your work is to estimate the answer before you compute it. Then ask if the answer you actually got seems in the ballpark.

8. Savor the solution. Savor the times when you're getting correct answers to most of the problems in the textbook. Relish the times when you feel relaxed and confident as you work or when you look over the last few pages and they seem easy. Then remember these times whenever you feel math or science anxiety.

master student

margaret mead

author, anthropologist, and feminist, was associated with the American Museum of Natural History from 1926 until her death

Mother thought about every place we lived not only in terms of its schools, but also as a more or less promising source of "lessons."

Whatever form such lessons took—drawing, painting, carving, modeling, or basketry—she thought of them as a supplement to formal education within the context of the most advanced educational theories. In Hammonton I had music lessons and also lessons in carving, because the only artist the town boasted was a skillful wood-carver. In Swarthmore we were taught by an all-round manual training teacher under whose tutelage I even built a small loom. In Bucks County I had painting lessons from a local artist and later from an artist in New Hope. And one year Mother had a local carpenter teach Dick and me woodworking. She was completely eclectic about what we were taught in these lessons, provided the person who was teaching us was highly skilled.

Looking back, it seems to me that this way of organizing teaching and learning around special skills provided me with a model for the way I have always organized work, whether it has involved organizing a research team, a staff of assistants, or the available informants in a native village. In every case I try to find out what each person is good at doing and then I fit them together in a group that forms some kind of whole. . . .

Living on the farm—and we were told that we lived there because Grandma believed every child had a right to grow up on a farm—opened our eyes to a great diversity of experience. There was always another family in the farmer's house, and we often had maids with little children. When the threshers came, there were twenty to sit down in the farmer's kitchen, and we all helped. My father taught me how to top off shocks of wheat as it was done in Ohio and then left me with the task of showing the men how to do it without making them mad. . . .

In school I always felt that I was special and different, set apart in a way that could not be attributed to any gift I had, but only to my background—to the education given me by my grandmother and to the explicit academic interests of my parents. I felt that I had to work hard to become part of the life around me. But at the same time I searched for a greater intensity than the world around me offered and speculated about a career. At different times I wanted to become a lawyer, a nun, a writer, or a minister's wife with six children. Looking to my grandmother and my mother for models, I expected to be both a professional woman and a wife and mother.

From Blackberry Winter *by Margaret Mead*
Copyright © 1972 by Margaret Mead
By permission of
William Morrow & Company, Inc.

QUIZ

1 *List and briefly describe three strategies for critical thinking.*

2 *Explain what is meant in this chapter by* aha.

3 *Define* serendipity *and give an example.*

4 *Summarize the difference between divergent and convergent thinking.*

5 *Define the word* dilemma. *Then explain one strategy for responding to dilemmas.*

6 *List and explain three qualities of a critical thinker.*

7 *Define* all-or-nothing thinking *and give an example.*

8 *Explain two ways that using a computer can help you become a more effective thinker.*

9 *Name at least one fallacy involved in this statement: "Everyone who's ever come to this campus has agreed that this is the best school in the state."*

10 *Name two core skills for critical thinking and give one example of each.*

JOURNAL ENTRY #46
DISCOVERY/INTENTION STATEMENT

Write a short statement about your current level of skill in creative and critical thinking.

I discovered that I . . .

_____

_____

Now choose three suggestions from this chapter to use during the next week. Along with each suggestion, note a possible benefit that could come from applying the suggestion.

I intend to . . .

_____

_____

_____

_____

Name _____ Date _____/_____/_____

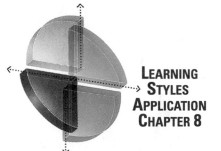

**LEARNING
STYLES
APPLICATION
CHAPTER 8**

Style 1

Describe a major decision you face in your life right now. Examples are decisions about what courses to take next quarter or what career you will choose. Describe how you have made such decisions in the past. List techniques that worked well for you, along with those that did not.

Style 2

List 10 specific suggestions from this chapter that could help you think through your options and make the decision you listed for Style 1.

Style 3

From the list of suggestions you made for Style 2, choose three that you will definitely apply. Describe how you will use each technique.

Style 4

After experimenting with the three techniques you chose, evaluate how well they worked for you. Then describe any ways you could modify these techniques to make them work more effectively.

Bibliography

■ **Endnotes**

[1]Arthur Koestler, *The Act of Creation* (New York: Dell, 1964).

[2]Peter Facione, *Critical Thinking: What It Is and Why It Counts* (Millbrae, CA: California Academic Press, 1996).

[3]Vincent Ryan Ruggiero, *Becoming a Critical Thinker* (Boston: Houghton Mifflin, 1996).

[4]Mortimer J. Adler and Charles Van Doren, *How to Read a Book* (New York: Simon & Schuster, 1940).

[5]Walter J. Kaufman, *From Decidophobia to Autonomy: Without Guilt and Justice* (New York: Delta, 1975).

■ **Additional Reading**

Barry, Vincent. *Looking at Ourselves: An Introduction to Philosophy,* Belmont, CA: Wadsworth, 1977.

Copi, Irving M. *Introduction to Logic,* New York: Macmillan, 1972.

LeBoeuf, Michael. *Imagineering: How to Profit from Your Creative Powers,* New York: McGraw-Hill, 1980.

Pirsig, Robert. *Zen and the Art of Motorcycle Maintenance,* New York: Bantam, 1976.

Ries, Al, and Jack Trout. *Positioning: The Battle for Your Mind,* New York: McGraw-Hill, 1980.

9

writing

In this chapter...

discover ways to efficiently approach a task faced by every student—writing. Get past fear and frustration with an organized, three-phase strategy. Also tap into the Internet, discover buried treasure by using the library, and approach public speaking with newfound skill. In the process, avoid some common writing traps, including sexism and plagiarism.

JOURNAL ENTRY #47
DISCOVERY STATEMENT

Recall a writing assignment you were asked to complete this term. Evaluate the process you used to complete the writing, listing anything you would like to do differently for your next writing project. (For example, you might want to avoid a last-minute deadline crunch or to use your research time more effectively.)

_____
_____
_____
_____
_____
_____
_____
_____
_____
_____

Now preview this chapter for any strategies that can help you gain your desired outcomes. List five strategies here.

_____
_____
_____
_____
_____
_____
_____
_____
_____

LEARNING TO WRITE WELL PAYS. Writing effectively can help you express yourself powerfully and persuasively. Writing helps you organize information and adapt your ideas to different audiences. It can also help you give clear instructions—a task that occupies much of our waking time. By becoming a skilled writer, you can become a better thinker, speaker, reader, and listener.

Writing well pays

Good writing is a marketable skill. To verify this, flip through the "Help Wanted" section in a large Sunday newspaper. Note how many job descriptions call for good writing skills.

Writing is also a powerful way to learn. Professional writers report that one of the joys of their craft is the repeated opportunity to explore new fields. They constantly learn new subjects by researching and writing about them. They know that you can literally write your way into a subject. Through writing, you can get a much clearer picture of what you know, what you don't know, and where to look for the missing pieces.

Writing is an essential skill in the age of information. Computers have made it possible to store and retrieve data on a vast scale. Today the human race mass-produces information. This barrage of information is not always helpful. It's possible to get lost in stacks of computer printouts, professional journals, newspapers, magazines, and books.

Writing can help. When you write, you not only gather information; you also assess it. You sift through the data, play with it, and sort it out. You look for relationships among facts and choose ideas that are useful to you. Through writing, you turn *data* into *insight*.

> **" "**
>
> *In truth, the innate human need that underlies all writing, the need to give shape to your experience, is a gift we all possess from earliest childhood.*
> –GABRIELE LUSSER RICO

> **" "**
>
> *You do not know what is in you—an inexhaustible fountain of ideas.*
> –BRENDA UELAND

> **" "**
>
> *You know, when we are kids we make up things, we write, and for me the puzzle is not that some people are still writing; the real question is why did the other people stop?*
> –WILLIAM STAFFORD

Phase 1:

Creating something from nothing

Getting ready to write

I t's easy to put off writing until the last minute, when anxiety forces you to commit words to paper. There are easier ways to get a writing project done. This chapter outlines a three-phase process for writing any paper or speech:

1. Creating something from nothing— Getting ready to write

2. Getting down to it— Writing the first draft

3. Polishing your creation— Revising your draft

Every writer has an individual style. Even though this article lays out the process step by step, remember that writing is highly personal. You might go through the steps in a different order or find yourself working on several at once.

Step 1: List and schedule writing tasks

You can break the goal—a finished paper—into smaller steps that you can tackle right away. Estimate how long it will take to complete each step. Start with the date your paper is due and work backward to the present. Say that the due date is December 1 and you have about three months to write the paper. List November 20 as your target completion date, plan what you want to get done by November 1, then list what you want to get done by October 1.

Here's a list of possible writing tasks. Each is an event to schedule.

> Generate ideas
> Refine your initial ideas
> Select a topic
> Choose a working title
> Write a thesis statement
> Consider audience, purpose, and content
> Do initial research
> Outline
> Research
> Complete first draft
> Complete second draft
> Complete third draft
> Proofread and prepare the final copy

Step 2: Generate ideas

Brainstorm with a group. There's no need to create in isolation. Forget the myth of the lonely, frustrated artist rehashing ideas alone in a dark Paris cafe. You can harness the natural creative power of a group to your favor. For ideas about ways to brainstorm, see page 206.

Speak it. To get ideas flowing, start talking. Admit your confusion or lack of a clear idea. Then just speak. By putting your thoughts into words, you'll start thinking more clearly. Novelist E. M. Forster said, "Speak before you think is creation's motto."

Use free writing. Free writing, a technique championed by writing teacher Peter Elbow[1], sends a depth probe into your creative mind. This is one way to bypass your internal censors, those little voices in your head that constantly say, "That sentence wasn't very good. Why don't you stop this before you get hurt?"

There's only one rule in free writing: Write without stopping. Set a time limit— say, 10 minutes—and keep your pencil in motion or your fingers dancing across the keyboard the whole time.

Give yourself permission to keep writing, even if you don't think it's very good, even if you want to stop and rewrite. There's no need to worry about spelling, punctuation, or grammar. It's OK if you stray from the initial subject. Just keep writing. Now you're starting to get ideas down on paper.

Step 3: Refine initial ideas

Select a topic and working title. It's easy to put off writing if you have a hard time choosing a topic. However, it is almost impossible to make a wrong choice at this stage. The best way to choose is to just do it.

Using your instructor's guidelines for the paper or speech, sit down and make a list of topics that interest you. Write as many of these as you can think of in two minutes. Then choose one. If you can't decide, use scissors to cut your list into single items, put them in a box, and pull one out. To avoid getting stuck on this first step, set a precise deadline for yourself: "I will choose a topic by 4 p.m. on Wednesday."

The most common pitfall is selecting a topic that's too broad. "Harriet Tubman" is not a useful topic for your American history paper. Instead, consider "Harriet Tubman's activities as a Union spy during the Civil War."

Write a thesis statement. Clarify what you want to say by summarizing it in one concise sentence. This sentence is called a thesis statement, and it refines your working title. It also helps in making a preliminary outline.

You might write a thesis statement such as "Harriet Tubman's activities with the Underground Railroad led to a relationship with the Union army during the Civil War." A statement that's clear and to the point can make your paper easier to write. Remember that it's OK to rewrite your thesis statement as you learn more about your topic.

A thesis statement is different from a topic. Like newspaper headlines, a thesis statement makes an assertion or describes an action. It is expressed in a complete sentence, including a verb. "Diversity" is a topic. "Cultural diversity is valuable" is a thesis statement.

Step 4: Consider audience, purpose, and content

Writing flows from a purpose. This means your writing is more effective when you know exactly what your purpose is.

Clarify the purpose of your assignment with your instructor. Think about how you'd like your reader or listener to change after considering your ideas. Do you want her to think differently, to feel differently, or to take a certain action? Your writing strategy is greatly affected by how you answer these questions.

If you want someone to think differently, make your writing clear and logical. Support your assertions with evidence. If you want someone to feel differently, consider crafting a story. Write about a character your audience can sympathize with, and tell how she resolves a basic problem. And if your purpose is to move the reader into action, explain exactly what steps to take and offer a solid benefit for doing so.

Your writing can be more powerful if you work with a specific audience in mind. Audience analysis is complex. However, answering these questions helps writers stay on track: Who is your primary audience? What does your audience already know about this subject? What is their attitude toward this subject? How will they use this information?

Step 5: Do initial research

At this stage, your research is not about uncovering specific facts about your topic. That comes later. Now you want to get an overview of the subject. Find out the structure of your topic—its major divisions, issues, or branches. Say you want to persuade the reader to vote for a certain candidate. Then learn enough about this person to state her stands on key issues and summarize her background.

Step 6: Outline

Many people shun outlining. They forget that the primary purpose of an outline is to save time. It's much like plotting a route when you travel to a new place. When you follow a map, you avoid getting lost. Likewise, an outline keeps you from wandering off the topic.

To start an outline, gather a stack of 3x5 cards and brainstorm ideas you want to include in your paper. Write one idea per card.

Then experiment with the cards. Group them into separate stacks, each stack representing one major category. After that, arrange the stacks in order. Finally, arrange the 3x5s within each stack in a logical order. Rearrange cards until you discover an organization you like.

If you write on a computer, consider using outlining software. These programs allow you to record and rearrange ideas on the screen, much like the way you'd create and shuffle 3x5 cards.

Step 7: Research

You can find information about research skills in Chapters Four and Five of this book. Following are added suggestions.

Use 3x5 cards. If 3x5 cards haven't found their way into your life by now, joy awaits you. These cards work wonders in researching. Just write down one idea per card. This makes it easy to organize—and reorganize—your ideas.

Organizing research cards as you create them saves time. Use rubber bands to keep source cards separate from information cards and to maintain general categories.

You can also save time in two other ways. First, copy all information correctly. Always include the source code and page number on information cards. Second, write legibly and use the same format for all your cards.

In addition to source cards and information cards, generate idea cards. If you have a thought as you are researching, write it down on a card. Label these cards clearly as your own ideas.

An alternative to 3x5 cards is a computer outlining or database program. Some word processing packages also include features that can be used for note taking.

Sense the time to begin writing. A common mistake of beginning writers is to hold their noses, close their eyes, and jump into the writing process with both feet and few facts. Avoid this temptation by gathering more information than you can use.

On the other hand, you can begin writing even before your research is complete. The act of writing creates ideas and reveals holes in research.

Finding a natural place to begin is one signal to begin writing. This is not to say that the skies will suddenly open and your whole paper, flanked by trumpeting angels, will appear before your eyes. You might get a strong sense of how to write just one small section of your paper. When this happens, write.

EXERCISE #30
FREE WRITING

Think about a paper or other writing project you've been assigned. Pick a limited topic related to that project. Or pick any topic you'd like to write about.

With your topic in mind, write for 10 minutes. Follow the guidelines for free writing: Jot down phrases, sentences, single words, pictures—anything that comes to mind, in any order. Imagine yourself talking about this topic to a friend over a cup of coffee. Write down what you would say. Just keep your hand moving.

Remember that this writing sample is not for keeps, and you won't show it to anybody. Anything that comes out is OK for now.

Set a timer and go for it. On a separate sheet of paper, write for a full 10 minutes. After you're finished, go back and circle any passages you like. Consider filing these for use in future writing projects.

EXERCISE #31
CREATE A WORKING TITLE

Using mind maps, 3x5 cards, or other materials you feel comfortable with, create specific, narrowed working titles for the following subjects:

> *Fashion models*
> *World hunger*
> *Garbage*
> *American cars*
> *Space travel*
> *Loud music*
> *Television*

For example:
Subject: Sports
Working title: The effect of the increased popularity of jogging on the health of the population of Little Rock, Arkansas.

Now sharpen your thinking about each topic by writing a possible thesis statement for each working title. Remember that an effective thesis statement is a complete sentence that makes an assertion about a topic.

Phase2:
Getting down to it—
Writing the first draft

If you've followed the steps in the previous article, you've already done much of the hard work. Now you can relax into writing your first draft.

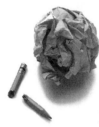

Just gather your notes, arranged to follow your outline. Now, write about the ideas in your notes. Write in paragraphs, one idea per paragraph. If you have organized your notes logically, related facts will appear close to each other.

As you complete this task, keep the following suggestions in mind.

Remember that the first draft is not for keeps

Again, give yourself permission to turn out a first draft that doesn't meet your standards. The only thing that counts now is quantity—not quality. You can save quality control for later, when you revise. Your goal at this point is simply to generate lots of material.

So don't worry about grammar, punctuation, or spelling as you write your first draft. Write as if you were explaining the subject to a friend. Let words flow. The very act of writing will release creative energy.

It's perfectly all right to crank out a draft that you heavily rewrite or even throw away later. The purpose of a first draft is merely to have something to work with—period. For most people, that's a heck of a lot better than facing a blank page. You will revise this rough draft several times, so don't worry if the first draft seems rough or choppy.

Write freely

Many writers prefer to get their first draft down quickly. Their advice is to just keep writing, much as in free writing. You can pause occasionally to glance at your notes and outline. The idea is to avoid stopping to edit your work. You can save that for the next step.

Another option is to just write a first draft without referring back to your notes and outline. If you've immersed yourself in the topic, chances are that much of the information is already bubbling up near the surface of your mind anyway. Later, when you edit, you can go back to your notes and correct any errors.

Keep in mind, too, that there's no obligation to write straight through, following your outline from the beginning to the end. Some professional writers prefer to write the last chapter of a novel or last scene of a play first. With the ending firmly in mind, they can guide the reader through all the incidents that lead to it. You may feel more comfortable with certain aspects of your topic than others. Dive in where you feel most comfortable. Then you'll be warmed up for the other sections of your paper.

Be yourself

As you write, let go of the urge to sound "official" or "scholarly." Write not to the teacher, but to an intelligent student or someone you care about. Visualize this person and choose the three or four most important things you'd say to her about the topic. This helps you avoid the temptation to write merely to impress.

In short, be honest and be yourself. Write the way you talk. For instance, if you attempt to use words that aren't part of your vocabulary, simply for the sake of using bigger or more obscure words, the result will be a paper that is difficult to read. Stick with what is natural.

The other side of this coin is that we can't really write the way we speak. The spoken word is accompanied by facial expressions and gestures, as well as changes in voice tone, pitch, and volume. Slang expressions used in everyday speech are not appropriate in academic writing. Compensate for elements peculiar to the spoken language by being clear and concise and by providing smooth, logical transitions from subject to subject.

Let your inner writer take over

There may be times during a first draft that you feel ideas come without stopping. It may feel as if the ideas are just running through you, flowing from head to hand without conscious effort on your part. This is a natural "high" similar to states that accomplished athletes, musicians, and artists have reported. Writer Natalie Goldberg[2] says that in such moments you are in touch with your "inner writer." Such "peak experiences" can yield moments of pure joy. Often those moments come just after a period of feeling stuck. Welcome getting stuck. A breakthrough is not far behind.

Ease into it

Some people find it works well to forget the word *writing*. Instead, they ease into the task with activities that help generate ideas. You can free-associate, cluster, meditate, daydream, doodle, draw diagrams, visualize the event you want to describe, talk into a tape recorder—anything that gets you started.

Make writing a habit

Inspiration is not part of the working vocabulary for many professional writers. Instead of waiting for inspiration to strike, they simply make a habit of writing at a certain time each day. You can use the same strategy. Simply schedule a block of time to write your first draft. The very act of writing can breed inspiration.

Respect your deep mind

Part of the process of writing takes place outside our awareness. There's nothing mysterious about this. Many creative people report that ideas come to them while they're doing something totally unrelated to writing. Often this happens after they've been grappling with a question and have reached a point where they feel stuck. It's like the composer who said, "There I was, sitting and eating a sandwich, and all of a sudden this darn tune pops into my head." You can trust your deep mind. It's writing while you eat, sleep, and brush your teeth.

Get physical

Writing is physical, like jogging or playing tennis. You can move your body in ways that tune in to the flow of your ideas. While working on the first draft, take breaks. Go for a walk. Speak or sing your ideas out loud. From time to time, take a break to relax and breathe deeply. Also experiment with standing up as you write, adapting your work area for that purpose as explained in a previous chapter.

Use affirmations and visualizations

Write with the idea that the finished paper or speech is inside you, waiting to be released. Affirmations and visualizations can help you here. Imagine what your finished paper will look like. Construct a detailed mental picture of the title page and major sections of the paper. See a clean, typed copy and imagine how it will feel to hold the paper and flip through the pages.

Then support your writing by sprinkling your self-talk with statements that affirm your abilities. For example: "I express myself clearly and persuasively." "I am using an effective process to write my paper." "I will be pleased with the results."

Hide it in your drawer for a while

Rewrite. Then rewrite your rewrite. Then rewrite that one. This is the critical part of writing for most writers—geniuses included. Paper is cheap.

Schedule time for rewrites before you begin, and schedule at least one day between revisions so you can let the material sit. On Tuesday night, you might think your writing sings the song of beautiful language. On Wednesday, you will see that those same words, like the phrase "sings the song of beautiful language," belong in the trash basket.

Ideally, a student will revise a paper two or three times, make a clean copy of those revisions, then let the last revised draft sit for at least three or four days. The brain needs that time to disengage itself from the project. Obvious grammatical mistakes, awkward constructions, and lapses in logic are hidden from us when we are in the middle of the creative process. Give yourself time to step back.

So after you've completed your first draft, schedule time to be away from it. Put your draft away. With a few minutes', a few hours', or a few days' worth of perspective, you'll find it easier to get on to the next step: polishing your creation.

Phase 3:

Polishing your creation–

Revising your draft

When you wrote your first draft, you turned off your internal critic. Now that you've moved into revising, a third step of writing, you can put on your critic's hat. You're shifting roles.

The purpose here is not to beat yourself up or bruise your paper. Rather, you revise to let the fire of your ideas glow through the haze of creation.

One definition of a writer is simply anyone who rewrites. Some people who write for a living will rewrite a piece seven, eight, or even more times. Ernest Hemingway rewrote the last page of *A Farewell to Arms* 39 times before he was satisfied with it. When asked what the most difficult part of this process was, he simply said, "Getting the words right."

People who rewrite care. They care about the reader. They care about precise language and careful thinking. And people who rewrite care about themselves. They know that the act of rewriting teaches them more about the topic than almost any other step in the process. For that reason, rewriting can be a real joy.

There's a difference in pace between writing a first draft and revising it. Keep in mind the saying "Write in haste, revise at leisure." When you edit and revise, slow down and take a microscope to your work. One guideline is to allow 50 percent of writing time for planning, research, and writing the first draft. Then give the remaining 50 percent to revising.

An effective way to revise your paper is to read it out loud. The eyes tend to fill in the blanks in our own writing. The combination of voice and ears forces us to pay attention to the details. Reading aloud to a friend is powerful too. So is having a friend read your paper aloud to you.

Another revision technique is to have a friend revise your paper. This is never a substitute for your own revision, but a friend can often see mistakes you miss.

Reading aloud and having a friend edit your paper are techniques that can help you in each phase of rewriting. Those phases are *cut, paste, fix, prepare,* and *proof.*

Step 1: Cut

Writer Theodore Cheney[3] suggests that an efficient way to begin revising is to cut the passages that don't contribute to your purpose. Right now it may not pay to polish individual words, phrases, and sentences— especially if you decide later that you don't need them. To save time, decide now what words you want to keep and what you want to let go.

Look for excess baggage. Avoid at all costs and at all times the really, really terrible mistake of using way too many unnecessary words, a mistake that some student writers often make when they sit down to write papers for the various courses in which they participate at the fine institutions of higher learning which they are fortunate to attend. (Example: The previous sentence could be edited to "Avoid using unnecessary words.")

Approach your rough draft as if it is a chunk of granite from which you will chisel the final product. In the end, much of your first draft will be lying on the floor. What is left will be the clean, clear, polished product.

Sometimes the revisions are painful. Sooner or later, every writer invents a phrase that is truly clever but makes no contribution to the purpose of the paper. It is difficult to eliminate these phrases. They play to our pride. We all want to demonstrate how witty we are. Those clever phrases look at us with big, watery doe eyes and beg for life. "I'm cute," they say. "I show everyone how smart you are. Please let me stay in your paper." Grit your teeth and let them go.

Keep in mind that cutting a passage means for now, for this paper, for this assignment. You may want to keep a file of deleted writing and label it "Possible Gems." You may find ideas for future papers in this file. Also, knowing that your deleted passages are safely tucked away can make it easier to let go of them.

So, cut unnecessary sections, pages, paragraphs, sentences, words, and letters. Delete. Prune. Winnow. Reduce. Tighten. Some editors say that 75 percent of their job is doing this alone.

This step may mean cutting out some of your pet words and phrases. That may hurt at first. Soon, though, you'll discover the power of this process. The payoffs are clarity and sparkle. Sometimes all that's needed to bring a passage to life is to winnow out the chaff—the extra, unnecessary words. It's much like wiping off a dirty light bulb. Now the clear light of your message can shine forth with more brilliance.

Note: For maximum efficiency, make the larger cuts first—sections, chapters, pages. Then go for the smaller cuts—paragraphs, sentences, phrases, words.

Step 2: Paste

In deleting passages, you've probably removed some of the original transitions and connecting ideas from your draft. The next task is to rearrange what's left of your paper so it flows logically.

Now that you've cut words, look at what remains. Are the concepts presented in a logical order? Does one point flow into the next? Will it hang together for the reader? Or will the reader feel that points are being made in a random order? Look for consistency within paragraphs, logical transitions from paragraph to paragraph and from section to section.

If your draft doesn't hang together, then reorder your ideas. Imagine yourself with a scissors and glue. You're going to cut the paper into scraps—one scrap for each point. Then you're going to paste these points down in a new, more logical order.

If you're writing by hand or with a typewriter, consider cutting and pasting for real. This is a time-honored technique. Or, if you're writing with a word processor, you can ask the computer to do the cutting and gluing for you.

This is where it can pay to have other people read your draft. Someone who is fresh to your topic will not have the same assumptions and biases you bring to the paper. This person can help you define what's needed to make your ideas hang together for the reader. Another way to do so is to read your paper out loud, either to yourself or someone else. In the process, gaps in logic will become more clear.

Remember that you are not your draft. When other people criticize or edit your work, they're not attacking you. They're just commenting on your paper. With a little practice, you can actually learn to welcome feedback.

Step 3: Fix

Now it's time to look at individual words and phrases.

In general, write with nouns and verbs. Relying too much on adjectives and adverbs weakens your message and adds unnecessary bulk to your writing. Write about the details, and be specific. Also, use the active rather than the passive voice.

1. Instead of writing in the passive voice:
   A project was initiated.
   You can make it active by writing:
   The research team began a project.

2. Instead of writing verbosely:
   After making a timely arrival and perspicaciously observing the unfolding events, I emerged totally and gloriously victorious.
   You can write as Julius Caesar did:
   I came, I saw, I conquered.

3. Instead of writing vaguely:
   The speaker made effective use of the television medium, asking in no uncertain terms that we change our belief systems.
   You can write specifically:
   The reformed criminal stared straight into the television camera and shouted: "Take a good look at what you're doing! Will it get you what you really want?"

Next, go through the paper again, paying attention to grammar and spelling. Also define any terms the reader may not know and put them into plain English whenever you can. These are touches that polish your writing.

Step 4: Prepare

In a sense, any paper is a sales effort. If you hand in a paper with wrinkled jeans, its hair tangled and unwashed, and its shoes untied, your instructor is less likely to buy.

To avoid this situation, type your paper following an acceptable format for margin widths, footnotes, title pages, and other details. Use quality paper for your final version. For an even more professional appearance, bind your paper with a paper or plastic cover. This shows that you take care with your work.

Step 5: Proof

Reading your paper out loud is one way to spot awkward sentences. Another option is to ask a friend to proof your paper. Be sure to ask someone who is competent and will give you candid feedback.

Also read over your paper with an eye for grammar. Many dictionaries include useful summaries of grammar principles. Another resource is the Grammar Hotline at 1-805-378-1494.

As you ease down the homestretch, read your revised paper one more time. This time, go for the big picture and look for the five elements of effective writing:

- A clear thesis statement that captures the main point of the paper.
- Sentences or paragraphs that orient the reader. These introduce your topic, guide the reader through the major sections of your paper, and summarize your conclusions.
- Details that support your conclusions. These can include quotations, examples, and statistics.
- Lean sentences that are purged of needless words.
- Plenty of action verbs and concrete, specific nouns.

When you're finished proofreading and have your final copy in hand, take a minute to savor the experience. You've just witnessed something of a miracle—the mind attaining clarity and resolution. That's the aha! in writing.

PRACTICING
CRITICAL THINKING #17

Choose a subject about which you have some detailed or advanced knowledge. Explain a topic in that field for someone who knows nothing about it. Put your explanation in writing.

Next, field-test your explanation. Present it to a sample member of your chosen audience, perhaps a relative or friend. Based on your field test, describe how you could revise your presentation to make it more effective. Summarize your ideas in the space below. Also reflect on what it means to say that your presentation is "effective."

_____

_____

_____

_____

_____

JOURNAL ENTRY #48
DISCOVERY STATEMENT

This Journal Entry is for people who avoid writing. As with any anxiety, approach writing anxiety by accepting it fully. Realize that it's OK to feel anxious about writing. That feeling is shared by others, and many people have worked with it successfully.

Begin by telling the truth. Describe exactly what happens when you start to write. What thoughts or images run through your mind? Do you feel any tension or discomfort in your body? Where? Let the thoughts and images come to the surface without resistance. Complete the following statement:

When I begin to write, I discover that I . . .

_____

_____

_____

Seven steps to
nonsexist writing

Picture a country that is dominated by women. The vast majority of people in positions of power are female. This includes executives, administrators, managers, police officers, judges, physicians, and lawyers. Ninety-nine percent of this country's elected officials are women. In fact, the country has never had a male president. In the country's 200-year history, only two men have sat on the Supreme Court. Most of the announcers on radio and television are female. And during marriage ceremonies, it's the custom for a minister (almost always a woman) to say, "I now pronounce you woman and husband."

Now imagine that you're reading a popular book about the history of this society. You might find a passage like this one:

The story of this country is a tale of uncommon courage. We can remember the women who fought to free our country from colonial domination and the women who drafted its constitution. Our proud foremothers guided this country from infancy into the splendor of full-fledged womanhood. And the spirit of this country is still unshakable, thanks to the women who guide it now.

Men reading these words may well feel excluded—and for good reason. Judging from the way this passage was written, it's hard to imagine that men even exist.

Now return to our world. You're likely to find examples of a similar problem—only this time, it's women who are being left out.

The lesson is clear: Use language that includes both women and men. Carrying out this suggestion can be tricky, even when we have the best intentions. Following are some paths you can follow to writing that's gender-fair—without twisting yourself in verbal knots.

1. Use gender-neutral terms. Instead of writing *policeman* or *chairman*, for example, use *police officer* or *chairperson*. In many cases there's no need to identify the gender or marital status of a person. This allows us to dispose of expressions such as *female driver*, *little woman*, and *lady doctor*.

2. Use examples that include both men and women. Good writing thrives on examples and illustrations. As you search for details to support the main points in your papers, include the stories and accomplishments of women as well as men.

3. Alternate pronoun gender. In an attempt to be gender-fair, some writers make a point of mentioning both sexes when they refer to gender.

Another option is to alternate the gender of pronouns throughout a text—the strategy used in this book. For example, you can use masculine pronouns in odd-numbered chapters of a book and feminine pronouns in even-numbered chapters.

4. Switch to plural. With this strategy, a sentence such as *The writer has many tools at his disposal* becomes *Writers have many tools at their disposal.*

5. Avoid words that imply sex role stereotypes. Included here are terms such as *tomboy, sissy, office boy, waitress, advertising man, maneater, mama's boy, anchorman, old lady, powder puff,* and *handyman.*

6. Use parallel names. When referring to men and women, use first and last names consistently. In the same paper, for instance, avoid referring to *President Bill Clinton and his wife.* An alternative is to mention the woman's full name: *Hillary Rodham Clinton.*

7. Visualize a world of sexual equality. Our writing is a direct reflection of the way we perceive the world. As we make a habit of recognizing women in roles of leadership, our writing can reflect this shift in viewpoint. That's a powerful step toward gender-fair writing.

PEOPLE AT WORK

GIVING CREDIT WHERE CREDIT IS DUE—

Avoiding the high cost of

plagiarism
plagiarism
plagiarism
plagiarism

There's a branch of law known as *intellectual property*. This field is based on the idea that original work—speeches, publications, and artistic creations—are not free for the taking. Anyone who borrows from these works is obligated to acknowledge the work's creator. This is the purpose behind copyrights, patents, and trademarks.

Using another person's words without giving proper credit is called *plagiarism*. This is a real concern for anyone who writes, including students. Plagiarism can have big-time consequences, ranging from a failing grade to expulsion from school.

To avoid plagiarism when writing a research paper, take care as you take notes. If you use a direct quote from another writer or speaker, put that person's words in quotation marks. Also note the details about the source of the quotation: publication title, publisher, date, and page number. Many instructors will ask you to add to your paper footnotes or endnotes that include this information. If you use index cards to take notes, include source information on each card with a quotation.

Instead of using a direct quote, you might choose to paraphrase an author's words. Credit paraphrases in the same way you credit direct quotes.

Keep in mind that paraphrasing is not copying a passage word for word and then deleting or rearranging a few phrases to disguise the fact. Consider this paragraph:

Higher education also offers you the chance to learn how to learn. In fact, that's the subject of this book. Employers value the person who is a "quick study" when it comes to learning a new job. That makes your ability to learn a marketable skill.

Following is an improper paraphrase of that passage:

With higher education comes the chance to learn how to learn. Employers value the person who is a "quick study" when it comes to learning a new job. That makes your ability to learn a marketable skill.

A better paraphrase of the same passage would be:

The author notes that when we learn how to learn, we gain a skill that's valued by employers.

Out of a concern for avoiding plagiarism, some students go overboard crediting their sources. You do not need to credit wording that's wholly your own. Nor do you need to credit general ideas. For example, the suggestion that people use a to-do list to plan their time is a general idea. When you use your own words to describe to-do lists, there's no need to credit a source. But if you borrow someone else's wording to explain this idea, do give credit.

SUPERCHARGE YOUR COMPUTER
with the Internet

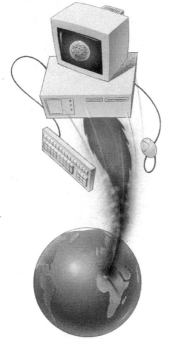

The Internet is a network of computer networks, used by millions of people across the world. Functionally speaking, the Internet is a huge community of people who communicate with one another in a way that looks like anarchy. No one person or group owns or operates the Internet. There are some volunteer boards that oversee certain aspects of Internet operation, but no one is really in control.

This phenomenon grew from a computer system created by the U.S. Department of Defense in the late 1960's. The original idea was to create a network so complex and resilient, it could survive a nuclear attack. In the meantime, people in many government agencies found the network to be a useful way of staying in touch with one another. Eventually colleges and universities joined in, followed by large online services and computer-savvy individuals. Today almost anyone with a computer can tap into this network, now known as the Internet.

The Internet is what people usually mean when they refer to the information superhighway. Perhaps a more apt analogy would be the "information jungle." Imagine a library with millions of books and no central card catalog—a place where anyone can bring in materials and arrange the shelves any way she wants. That's something like the way information is stored on the Internet.

As you can imagine, finding your way through this jungle can be a challenge. Yet there are potential rewards. Through the Internet you can access millions of files with text, graphics, sound, animation, or even video clips. You can communicate with anyone else who has an Internet connection. And new software is making it easier for people to find exactly what they want on the "Net."

The Internet is so vast and dynamic that any statements made about it could become outdated. For the latest information, go directly to the Internet itself.

Features of the Internet

Over the last few years, several features of the Internet have become especially popular.

FAQs

When you're exploring the Internet, keep an eye out for files with the acronym *FAQ* in the title. Those letters are short for Frequently Asked Questions, documents written in a question-answer format that offer overviews of a topic. With a little searching, you can find FAQs that answer common questions about the Internet.

Electronic mail

Through the Internet you can instantly send messages to anyone with an e-mail address and receive replies from that person. This might be the most widely used feature of the Internet to date. Almost every country in the world can now accommodate e-mail through the Internet.

Telnet

Telnet is an Internet feature that allows you to access a remote computer from the comfort of your own keyboard. For example, you might tap into a library's listing of materials—just as if you were sitting at a computer terminal in that library. This can be a tremendous time-saver when you do research. You can locate information and ideas from around the planet without leaving your personal computer.

Chat rooms

Go to the Internet to connect with others who share your interests. Through commercial online services and other Internet connections, you can enter "chat rooms." These services allow people to carry on real-time conversations by typing messages to each other at their computers. Chat rooms exist for almost any subject—from astronomy to zoology. Use them to make contacts and monitor the latest developments in your field.

Bulletin boards and newsgroups

Many bulletin boards exist in an area of the Internet called Usenet. Here people can post messages and articles in public files that you can access. From your computer, you can log on to a bulletin board, read messages at your leisure, and even add a contribution of your own. As with chat rooms, bulletin boards exist on countless subjects. Some specialized bulletin boards are called newsgroups.

Transferring files

On the Internet you can find thousands of files that are free for the taking. These files run the gamut, from games to computer virus detectors and everything in between. Using File Transfer Protocol (FTP), you can copy such files from a remote computer to your own computer. Actually, the term *FTP* refers to a method of transferring files and to a type of site on the Internet.

Accessing the Internet

Currently there are four ways for you to access the Internet. One option is a direct connection—usually reserved for large organizations with sophisticated computer systems. You might be able to find a direct connection through your school.

Another method is a SLIP/PPP account, which hooks you up to a computer network with a direct Internet connection. (SLIP stands for Serial Line Interface Protocol, and PPP for Point-to-Point Protocol.) Private businesses operate these accounts and offer access to the Internet for a monthly fee.

Commercial online services such as America Online, Compuserve, Prodigy, and e-World are another option. Access to certain areas of the Internet might be limited through these services.

Finally, you can purchase a shell account from companies that provide Internet access, usually for a flat monthly fee. Shell accounts display only text, not graphics.

To locate an Internet service provider, check computer magazines or your local phone book. Before signing up for a service, find out if they'll provide the software you need. Ask in particular about programs that allow you to browse the Internet and search for specific sites. Netscape Navigator and Mosaic are two widely used titles.

You can always sign up for a service on a trial basis. Review the software and instructional materials that the service provides. Send an e-mail request to the customer service department and see how well they respond. Also, avoid long-distance charges by choosing a service that provides a local access number.

Finding what you want

Currently you can navigate the Internet with four major tools. Their names prove that even computer programmers can have a sense of humor. One tool is called Archie, which allows you to search the Internet for names of files that you can copy to your computer. With Gopher, you can "burrow" through the Internet via a series of menus. WAIS searches for files according to key words in their content.

The area of the Internet that's received the most publicity is the World Wide Web, which is growing about 341,000 percent each year. This is the flashiest region of the Internet and popular with people who know little about computers. Information on the Web is organized and displayed as colorful "pages." You can move through pages in any sequence by clicking on highlighted or underlined words called hyperlinks. Never mind that pages might originate from computers separated by thousands of miles. Pages from any source show up on your screen in a matter of seconds or minutes.

Connecting to the Internet can transform your computer from a fancy, high-priced typewriter to a gateway to the planet. Another enjoyable fact about the Internet is its newness. Many people are just learning to use it right now. Join them for the ride. You might find uses for the Internet that no one has invented yet—including uses that promote your success at school and at work.

Library:
The buried treasure

Books. That's what most people imagine when a library is mentioned. Books occupy a lot of space in a library, but they are only part of what is really there.

Most libraries have books. Many also have records, art work, maps, telephone directories for major cities, audiovisual equipment, newspapers, microfiche, microfilm, and audio- and videocassettes. You may also find computers and computer software, slide programs, film strips, magazines, dictionaries and encyclopedias of all varieties, research aids, computer searches, and—people.

Libraries range widely in size. Most have the same purpose. They exist to help you find information—facts, opinions, or ideas.

Getting familiar with the resources and services in a library is crucial to the success of most students. It can enhance your reading skills, expand your vocabulary, increase your self-confidence, and save you time. Even more valuable for some is the convenient, comfortable, quiet, and dependable atmosphere for studying.

The best resource is not made of paper

People who work in libraries are trained explorers. They know how to search out information that might be located in several different places. They can also act as a guide for your own expedition into the data jungle. Their purpose is to serve you. Ask for help.

Most libraries have a special reference librarian who can usually let you know right away if the library has what you need. He may suggest a different library or direct you to another source, such as a business, community agency, or government office.

You can save hours by asking.

Any book you want

Most libraries now can provide nearly every book you could ever want through inter-library loans. This sharing of materials gives even the smallest library access to millions of books. Just ask that the book be borrowed from another library. Keep in mind that this may involve a small fee and could take anywhere from a few days to a few months. It pays to plan for this time when doing research.

Periodicals

Which magazines and newspapers a library carries depends mostly on the size, type, location, and purpose of the library. A neighborhood branch of a public library may have copies of the local paper and magazines right from the grocery store aisle. A library in a business school is more likely to have the *Wall Street Journal* and trade journals for accountants and business managers. Law libraries subscribe to magazines that would probably bore the socks off a veterinarian.

Reference materials

The library catalog lists books available in that library and their location. These listings used to be kept on cards, and in some libraries they still are. Today many libraries catalog their materials on computer or microfilm.

A computerized catalog gives you more flexibility in searching for materials. For example, you can type in a key word and ask the computer to search for all listings with that word. Some of these systems will also allow you to see if the title is on the shelf or checked out. They may even allow you to put a hold on a book or recording.

In any case, the catalog is an alphabetical listing that is cross-referenced by subject, author, and title. Each listing carries the author's name, the title, the publisher, the date of publication, the number of pages and illustrations, the Library of Congress or Dewey decimal system number (for locating the book), and sometimes a brief description of the book.

Books in Print is a list of most books currently available for sale in the United States. Like the card catalog, it is organized by subject, author, and title. (Note that this resource is not a guide to the materials in any particular library.)

The Reader's Guide to Periodical Literature indexes articles found in many magazines. Searching by subject, you can find titles of articles. The magazine name, date, volume, and page numbers are listed. If you want an older magazine, many libraries require that you fill out a form requesting the magazine so it can be retrieved from storage in closed stacks.

Other guides to what has been recently published include: *New York Times Index, Business Periodicals Index, Applied Science and Technology Index, Social Sciences Index, Accountants' Index, General Science Index, Education Index, Humanities Index,* and *Art Index.* These indices help you find what you want in a hurry.

More recently, such indices have become available on microfilm or compact disc. These include *Magazine Index, Business Index, InfoTrac, Newsbank,* and *Medline.* The information these sources provide is the same as the traditional bound indices. Yet many people find them quicker and easier to use, and often they are more current than printed indices.

Abstracts are publications that summarize current findings in specific fields. You can review condensed versions of specialized articles by reading, for example, *Chemical Abstracts, Psychological Abstracts,* or *Sociological Abstracts.*

Pamphlets and clippings are usually stored in file cabinets organized by subject. This section contains information from the U.S. Government Printing Office, state and local governments, and newspaper and magazine clippings.

Facts about virtually anything you can imagine are waiting in almanacs and publications from government departments such as Labor, Commerce, and Agriculture.

The U.S. Government Printing Office is the largest publisher in the world. *The Monthly Catalog* of its printings takes up several feet of shelf space.

Articles listed in indices or *Reader's Guide* that are not available at a particular library are usually available through interlibrary loan for a small fee.

General and specialized encyclopedias are also found in the reference section. Find what you want to know about individuals, groups, places, products, words, or other books. Specialized examples include: *Cyclopedia of World Authors, Grove's Dictionary of Music and Musicians, Encyclopedia of Religion and Ethics, Encyclopedia of Associations, Thomas Register of American Manufacturers,* and *Encyclopedia of World Art.*

Dictionaries of all sizes and specialties are also available in the library. Many disciplines (medicine, computer science, engineering) have their own dictionaries.

Of special value to your writing projects is the thesaurus, a type of dictionary. This is one place to check for words (synonyms) that have a similar meaning to the word you look up. Instead of standard definitions, a thesaurus provides fast relief when you just can't think of the word you want.

Computer networks now provide information and resource materials to many libraries. DIALOG, ERIC, ORBIT, and BSR are four major electronic information vendors, and each network contains several dozen databases. Up-to-the-minute reports (stock prices set in the past 15 minutes, yesterday's *New York Times* stories) can be retrieved almost instantly on a computer terminal.

Ironically enough, one place to learn about electronic researching is with some old-fashioned reference books. These include the *Encyclopedia of Information Systems and Services* and *Directory of Online Databases.*

**EXERCISE #32
FIND IT**

Most libraries have the answers to the following questions. Go exploring. If you search for the answers and can't find them on your own, ask one of the librarians for help.

1. What are a dozen words that mean about the same thing as the word power?

2. What is the Library of Congress number (which is used to locate books in many libraries) for the novel 1984 by George Orwell? (Give the Dewey decimal number if that is the system used in your library.)

3. Is the book The Lazy Man's Guide to Enlightenment still in print? If so, who is the publisher?

4. What are three magazine articles, published since last year, that discuss methods to prevent or treat cancer?

5. Who manufactures nails and tacks? List three companies you could contact if you wanted one million nails made to your specifications.

6. What computer search capabilities are available at two libraries you can use? List the names of the two libraries and briefly describe information they can access directly by computer.

Some useful things to know

To save research time, plan a strategy. That means asking pointed questions about your topic and knowing what kind of information you're looking for.

Say that the purpose of your paper is to persuade students to use personal computers. Begin by asking typical questions a reader might: "What can a computer really do for me?", "How much do they cost?", "Can I get along fine without one?"

Next, choose, in general, what type of sources you want to consult and in what order. For help in completing this step, ask a librarian. If you're still unsure about what you're looking for, explain to the librarian the context of your paper. Describe the subject and purpose of the questions you want to answer.

Use the index in the back of books or last volume of encyclopedias to save time when searching for information.

Look in the front of reference materials for guidelines on how to use them. Often this section will tell you what abbreviations mean and how the entries in that volume were selected.

Look for the most specific items first. Then generalize if needed. For example, if you are looking for a user's manual for a particular word processing program, look under the name of that program. If that doesn't work, then look under the more general category of "word processing."

Remember that any specific subject has a corresponding set of specialized reference materials. For example, if you're looking for an introduction to the thought of Spinoza, the philosopher, you can look in the *Encyclopedia of Philosophy.*

Keep in mind the full range of sources for finding facts. Many of these were mentioned above: encyclopedias, indexes, the library catalog, computer databases, magazines and journals. You can also use abstracting services, which summarize published and unpublished articles on paper, microfiche, or microfilm. An example is ERIC (the Educational Resources Information Center), which specializes in information about education.

Look through nonprint materials. These include audio- and videotapes, videodiscs, films, slides, and filmstrips.

Other information sources are outside the library. They include corporations and professional organizations, museums, and historical societies. You can also write or talk directly with people who know a lot about a given subject. Often a librarian can guide you to such resources in the community.

Use magazines for purposes other than researching a paper. Use them to find tips for how to quit smoking, build bookshelves, or knit a sweater. You can also find product ratings that provide valuable information about major purchases, such as a car or stereo.

The library exists for your benefit, waiting only for you to use it. Happy treasure hunting.

EXERCISE #33
CATALOG RECONNAISSANCE

Look at every page in your school catalog—quickly. Notice what is new, interesting, or puzzling. Locate your major program description and notice the courses you are required to take for graduation. Find out more about courses you know nothing about. If you see that you have to take macroeconomics to graduate, find out how that differs from microeconomics and accounting.

Locate the major program that is most different from yours. Look through the courses students in that major are required to take. Pick out a course that looks interesting, even though it is different from anything you ever thought you'd take. Find out more about that course.

Writing and delivering speeches

Polishing your speaking skills can help you think on your feet and communicate clearly. These are skills you will use during school and in any career you choose.

Organizing your speech

Some people tune out during a speech. Just think of all the times you have listened to instructors, lecturers, politicians, and others. Think of all the wonderful daydreams you have had during their speeches. Your audiences are like you.

The way you organize your speech can determine the number of people in your audience who stay with you until the end.

Speeches are usually organized in three main parts: the introduction, the main body, and the conclusion.

Introduction

The introduction sets the stage for your audience. This is the time you make clear to the audience where you are taking them (to "tell them what you're going to tell them"). Unless you are a brilliant presenter, such as Jesse Jackson or Mario Cuomo, avoid rambling speeches with no clear organization. They put audiences to sleep.

The following introduction, for example, tells exactly what is coming. The speech has three distinct parts, each in logical order.

Cock fighting is a cruel sport. I intend to describe exactly what happens to the birds, tell you who is doing this, and show you how you can stop this inhumane practice.

To make an effective speech, be precise about your purpose. Speeches can inform, persuade, motivate, or entertain. Choose what you want to do, and let your audience know what you intend.

When the choice is yours, talk about things that hold your interest. Include your personal experiences. Your enthusiasm will reach the audience.

Start with a bang! Compare the following two introductions to speeches on the subject of world hunger. Example number one:

I'm very honored to be here with you today. I intend to talk about malnutrition and starvation. First, I want to outline the extent of these problems, then I will discuss some basic assumptions concerning world hunger, and finally, I will propose some solutions.

You can almost hear the snores from the audience. Example number two:

More people have died from hunger in the past five years than have been killed in all the wars, revolutions, and murders in the past 150 years. Yet there is enough food to go around. I'm honored to be with you today to discuss the problem . . . .

Most people pay attention to the first few seconds of a speech, so this is a good time to highlight your best points. One practical note: Before you begin, be sure you have the audience's attention. If people are still filing into the room or adjusting seats, they're not ready to listen.

Main body

The main body of the speech is the content—70 to 90 percent of most speeches. In the main body, you will develop your ideas much the way you develop a written paper. (This is where you "tell them.")

In speeches, transitions are especially important. Give your audience a signal when you change points: "On the other hand, until the public realizes what is happening to children in these countries . . ." or "The second reason hunger persists is . . . ."

In long speeches, recap from time to time and preview what's to come. Using facts, descriptions, expert opinions, statistics, and other concrete details will help you hold audience attention.

Conclusion

At the end of the speech, summarize your points and draw your conclusion ("tell them what you've told them"). You started with a bang, so finish with drama.

The first and last parts of a speech are the most important. Make it clear to your audience when you've reached the end. Avoid endings such as "This is the end of my speech" or "Well, I guess that's it." A simple stand-by is "So, in conclusion I want to reiterate three points: First . . . ." When you are finished, stop talking.

Using notes

Some professional speakers recommend writing key words on a few 3x5 cards. They make it easy to keep your speech in order. Number the cards so that if you drop them, you can quickly put them in order again. As you finish the information on each card, move it to the back of the pile. Write information clearly and in letters large enough to be seen from a distance.

The disadvantage of the 3x5 card system is that it involves a lot of card shuffling. Some speakers prefer to use standard outlined notes. Another option is mind mapping. Even an hour-long speech can be mapped on one sheet of paper. You can also use memory techniques to memorize the outline of your speech.

Ways to practice

The key to successful public speaking is practice. When you practice, do so in a loud voice. Your voice sounds different when you talk loudly, and this can be unnerving. Get used to it before the big day.

If possible, practice in the room where you will deliver your speech. Hear what your voice sounds like over a sound system. If you can't practice your speech in the actual room, at least visit the site ahead of time. Also list materials you will need for your speech, including audiovisual aids.

To get the most out of your practice, record your speech and listen to it. Better yet, videotape your presentation. Many schools have video equipment available for students' use. Check the library.

When practicing, listen for repeated phrases: *you know, kind of, really*, plus any little *uh's, umm's*, and *ah's*. To get rid of these mannerisms, simply tell yourself that you intend to notice every time they pop up in your daily speech. When you hear them, tell yourself that you don't use those words anymore. Also ask someone else to monitor your speech for these phrases. Eventually, they can disappear.

Practice your speech in front of friends or while looking in the mirror. Speaking before one or two friends builds confidence; it can be more demanding than talking in front of a large group. You can also practice by speaking up often in class.

Use stress reduction techniques before and during your speech. Practice them ahead of time. Then, before you speak, visualize yourself in the room successfully giving the speech.

When you practice your speech, avoid delivering it word for word, as if you were reading a script. Know your material and present the information in a way that is most natural for you. Diligent practice relieves you of having to rely heavily on your notes.

One more note about getting ready: If you want to get your message across, dress appropriately. Dress up to speak before the Association of University Presidents—unless they're having a picnic.

Delivering the speech

For some beginners, the biggest problem in delivering a speech is nervousness. If this is your concern, give yourself a hand by knowing your material inside out.

Nervousness is common. You can deal with it by noticing it. Tell yourself, "Yes, my hands are clammy. I notice that my stomach is slightly upset. My face feels numb." Allow these symptoms to exist. Experience them fully. When you do, those symptoms often become less persistent. Use Power Process #3: "Love your problems."

Also use Power Process #2: "Be here now." Be totally in the present moment. Notice how the room feels. Notice the temperature and lighting. See the audience. Look at them. Make eye contact. Notice all your thoughts about how you feel and gently release them.

Another technique is to look at your audience and imagine them all dressed as clowns. Chances are that if you lighten up and enjoy your presentation, so will the audience.

Also, focus on the audience rather than on your own comfort level. Look for signals that they are at ease and fully receiving your message.

When you speak, talk loudly enough to be heard. To help yourself project, avoid leaning over your notes or the podium.

Also maintain eye contact. When you look at people, they become less frightening. Remember that it is easier to listen to someone who looks at you. Find a few friendly faces around the room and imagine that you are talking to them individually. If you notice a side conversation in the room, continue speaking and look directly at the people who are visiting.

You can increase the impact of words by keeping track of the time during your speech. Better to end early than run late. The conclusion of your speech is what is likely to be remembered, and you might lose this opportunity if people are looking at the clock.

Use audiovisual aids, flip charts, and other props whenever possible.

Only a fraction of our communication is verbal. Be aware of what your body is telling your audience. Contrived or staged gestures will look dishonest. Be natural. If you don't know what to do with your hands, notice that. Then don't do anything with them.

Pause when appropriate. Beginners sometimes feel they have to fill every moment with the sound of their voice. Let your audience take a mental deep breath from time to time. And lighten up. Friendliness and humor are usually appropriate. There are few reasons to take yourself too seriously.

After you speak

Review and reflect upon your performance: Did you finish on time? Did you cover all the points you intended to cover? Was the audience attentive? Did you handle any nervousness effectively? What can you do to improve your performance and delivery next time?

Welcome evaluation from others. Most of us find it difficult to hear criticism about our speaking. Be aware if you resist such criticism, then let go of your resistance. Listening to feedback will increase your skill.

POWER PROCESS # 9

Be a fool

A powerful person has the courage to be a fool. This idea can work for you because you already are a fool. Don't be upset. All of us are fools, at one time or another. There are no exceptions. If you doubt it, think back to that stupid thing you did just a few days ago. You know the one. Yes . . . that one. It was embarrassing and you tried to hide it. You pretended you weren't a fool. This happens to everyone.

People who insist they have never been fools are perhaps the biggest fools of all. We are all fallible human beings. Most of us, however, spend too much time and energy trying to hide our fool-hood. No one is really fooled by this—not even ourselves. What's more, whenever we pretend to be something we're not, we miss part of life.

For example, many people never dance because they don't want to look ridiculous. They're not wrong. They probably will look ridiculous. That's the secret of being a fool.

It's OK to look ridiculous dancing. It's all right to sound silly singing to your kids. Sometimes it's OK to be absurd.

Being a fool is not being foolhardy

And sometimes it's not OK to be absurd. Power Process #9 comes with a warning label: Being a fool does not mean we get to escape responsibility for our actions. "Be a fool" is not a suggestion to get drunk at a party and make a fool of yourself. It is not a suggestion to act the fool by disrupting class. It is not a suggestion to be foolhardy or to "fool around."

"Be a fool" means recognizing that foolishness, along with dignity, courage, cowardice, grace, clumsiness, and other qualities, is a human characteristic. We all share it. You might as well risk being a fool because you already are one, and nothing in the world can change that. Why not enjoy it once in a while?

Consider the case of the person who won't dance because she's afraid she'll look foolish. This same person will spend an afternoon tripping over her feet on a basketball court. If you say that her jump shot from the top of the key looks like a circus accident, she might even agree.

"So what?" she might say. "I'm no Michael Jordan." She's right. On the basketball court, she is willing to be a fool in order to enjoy the game.

She is no Ginger Rogers, either. For some reason, that bothers her. The result is that she misses the fun of dancing. (Dancing badly is as much fun as shooting baskets badly—and maybe a lot more fun.)

There's one sure way to avoid being a fool, and that's to avoid life. The writer who never finishes a book will never have to worry about getting negative reviews. The center fielder who sits out every game is safe from making any errors. And the comedian who never performs in front of an audience is sure to avoid telling jokes that fall flat. The possibility of succeeding at any venture increases when we're comfortable with making mistakes—that is, with being a fool.

Be willing to take risks

Again, remember the warning label. Power Process #9 does not suggest that the way to be happy in life is to do things badly. Mediocrity is not the goal. The point is that mastery in most activities calls for willingness to do something new, to fail, to make corrections, to fail again, and so on. On the way to becoming a good writer, be willing to be a bad writer.

Consider these revised clichés: Anything worth doing is worth doing badly at first. Practice makes improvement. If at first you don't fail, try again.

Most artists and athletes have learned the secret of being foolish. Comedians are especially well versed in this art. All of us know how it feels to tell a joke and get complete silence. We truly look and feel like fools. Professional comedians risk feeling that way for a living. Being funny is not enough for success in the comedy business. A comedian must have the courage to face failure.

Courage is an old-fashioned word for an old-fashioned virtue. Traditionally, people have reserved that word for acts of the high and mighty—the campaigns of generals and the missions of heroes.

This concept of courage is fine, but it can be limiting and rob us of seeing courage in everyday actions. Courage is the kindergartner whose heart is pounding as she waves good-bye to her parents and boards the bus for her first day of school. Courage is the 40-year-old man who registers for college courses after 20 years away from the classroom.

For a student, the willingness to be a fool means the willingness to take risks, to experiment with new skills, to grow. The rewards are expanded creativity, more satisfying self-expression, and more joy.

An experiment for you

Here's an experiment you can conduct to experience the joys of fool-hood. The next time you do something silly or stupid, experience the feeling. Don't deny it. Don't cover it up. Notice everything about the feeling, including the physical sensations and thoughts that come with it. Acknowledge the foolishness. Be exactly who you are. Explore all the emotions, thoughts, images, and sensations surrounding your experience.

Also remember that we can act independently of our feelings. Courage is not the absence of fear but the willingness to act even when you feel fear. We can feel homesick and still choose to do homework. We can feel a fear of public speaking and still walk up to the microphone.

When we fully experience it, the fear of being foolish loses its power. Then we have the freedom to expand and grow.

Be willing to be a fool.

PRACTICING CRITICAL THINKING #18

Review the article "Supercharge your computer with the Internet." Think about the implications of this new technology. Write three possible scenarios describing how the Internet could affect the way you live and work in the year 2010. Choose a best-case scenario, a worst-case, and a most probable case.

Write your scenarios on a separate sheet of paper. Then focus on your most probable scenario. What could change it to become a best-case or worst-case scenario? Next, summarize your scenarios and your answers to this question.

JOURNAL ENTRY #49 INTENTION STATEMENT

Participating in class is an excellent way to practice speaking in public. On a separate sheet of paper, write an Intention Statement concerning how you intend to participate in class in order to experience talking to a group of people. Be specific about which class you intend to speak in, how you will set up the opportunity to speak (i.e., having questions ready, sitting in front, asking to give a presentation, etc.), and how you intend to record your observations of the experience.

JOURNAL ENTRY #50 DISCOVERY STATEMENT

Think back to a time when you were called upon to answer a question in class or speak before a group. On a separate sheet of paper, write down what you remember about that situation. Describe your physical sensations, the effectiveness of your presentation, feedback from the audience, and so forth.

master student

w i l l i a m   n o l e n
*surgeon and author, practiced medicine
for years. He wrote several popular books,
and his articles have appeared in many
leading magazines.*

In contrast to my four relatively miserable years at Holy Cross, I enjoyed, for the most part, the four years at Tufts Medical School. . . .

For almost the first time in my academic career I was studying material that I knew was going to be of value to me the rest of my life. Anatomy was a course that required mostly brute memory. It wasn't easy to remember where the deltoid muscle began, where it ended, what muscles were next to it, and what blood vessels and nerves nourished it and made it work, but I could see the practicality of having all that information tucked away in my mind. So I studied, not only because I wanted a decent grade but because I wanted to be a knowledgeable doctor.

Like most pre-med students I had resented the time I spent in college on subjects which seemed unrelated to my future as a doctor. I know now that my attitude was based in immaturity. College is a place where a student ought to learn not so much how to make a living, but how to live. In the 1970's we're trying to reduce the time . . . [students have] to spend becoming a doctor. Some medical schools will accept students after three years of college—others are combining the fourth year of medical school with the internship. It's possible in some programs to acquire an M.D. degree six years after high school graduation, rather than the usual eight.

The purpose in shortening medical education is to produce more doctors. Personally, I don't think it will work. With every year that passes there is more and more knowledge that a doctor should have. How in the world can we expect students to learn more in less time?

What will happen, I'm afraid, is that we'll start producing pure technicians. If anything is to be eliminated from the would-be doctor's education, it won't be biochemistry, anatomy or pharmacology; it will be the course in Shakespeare, the year of philosophy, the semesters of French. One of the major problems in medicine now is that doctors tend to have depth but no breadth to their knowledge. There is a saying, well known to all medical students, that the General Practitioner is a doctor who learns less and less about more and more, until he eventually knows nothing about everything; the specialist is the man who learns more and more about less and less, until he eventually knows everything about nothing. This is the age of the specialist, and because their interests are so narrow, the specialists tend to see patients as faceless carriers of disease, technical problems to be solved, rather than as human beings. What we need in medicine are doctors who are more the artist and less the scientist. I don't think that shortening medical education will produce them.

1 It is important to list and schedule all writing tasks before you do any work on writing a paper. True or False. Explain your answer.

2 What are at least three methods that can assist you in writing the first draft of a paper?

3 Free writing is based on writing as much as you can for a specified time period, stopping only occasionally to edit your work. True or False. Explain your answer.

4 Describe at least three ways to create "gender fair" writing.

5 Describe at least three techniques for practicing and delivering a speech.

6 Name and briefly define two popular features of the Internet.

7 Rewrite the following sentence so that it is gender-neutral: "Any writer can benefit from honing his skill at observing people."

8 *Define* plagiarism *and explain ways to avoid it.*

9 *When delivering a speech, it's often effective to make direct eye contact with members of your audience. True or False. Explain your answer.*

10 *Which of the following is an effective thesis statement?*

    (A) Two types of thinking.
    (B) Critical thinking and creative thinking go hand in hand.
    (C) The relationship between critical thinking and creative thinking.

JOURNAL ENTRY #51
DISCOVERY/INTENTION STATEMENT

Review the suggestions for writing offered throughout this chapter and list at least one that you already use.

    I discovered that I . . .

_____

_____

    Now choose one suggestion that could make a huge difference in your effectiveness at writing. Describe that suggestion and explain exactly how you intend to use it.

    I intend to . . .

_____

_____

_____

_____

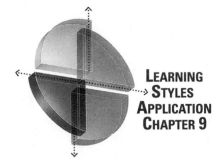

**LEARNING
STYLES
APPLICATION
CHAPTER 9**

Complete the following exercises on a separate sheet of paper.

Style 1

Think about how you've approached writing assignments in the past. If you could instantly change any one thing about the way you write, what would it be? Perhaps you'd like to generate first drafts more quickly or avoid last-minute crunches before the assignment is due. Describe a specific change you'd like to make.

Style 2

List 10 suggestions from this chapter that could help you make the change you listed for Style 1.

Style 3

From the 10 suggestions you listed for Style 2, choose five to use in a writing task you now face. Describe how you will use each suggestion.

Style 4

Imagine that you are going to teach a course in effective writing. Create an outline for this course, based on what you learned from reading this chapter and applying your chosen techniques.

Bibliography

■ Endnotes

[1]Peter Elbow, *Writing with Power: Techniques for Mastering the Writing Process* (New York: Oxford University, 1981).

[2]Natalie Goldberg, *Writing Down the Bones: Freeing the Writer Within* (Boston: Shambhala, 1986).

[3]Theodore Cheney, *Getting the Words Right: How to Revise, Edit & Rewrite* (Cincinnati, OH: Writer's Digest, 1983).

■ Additional Reading

Bartlett, John G. *Familiar Quotations*, Boston: Little, Brown, 1980.

Dumond, Val. *The Elements of Nonsexist Usage*, New York: Prentice-Hall, 1990.

McCutcheon, Randall. *Can You Find It?* Minneapolis: Free Spirit, 1989.

Murray, Donald M. *Write to Learn*, New York: Holt, Rinehart and Winston, 1987.

Osborn, Susan. *Dial An Expert: The Consumer's Sourcebook of Free & Low Cost Expertise Available by Phone*, New York: McGraw-Hill, 1986.

Rico, Gabriele Lusser. *Writing the Natural Way*, Los Angeles: J. P. Tarcher, 1983.

Roth, Audrey J. *The Research Paper: Process, Form & Content*, Belmont, CA: Wadsworth, 1989.

Strunk, William, Jr., and E. B. White. *The Elements of Style*, New York: Macmillan, 1979.

Ueland, Brenda. *If You Want To Write: A Book About Art, Independence and Spirit*, St. Paul, MN: Graywolf, 1987.

relations

In this chapter...

■ look for a wealth of suggestions to prevent misunderstanding, resolve conflict, handle complaints, and even accept compliments. Learn new ways to respond when you experience emotional pain or when you encounter instructors you can't stand. Also begin using **integrity** (the skill of making promises and keeping agreements) as a tool for transforming your life, and tap into your **leadership** abilities.

JOURNAL ENTRY #52
DISCOVERY STATEMENT

Describe a time when you experienced an emotionally charged conflict with another person. Were you able to resolve this conflict effectively? If so, list the strategies you used to resolve the conflict. Also list any different outcomes you would like to achieve the next time you experience conflict with another person.

_____

_____

_____

_____

_____

_____

Now scan this chapter for ideas that can help you get across your feelings more skillfully in such situations. List several ideas here.

_____

_____

_____

_____

_____

_____

_____

hips

The communication loop

COMMUNICATION IS OFTEN GARBLED when we try to send and receive messages at the same time. One effective way to improve your ability to communicate is to be aware of when you are the receiver and when you are the sender. If you are receiving (listening), then just receive. Avoid switching into the sending mode. When you are sending (talking), stick with it until you are finished.

If the other person is trying to send a message when you want to be the sender, you have at least three choices: stop sending and be the receiver, stop sending and leave, or ask the other person to stop sending so you can send. It is ineffective to try to send and receive at the same time.

This becomes clear when we look at what happens in a conversation. When we talk, we put thoughts into words. Words are a code for what we experience. This is called *encoding*. The person who receives the message takes our words and translates them into his own experience. This is called *decoding*.

A conversation between two people is like communication between two telegraph operators. One encodes a message and sends it over the wire. The operator at the other end receives the coded signal, decodes it, evaluates it, and sends back another coded message. The first operator decodes this message and sends another. The cycle continues. The messages look like this:

1 ..--..--.-.-	3 --.--..---	OPERATOR 1
2 --.-..-..	4 -..- --...-.	OPERATOR 2

> **" "**
> *Candor is a compliment; it implies equality. It's how true friends talk.*
> –PEGGY NOONAN

> **" "**
> *The origin of all conflict between me and my fellow men is that I do not say what I mean, and that I do not do what I say.*
> –MARTIN BUBER

> **" "**
> *You have two ears and one mouth. Remember to use them in more or less that proportion.*
> –PAULA BERN

In this encoding-decoding loop you continually switch roles. One minute you send, the next you receive. It's a problem when both operators send at the same time. Neither operator knows what the other one sent. Neither can reply. Communication works best when each of us has a complete chance to send, sufficient time to comprehend, and plenty of time to respond.

There are other problems in communication. As psychotherapist Virginia Satir[1] reminds us, only a small percentage of communication is verbal. All of us send messages with our bodies and with the tone of our voices. Throw in a few other factors, like a hot room or background noise, and it's a wonder we communicate at all.

Another problem is that the message sent is often not the message received. This process of continually encoding and decoding words can result in the simplest message's being muddled. For some, *chair* conjures up the image of an overstuffed rocking recliner. Others visualize a metal folding chair. And some people think of the person who "chairs" a meeting. If simple things like this can be misunderstood, it's easy to see how more complex ideas can wreak havoc on communication. For example, a "good teacher" can mean someone who is smart, entertaining, easy, challenging, creative—or a hundred other things.

Communicating effectively means getting on the same wavelength. Even then, it helps to keep checking with each other to make sure we are talking about the same thing.

These difficulties are never fully overcome. They can be partially alleviated by using effective communication techniques and by having a sincere intention to understand one another.

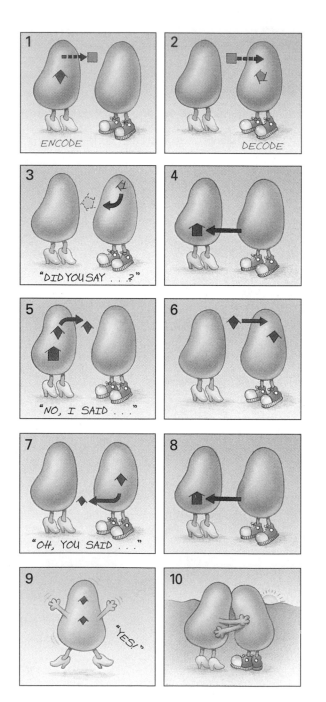

The communication loop

LISTENING

You observe a person in a conversation who is not talking. Is he listening? Maybe. Maybe not. He may be preparing his response or daydreaming. Listening is not easy. Doing it effectively requires concentration and energy.

It's worth it. Listening well promotes success in school—more powerful notes, more productive study groups, better relationships with students and instructors. A skilled listener is appreciated by friends, family, and business associates. The best salespeople and managers are the best listeners. People love a good listener. Through skilled listening, you gain more than respect. You gain insight into other people. You learn about the world and about yourself.

To be a good listener, decide to listen. Once you've made this choice, you can use the following techniques to be a more effective listener. These ideas are especially useful in times of high emotional tension.

Nonverbal listening

Much of listening is nonverbal. Here are five guidelines for effective nonverbal listening.

1. Be quiet. Silence is more than staying quiet while someone is speaking. Allowing several seconds to pass before you begin to talk gives the speaker time to catch his breath or gather his thoughts. He may want to continue. Someone who talks nonstop might fear he will lose the floor if he pauses.

If the message being sent is complete, this short break gives you time to form your response and helps you avoid the biggest barrier to listening—listening with your answer running. If you make up a response before the person is finished, you miss the end of the message—which is often the main point.

Pausing for several seconds might be inappropriate. Ignore this suggestion completely when someone asks in a panic where to find the nearest phone to call the fire department.

2. Maintain eye contact. Look at the other person while he speaks. It demonstrates your attention and it helps keep your mind from wandering. Your eyes also let you "listen" to body language and behavior. When some of us remove our glasses, we not only can't see—we can't hear.

Avoid staring too long. The speaker might think he is talking to a zombie. Act appropriately.

This idea is not an absolute. People from some cultures are uncomfortable with sustained eye contact. Others learn primarily by hearing; they can listen more effectively by turning off the visual input once in a while. Keep in mind the differences among people.

3. Display openness. You can communicate openness by your facial expression and body position. Uncross your arms and legs. Sit up straight. Face the other person and remove any physical barriers between you, such as a pile of books.

4. Listen without response. This doesn't mean you should never respond. It means wait.

When listening to another person, we often interrupt with our stories, opinions, suggestions, and inappropriate comments:

"Oh, I'm so excited. I just found out that I am nominated to be in *Who's Who in American Musicians.*"

"Yeah, that's neat. My uncle Elmer got into *Who's Who in American Veterinarians.* He sure has an interesting job. One time I went along when he was treating a cow and . . . . "

Watch your nonverbal responses too. A look of "Good grief!" from you can keep the other person from finishing his message.

5. Send acknowledgments. It is important to periodically let the speaker know you are still there. Your words or nonverbal gestures of acknowledgment let the speaker know you are interested and that you are with him and his message. These include "Umhum," "OK," "Yes," and head nods.

These acknowledgments do not imply your agreement. If people tell you what they don't like about you, your head nod doesn't mean you agree. It just indicates that you are listening.

Verbal listening

Sometimes speaking promotes listening.

1. Feed back meaning. Paraphrase the communication. This does not mean parroting what another person says. Instead, briefly summarize. Feed back what you see as the essence of that person's message: "Let me see if I understood what you said . . ." or "What I'm hearing you say is . . . ." (Psychotherapist Carl Rogers[2] referred to this technique as *reflection*.) Often the other person will say, "No, that's not what I meant. What I said was . . . ."

There will be no doubt when you get it right. The sender will say, "Yeah, that's it," and either continue with another message or stop sending when he knows you understand.

If you don't understand the message, be persistent. Ask the person to please repeat what he said; then paraphrase it again. Effective communication involves a feedback loop.

Be concise. This is not a time to stop the other person by talking on and on about what you think you heard.

2. Listen beyond words. Be aware of nonverbal messages and behavior. You may point out that the speaker's body language seems to be the exact opposite of his words. For example, "I noticed you said you are excited, but you look very bored."

Keep in mind that the same nonverbal behavior can have different meanings, depending on the listener's cultural background. Someone who looks bored may simply be listening in a different way.

The idea is to listen not only to the words, but also to the emotion behind the words. Sometimes that emotional message is more important than the verbal content.

3. Take care of yourself. People seek out good listeners, and there are times when you don't want to listen. You may be busy or distracted with your own concerns. Be honest. Don't pretend to listen. You can say, "What you're saying is important, and I'm pressed for time right now. Can we set aside another time to talk about this?" It's OK not to listen.

4. Listen for requests and intentions. "This class is a waste of my time." "Our instructor talks too fast." An effective way to listen to complaints is to look for the request hidden in them.

"This class is a waste of my time" can be heard as "Please tell me what I'll gain if I participate actively in class." "The instructor talks too fast" can become "What strategies can I use for taking notes when the instructor covers the material rapidly?"

We can even transform complaints into intentions. Take the complaint "The parking lot by the dorms is so dark at night that I'm afraid to go to my car." This complaint can result in a project—installing a light in the parking lot.

Viewing complaints this way gives us more choices. When the complaint becomes a request or an intention, we can decide whether to grant the request or take on the project. That's more powerful than responding to a complaint with defensiveness ("What does he know anyway?"), resignation ("It's always been this way and always will be"), or indifference ("It's not my job").

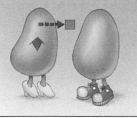

The communication loop

SENDING

We have been talking for years, and we usually manage to get our messages across. There are times, though, when we don't. Often these times are emotionally charged. Sometimes we feel wonderful or rotten or sad or scared and we want to express it. Emotions can get in the way of the message. Described below are four techniques for delivering a message through tears, laughter, fist-pounding, or hugging. They are: replacing "You" messages with "I" messages, avoiding questions that aren't really questions, noticing nonverbal messages, and noticing barriers to communication.

The "I's" have it!

It can be difficult to disagree with someone without his becoming angry or your becoming upset. When conflict occurs, we often make statements about the other person, or "You" messages:

"You are rude."

"You make me mad."

"You must be crazy."

"You don't love me anymore."

This kind of communication results in defensiveness. The responses might be:

"I am not rude."

"I don't care."

"No, *you* are crazy."

"No, *you* don't love *me!*"

"You" messages are hard to listen to. They label, judge, blame, and assume things that may or may not be true. They demand rebuttal. Sometimes even praise can be an ineffective "You" message. "You" messages don't work.

When communication is emotionally charged, psychologist Thomas Gordon[3] suggests that you consider limiting your statements to descriptions about yourself.

Replace "You" messages with "I" messages.

"You are rude" might become "I feel upset."

"You make me mad" could be "I feel angry."

"You must be crazy" can be "I don't understand."

"You don't love me anymore" could become "I'm afraid we're drifting apart."

Suppose a friend asks you to pick him up at the airport. You drive 20 miles and wait for the plane. No friend. You decide your friend missed his plane, so you wait three hours for the next flight. No friend. Perplexed and worried, you drive home. The next day, you see your friend downtown.

"What happened?" you ask.

"Oh, I caught an earlier flight."

"You are a rude person," you reply.

Look for the facts, the observable behavior. Everyone will agree that your friend asked you to pick him up, he did take an earlier flight, you did not receive a call from him. But the idea that he is rude is not a fact, it's a judgment.

He may go on to say, "I called your home and no one answered. My mom had a stroke and was rushed to Valley View. I caught the earliest flight I could get." Your judgment no longer fits.

When you saw your friend, you might have said, "I waited and waited at the airport. I was worried about you. I didn't get a call. I feel angry and hurt. I don't want to waste my time. Next time, you can call me when your flight arrives and I'll be happy to pick you up."

"I" messages don't judge, blame, criticize, or insult. They don't invite the other person to counterattack with more of the same. "I" messages are also more accurate. They report our own thoughts and feelings.

"I" messages may feel uncomfortable or forced at first. That's OK. Use the five ways to say "I'" explained in this chapter. With practice, you'll feel more at home with this technique.

Questions are not always questions

You've heard these "questions" before. A parent asks, "Don't you want to look nice?" Translation: "I wish you'd cut your hair, lose the blue jeans, and put on a tie." Or how about this question from a spouse: "Honey, wouldn't you love to go to an exciting hockey game tonight?" Translation: "I already bought tickets."

We use questions that aren't questions to sneak our opinions and requests into conversations, without owning up to them publicly.

"Doesn't it upset you?" means "It upsets me," and "Shouldn't we hang the picture over here?" means "I want to hang the picture over here."

Communication improves when we say, "I'm upset," "Let's hang the picture over here," and "The game begins at eight."

Notice nonverbal messages

How you say something can be more important than what you say.

Your tone of voice and your gestures can support, modify, or contradict your words. Your posture, the way you dress, how often you shower, and even the poster hanging on your wall can negate your words before you say them.

Most nonverbal behavior is unconscious. We can learn to be aware of it. Then we can choose our nonverbal messages. The key is to be clear about our intention and purpose. When we know what we want to say and are committed to getting it across, our inflections, gestures, and words work together and send a unified message.

Notice barriers to sending your message

Sometimes fear stops us from sending messages. We are afraid of other people's reactions, sometimes justifiably. Being truthful doesn't mean being insensitive to others' reactions. Tact is a virtue; letting fear prevent communication is not.

Assumptions also can be used as excuses for not sending messages. "She already knows this," we tell ourselves. "I told her last week." You may have sent the message last week, but sometimes people don't receive messages and sometimes they don't remember. Reminders can be useful.

Predictions of failure also can be barriers to sending. "She won't listen," we tell ourselves. That statement may be inaccurate. Perhaps the other person senses that we're angry and listens in a guarded way. Or perhaps the other person is listening and sending nonverbal messages we don't understand.

Or we might predict, "She'll never do anything about it if I tell her." Again, assuming can kill your message before you send it.

It's easy to make excuses for not communicating. If you have fear or some other concern about sending a message, be aware of it. Don't expect the concern to go away. Realize that you can communicate even with your

concerns. You can choose to make them a part of the message: "I am going to tell you how I feel, and I'm afraid you will think it's stupid."

Talking to someone when you don't want to could be a matter of educational survival. A short talk with an adviser, teacher, friend, or family member may solve a problem that jeopardizes your education.

Notice your barriers and make choices that promote your success.

Five ways to say "I"

An "I" message can include any or all of the following five parts. Be careful when including parts four and five since they contain hidden judgments or threats.

1. Observation. Describe the facts—the indisputable, observable realities. Talk about what you—or anyone else—can see, hear, smell, taste, or touch. Avoid judgments, interpretations, or opinions. Instead of saying "You're a slob," say "Last night's lasagna pan was still on the stove this morning."

2. Feelings. Describe your own feelings. It is easier to listen to "I feel frustrated" than to "You never help me." Talking about how you feel about another's actions can be valuable feedback for that person.

3. Wants. You are far more likely to get what you want if you say what you want. If someone doesn't know what you want, he doesn't have a choice about helping you get it. Ask clearly. Avoid demanding or using the word *need*. Most people like to feel helpful, not obligated. Instead of "Do the dishes when it's your turn, or else!" say "I want to divide the housework fairly."

4. Thoughts. Communicate your thoughts, and use caution. Beginning your statement with an "I" doesn't qualify it as an "I" message. "I think you are a slob" is a "You" judgment in disguise. Instead, say "I'd have more time to study if I didn't have to clean up so often."

5. Intentions. The last part of an "I" message is a statement about what you intend to do. Have a plan that doesn't depend on the other person. For example, instead of "From now on we're going to split the dishwashing evenly," you could say "I intend to do my share of the housework and leave the rest undone."

EXERCISE #34
WRITE AN "I" MESSAGE

Pick something about school that irritates you. Pretend you are talking to the person who is associated with this irritation.
First, write what you would say as a "You" message.

_____

_____

_____

_____

Now write the same complaint as an "I" message. Include at least the first three of the elements suggested in "Five ways to say 'I.'"

_____

_____

_____

_____

_____

JOURNAL ENTRY #53
DISCOVERY/INTENTION STATEMENT

Think about one of your relationships for a few minutes. It might be with a parent, sibling, spouse, child, friend, hairdresser, etc. In the space below, write about some things that are not working in the relationship. What bugs you? What do you find irritating or unsatisfying?
Now think for a moment about what you want from this relationship. More attention? Less nagging? More openness, trust, security, money, or freedom? After describing what you want from the relationship, describe a suggestion from this chapter you could use to make the relationship work.

_____

_____

_____

_____

_____

_____

_____

As long as we are in a relationship, there is the potential for lasting happiness—and for serious conflict. This applies at work, in the classroom, and at home. The simple fact is that relationships are not always smooth sailing.

That fact is a gift. We can be thankful that we get plenty of opportunities to practice conflict resolution. It's one of the most practical skills we'll ever learn.

Following are several strategies that can help you resolve conflict. As a way to bring these ideas to life, think of ways to apply them right now. Before going further, bring to mind someone with whom you are currently in conflict. And as you read, see these ideas working for you.

Let it get worse before it gets better

Sometimes a conflict needs to escalate so that everyone is truly aware of it. Many people are reluctant to do this. That's understandable—and it can prevent us from getting to the bottom of the problem.

Often it is not necessary for a conflict to get worse. Yet our willingness to allow this possibility gives us freedom to clear the air.

Lay your cards on the table

One of the most effective strategies for resolving any problem is to outline the problem clearly. By using "I" statements, which are explained in this chapter, you tell people what you observe, feel, think, want, and intend to do. This can be a careful and thorough way to get your message across.

We are often reluctant to lay all this out on the table. This very reluctance holds some problems in place.

The fine art of con

Step back from the conflict

Instead of trading personal attacks during a conflict, step back. Defuse the situation by approaching it in a neutral way. Define the conflict as a problem to be solved, not as a contest to be won. Detach. Give up being "right" and aim for being effective instead.

The trick here is to state the problem in a way that grants choice to all parties involved. You could say something like this: "We have a situation here that isn't working for either of us. Please tell me what you think the problem is and what is needed to solve it. Then I'll share my perspective. Let's talk until we find a solution that works for both of us."

Just speak

When we're locked in combat with someone, it's tempting to hold back—to say only a fraction of what we're thinking or feeling. This can be one more way to keep the conflict alive.

An alternative is to "empty our buckets"—to let the words and the feelings flow without editing. In this case, we don't worry about making a perfect "I" statement. We just say the first things that come to mind. This is one way to get all our cards on the table.

Commit to the relationship

The thorniest conflict usually happens between people who genuinely care for each other. It's hard to be in conflict when the relationship doesn't matter to us.

Begin by affirming your commitment to the other person: "I care about you, and I want this relationship to last. So I'm willing to do whatever it takes to resolve this problem." Also ask the other person for a similar commitment. This strategy can go a long way in fixing even the most serious problems.

You might be unsure of your commitment to the relationship. If so, postpone any further communication for now. Take some time to be alone and consider the value of this relationship to you.

People engaged in conflict often stop seeing each other. Many times we increase the odds of solving the problem when we stay in a relationship.

Back up to common ground

Conflict heightens the differences between people. When this happens, it's easy for them to forget how much they still agree with each other. As a first step in resolving conflict, back up to common ground. List all the points on which you are not in conflict: "I know that we disagree about how much to spend on a new car, but we do agree that the old one needs to be replaced." Often such comments put the problem in perspective and pave the way for a solution.

flict resolution

Listen for the request in the complaint

People complain to us when they want something different from us. And when we take the complaint at face value, we may feel blamed or put down.

Go deeper. Listen for the request that's behind the complaint. If a friend complains that you always interrupt her, take it as a request: "Please let me finish what I'm saying before you speak." This makes it easier to respond to the request—not the accusation or the anger.

Slow down the communication

In times of great conflict, people often talk all at once. Words fly like speeding bullets, and no one is really listening. Such discussions generate a lot of heat and little light. Chances for resolving the conflict take a nosedive.

When this happens, choose to either listen or talk—not both at the same time. Just send your message. Or just receive the other person's message. Usually this slows down the pace, clears the smoke, and allows people to become more levelheaded.

To slow down the communication even more, take a break. Depending upon the level of conflict, that might mean anything from a few minutes to a few days.

A related suggestion is to do something nonthreatening together. Share an activity with others that's not a source of conflict.

Be a complete listener

Often in times of conflict, we say one thing and mean another. So before responding to what the other person says, use active listening. Check to see if you have correctly received that person's message: "What I'm hearing you say is . . . . Did I get it correctly?"

Listening completely can also include asking for more. Often people will stop short of their bottom-line message. Encourage them to continue by asking for it: "Anything else that you want to say about that? Is something more on your mind right now?"

Get to the point— then elaborate

Sometimes people in conflict build up to their main points cautiously. This technique works well for actors on stage who want to add drama to a scene. It doesn't work so well for the rest of us, especially when we're in conflict.

Making our listeners wait in suspense while we saunter up to our message can lead to a problem: During the interval, other people might make up something far worse than what we really intend to say. As an alternative, get to your point right away. When that's done, there's usually time to provide supporting details.

Recap your message

As we send messages in times of conflict, we may talk for a long time. Sometimes people in emotional stress can't take it all in. And even if they get our whole message, they may not understand which of our points is most important.

You can follow that homespun advice given to professional speakers: First, tell 'em what you're going to say. Then tell 'em. And then tell 'em what you told 'em.

Before you yield the floor to someone else, "tell 'em what you told 'em." Review your main messages and repeat your key requests.

Use a mediator

Even an untrained mediator—someone who's not a party to the conflict—can do much to decrease tension. Mediators can help all those involved in the problem get their points of view across. Here the mediator's role is not to give advice but to keep the discussion on track and moving toward a solution.

Allow for cultural differences

People from different cultures use different methods for solving problems. When it seems to you that other people are sidestepping or escalating a conflict, consider whether your reaction is based on cultural bias.

Apologize or ask for forgiveness

Often a conflict arises from our own errors. Usually we don't do these things on purpose. They're just mistakes.

Others may move quickly when we acknowledge this fact, apologize, and ask for forgiveness. This is "spending face"—an alternative to the age-old habit of "saving face." Here we simply admit that we are less than perfect and own up to our goof-ups.

Write a letter and send it

What can be difficult to say to another person face-to-face might be effectively communicated in writing. When people in conflict write

letters to each other, they automatically apply many of the suggestions in this article. Letter writing is a way to slow down the communication and ensure that only one person at a time is sending a message.

One drawback: It's possible for people to misunderstand what you say in a letter. To avoid further problems, make clear what you are not saying: "I am saying that I want to be alone for a few days. I am not saying that I want you to stay away forever."

Before you send your letter, put yourself in the shoes of the person who will receive it. Imagine how your comments could be misinterpreted. Then rewrite your letter, correcting any areas that are likely to be misinterpreted.

Write a letter and don't send it

Sometimes we feel compelled to blame other people or speak to them angrily. This is likely to fan the flames instead of resolve the conflict.

If this happens, consider a way to get the problem off your chest and the upset out of your system—without beating up the other person: Write the nastiest, meanest letter you can imagine. Let all of your frustration, anger, and venom flow onto the page. Be as mean and blaming as you can. When your pen has cooled off, see if there is anything else you want to add.

Now, take the letter and destroy it. Your writing has served its purpose. Chances are that you've calmed down and are ready for some skilled conflict resolution.

Permit the emotion

Crying is OK. Being upset is all right. Feeling angry is often appropriate. Allowing other people to see the strength of our feelings can go a long way in clearing up the conflict. Emotion is part of life and certainly an important part of any communication.

Just allow the full range of your feeling. Often what's on the far side of anger is love. When we clear out the resentment and hostility, we might find genuine compassion taking its place.

Videotape the disagreement

This is an option for the brave—those who really want feedback on their conflict resolution skills. With the agreement of all parties involved, set up a camera and videotape your conversation.

Later, play back the tape and review your side of the conversation. Look for any ways that you perpetuated the upset. Spot anything you did or said to move the problem toward a solution.

In the midst of a raging argument, when emotions run high, it's almost impossible to see ourselves objectively. Let the video camera be your unbiased observer.

Agree to disagree

Sometimes we say all we have to say. We do all the problem solving we can do. We get all points of view across. And the conflict remains, staring us in the face.

What's left is to recognize that honest disagreement is a fact of life. We can peacefully coexist with other people—and respect them—even though we don't agree on fundamental issues. Conflict can be accepted even when it is not resolved.

Do nothing

Sometimes we worsen a conflict by insisting that it be solved immediately. It can be wise to sit tight and wait things out. Some conflicts resolve themselves with the passage of time.

See the conflict within you

Sometimes conflict we see in the outside world has its source in the world behind our eyeballs. A cofounder of Alcoholics Anonymous put it this way: "It is a spiritual axiom that every time we are disturbed, no matter what the cause, there is something awry with us."

It's been said that nobody can hurt us as much as our own thoughts can. When we're angry or upset, we can take a minute to look inside. Perhaps we were ready to take offense, waiting to pounce on something the other person said. Perhaps, without realizing it, we did something to create the conflict. Or maybe the other person is simply saying what we know to be true—and don't want to admit.

When these things happen, we can shine a light on ourselves. A simple spot-check on our thinking might help the conflict disappear—right before our eyes.

Conflict resolution in a nutshell

Conflict can lead to anger, hostility, and further conflicts. Or it can be used as a powerful opportunity for solving problems. For example, you can handle conflict by denying the problem exists, smoothing it over, or trying to overpower the other person. These lead to win/lose situations. When you resolve conflict through collaboration and compromise, you can achieve win/win solutions.

Here are seven steps to transform a conflict into a solution in which both parties win.

1. State the problem. Using "I" messages (page 264), explain the problem. Allow the other person to do the same. You may have different problems. This is the time to clearly define the conflict. It's hard to fix something before everyone agrees on what's broken.

2. Understand all points of view. If you want to defuse tension or defensiveness, set aside your opinions for a moment. Take the time to understand the other points of view. Sum up those points of view in words that the other parties can accept. When people feel they've been heard, they're often more willing to listen.

3. Brainstorm solutions. Dream up as many solutions as you can. Be outrageous. Don't evaluate them. Quantity, not quality, is the key. If you get stuck, restate the problem and continue brainstorming.

4. Evaluate the solutions. Discard the unacceptable ones. This step will require time and honesty. Talk about which solutions will work and how difficult they will be to implement. You may hit upon a totally new solution.

5. Choose the solution. Choose the one most acceptable to all. Be honest.

6. Implement. Decide who is going to do what by when. Then keep your agreements.

7. Re-evaluate. Review the effectiveness of your solution. If it works, pat yourselves on the back. If not, be open to making changes or implementing a new solution.

PRACTICING
CRITICAL THINKING #19

Discuss a controversial issue of your choosing with a small group of friends or classmates. At several points in your discussion, stop to evaluate your group's critical thinking. Answer the following questions:

- Are we staying open to opposing ideas—even if we initially disagree with them?
- Are we asking for evidence for each key assertion?
- Are we adequately summarizing one another's point of view before we analyze it?
- Are we foreseeing the possible consequences of taking a particular stand on any issue?
- Are we considering more than one solution to problems?
- Are we willing to change our stands on issues or suspend judgement when appropriate?
- Are we being systematic as we consider the issues?

PRACTICING
CRITICAL THINKING #20

The following exercise offers you a chance to interpret and categorize different views on an issue. This exercise can be done with any number of people. When more people take part, you are more likely to gain a wider range of opinions.

Select a topic—for example, the recent war in the Balkan territories, including Bosnia-Herzegovina. Ask everyone to spend five minutes writing down their opinions about this issue. Ask them to recall articles they read, reports they heard, or experiences they had during this war. Each opinion can be recorded on one 3x5 card. Examples might include:

- This war shows that centuries of ethnic hatred cannot be stopped by a single diplomatic effort.
- The United States should have acted more decisively and sooner to help resolve this conflict.
- Any peace accord reached in this part of the world is likely to unravel within a few years.

Write as many opinions as you can in five minutes. Whenever possible, include reasons and evidence for your opinions. All your thoughts about the issue are important.

Now spread all the 3x5 cards out on a desk or the floor. Ask everyone to take 10 minutes and walk around and read what other people have written. Whenever you find an opinion that intrigues you or leads you to think about the issue in a new way, write that opinion on a 3x5 card.

After reviewing all the opinions, reasons, and evidence, return to your own cards and pick up the ones you still agree with after reading everyone else's cards. Now you have in hand the cards that reflect your current opinion about this issue.

After this process, you may have decided that some of your former opinions have little value. They stayed on the floor. You could also decide that other opinions need substantial change.

At this point, review the stack of cards you now hold in your hands. These cards represent your considered opinion about the topic. You might have only the cards you initially wrote (no changes in your opinions about the topic) or a combination of your own and others' opinions (some change in your thoughts about the topic) or completely new cards (a total shift in your opinion about the topic).

Keep in mind that opinions on any topic are subject to change in the light of further reasoning and new evidence. This is often the result of high-quality critical thinking. Change may occur when you discover new information, when you see the topic from a new vantage point, have new experiences in life, or see greater significance in something that you missed before.

On a separate sheet of paper, write a Discovery Statement about what you learned about yourself through this exercise. Describe any qualities of a critical thinker that you displayed. Also list the critical thinking qualities or skills you used.

Emotional pain is not a sickness

Emotional pain has gotten a bad name. This type of slander is undeserved. There is nothing wrong with feeling bad. It's OK to feel miserable, depressed, sad, upset, angry, dejected, gloomy, or unhappy.

It may not be pleasant to feel bad, but it can be good for you. Often, the appropriate way to feel is bad. When you leave a place you love, sadness is natural. When you lose a friend or lover, misery might be in order. When someone treats you badly, it probably is appropriate to feel angry.

Some people will try almost anything to avoid feeling bad, even if the cure is worse than the sadness. This kind of behavior is promoted by messages we get every day.

It started when we were children and adults told us: "Oh, please don't cry" or "Stop that crying right now!" or "Oh, cheer up." Later in life, we got similar advice: "Sleep on it, you'll feel better in the morning." "Have a drink. It's a great way to relax." "Take two of these pills and you'll feel great."

These messages usually come from well-meaning people who don't want you to feel too bad.

Unless you are suicidally depressed, it is almost impossible to feel too bad. Feeling bad for too long can be a problem. If depression, sadness, or anger persists, get help. Otherwise, allow the feelings. They're usually appropriate and necessary for personal growth.

When a loved one dies, it is necessary to grieve. The grief might appear in the form of depression, sadness, or anger. There is nothing wrong with extreme emotional pain. It is natural, and it doesn't have to be fixed.

When feeling bad becomes a problem, it is usually because you didn't allow yourself to feel bad. So the next time you feel rotten, go ahead and feel rotten. It will pass, and it will probably pass more quickly if you don't fight it or pretend it doesn't exist. Here are some good ways to feel bad.

Give yourself permission. Most of us have been taught from the time we were little not to feel bad. Send yourself a reverse message. Say to yourself, out loud if you can, "It's all right for me to feel the way I do" or "I feel bad and that is good."

Don't worry about reasons. Sometimes we allow ourselves to feel bad if we have a good reason. For example: "Well, I feel very sad, but that is because I just found out my best friend is moving to Madagascar." It's all right to know the reason why you are sad, and it is fine not to know. You can feel bad for no apparent reason. The reason doesn't matter.

Set a time limit. If you are concerned about feeling bad, if you are worried that you need to "fix it," give yourself a little time. Before you force yourself not to feel the way you feel, set a time limit. Say to yourself, "I am going to give myself until Monday at noon, and if I don't feel better by then, I am going to try to fix myself." Sometimes, it is appropriate to fix a bad feeling. There might be a problem that needs a solution. You can use feeling bad as your motivation to solve the problem. And sometimes it helps to just feel bad for a while.

Tell others. Sometimes other people—friends or family, for example—have a hard time letting you feel bad. They might be worried that they did something wrong and want to make it better. They want you to quit feeling bad. Tell them you will. Assure them that you will feel good again but that, for now, you just want to feel bad.

This is no joke. Sometimes students think this whole idea of allowing yourself to feel bad is a joke, reverse psychology, or something. It isn't. This suggestion is based on the notion that good mental health is possible only if you allow yourself to feel the full range of your emotions.

You deserve compliments

For some people, compliments are more difficult to accept than criticisms. Here are some hints for handling compliments.

1. Accept the compliment. We sometimes respond to praise with, "Oh, it's really nothing" or "This old thing? I've had it for years." This response undermines both you and the person who sent the compliment.

2. Choose another time to deliver your own compliments. Automatically returning a compliment can appear suspiciously polite and insincere.

3. Let the compliment stand. "Do you really think so?" questions the integrity of the message. It can also sound as if we're fishing for more compliments. Accepting compliments is not the same as being conceited. You are worthy and capable. Allow people to acknowledge that.

Relationships can work

ometimes relationships work exceptionally well; sometimes they don't. Of all the factors that affect relationships, the biggest is communication (which is discussed in this chapter). Here's a list of other factors that can benefit or damage your relationships.

Do tell the truth. Life is complicated when you don't. For example, if you think a friend is addicted to drugs, telling him so in a supportive, nonjudgmental way is a sign of friendship. Psychotherapist Sidney Jourard[4] referred to such openness and honesty as *transparency* and wrote eloquently about how it can heal and deepen relationships.

Do support others. Encourage fellow students to reach their goals and be successful. Respect their study time. Helping them to stay on purpose can help you as well.

Don't pry. Being a good listener is invitation enough for fellow students to share their problems, feelings, and personal goals.

Don't borrow . . . too much. Borrowing a book or a tennis racket may seem like a small thing. Yet these requests can become a sore point in a relationship. Some people have difficulty saying no and resent lending things. Consider keeping borrowing to a minimum.

Do divide chores. Whether it's a class project or a household chore, do your part. Frustrations result when people fail to agree upon a fair division of work.

Don't gripe. There is a difference between griping and sharing problems. Gripers usually don't seek solutions. They just want everyone to know how unhappy they are. Sharing a problem is an appropriate way of starting the search for a solution.

Do write a letter. Sometimes it's not easy to express ourselves face-to-face, so write a letter. Even if you never send it, you've rehearsed what you want to say.

Do get involved. Being involved in extracurricular activities is a great way to meet people with common interests. If you commute and have little time for these activities, study at the library, eat at the cafeteria, or relax at the student union. You may be surprised at how many friends you make.

Don't brag. Other students are turned off by constant references to how much money you have, how great your boyfriend is, your social successes, or your family's accomplishments. There is a difference between sharing excitement and being obnoxious.

Do detach. Allow others to accept responsibility for their problems. Pitying them, getting upset along with them, or assuming responsibility for solving the problem is not helpful.

Do allow people to be upset. Trying to joke people out of their anger, discounting their frustration, or minimizing their disappointment invalidates their feelings. You can best support them by allowing them to experience their emotions.

Do ask for help. One of the central messages of this book is that you are not alone. You can draw on the talent, strength, and wisdom of other people. People often respond to a genuine request for help.

Do share yourself. When we brood on negative thoughts and refuse to speak them out loud, we lose perspective. And when we keep joys to ourselves, we diminish our satisfaction. A solution is to regularly share what we think and feel. Imagine a community where people freely and lovingly speak their minds—without fear or defensiveness. That can be your community.

Don't preach. This piece of advice might seem funny at the end of a sermon of do's and don'ts. Sometimes people ask for advice. It's OK to share your values and opinions. It's not OK to pretend you know what's best for someone else. Don't try to reform the world.

Relationships change

Relationships change, and the changes can be painful. Be prepared. Forget about buying broken heart insurance. You are too high a risk. In fact, any time you choose to care about another person, you risk a painful, but rarely fatal, broken heart.

Relationships grow and die. Lovers and spouses leave. Children grow up and move away. Parents die. We may even surpass the people we once looked to as models; that's a kind of loss too. All these events can lead to pain.

Pain is a part of living and can be dealt with in ways that help us learn. When an important relationship ends and you feel bad, allow yourself to experience that feeling. It is appropriate to be miserable when you are. It's normal to cry and express your feelings. It is also possible to go to class, study, work, eat, sleep, get your laundry done, and feel miserable at the same time.

Sometimes emotional pain is intense. If you feel absolutely rotten, useless, ugly, and unlovable, look in the mirror and tell yourself over and over again how rotten, useless, ugly, and unlovable you are. It might be hard to berate yourself for very long and keep a straight face. (Apply this suggestion with care.)

One option is to throw a pity party and talk about how rotten things have been going for you. Be prepared for your depressed mood to change quickly.

If you are determined to feel sorry for yourself, go all the way. Increase your misery by studying a few extra hours. This method works especially well on a Saturday night. You can get the most out of being depressed and deprived while everyone else is out having fun.

It could go like this: You get some extra studying done and start feeling like a good student. Maybe you are more worthwhile than you thought. You fight it, but you can't help feeling pleased with yourself. The pain subsides. Feeling good about yourself has an interesting side effect: Usually others start feeling good about you too.

Another way to work through this kind of pain is to do something. Do anything. Exercise. Mop the kitchen floor, clean out your dresser drawers, iron your shirts.

This sounds ridiculous, but it works. Remember that your purpose is not to avoid pain, but to see it from a more balanced viewpoint. Japanese psychiatrist Morita Masatake[5], a contemporary of Sigmund Freud, based his whole treatment approach on this insight: We can face our emotional pain directly and still take constructive action. One of Masatake's favorite suggestions for depressed people was that they tend a garden.

Do things with other people. Include old friends. Make new friends. It's rarely effective to become a hermit. Talking to people is a way of healing.

You can also use the Power Processes when you feel pain. Tell the truth about your feelings and fully experience them. Embrace this barrier and "be here now" with it. Surrender to your negative feelings. Yes, it can be difficult to practice the Power Processes at times like this. And when your practice becomes this intense, it can yield the most learning.

Writing about your feelings and what you're learning through the pain can also bring perspective. Your journal is one friend who is on call 24 hours each day, every day of the year. You can approach this friend in any mood and say anything at all. Now that's unconditional acceptance.

If you feel severely depressed and stay that way, talk to someone. If friends and family can't help, then remember that most colleges and communities have counselors available. Take action. Depression can affect your health, and it can be alleviated.

Emotional pain does not last forever. Often it ends in a matter of weeks. One case disappeared in four hours and 12 minutes.

There's no need to let a broken heart stop your life. Though you can find buckets of advice on the subject, just remember a simple and powerful idea: "This, too, shall pass."

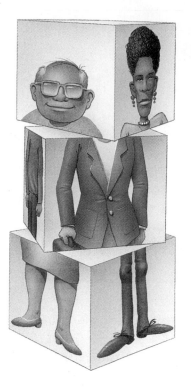

Create your instructor

There are "poor" instructors, and there are as many definitions of *poor instructor* as there are students.

For some students, *poor* means "boring," "rude," or "insensitive." Or maybe it's an instructor who blows his nose every five minutes, stuffs the dirty Kleenex in his pocket, and wears an aftershave that could halt a hamster at 30 paces.

Faced with such facts, you have some choices. One is to label the instructor a dud, dweeb, geek, or airhead and let it go at that. When you choose this solution you get to endure class, complain to other students, and wait for a miracle. This choice puts you at the mercy of circumstance. It gives your instructor responsibility for the quality of your education, not to mention responsibility for giving you value for your money.

You do not have to give away your power. Instead, you can take responsibility for your education. Use any of the following techniques to change the way you experience your instructors. In effect, you can "create your instructors." Here's how.

Research the instructor. There are formal and informal sources of information you can turn to before you register for class. One is the school catalog. Alumni magazines or newsletters or the school newspaper may have run articles on teachers. In some schools, students circulate informal evaluations of instructors. Also talk to students who have taken courses from the instructor.

Or introduce yourself to the instructor. Visit him during office hours and ask about the course. Doing so can help you get the flavor of the class and clues to his teaching style.

Show interest in class. Students give teachers moment-by-moment feedback in class. That feedback comes through posture, eye contact, responses to questions, and participation in class discussions. If you find a class boring, re-create the instructor through a massive display of interest. Ask lots of questions. Show enthusiasm through nonverbal language—sitting up straight, making eye contact, taking detailed notes.

Take responsibility for your attitude. Maybe your instructor reminds you of someone you don't like—your annoying Uncle Fred, a rude store clerk, or the fifth-grade teacher who kept you after school. Your attitudes are in your own head and beyond the instructor's control.

An instructor's beliefs about politics, religion, or feminism are not related to teaching ability. Likewise, using a formal or informal lecture style does not indicate knowledge of subject matter. Knowing such things will help you let go of negative judgments.

Get to know the instructor better. You might be missing the strong points of an instructor you don't like. Meet with your instructor during office hours. Ask questions you didn't get answered in class. Teachers who seem boring in class can be fascinating in person. Prepare to notice your pictures and let them go.

Separate liking from learning. You don't have to like an instructor to learn from one. Focus on content instead of form. Form is the way something is organized or presented. If you sit through a three-hour class irritated at the sound of an instructor's voice, you're focusing on the form of his presentation. When you put aside your concern about his voice and rivet your attention on the points he's making, you're focusing on content.

Personal preferences can get in the way too. That happens when you don't like the instructor's clothes, hairstyle, political views, or taste in music. If you see this happening, note your response without judgment. Then gently return your attention to the class content.

Form your own opinion about each instructor. Students talk about teachers, and you may hear conflicting reports. Decide for yourself.

Seek alternatives. You may feel more comfortable with another teacher's style or way of organizing the same subject. Consider changing teachers, asking another teacher for help outside class, or attending an additional section taught by another instructor.

You can also learn from other students, other courses, tutors, study groups, books, and tapes. You can be a master student, even when you have teachers you don't like. Your education is your creation.

Avoid excuses. Instructors know them all. Most teachers can see a snow job coming before the first flake hits the ground. Accept responsibility for your own mistakes, and avoid thinking you can fool the professor. When you treat instructors honestly, you are more likely to get the same treatment in return.

Submit professional work. Prepare papers and projects as if you were submitting them to an employer. Pay attention to form. Imagine that a promotion and raise will be determined by your work. Instructors often grade hundreds of papers during a term. Your neat, orderly, well-organized paper can lift an instructor's spirits after a long night of deciphering gibberish.

Arrive early for class. You can visit with your instructor and get to know him better. You can review notes and prepare for class. Being on time demonstrates your commitment and interest.

Accept criticism. Learn from your teachers' comments about your work. It is a teacher's job to correct. Don't take it personally.

Use conference time effectively. Instructors are usually happy to answer questions about class content. To get the most out of conference time, be prepared to ask those questions. Bring your notes, text, and other materials you need.

During this session you also can address more difficult subjects, such as grades, attendance policies, lecture styles, term papers, or personality conflicts.

Instead of trying to solve a serious problem in the few minutes before or after class, set up a separate meeting. The instructor might feel uncomfortable discussing the problem in front of the other students.

Using the communication techniques suggested in this chapter can make your conference more effective.

Use course evaluations. In many classes you'll have an opportunity to evaluate the instructor. When you're asked to do so, respond honestly. Write about the aspects of the class that did not work well for you. Offer specific ideas for improvement. Also note what did work well.

Formal evaluations often come late in the course, after final tests and assignments. This may lead students to gloss over evaluations or give only vague feedback. If you want your feedback to make a difference, treat this evaluation as you would an assignment.

Take further steps, if appropriate. Sometimes severe conflicts develop between students and instructors. Feedback from students may not be enough to resolve it. In such cases, you might decide to file a complaint or ask for help from a third party, such as an administrator.

If you do, be prepared to document your case in writing. When talking about the instructor, offer details. Describe specific actions that created problems for the class. Stick to the facts—that is, to events that other class members can verify.

Your school may have specific grievance procedures to use in these cases. Before you act, understand what the policies are.

You are a consumer of education. You have a right and a responsibility to complain if you think you have been treated unfairly.

Employy your word

When you speak and give your word, you are creating—literally. Your speaking brings life to your values and purpose. In large part, others know who you are by the words you speak and the agreements you make. You can learn who you are by observing which commitments you choose to make and which ones you avoid.

Giving your word makes things happen. Circumstances, events, and attitudes fall into place. The resources needed to accomplish whatever was promised become available. What makes it happen is promising a result.

The person you are right now is, for the most part, a result of the choices and agreements you've made in your life. Your future is largely determined by the choices and agreements you make from now on. Giving your word is a big step in creating your future.

The world works by agreement

There are over 5 billion people on planet Earth. We live on different continents, in different nations, and communicate in different languages. We have diverse political ideologies and subscribe to various social and moral codes.

This complex planetary network is held together by people keeping their word. Agreements minimize confusion, prevent social turmoil, and keep order. Projects are finished, goods are exchanged, and treaties are made. People, organizations, and nations know what to expect when agreements are kept. When people keep their word, the world works.

Agreements are the foundation of many things that are often taken for granted. Words, our basic tool of communication, work only because we agree about their meanings. A pencil is a pencil only because everyone agrees to call a thin, wood-covered column of graphite a pencil. We could just as easily call them ziddles. Then you might hear someone say, "Do you have an extra ziddle? I forgot mine."

Money exists only by agreement. If we leave a $100 MONOPOLY® bill (play money) on a park bench next to a real $100 bill (backed by the U.S. Treasury), one is more likely to disappear than the other. The only important difference between the two pieces of paper is that everyone agrees that one can be exchanged for goods and services and the other cannot. Shopkeepers will sell merchandise for the "real" $100 bill because they trust a continuing agreement.

Relationships work by agreement

Relationships are built on agreements. They begin with our most intimate personal contacts and move through all levels of families, organizations, communities, and nations.

When we break a promise to be faithful to a spouse, to help a friend move to a new apartment, or to pay a bill on time, relationships are strained and the consequences can be painful. When we keep our word, relationships are more likely to be satisfying and harmonious. Expectations of trust and accountability develop. Others are more likely to keep their promises to us.

Perhaps our most important relationship is the one we have with ourselves. Trusting ourselves to keep our word is enlivening. As we experience success, our self-confidence increases.

When we commit to complete an assignment and then keep our word, our understanding of the subject improves. So does our grade. We experience satisfaction and success. If we break our word, we create a gap in our learning, a lower grade, and possibly negative feelings.

Ways to make and keep agreements

Being cautious about making promises can improve the quality of our lives. Making only those promises that we fully intend to keep improves the likelihood of reaching our goals. It helps to ask ourselves what level of commitment we have to a particular promise.

At the same time, if we are willing to risk, we can open new doors and increase our possibilities for success. The only way to be certain we keep all of our agreements is either to make none, or to make only those that are absolutely guaranteed. In either case, we are probably cheating ourselves. Some of the most powerful promises we can make are those that we have no idea how to keep. We can stretch ourselves and set goals that are both high and realistic.

If we break an agreement, we can choose to be gentle with ourselves. We can be courageous, quickly admit our mistake to the people involved, and consider ways to deal with the consequences.

Examining our agreements can improve our effectiveness. Perhaps we took on too much—or too little. Perhaps we did not use all the resources that were available to us—or we used too many. Perhaps we did not fully understand what we were promising. When we learn from both our mistakes and our successes, we become more effective at employing our word.

Move up the ladder of powerful speaking

The words used to talk about whether or not something will happen fall into several different levels. We can think of each level as one rung on a ladder—the ladder of powerful speaking. As we move up the ladder, our speaking becomes more effective.

- The lowest rung on the ladder is *obligation*. Words used at this level include *I should, he ought to, someone better, they need to, I must,* and *I had to.* Speaking this way implies that people and circumstances other than ourselves are in control of our lives. When people live at the level of obligation, they often feel passive and helpless to change anything.

Note: When we move to the next rung, we leave behind obligation and advance to self-responsibility. All of the rungs to come can build on and reinforce each other. Rather than leave them behind, we can rely on them as we move up the ladder of powerful speaking.

- The next rung up is *possibility.* At this level, we examine new options. We play with new ideas, possible solutions, and alternative courses of action. As we do so, we learn that we can make choices that dramatically affect the quality of our lives. We are not the victims of circumstance. Phrases that signal this level include *I might, I could, I'll consider, I hope to,* and *maybe.*

- From possibility we can move to another rung, called *preference.* Here we begin the process of choice. The words *I prefer* signal that we're moving toward one set of possibilities over another, perhaps setting the stage for eventual action.

- Above preference is a rung called *passion.* Again, certain words signal this level: *I want to, I'm really excited to do that, I can't wait.* Possibility and passion are both exciting places to be. Even at these levels, though, we're still far from action. Many people want lots of things and have no specific plan to get them.

- Action comes with the next rung: *planning.* When people use phrases such as *I intend to, My goal is to, I plan to,* and *I'll try like mad to,* they're at the level of planning. The Intention Statements you write in this book are examples of planning.

- The highest rung on the ladder is *promising.* This is where the power of your word really comes into play. At this level, it's common to use phrases such as these: *I will, I promise to, I am committed, you can count on it.* This is where we bridge from possibility and planning to action. Promising brings with it all the rewards of keeping your word.

EXERCISE #35
MOVE FROM OBLIGATION TO CHOICE

This exercise is about becoming more precise in your use of language—specifically, about drawing a distinction between the concepts of obligation and choice. The point is that we often limit ourselves unnecessarily when thinking about what we have to do or what we think we can't do. (For more ideas on this subject, look back to Power Process #5: "I create it all.")

Part 1

Take a look at all aspects of your life (family, friends, school, work) and complete each of the following sentences with whatever comes to mind.

I have to _____

I ought to _____

I should _____

I can't _____

I really must _____

I just couldn't _____

I am not able to _____

I have to _____

I can't _____

I shouldn't _____

Part 2

Review each of the previous sentences, cross off the first two or three words, and replace them with one of the following groups of words:

"I want to . . ."   "I choose to . . ."
"I don't want to . . ."   "I choose not to . . ."

7 Steps to effective complaints

Sometimes skill in relationship-building means making a complaint. Whining, blaming, pouting, kicking, and spitting usually don't get results. Here are some guidelines for complaining effectively.

1. Go to the source. Start with the person who is most directly involved with the problem.

2. Present the facts without blaming anyone. Your complaint will carry more weight if you document the facts. Keep track of names and dates. Note what actions were promised and what results actually occurred.

3. Go up the ladder to people with more responsibility. If you don't get satisfaction at the first level, go to that person's direct supervisor. Requesting a supervisor's name will often get results. Write a letter to the company president.

4. Ask for commitments. When you find someone who is willing to solve your problem, get him to say exactly what he is going to do and when.

5. Use available support. There are dozens of groups, as well as government agencies, willing to get involved in resolving complaints. Contact consumer groups of the Better Business Bureau. Trade associations can sometimes help. Ask city council members, county commissioners, state legislators, and senators and representatives. All of them want your vote, so they usually are eager to help.

6. Take legal action if necessary. Small-claims court is relatively inexpensive, and you don't have to hire a lawyer. These courts can handle cases involving small amounts of money (up to $1000 or $2000 usually). Legal aid offices can sometimes answer questions.

7. Don't give up.

CRITICISM *really can be constructive*

Although receiving criticism is rarely fun, it is often educational. Here are some ways to get the most value from it.

1. Avoid finding fault. When your mind is occupied with finding fault in others, you aren't open to hearing constructive comments about yourself.

2. Take it seriously. Some people laugh or joke to cover their anger or embarrassment at being criticized. Humor can be mistaken for a lack of concern.

3. React to criticism with acceptance. Most people don't enjoy pointing out another's faults. Denial, argument, or joking make it more difficult for them to give honest feedback. You don't have to agree with criticism to accept it calmly.

4. Keep it in perspective. Avoid blowing the criticism out of proportion. The purpose of criticism is to generate positive change and self-improvement. There's no need to beat yourself with it.

5. Listen without defensiveness. You can't hear the criticism if you're busy building your case.

We are all leaders

o matter what our station in life, at some point most of us become leaders.

Many people mistakenly think that leaders are only those with formal titles like supervisor or manager. In fact, some leaders have no such titles. Some have never supervised others. Like Gandhi, some people change the face of the world without ever reaching a formal leadership position.

Most of us may not alter the course of human events. Even so, we constantly influence what happens in our classrooms, offices, communities, and families. We do this through our actions and words. We are constant, though unconscious, leaders.

To become more effective leaders, we can understand the many ways we influence others. The following strategies can help us have a positive impact on our children, parents, friends, schools, employers, and employees. They can help us relate to our politicians, our places of worship, our cities, our states, and our planet.

Own your leadership

Let go of the reluctance that many people feel toward assuming leadership. It's impossible to escape leadership. Every time you speak, you lead others in some small or large way. Every time you take action, you lead others through your example.

Every time you ask someone to do something, you are in essence leading her. Leadership becomes more effective when it is consciously applied.

Be willing to be uncomfortable

Leaders are often not appreciated or even liked. They often feel isolated, cut off from their colleagues. With that can come self-doubt and even fear.

Leadership is a courageous act. Before you take on a leadership role, be aware that such feelings may happen to you. Also remember that none of them needs to stop you from leading.

Allow huge mistakes

The more important and influential you are, the more likely your mistakes will have huge consequences. The chief financial officer for a large company can make a mistake that costs thousands or even millions of dollars. A physician could make a mistake that costs a life. As commander-in-chief of the armed forces, the president of a country can make a decision that costs thousands of lives.

At the same time, these people are in a position to make a huge difference—to save thousands of dollars or lives through their power and influence.

People in leadership positions become paralyzed and ineffective if they fear making a mistake. It's necessary for them to act even when information is incomplete or when they know a catastrophic mistake is possible.

Take on big projects

Leaders make promises. And effective leaders make big promises. These words— *I will do it; you can count on me*— distinguish a leader.

Look around your world to see what needs to be done and then take it on. Consider taking on the biggest project you can think of—ending world hunger, eliminating nuclear weapons, wiping out poverty, promoting universal literacy. Think about how you'd spend your life if you knew you could make a difference in these overwhelming problems. Then take the actions you considered. See what a difference they make for you and others.

Tackle projects that stretch you to your limits—projects that are worthy of your time and talents.

Provide feedback

An effective leader is a mirror to others. Share what you see. Talk with others about what they are doing effectively—and what they are doing ineffectively.

Keep in mind that people may not enjoy your feedback. In fact, some would probably rather not hear it at all.

Two things can help. One is to let people know up front that if they sign on to work with you, they can expect feedback. Also give your feedback with skill. Use "I" messages as explained in this chapter. Back up any criticisms with specific observations and facts. When people complete a task with real skill, point that out too.

Paint a vision

Help others see the big picture, the ultimate purpose of a project. Speak a lot about the end result and the potential value of what you're doing.

There's an ancient saying: "Without vision, the people perish." Long-term goals usually involve many intermediate steps. Unless we're reminded of the purpose for those day-to-day actions, our work can feel like a grind. Leadership is the art of helping others lift their eyes to the horizon—keeping them in touch with the ultimate value and purpose of a project. Keeping the vision alive helps their spirits soar again.

Model your values

"Be the change you want to see" is an apt motto for leaders. Perhaps you want to see integrity, focused attention, and productivity in the people around you. Begin by modeling these qualities yourself.

Enthusiasm is catching. Having fun while being productive is contagious. If you bring these qualities to a project, others may follow suit.

Make requests—lots of them

An effective leader is a request machine. She asks a tremendous amount of others. Making requests—both large and small—is an act of respect. When we ask a lot of others, we demonstrate our respect for them and our confidence in their abilities.

At first, some people might get angry when we make requests of them. Over time, many of them see that requests are compliments, opportunities to expand their skills. Ask a lot from others, and they may well appreciate you for it.

Follow up

What we don't inspect, people don't respect. When other people agree to do a job for you, follow up to see how it is going. This can be done in a way that communicates your respect and interest—not your fear that the project may flounder. Display a genuine interest in other people and their work, and it's likely that they will see you as a partner in achieving a shared goal.

Focus on the problem, not the person

Sometimes projects do not go as planned. Big mistakes occur. If this happens, focus on the project and the mistakes—not the personal faults of your colleagues. People do not make mistakes on purpose. If they did we would call them on-purposes, not mistakes.

Most people will join you in solving a problem if your focus is on the problem, not on what they did wrong.

Acknowledge others

Spend time in genuine appreciation of the energy and creativity that others have put into their work. Take the time to be interested in what they have done and to care about the results they have accomplished. Thank them with your eyes, your words, the tone of your voice, and your appreciation.

Share credit

As a leader, constantly give away the praise and acknowledgment that you receive. When you're congratulated for your performance, pass it on to others. Share the credit with the group.

When you're a leader, the results you achieve depend on the efforts of many. Acknowledging that fact often is more than telling the truth—it's essential if you want to count on others' support in the future.

Delegate

We often see delegation as a tool that's available only to those above us in the chain of command. Actually, delegation up or across an organization can be the most effective.

Consider delegating a project to your boss or teacher. That is, ask her to take on a job that you would like to see accomplished. This may be a job that you cannot do, given your position in the company or class.

The same strategy works in a variety of contexts. Ask a coworker or classmate to take on a job that you'd like to see done. Ask the same of your family or friends. Delegate tasks to the mayor of your town, the governor of your state, and the leaders of your country.

In summary, take on projects that are important to you. Then find people who can lead the effort. You can do this even when you have no formal role as a leader.

Communicate assertively— not aggressively

Aggressive behavior is not generally effective in relationships. People who act aggressively are domineering. They get what they want by putting other people down. When they win, other people lose.

Assertive behavior is a sign of a healthy, strong leader. Assertive people are confident and respectful of others as well as themselves. They ask directly for what they want without feeling embarrassed or inadequate. When they fail to get what they want, their self-esteem does not suffer.

Many people don't act assertively for fear they will appear aggressive. However, passive behavior—neither assertive nor aggressive—can get us nowhere. By remaining quiet and submissive, we allow others to infringe on our rights.

When others run our lives, we fail to have the lives we want. The alternative is to ask for what we want, appropriately and assertively.

Listen

Sometimes it seems that effective leaders talk a lot. Chances are, they also listen a lot.

As a leader, be aware of what other people are thinking, feeling, and wanting. Listen fully to the concerns and joys of others. Before you criticize their views or make personal judgments, take time to understand what's going on inside others.

This is not merely a personal favor to the people you work with. The more you know about your coworkers or classmates, the more effectively you can lead them.

Practice

Leadership is an acquired skill. No one is born knowing how to make requests, give feedback, create budgets, do long-range planning, or delegate tasks. We learn these things over time, with practice, by seeing what works and what does not.

At times leadership is a matter of trial and error and flying by the seat of our pants. As a leader, you may sometimes feel you don't know what you're doing. That's OK. Sometimes a powerful course of action is discovered in midstream—not known in advance. We can act as leaders even when we don't feel like leaders. As a path of constant learning, leadership calls for all the skills of master students.

Look for areas where you can make a difference and experiment with these strategies. Right now there's something worth doing that calls for your leadership. Take action now and others will join you.

Exercise #36
V.I.P.'s (Very Important Persons)

Step 1
Under the column below titled "Name," write the names of at least five people who have positively influenced your life. They may be relatives, friends, teachers, or perhaps someone you have never met. (Complete each step before moving on.)

Step 2
In the next column, rate your gratitude for this person's influence. (From 1 to 5, with 1 being a little grateful and 5 being extremely grateful.)

Step 3
In the third column, rate how fully you have communicated your appreciation to this person. (Again, 1 to 5, with 1 being not communicated and 5 being fully communicated.)

Step 4
In the final column, put a U beside the persons with whom you have unfinished business (important communication that you have not taken an opportunity to send).

Name	Grateful (1-5)	Communicated (1-5)	U?
1.			
2.			
3.			
4.			
5.			
6.			
7.			
8.			

Step 5
Now select two persons with U's beside their names and write them a letter. Express the love, tenderness, and joy you feel toward them. Tell them exactly how they have helped change your life and how you are glad they did.

Step 6
You also have an impact on others. Make a list of people whose lives you have influenced. Consider sharing with these people why you enjoy being part of their lives.

Journal Entry #54
Discovery/Intention Statement

There are things we think about telling people, but don't. Examine your relationships and complete the following statements.

I realize that I am not communicating

about _____

with _____.

I realize that I am not communicating

about _____

with _____.

I realize that I am not communicating

about _____

with _____.

I realize that I am not communicating

about _____

with _____.

Now choose one idea from this chapter that can open communication with these people in these areas. Describe below how you will use this idea.

I intend to . . .

_____
_____
_____
_____
_____
_____
_____
_____
_____
_____
_____
_____

master student

golda meir

a pioneer in the creation of Israel,
was elected its fourth prime minister

I started school in a huge, fortresslike building on Fourth Street near Milwaukee's famous Schlitz beer factory, and I loved it. I can't remember how long it took me to learn English (at home, of course, we spoke Yiddish, and luckily, so did almost everyone else on Walnut Street), but I have no recollection of the language ever being a real problem for me, so I must have picked it up quickly. I made friends quickly, too. Two of those early first- or second-grade friends remained friends all my life, and both live in Israel now. One was Regina Hamburger (today Medzini), who lived on our street and who was to leave America when I did; the other was Sarah Feder, who became one of the leaders of Labor Zionism in the United States . . . .

More than fifty years later—when I was seventy-one and a prime minister—I went back to that school for a few hours. It had not changed very much in all those years except that the vast majority of its pupils were now black, not Jewish, as in 1906. They welcomed me as though I were a queen. Standing in rows on the creaky old stage I remembered so well, freshly scrubbed and neat as pins, they serenaded me with Yiddish and Hebrew songs and raised their voices to peal out the Israeli anthem "Hatikvah" which made my eyes fill with tears. Each one of the classrooms had been beautifully decorated with posters about Israel and signs reading SHALOM (one of the children thought it was my family name), and when I entered the school, two little girls wearing headbands with Stars of David on them solemnly presented me with an enormous white rose made of tissue paper and pipe cleaners, which I wore all day and carefully carried back to Israel with me.

Another of the gifts I got that day in 1971 from the Fourth Street School was a record of my grades for one of the years I had spent there: 95 in reading, 90 in spelling, 95 in arithmetic, 85 in music, and a mysterious 90 in something called manual arts, which I cannot remember at all. But when the children asked me to talk to them for a few minutes, it was not about book learning that I chose to speak. I had learned a lot more than fractions or how to spell at Fourth Street, and I decided to tell those eager, attentive children—born, as I myself had been, into a minority and living, as I myself had lived, without much extravagance (to put it mildly)—what the gist of that learning had been. "It isn't really important to decide when you are very young just exactly what you want to become when you grow up," I told them. "It is much more important to decide on the way you want to live. If you are going to get involved with causes which are good for others, not only for yourselves, then it seems to me that that is sufficient, and maybe what you will be is only a matter of chance." I had a feeling that they understood me.

From My Life
by Golda Meir
Copyright © 1975 by Golda Meir
Reprinted by permission of George Weidenfeld & Nicolson Limited

1 The fact that a disagreement is getting worse means that there's little hope for conflict resolution.
   True or False. Explain your answer.

2 What is the difference between encoding and decoding as explained in this chapter?

3 One suggested guideline for nonverbal listening is to respond frequently to the speaker.
   True or False. Explain your answer.

4 What characteristic distinguishes the top five rungs of the ladder of powerful speaking from the bottom rung?

5 The suggested techniques for verbal listening include which of the following?

       (A) Parrot exactly what another person says.
       (B) Pay attention to the speaker's words and not other emotions behind the words.
       (C) Put your own wants aside in order to listen attentively.
       (D) Look for the requests hidden in complaints.
       (E) Use facial gestures to show your reactions.

6 Describing your feelings is an effective part of an "I" message. True or False. Explain your answer.

7 List the five parts of an "I" message (the five ways to say "I").

8 *Give some examples of how you can "create" your instructor.*

9 *Reword the following complaint as a request: "You always interrupt when I talk!"*

10 *Few of us get the chance to be leaders. True or False. Explain your answer.*

JOURNAL ENTRY #55
DISCOVERY/INTENTION STATEMENT

Review what you learned in this chapter about listening and describe your current level of skill as a listener.

I discovered that I . . .

_____

_____

Now choose a suggestion from this chapter that could immediately apply to one of your current relationships. Describe how you will apply this suggestion.

I intend to . . .

_____

_____

_____

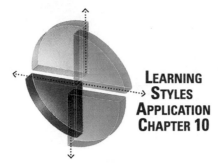

**LEARNING
STYLES
APPLICATION
CHAPTER 10**

Complete the following exercises on a separate sheet of paper.

Style 1

Think of a conflict you are experiencing right now with an important person in your life. (If you cannot think of one, recall a conflict you've experienced in the past.) Do you think that any of the ideas in this chapter could help you resolve this conflict? Explain your answer.

Style 2

After reviewing this chapter, choose 10 specific suggestions that could help you resolve the conflict you listed for Style 1.

Style 3

From the 10 suggestions you listed for Style 2, choose five you will definitely commit to using. Describe when and where you plan to use each suggestion.

Style 4

Explain how you will approach conflict resolution differently having read this chapter and having applied several of its ideas.

Bibliography

▇ Endnotes

[1] Virginia Satir, *Peoplemaking* (Palo Alto, CA: Science and Behavior, 1972).

[2] Carl Rogers, *On Becoming a Person* (Boston: Houghton Mifflin, 1961).

[3] Thomas Gordon, *Parent Effectiveness Training: The Tested New Way to Raise Responsible Children* (New York: New American Library, 1975).

[4] Sidney Jourard, *The Transparent Self* (New York: Van Nostrand, 1971).

[5] David Reynolds, *Morita Psychotherapy* (Berkeley, CA: University of California, 1976).

▇ Additional Reading

Driekurs, Rudolf, and Vicki Soltz. *Children: The Challenge*, New York: Dutton, 1964.

Gordon, Thomas. *Parent Effectiveness Training: The Tested New Way to Raise Responsible Children*, New York: New American Library, 1975.

Keyes, Ken, Jr. *A Conscious Person's Guide to Relationships*, Coos Bay, OR: Living Love, 1979.

Keyes, Ken, Jr. *The Hundredth Monkey*, Coos Bay, OR: Vision, 1982.

Lerner, Harriet G. *The Dance of Anger*, New York: Harper and Row, 1989.

Montagu, Ashley. *The Natural Superiority of Women*, New York: Macmillan, 1974.

U.S. Department of Education, Office for Civil Rights. *Sexual Harassment: It's Not Academic*, Washington, DC: Government Printing Office, 1988.

health

In this chapter...

■ see your body as an **incredible machine** that deserves at least as much attention as your car. Choose ways to **fuel, move, rest, observe,** and **protect** your machine so that it serves your success in school. Also consider the **truth about drugs** and consider that **surrendering** can be a path to satisfaction instead of defeat.

**JOURNAL ENTRY #56
DISCOVERY STATEMENT**

On a separate sheet of paper, make a quick list of your activities during the last 48 hours, including the foods you ate at each meal. Circle any activities on your list that promoted your health. Underline any activities that could detract from your health. Sum up your discoveries here.

I discovered that . . .

_____
_____
_____
_____
_____
_____

Now scan this chapter for any strategies you can use immediately to sustain your health-producing behavior or change any health-defeating behaviors. List three strategies you want to read about in more detail.

_____
_____
_____
_____
_____
_____
_____
_____

Take care of your machine

SOME PEOPLE ARE OFFENDED by the notion that a body is a machine. This analogy is made with great respect for our bodies and with the understanding that we are more than our bodies. We have a mind and a soul that are certainly separate from our bodies even though they are connected. And, in order to house the mind and soul, we have a body—a fantastic machine.

Our machines are truly incredible. They often continue to operate despite abuse. We pollute them, dent them, run them too hard, let them sit idle for years, even wreck them, and still they continue to run—most of the time. Ironically, we can also take excellent care of our machines, only to have them quit on us just when we need them.

To an extent greater than most of us imagine, we choose our level of health. You can promote your health by taking definite steps.

When we buy a car or a new appliance, we generally look at the owner's manual. We study it to find out just how this new machine works. We make sure we understand all the features and what is needed to properly maintain the equipment.

The following suggestions are accepted by almost all experts on health. Study them as if they made up an owner's manual for a priceless machine, one that can't be replaced, one that your life depends on. That machine is your body.

> " "
> *Emotion, which is suffering, ceases to be suffering as soon as we have a clear picture of it.*
> –BARUCH SPINOZA

> " "
> *To be somebody you must last.*
> –RUTH GORDON

> " "
> *Disease is not only suffering, but also the body fighting to restore itself to normal–a sort of healing source within.*
> –HIPPOCRATES

Your machine:
Fuel it

It is a cliché, but it's true: You are what you eat. The brain needs nutrients to function properly. What you eat can have immediate and long-term effects on your performance as a student. That giant jelly donut can make you drowsy within minutes, and a steady diet of them can affect the amount of energy you have to meet and juggle the demands of classes, jobs, extracurricular activities, family, and other activities.

There have been hundreds of books written about nutrition. One says don't drink milk. Another says buy a cow. Some say load up on 5,000 milligrams of vitamin C a day. Others say avoid oranges. This debate can be confusing. There is, however, some agreement among nutritional scientists.

A list of guidelines was developed by a committee of experts and published by the U.S. Senate. You'll find it on page 299. Though you might find a healthier diet, you can do well by following these guidelines.

Weight control is a problem for millions, and self-starvation can be as dangerous as obesity. Both conditions can be controlled. Working with others who have similar problems is often effective and brings lasting results.

If you are overweight, avoid people, groups, diets, or chemicals that claim a quick fix. Even if that "Lose 20 pounds in 20 days!" diet works, you're likely to gain the weight back in a few weeks—plus a few extra pounds.

The formula for weight loss is simple: Eat better food, eat less food, and exercise. And to maintain your health, avoid losing more than two pounds per week.

Though the formula is simple, using it is sometimes not so simple. Local newspapers and the Yellow Pages list classes, support groups, and professionally run programs that can help you to reduce and then maintain your ideal weight.

There are two eating disorders that affect many students. *Bulimia* is a serious illness that runs in cycles of excessive eating and forced purges. A person with this disorder might gorge on a large pizza, a dozen donuts, or a gallon of ice cream, then force himself to vomit. Or he might compensate for overeating by using excessive laxatives, enemas, or diuretics.

Anorexia nervosa is an illness characterized by starvation, either through extended fasts or by eating only one food for weeks at a time. Both of these conditions can be addictive disorders that call for treatment. Contact either of the organizations listed below for further information and help.

National Association of Anorexia
Nervosa and Associated Disorders
(847) 831-3438

Anorexia Nervosa and Related
Eating Disorders, Inc.
(541) 344-1144

Your machine:
Move it

Regular exercise can improve your performance in school. Your brain usually functions better if the rest of your body is in shape, and the right kind of exercise is an effective way to dissipate the tension that you build up hunched over a keyboard hammering out a term paper.

Our bodies were meant to exercise. The world ran on muscle back in the days when we had to track down a woolly mammoth every few days, kill it, and drag it back to the cave. Now we can grab a burger at the drive-up window. It's convenient, but it doesn't do much for our deltoids, quadriceps, and other muscles. The heart is a muscle that can get fat too. A fat belly may be unattractive. A fat heart can be lethal.

Lean muscles absorb nutrients more efficiently than muscles marbled with fat. The best reason to get in shape isn't to improve how you will look in designer jeans. With lean muscles, you function better at whatever you do, whether it's mammoth hunting or boning up on math.

Sometimes people who are out of shape or overweight think they cannot change. The human body can change. Inside even the most dilapidated body there is a trim, healthy, energized body that wants to escape.

Begin by taking a First Step. Tell the truth about the problem and declare your desire to change. You can make real progress in a matter of weeks. Sticking to an exercise schedule for just three weeks can bring rewards. Remember, dieting alone doesn't create lean muscles and a strong heart. The only way to get lean is by moving.

You don't have to train for the Boston Marathon, however. It's not even smart, unless you're in great shape. Do something you enjoy. Start by walking briskly 15 minutes every day. Increase that time gradually and add a little running.

Once you're in reasonable shape, you can stay there by doing three 20- to 30-minute sessions a week of aerobic activity—the kind that elevates your heart rate to a faster and steady pace.

School can be a great place to get in shape. Classes may be offered in aerobics, swimming, volleyball, basketball, golf, tennis, and other sports.

> Before beginning any vigorous exercise program, consult a doctor. This is critical if you are overweight, over age 60, in poor condition, a heavy smoker, or have a history of health problems.

Your machine:
Rest it

Human bodies also need to rest. It is possible to drive people crazy or even to kill them by depriving them of sleep.

You might be tempted to drastically cut back on your sleep once in a while. All-nighters are common for some students. If you find you are indulging in them often, read Chapter Two for some time management ideas. Depriving yourself of sleep is a choice you can avoid.

Sometimes getting to sleep isn't easy, even when you feel tired. If you have trouble falling asleep, experiment with these suggestions:

- Exercise daily. For many people, this promotes sounder sleep.
- Keep your sleeping room cool.
- Take a warm bath, not a shower, just before bed.
- While lying in bed, practice relaxation techniques.
- If you can't fall asleep after 30 minutes, get up and study or do something else until you're tired.
- If sleeplessness persists, see a doctor.
- Avoid naps during the daytime.
- Sleep in the same place each night. When you're there, your body gets the message: "It's time to go to sleep."

How much sleep is enough? Your body knows when it's tired. Also look for signs of depression, irritability, and other emotional problems. Lack of sleep can interfere with your memory, your concentration, and your ability to stay awake in class. The solution is a good night's sleep.

You can sleep 12 hours a day and still not get enough rest if you are not managing stress effectively. School can be an especially stressful environment, so it is important that students know how to relax.

Stress is not always harmful. It can result from pleasant experiences as well as unpleasant ones. The excitement of a new term—new classes, new instructors, new classmates—can be fun and stressful at the same time.

Oddly enough, your body perceives excitement almost the same way it perceives fear. Both emotions produce rapid heart rates, increased adrenaline flow, and muscle contractions. Both emotions produce stress.

Stress, at appropriate times and at manageable levels, is normal and useful. It can sharpen our awareness and boost our energy just when we need it the most. When stress persists or becomes excessive, it is harmful.

Chances are, your stress level is too high if you consistently experience any of the following symptoms: irritability; depression; low productivity; strained relationships at work or home; health problems such as upset stomach, frequent colds, and low energy level; a pattern of avoiding tasks; difficulty falling asleep or staying asleep; feeling burned out at home or at work; feeling tense, nervous, or fearful.

Stress has both mental and physical components. The mental components include thoughts and worries; the physical components include illness and tension. The fact that stress has these two elements points to two broad strategies for managing it.

One of the best ways to deal with stressful thoughts is to manage our self-talk. We can notice and regulate the little voice in the back of our minds that is constantly giving us messages. Exercises that help us mentally rehearse success and visualize positive events increase the odds for positive results.

Methods of dealing with the physical element of stress include breathing exercises, relaxation techniques such as body scans and guided imageries, massage, and aerobic exercise.

Some schools offer training in these techniques. Free or reasonably priced classes also are available through community education programs, churches or synagogues, the YMCA, and local libraries.

Or read this book. It includes a number of relaxation and breathing exercises. Many of the Power Processes and techniques for letting go of test anxiety can help you manage stress.

If these techniques don't work within a few weeks, get help. There are trained relaxation therapists in most cities. Ask a doctor, counselor, or school dean for a referral. Also check with the student health service or counseling center at your school.

Stress management is a well-researched field. There is no need to continue to have a pain in your neck, a knot in your stomach, cold feet, or a dozen other symptoms of tension. Relax.

PRACTICING CRITICAL THINKING #21

This exercise is about clarifying the differences between facts (behaviors) and interpretations. A behavior is something factual and observable. For instance, arriving 10 minutes after a movie starts or pulling a dog's tail are both observable behaviors. In contrast, an interpretation is a conclusion we draw on the basis of observed behavior: "He's either too rude or too irresponsible to get to a movie on time." "She hates animals; just look at how she pulled that dog's tail."

Consider another example. "She shouted at me, left the room, and slammed the door" is a statement that describes behaviors. "She was angry" is an interpretation about the social significance or meaning of the behavior.

With this distinction in mind, brainstorm a list of behaviors you have observed in others when they were in conflict with you. List your observations below. Afterward, review your list and decide if some of the behaviors you noted are actually interpretations.

_____
_____
_____
_____
_____
_____
_____
_____
_____
_____
_____
_____
_____
_____
_____

Your machine:
Observe it

You are an expert on your body. Wherever you go, there it is. You are more likely to notice changes first. Pay attention to them. They often are your first clue about the need for repairs.

Watch for these signs:

1. Weight loss of more than 10 pounds in 10 weeks with no apparent cause.
2. A sore, scab, or ulcer that does not heal in three weeks.
3. A skin blemish or mole that bleeds, itches, or changes size, shape, or color.
4. Persistent or severe headaches.
5. Sudden vomiting that is not preceded by nausea.
6. Fainting spells.
7. Double vision.
8. Difficulty swallowing.
9. Persistent hoarseness or nagging cough.
10. Blood that is coughed up or vomited.
11. Shortness of breath for no apparent reason.
12. Persistent indigestion or abdominal pain.
13. A big change in normal bowel habits, such as alternating diarrhea and constipation.
14. Black and tarry bowel movements.
15. Rectal bleeding.
16. Pink, red, or unusually cloudy urine.
17. Discomfort or difficulty in urinating.
18. Lumps or thickening in a breast.
19. Vaginal bleeding between menstrual periods or after menopause.

If you are sick, get help. Even when you think it might not be serious, check it out. Without proper treatment, illness or injury can lead to serious problems. Begin with your physician or school health service.

Another resource is *Ask-a-Nurse*, a free phone service available in 38 states. Call 1-800-535-1111.

Your machine: *Protect it*

Protect against sexually transmitted diseases

Choices about sex can be life-altering. Sex is a basic human drive, and it can be wonderful. Sex can also be hazardous to your physical and psychological health. It pays to be clear about the pitfalls. These dangers include sexually transmitted diseases, unwanted pregnancies, and rape.

Technically, anyone who has sex is at risk of getting a sexually transmitted disease (STD). STDs are usually spread through sexual contact with an infected person. Some diseases, like Acquired Immune Deficiency Syndrome (AIDS), can be spread in other ways also.

There are more than 25 kinds of STDs. They are the most common contagious diseases in the United States, and they affect about one in every six adults. Here are some facts:

- Without treatment, some of these diseases can lead to blindness, infertility, cancer, heart disease, or even death.
- STDs can be harder to diagnose in women, and they can cause long-term damage to female reproductive organs. The risks are tubal pregnancies, miscarriages, and infertility. STDs can also be passed from an infected pregnant woman to the fetus she is carrying.
- STDs are often spread through body fluids that are exchanged during sex, including semen, vaginal secretions, and blood. Some STDs, such as herpes and genital warts, are spread by direct contact with infected skin.
- The more common STDs include chlamydia, gonorrhea ("clap"), syphilis, genital warts, genital herpes, and trichomoniasis. Sometimes there are no signs or symptoms of an STD, and the only way to tell if you're infected is to be tested by a health care professional.

AIDS is one of the most serious STDs, and it is different from the others in several respects. AIDS is the last stage of a viral infection caused by the Human Immunodeficiency Virus (HIV). A person with AIDS is unable to fight off many kinds of infections and cancers. Today, AIDS is fatal, and it may take researchers years to find a cure.

HIV is not just transmitted through sex. It can be caught by sharing needles used to inject drugs. The virus can also be passed from an infected pregnant woman to the fetus. Before 1985, HIV was sometimes spread through contaminated blood transfusions. Since March 1985, blood supplies have been screened for HIV, and transfusion is no longer considered a means of HIV infection.

Someone infected with HIV may feel no symptoms for months—sometimes years. Many times, the people who are spreading HIV don't even know they have it.

Public hysteria and misinformation still flourish about AIDS. You cannot get AIDS from touching, kissing, hugging, food, coughs, mosquitoes, toilet seats, hot tubs, or swimming pools. HIV is actually a weak virus that is transmitted in only a few ways.

Also, being infected with HIV is not an immediate death sentence. Some people live with HIV for years without developing AIDS, and even people with AIDS might live for years after developing the condition.

AIDS is not exclusive to male homosexuals, either. It is increasingly common among heterosexuals. AIDS cases among women have been increasing steadily, and AIDS is predicted to soon become one of the five leading causes of death among women. According to the U.S. Center for Disease Control, one in 500 college students is infected with HIV.

Our knowledge of AIDS is changing constantly. For the latest information, see the most recent publications from the Center for Disease Control or call the center's National AIDS Hotline: (800) 342-AIDS [in Spanish: (800) 344-7432; TDD: (800) 243-7889]. You can also visit the Center's site on the World Wide Web at http://www.cdc.gov/

STDs other than AIDS and herpes can be cured if treated early. Prevention is better.

The only way to be absolutely safe from STDs is to abstain from sex or to have sex exclusively with one person who is free of infection and has no other sex partners. Also avoid injecting illegal drugs. Sharing needles or other paraphernalia with other drug users is a high-risk behavior.

The more people you have sex with, the greater your risk. You are at risk even if you have sex only once with one person who is infected. If you have sex with several different people, get checked for STDs twice each year. Do so even if you have no symptoms.

If you choose to have sex with more than one partner, then protect yourself and others from STDs by practicing "safer sex." (The term *safe sex* is no longer used, since the choice to have multiple sex partners always poses a risk of infection.) Safer sex refers to a variety of methods that prevent the exchange of body fluids such as semen, vaginal fluid, and blood.

One such method is using condoms. These are thin membranes stretched over the penis prior to intercourse. Condoms prevent semen from entering the vagina. Both women and men can carry them and insist they be used.

For added protection, use a birth control foam, jelly, or cream along with condoms. Make sure these include a spermicide, preferably Nonoxynol-9. When used with condoms, Nonoxynol-9 might provide some protection against HIV infection.

While the use of condoms with spermicides can be effective, they are not guaranteed to be 100 percent effective. Condoms can break, leak, or slip off.

If you think you have an STD, call your doctor, student health service, or local STD clinic. If you think you might be infected with HIV, then avoid infecting others. Also seek counseling and further testing to find out if you really are infected.

You can also call the National STD Hotline (1-800-227-8922), the National AIDS Hotline (1-800-342-2437), or your state or local health department. These sources can give you the latest on how to prevent and treat STDs.

Protect against unwanted pregnancy

There are more ways to avoid pregnancy now than ever before, and new methods are being developed for both men and women. Following is some information that can help you and your partner avoid unwanted pregnancy. Supplement it with information from your doctor.

Abstinence is choosing not to have intercourse, and it is 100 percent effective in preventing pregnancy. Contrary to popular belief, many people exist happily without sexual intercourse. You may feel pressured to change your mind about this choice. If so, remember that abstinence, as birth control, is guaranteed only when it is practiced without exception.

"The pill" is a synthetic hormone that "tells" a woman's body not to produce eggs. To be effective, it must be taken every day for 21 days a month. Birth control pills must be prescribed by a doctor because the type of pill and the dose needed vary from one woman to the next. Side effects sometimes include slight nausea, breast tenderness, weight gain from water retention, and moodiness.

Though the pill is about 97 percent effective in preventing pregnancy, its long-term effects are still not known. Some women choose not take the pill because it poses too many health risks. Consult your doctor.

An *intrauterine device* (IUD) is a small metal or plastic device that is inserted in the uterus and left there for months at a time. It is about 94 percent effective in preventing fertilized eggs from developing. Side effects may include heavier menstrual flow, anemia, pelvic infection, perforation of the cervix or uterus, or septic abortion.

Many IUDs were removed from the market after lawsuits were filed against their manufacturers. Work closely with a doctor if you consider using an IUD.

A *diaphragm* is a shallow rubber dome that is covered with sperm-killing cream and inserted in the vagina. It fits over the cervix, which is the opening of the uterus, and prevents sperm from getting to the egg. A doctor must measure and fit the diaphragm. It must be inserted before intercourse and left in place for six to eight hours after intercourse. It is more than 80 percent effective.

A *contraceptive sponge* works something like a diaphragm. It is effective for 24 hours, and you can buy it over the counter at drug stores. Side effects might include odor, difficult removal, or allergic reactions. Sponges are more than 80 percent effective.

Foams, creams, tablets, suppositories, and *jellies* are chemicals that are placed in the vagina before intercourse and prevent sperm from getting to the egg. They are about 86 percent effective when used consistently.

When used carefully and consistently, *condoms* are 80 to 90 percent effective.

The *female condom* is a sheath of lubricated polyurethane with a ring on each end that is inserted into the vagina. This is a relatively new form of contraception, and not many studies exist to document its effectiveness. Ask your physician for the latest information about female condoms.

Another method, *natural family planning,* is based on looking for specific signs of fertility in a woman. (This is not to be confused with the rhythm method.) There are no side effects with natural family planning, and this method is gaining acceptance. Before you consider this method, however, talk to a qualified instructor.

The *rhythm method* involves avoiding intercourse during ovulation. It is about 80 percent effective. The problem with this method is that it is difficult to know for sure when a woman ovulates.

Douching is flushing the vagina with water or other liquid. Do not use it for birth control. Even if a woman douches immediately after intercourse, this method is ineffective. Sperm are quicker than humans are.

Withdrawal is the act of removing the penis before ejaculation occurs. This is also ineffective, since sperm can be present in pre-ejaculation fluid.

Sterilization is a permanent form of birth control, and one to avoid if you still want to have children. It is almost 100 percent effective.

Protect yourself against rape

Rape and other forms of sexual assault are all too common at schools, colleges, and universities. People often hesitate to report rape for many reasons, such as fear, embarrassment, and lack of credibility. Both women and men can take steps to prevent rape from happening in the first place. For example:

- Get together with a group of people and take a tour of the campus. Make a special note of danger spots, such as unlighted paths and unguarded buildings. Also note that rape can occur during daylight and in well-lit places.
- Ask if your school has escort services for people taking evening classes. These may include personal escorts, car escorts, or both. If you do take an evening class, ask if there are security officers on duty before and after the class.
- Take a course or seminar on self-defense and rape prevention. To find out where they're being held, check with your student counseling service, community education center, or local library.
- If you are raped, get to the nearest rape crisis center, hospital, student health service, or police station as soon as you can. It's wise to report the crime even if you don't want to press charges. Also arrange for follow-up counseling.

Date rape—the act of forcing sex on a date—is the most common form of rape on college campuses. Date rape is rape. It is a crime. It is particularly dangerous when neither the victim nor the perpetrator realizes a crime has taken place. A person who has been raped by a date might become depressed, feel guilty, have difficulty in school, lose a sense of trust, have sexual problems, or experience self-blame.

You can take steps to protect yourself by communicating clearly what you want and don't want. That means being assertive. It also pays to be cautious about using alcohol or drugs, and beware of dates who get drunk or high. You might also provide your own transportation on dates and avoid going to secluded places with people you don't know well.

It is never all right to force someone to have sex— on a date or anywhere else. We have the right to refuse to have sex with anyone, including dates. We also have the right to refuse sex with our partner, fiancé, or spouse.

Protect yourself against accidents

In North America, more than 4 million disabling injuries occur every year in the haven called the home, and more than 27,000 people die of accidents in their homes. Almost twice that many die in their cars. You can greatly reduce the odds of this happening to you.

1. Don't drive after drinking alcohol or using psychoactive drugs.

2. Drive with the realization that other drivers are possibly preoccupied, intoxicated, or careless.

3. Put poisons out of reach of children; label poison clearly. Poisoning takes a larger toll on people ages 15 to 45 than on children.

4. Keep stairs, halls, doorways, and other pathways clear of shoes, toys, newspapers, and other debris.

5. Don't smoke in bed.

6. Don't let candles burn unattended.

7. Keep children away from hot stoves, and turn pot handles inward.

8. Check electrical cords for fraying, loose connections, or breaks in insulation. Don't overload extension cords.

9. Keep a fire extinguisher handy.

10. Watch for ways that an infant or toddler could suffocate or choke—small objects that can be swallowed, old refrigerators or freezers that can act as air-tight prisons, unattended or unfenced swimming pools, kerosene heaters in tightly closed rooms, and plastic kitchen or clothing bags.

11. Install smoke detectors where you live and work. Most of these run on batteries that need occasional replacement. Follow the manufacturer's guidelines.

EXERCISE #37
SETTING YOUR BIO-ALARM

Sometimes, after only a few hours of sleep, we wake up feeling miserable. Other times, we bounce out of bed feeling terrific. How we feel in the morning often depends on how we program our bio-alarm clock the night before.

After a long night of studying, you may go to bed thinking, "I shouldn't have stayed up so late. I'll be exhausted tomorrow. I hope I hear the alarm in the morning." The next morning, you oversleep and miss class.

To wake up refreshed, experiment with the following.

Before going to bed, decide what time you want to get up in the morning. Now say aloud, "I am going to get up at 7 a.m." (or whatever time you choose).

Next, lie in bed and allow your body to relax. Imagine feeling heavy and sinking into the bed. Now softly say (out loud if possible), "I will wake naturally at 7 a.m. feeling refreshed, rested, and ready to start my day."

Then relax each part of your body, starting with your feet, then ankles, legs, lower back, and so forth until you are completely relaxed and asleep.

You will probably wake up feeling great, at exactly the time you chose. Set your alarm clock for five minutes later than usual and experiment with this exercise a few times. After a while, you may never have to wake up to the buzz again.

Seven Dietary Guidelines

1. Eat a variety of foods. Include fruits, vegetables, whole grains, breads, cereals, milk, cheese, yogurt, meats, poultry, fish, and eggs in your diet.

2. Maintain healthy weight. Overweight people tend to develop high blood pressure, heart disease, strokes, common diabetes, and certain cancers. To lose weight, eat less sugar and fat. Avoid alcohol. Eat slowly. Avoid second helpings. Eat smaller portions.

3. Choose a diet low in fat, saturated fat, and cholesterol. This is a good idea even if you are not overweight. High blood cholesterol is a health risk. Lean meat, fish, poultry, dried beans, and peas are low-cholesterol sources of protein. Limit your intake of eggs, organ meats, butter, cream, shortening, and oil. Broil, bake, or boil rather than fry. Cut off excessive fat before cooking meat.

4. Choose a diet with plenty of vegetables, fruits, and grain products. Include at least three servings of vegetables, two servings of fruit, and six servings of grain (preferably whole grain) products daily.

5. Use sugars in moderation. Obesity, impaired circulation, tooth decay, and other problems relate to excessive sugar in the diet. Many prepared foods contain excessive sugar. Do not select foods if sugar is listed as the first, second, or third ingredient on the label. Sometimes sugar is called corn syrup, dextrose, fructose, glucose, maltose, sucrose, honey, or molasses.

6. Use salt and sodium in moderation. Your body does need sodium chloride (salt). However, you need much less than most people eat and reduction will benefit those people whose blood pressure rises with salt intake. Use salt sparingly, if at all, in food preparation or at the table. Limit your intake of salty foods like pretzels, potato chips, cheese, salted nuts, pickles, and popcorn.

7. If you drink alcoholic beverages, do so in moderation. Moderate drinking is no more than one drink in one day for women, two for men. Some people should not drink at all. Too much alcohol may cause cirrhosis of the liver, inflammation of the pancreas, damage to the heart and brain, high blood pressure, hemorrhagic stroke, and increased risk for many cancers. Do not drink and drive.

JOURNAL ENTRY #57
INTENTION STATEMENT

For three minutes, brainstorm things you can do during the next month to improve your health. Use a separate sheet of paper for your brainstorm.

Next, pick three of your ideas that you can begin to use or practice this week. Finally, write an Intention Statement about how and when you intend to use them.

I intend to . . .

_____

_____

_____

_____

_____

JOURNAL ENTRY #58
INTENTION STATEMENT

Choose one habit related to your health that you would like to begin changing today. Write an Intention Statement about changing this habit so that your body can begin experiencing greater health.

I intend to . . .

_____

_____

_____

_____

_____

JOURNAL ENTRY #59
DISCOVERY STATEMENT

If you look and feel healthy, a greater awareness of your body can let you know what you're doing right. If you are not content with your present physical or emotional health, you may discover some ways to improve.

This exercise is a structured Discovery Statement that allows you to look closely at your health. As with the Discovery Wheel exercise in Chapter One: "First Step," the usefulness of this exercise is determined by your honesty and courage.

1. On a separate sheet of paper, draw a simple outline of yourself. You might have positive and negative feelings about various internal and external parts of your body. Label the parts, and include a short description of the attributes you like or dislike. For example: straight teeth, fat thighs, clear lungs, double chin, straight posture, etc.

2. The body you drew substantially reflects your past health practices. To discover how well you take care of your body, complete the following sentences.

EATING

1. The truth about what I eat is_____

_____

2. What I know about the way I eat is_____

_____

3. What I would most like to change about my diet is_____

_____

4. My eating habits lead me to be_____

_____

EXERCISE

1. The way I usually exercise is_____

_____

2. The last time I did 20 minutes or more of heart/lung (aerobic) exercise was_____

3. As a result of my physical conditioning I feel_____

_____

4. And I look_____

_____

5. It would be easier for me to work out regularly if I_____

_____

6. The most important benefit for me in exercising more is_____

_____

HARMFUL SUBSTANCES

1. My history of cigarette smoking is_____

_____

2. An objective observer would say my use of alcohol is_____

_____

3. In the last 10 days the number of alcoholic drinks I have had is_____

4. I would describe my use of coffee, colas, and other caffeine drinks as_____

5. I have used the following illegal drugs in the past week.

_____

6. When it comes to drugs, what I am sometimes concerned about is_____

7. I take the following prescription drugs._____

_____

RELATIONSHIPS

1. Someone who knows me fairly well would say I am emotionally

_____

2. The way I look and feel has affected my relationships by_____

_____

3. My use of drugs or alcohol has been an issue with_____

_____

4. The best thing I could do for myself and my relationships would be to _____

_____

SLEEP

1. The number of hours I sleep each night is_____

2. On weekends I normally sleep_____

3. I have trouble sleeping when_____

4. Last night I_____

5. The night before last I_____

6. The quality of my sleep is usually_____

_____

What concerns me more than anything else about my health is

_____

_____

_____

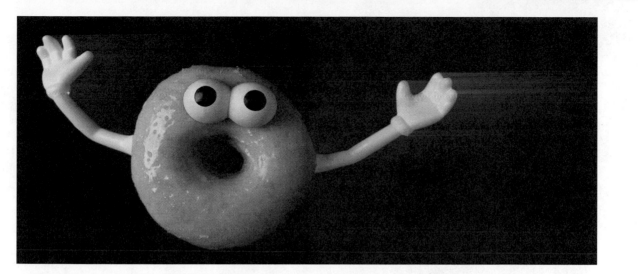

Crazed glazed donut runs amok

Editor's Note: For those of you who think this article might be a bit cutesy, please understand the theoretical and pedagogical rationale for its inclusion, which incorporated the purpose of puncturing the pretentiousness of pundits' puritanical prattle. This article is here to lighten up a subject that is so often approached with guilt and the solemnness of a final exam.

By Bill Harlan

PANCREAS CITY, IOWA— A glazed donut, apparently out of control, caused a multisugar pileup here early yesterday.

The entire state is reeling in lethargy, and the governor has called in extra fatty tissue.

The pileup occurred shortly after 9 a.m., when assistant brain cells in Hypothalamusville noticed an energy shortage. They telephoned the state procurement office in Right Hand with a request for a glazed donut.

Procurement officers delivered the donut to Mouth, two miles north of Throat, at 9:04 a.m. "We were only following orders," one said.

When the donut reached Stomach, the town was nearly deserted. "No one had been here since dinner the night before," a witness said. The donut raced straight through Duodenum Gap and into Intestine County.

Records indicate the energy level throughout the state did rise for more than a half hour. However, about 45 minutes after the donut was delivered, residents in Eyelid noticed what one witness described as "a sort of drooping effect." Within 90 minutes the whole state was in a frenzy. Energy levels dropped.

Tremors were reported in Hand. A suspicious "growl" was heard near Stomach.

By that time, confusion reigned in Pancreas. Officials there later claimed the donut was pure glucose, the kind of sugar that causes an immediate but short-lived energy boost. The glazed perpetrator apparently burned itself out in a metabolic rampage. Soon, only the smoking traces of burned glucose remained.

Minutes later, terror-stricken cells near Stomach began screaming, "Send down a candy bar." The cry was taken up throughout the state, as cells everywhere begged for more sugar.

For the rest of the day, the state reeled under an assault of caffeine and sugar. Three candy bars. Four soft drinks. Pie and coffee.

By evening, the governor's office had called up alcohol reserves.

"We've been recommending complex carbohydrates and small amounts of protein since Tuesday," said a highly placed source, who was reached on vacation at the Isle of Langerhans in Lake Pancreas. "Carbohydrates and proteins burn energy gradually, all day. An egg, some cereal, a piece of fruit, and this tragedy could have been avoided. Heck, a burger would have been better. This donut thing has got to stop."

This morning, a saddened state lies under a layer of fat.

"I'm guessing it will take a hard 10-mile run to get this mess cleaned up," an administrative assistant in Cerebellum said.

Officials in Legs could not be reached.

POWER PROCESS #11

Surrender

Life can be magnificent and satisfying. It can also be devastating. Sometimes there is too much pain or confusion. Problems can be too big and too numerous. Life can bring us to our knees in a pitiful, helpless, and hopeless state. A broken relationship with a loved one, a diagnosis of cancer, total frustration with a child's behavior problem, or even the prospect of several long years of school are situations that can leave us feeling overwhelmed—powerless.

In these troubling situations, the first thing we can do is admit that we don't have the resources to handle the problem. No matter how hard we try and no matter what skills we bring to bear, some problems remain out of our control. When this is the case, we can tell the truth. "It's too big and too mean. I can't handle it."

Releasing control, receiving help

Desperately struggling to control a problem can easily result in the problem controlling you. Surrender is letting go of being the master in order to avoid becoming the slave.

Once you have acknowledged your lack of control, all that remains is to surrender. Many traditions make note of this. Western religions speak of surrendering to God. Hindus say surrender to the Self. Members of Alcoholics Anonymous talk about turning their lives over to a Higher Power. Agnostics might suggest surrendering to the ultimate source of power. Others might speak of following their intuition, their inner guide, or their conscience. William James[1] wrote about surrender as a part of the conversion experience.

In any case, surrender means being open to help. Once we admit we're at the end of our rope, we open ourselves to receiving help. We learn that we don't have to go it alone. We find out that other people have faced similar problems and survived. We give up our old habits of thinking and acting as if we have to be in control of everything. We stop acting as general manager of the universe. In short, we surrender. And that opens a space for something new in our lives.

Surrender works

Surrender works for life's major barriers as well as for its insignificant hassles.

You might say, as you struggle to remember someone's name, "It's on the tip of my tongue." Then you surrender. You give up trying and say, "Oh well, it will come to me later." Then the name pops into your mind.

An alcoholic admits that he just can't control his drinking. This becomes the key that allows him to seek treatment.

A person with multiple sclerosis admits that she's gradually losing the ability to walk. She tells others about this fact. Now the people around her can understand, be supportive, and explore ways to help.

A man is devastated when his girlfriend abandons him. He is a "basket case," unable to work for days. Instead of struggling against this fact, he simply admits the full extent of his pain. In that moment, he is able to trust. He trusts that help will come and that one day he will be OK again. He trusts in his ability to learn and to create a new life. He trusts that new opportunities for love will come his way.

After trying unsuccessfully for years to have a baby, a couple finally surrenders and considers adoption. The woman then conceives in a few months.

After finding out she has terminal cancer, a woman shifts between panic and depression. Nothing seems to console her. Finally she accepts the truth and stops fighting her tragedy. She surrenders. Now at peace, she invests her remaining time in meaningful times with the people she loves.

A writer is tackling the first chapter of his novel, feeling totally in control. He has painstakingly outlined the whole plot, recording each character's actions on individual 3x5 cards. Three sentences into his first draft, he's spending most of his time shuffling cards instead of putting words on paper. Finally, he puts the cards aside, forgets about the outline, and just tells the story. The words start to flow effortlessly and he loses himself in the act of writing.

In each of these cases, the people involved learned the power of surrendering.

What surrender is not

Surrender is not resignation. It is not a suggestion to quit and do nothing about your problems. You have many skills and resources. Use them. You can apply all your energy to handling a situation and surrender at the same time. Surrender includes doing whatever you can in a positive, trusting spirit. Giving up is fatalistic and accomplishes nothing. So let go, keep going, and know that the true source of control lies beyond you.

Power Process #11 says, in effect, don't fight the current. Imagine a person rafting down a flowing river with a rapid current. She's likely to do fine if she surrenders control and lets the raft flow with the current. After all, the current always goes around the rocks. If she tries to fight the current, she could end up in an argument with a rock about where the current is going—and lose.

Detachment helps us surrender

Watching yourself with detachment can help your ability to surrender. Pretend that you are floating away from your body, and then watch what's going on from a distance.

Objectively witness the drama of your life unfolding as if you were watching a play. When you see yourself as part of a much broader perspective, surrender seems obvious and natural.

"Surrender" might seem inconsistent with Power Process #5: "I create it all." An old parable says that the Garden of Truth, the grand place everyone wants to enter, is guarded by two monsters—Fear and Paradox. Most of us can see how fear keeps us from getting what we want. The role of paradox may not be as clear.

The word *paradox* refers to two ideas that seem contradictory or absurd but may actually be true. It is our difficulty in holding these seemingly contradictory thoughts that sometimes keeps us out of the Garden of Truth. When we suspend the sovereignty of logic, then we may discover that ideas that seem contradictory can actually coexist. With application, we can see that both "surrender" and "I create it all" are valuable tools.

Some facts

There are more deaths, illnesses, and disabilities from substance abuse than from any other preventable health condition.

Male alcoholics take their own lives 11 times more frequently than other men. Women alcoholics kill themselves 16 times more often than do women who are not alcoholics.

Drug users consume three times the medical benefits and are five times as likely to file workers' compensation than their nonaddicted counterparts.

About 25 percent of all hospitalized patients have illnesses or injuries related to alcohol.

Between 25 and 40 percent of all general hospital patients are there because of complications related to alcoholism.

At least half of all people arrested for major crimes—including homicide, theft, and assault—were using illicit drugs at the time of their arrest.

The American Cancer Society estimates that cigarette smoking is responsible for 87 percent of lung cancer deaths.

About 5 million drug abusers and 18 million alcohol abusers need treatment, but only a fraction receive it.[2]

Alcohol, tobacco, and drugs: the truth

The truth is, getting high can be fun. In our culture, and especially in our media, getting high has become synonymous with having a good time. Even if you don't smoke, drink, or take drugs, you are certain to come in contact with people who do.

We are a drug-using society.

Drugs (legal and illegal), alcohol, tobacco, and caffeine are accepted and sought-after answers to practically any problem anyone has. Do you have a headache? Take a drug. Is it hard for you to fall asleep? Take a drug. Is it hard to stay awake? Take a drug. Are you depressed? Are you hyperactive? Are you nervous? Are you too skinny? Too fat? The often-heard answer is, "Take something." There is a brand of alcohol, a certain cigarette, or a faster-acting drug that can help.

There is a big payoff in using alcohol, tobacco, caffeine, prescription drugs, cocaine, heroin—or people wouldn't do it. The payoff is sometimes direct—relaxation, self-confidence, comfort, excitement, pleasure. At times, the payoff is not so obvious—avoiding rejection, masking emotional pain, peer group acceptance, rejecting authority.

Some people enjoy using drugs and alcohol so much they try to push these substances on to others: "Here, have another drink. Loosen up. Enjoy yourself." "I can't believe this stuff. Here, try some." "Come on, try it. Are you some kind of a lightweight?"

In addition to the payoff, there is a cost. For most people, the cost is much greater than the payoff. Yet they continue to abuse.

That cost goes beyond money. If cocaine, heroin, and other drugs don't make you broke, they can make you crazy. This is not necessarily the kind of crazy where you dress up like Napoleon, but the kind where you care about little else except finding more drugs—friends, school, work, and family be damned.

Lectures about why to avoid alcohol and drug abuse can be pointless. Ultimately, we don't take care of our bodies because someone says we should. We might take care of ourselves when we see that using a substance is costing us more than we're getting. You choose. It's your body. On the left side of this page are some facts—the truth—that can help you make choices about what to put into your body.

EXERCISE #38
ADDICTION, HOW DO I KNOW . . .

People who have problems with drugs and alcohol are great at hiding the problem from themselves and others. It is also hard to admit that a friend or loved one might have a problem.

The purpose of this exercise is to give you an objective way to look at your relationship to drugs or alcohol. This exercise is also useful in looking to see if a friend might be addicted. Addiction can be emotional and not physical. These are signals that let us know when drug or alcohol use has become abusive. Answer the following questions quickly and honestly with "yes," "no," or "n/a" (not applicable). If you are concerned about someone else, replace each "you" in the following questions with that person's first name.

_____ Are you uncomfortable discussing drug abuse or alcoholism?

_____ Are you worried about your drug or alcohol use?

_____ Are any of your friends worried about your drug or alcohol use?

_____ Have you ever hidden from a friend, spouse, employer, or coworker the fact that you were drinking? (Pretended you were sober? Covered up alchol breath?)

_____ Do you sometimes use alcohol or drugs to escape lows rather than to produce highs?

_____ Have you ever gotten angry when confronted about your use?

_____ Do you brag about how much you consume? ("I drank her under the table.")

_____ Do you think about or do drugs when you are alone?

_____ Do you store up alcohol, drugs, cigarettes, or caffeine (in coffee or soft drinks) so you are sure you won't run out?

_____ Does having a party almost always include alcohol or drugs?

_____ Do you try to control your drinking so that it won't be a problem? ("I drink only on weekends now," "I never drink before 5 p.m.," "I drink only beer.")

_____ Do you often explain to other people why you are drinking? ("It's my birthday," "It's my friend's birthday," "It's Veterans Day," "It sure is a hot day.")

_____ Have you changed your friends to accommodate your drinking? ("She's OK, but she isn't excited about getting high.")

_____ Has your behavior changed in the last several months? (Grades down? Lack of interest in a hobby? Change of values or what you think is moral?)

_____ Do you drink to relieve tension? ("What a day! I need a drink.")

_____ Do you have medical problems (stomach trouble, malnutrition, liver problems, anemia) that could be related to drinking?

_____ Have you ever decided to quit drugs or alcohol and then changed your mind?

_____ Have you had any fights, accidents, or similar incidents related to drinking or drugs in the last year?

_____ Has your drinking or drug use ever caused a problem at home?

_____ Do you envy people who go overboard with alcohol or drugs?

_____ Have you ever told yourself you can quit at any time?

_____ Have you ever been in trouble with the police after or while you were drinking?

_____ Have you ever missed school or work because you had a hangover?

_____ Have you ever had a blackout (a period you can't remember) after drinking?

_____ Do you wish that people would mind their own business when it comes to your use of alcohol or drugs?

Now count the number of questions you answered "yes." If you answered "yes" five or more times, talk with a professional. Five "yes" answers does not mean that you are an alcoholic or that you have a serious problem. It does point out that drugs or alcohol are adversely affecting your life. It is very important that you talk to someone with alcohol- and drug-abuse training. Do not rely on the opinion of anyone without such training.

If you answered this questionnaire about another person and you answered "yes" more than five times, your friend may need help. You probably can't provide that help alone. Seek out a counselor or a support group such as Al-Anon. (Call the local Alcoholics Anonymous chapter for an Al-Anon meeting near you.)

Seeing the full scope of addiction

Substance abuse—that is, addiction to a chemical in alcohol or drugs—is only part of the picture. People can also be addicted to food, gambling, sugar, spending money, sex, unhealthy relationships, and even work.

Here are some guidelines that can help you decide if addiction is a barrier for you right now. Most addictions share some key features[3]:

- Compulsive use of the substance or indulgence in the activity.
- Continued use or activity in spite of adverse consequences.
- Preoccupation with getting and keeping the substance or doing the activity.
- A loss of control over the substance or activity.
- A pattern of relapse—vowing to quit or limit the activity or substance and continually failing to do so.

The same basic features can be present in anything from cocaine use to compulsive gambling. All this can add up to a continuous cycle of abuse.

It's these common features that prompt many people to call some forms of addiction a disease. The American Medical Association formally recognized alcoholism as a disease in 1956.

Some people do not agree that alcoholism is a disease or that all addictions can be labeled with that term. You don't have to wait until this question is settled before examining your own life.

What to do

If you have a problem with addiction, consider getting help. Your problem may be your own addiction or perhaps the behavior of someone you love. In any case, consider acting on several of these suggestions.

1. Admit the problem. People with active addictions are a varied group—rich and poor, young and old, successful and unsuccessful. Often these people do have one thing in common: They are masters of denial. They deny they are unhappy. They deny they have hurt anyone. They are convinced they can quit any time they want. They sometimes become so adept at hiding the problem from themselves that they die.

2. When you use, pay attention. If you do use a substance compulsively or behave in compulsive ways, do it with awareness. Then pay attention to the consequences. Act with deliberate decision rather than out of habit or pressure from others.

3. Look at the costs. There is always a tradeoff. You may feel great after 10 beers, and you will probably remember that feeling. No one feels great the morning after 10 beers, but it seems easier to forget pain. Often people don't notice how bad alcoholism, drug addiction, or other forms of addiction make them feel.

4. Instead of blaming yourself, take responsibility for recovery. Nobody plans to become an addict. If you have pneumonia, you can recover without guilt or shame. Approach an addiction in yourself or others in the same way. You can take responsibility for your recovery without blame, shame, or guilt.

5. Get help. Many people find that addiction is not a condition they can treat alone. Addictive behaviors are often symptoms of an illness that needs treatment.

Two broad options exist for getting help with addiction. One is the growing self-help movement. The other is formal treatment. People recovering from addiction often combine the two.

Many self-help groups are modeled after Alcoholics Anonymous. AA is made up of recovering alcoholics and addicts. These people understand the problems of abuse firsthand, and they have a systematic, 12-step approach to living without it. With over a million members, this is one of the oldest and most successful self-help programs in the world. Chapters of AA welcome people from all walks of life, and you don't have to be an alcoholic to attend most meetings. Programs based on AA principles exist for many other forms of addiction as well.

Some people feel uncomfortable with the AA approach. Other resources exist for these people, including private therapy and group therapy. Also investigate organizations such as Women for Sobriety, the Secular Organizations for Sobriety, and Rational Recovery Systems. Use what works for you.

Treatment programs are available in almost every community. They may be residential (you live there for weeks or months at a time) or outpatient (you visit several hours a day). Find out where these treatment centers are located by calling a doctor, mental health professional, or a local hospital.

Alcohol and drug treatment are now covered by many health insurance programs. If you don't have insurance, it is usually possible to arrange some other payment program. Cost is no reason to avoid treatment.

PRACTICING
CRITICAL THINKING #22

The advice about health we receive in the popular press often seems contradictory. For example, one expert claims that running is an ideal form of exercise. Another authority warns about dangers of injury from jogging and recommends walking instead.

Choose one health topic on which you see diverging viewpoints. Explain each point of view, then see if you can construct a new viewpoint that reconciles the conflicting opinions—or at least clarifies the nature of the disagreement. Summarize your viewpoint on a separate sheet of paper. Upon closer examination, you might conclude that experts may not really be in disagreement, considering the ways that they qualify their opinions.

Where to turn for more information on recovery

You can begin with your doctor, school health care center, or local chapter of Alcoholics Anonymous. You can also contact:

African American Family Services
1-612-871-7878

Alcoholics Anonymous
World Services
1-212-870-3400

National Black
Alcoholism Council
1-315-735-3551

National Institute on
Drug Abuse Hotline
1-800-662-4357

National Clearinghouse for
Alcohol and Drug Information
1-800-729-6686

National Council on Alcoholism
and Drug Dependence, Inc.
1-212-206-6770

National Coalition of Hispanic
Health & Human Services
1-202-387-5000

National Association of Native
American Children of Alcoholics
1-206-467-7686

PRIDE Drug Information Line
1-800-853-7867

Rational Recovery Systems
1-800-303-2873

Women for Sobriety
1-215-536-8026

master student

may lemke

raised five children previous to working with Leslie

The Milwaukee County General Hospital had a serious problem: a six-month-old infant named Leslie. Mentally retarded and without eyes, the baby also had cerebral palsy. He was a limp vegetable, totally unresponsive to sound or touch. His parents had abandoned him.

The hospital staff didn't know what to do—until a pediatrician mentioned May Lemke, a nurse-governess living nearby. A nurse telephoned May and explained that in all likelihood Leslie would die in a short time. "Would you help us by taking care of him while he lives?" the nurse asked.

"If I take him he certainly will not die, and I will take him," May replied. . . .

When May accepted the baby, she accepted him as just that, a baby—no different from the others—to be taught and loved. . . .

Year after year she cared for him, but there was no movement. No smile. No tears. No sound. . . .

The Lemkes then had a chain-link fence erected along the side of their property, and May stood Leslie next to it,

thrusting his fingers through the openings. After several weeks he finally got the idea of letting the fence support him. He stood. He was 16 . . . .

One day she noticed Leslie's index finger moving against a taut piece of string around a package, as if plucking it. Was this a sign? she wondered. What did it mean?

Music! she exclaimed to herself. That's it. Music. From then on the Lemke house was filled with music from the record player, the radio and the TV. Hour after hour the music played. Leslie gave no indication that he was listening.

May and her husband Joe bought an old upright piano for $250.00 and placed it in Leslie's bedroom. Repeatedly, May pushed his fingers against the keys to show him that his fingers could make sounds. He remained totally indifferent.

It happened in the winter of 1971. May was awakened by the sound of music. It was 3 a.m. Someone was playing Tchaikovsky's Piano Concerto No. 1. She shook Joe. "Did you leave the radio on?" she asked.

"No," he said.

"Then where's the music coming from?" She swung out of bed and turned on a living room light. It dimly illuminated Leslie's room. Leslie was at the piano. May saw a smile glowing on his face.

He had never before gotten out of bed on his own. He had never seated himself at the piano. He had never voluntarily or deliberately struck the keys with his fingers. Now he was actually playing a concerto—and with deftness and confidence . . . .

"Coming out" musically opened the door for all kinds of emotions and developments. Occasionally a single word popped from his mouth. Then one afternoon some children were playing on the other side of the chain-link fence, and May asked them what they were doing. One of them answered, "We're having fun." Leslie took a few steps along the fence. "I'm having fun," he said in a thick but understandable voice. It was his first complete sentence . . . .

As news of Leslie's talent traveled, groups requested him for concerts. May pondered the invitations; then she decided that public appearances would be valuable to Leslie. . . .

There are still many things that Leslie cannot do. Those fingers that perform so brilliantly at the keyboard cannot use a knife or fork. Conversation does not flow easily. But ask what music means to him and he replies with a voice that is firm. "Music," says Leslie, "is love."

Excerpted with permission from "The Miracle of May Lemke's Love" by Joseph P. Blank, Reader's Digest *October 1982. Copyright © 1982 by the Reader's Digest Assn., Inc.*

1 *The strategies suggested for dealing with stress do not include:*

   (A) Manage self-talk.
   (B) Practice relaxation techniques.
   (C) Cut back in exercising.
   (D) Mentally rehearse success and visualize positive events.
   (E) Check with the student health service.

2 *How is surrender, as discussed in Power Process #11, different from giving up?*

3 *A person infected with HIV may feel no symptoms for months—sometimes years. True or False. Explain your answer.*

4 *Define* date rape *and describe at least two ways to prevent it.*

5 *List at least three dietary guidelines that can contribute to your health.*

6 *One of the suggestions for dealing with addiction is "When you use, pay attention." This implies that it's OK to use drugs compulsively, as long as you do so with full awareness. True or False. Explain your answer.*

7 *Name at least three methods for preventing unwanted pregnancy.*

8 The only way to be absolutely safe from STDs is to abstain from sex. True or False. Explain your answer.

9 Name two characteristics shared by most forms of addiction.

10 Stress is always harmful. True or False. Explain your answer.

JOURNAL ENTRY #60
DISCOVERY/INTENTION STATEMENT

Review what you learned in this chapter about the way you take care of your "machine."

I discovered that I . . .

_____

_____

Choose one health-related behavior you want to change. Describe when and where you will do this activity.

I intend to . . .

_____

_____

JOURNAL ENTRY #61
DISCOVERY STATEMENT

After reading Power Process #10: "Employ your word" in Chapter Ten, on a separate sheet of paper list one problem in your life and how it could be related to broken agreements. Begin with this phrase: I discovered that I . . .

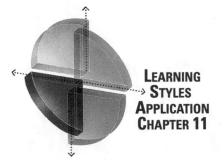

LEARNING STYLES APPLICATION CHAPTER 11

Complete the following exercises on a separate sheet of paper.

Style 1

Name one specific health benefit you'd like to gain. Possibilities include decreased stress, lower weight, or an increased energy level.

Style 2

List 8 ideas from this chapter that could help you gain the benefit you just listed.

Style 3

Create an action plan for using the ideas you listed for Style 2. Write 5 to 7 Intention Statements and set a date for taking each action.

Style 4

After carrying out your plan, consider how well it worked for you. Which actions do you intend to continue on a regular basis? Are there any new actions you intend to take or any changes you want to make in your action plan? Write answers to both of these questions.

Bibliography

Endnotes

[1]William James, *The Varieties of Religious Experience: A Study in Human Nature* (New York: New American Library, 1902).

[2]Brandeis University Institute for Health Policy, *Substance Abuse: The Nation's Number One Health Problem* (The Robert Wood Johnson Foundation, 1993).

[3]American Psychiatry Association, *Diagnostic and Statistical Manual of Psychoactive Substance Abuse Disorders,* 4th ed. (Washington, DC: 1994).

Additional Reading

Cousins, Norman. *Anatomy of an Illness as Perceived by the Patient,* New York: Bantam Books, 1981.

Johnson, Vernon E. *I'll Quit Tomorrow,* New York: Harper and Row, 1980.

Pennebaker, James W. *Opening Up: The Healing Power of Confiding in Others,* New York: Morrow, 1990.

Robbins, John. *Diet For A New America,* Walpole, NH: Stillpoint, 1987.

Ryan, Regina Sara, and John W. Travis, M.D. *Wellness Workbook: A Guide to Attaining High Level Wellness,* Berkeley, CA: Ten Speed Press, 1981.

Silber, Sherman J., M.D. *How Not to Get Pregnant: Your Guide to Simple, Reliable Contraception,* New York: Scribner, 1987.

Vickery, Donald M., M.D., and James Fries, M.D. *Take Care of Yourself: The Consumer's Guide to Medical Care,* Reading, MA: Addison-Wesley, 1986.

Weil, Andrew. *Health and Healing,* Boston: Houghton Mifflin, 1988.

Weil, Andrew. *Natural Health, Natural Medicine,* Boston: Houghton Mifflin, 1995.

Whittemore, Gerard. *Street Wisdom for Women: A Handbook For Urban Survival,* Boston: Quinlan Press, 1986.

Yoder, Barbara. *The Recovery Resource Book,* New York: Fireside, 1990.

what next?

Now that you're done...

with this course, consider turning the skills that you've learned into lifelong habits. Also make full use of school and community resources, and bring your inner resources to life by choosing attitudes that promote your success. Along the way, gain tools for choosing majors, planning careers, changing schools, and traveling via computer. In addition, find a path to personal satisfaction by contributing to others, and discover a process that enhances the power of every idea in this book—"Be it."

JOURNAL ENTRY #62
DISCOVERY STATEMENT

Complete the following sentences with the first thoughts that come to mind.

From this chapter, I want . . .

_____
_____
_____
_____
_____
_____
_____
_____

From my life, I want . . .

_____
_____
_____
_____
_____
_____
_____
_____
_____

IF YOU USED THIS BOOK, if you actively participated in reading the contents, writing the journals, doing the exercises, practicing critical thinking, completing the learning style applications, and applying the suggestions, then you have had quite a journey. You are on a path of growth toward becoming a master student. Now what? What's the next step?

Now that you're done — Begin

The world is packed with opportunities for master students. If you excel in adventure, exploration, discovery, and creativity, you will never lack for possibilities. If you want to continue to grow and to continue to learn how to learn, the choices are endless.

You are on the edge of a universe so miraculous and full of wonder that your imagination at its most creative moment cannot encompass it. Paths are open to lead you to worlds beyond your wildest dreams.

If this sounds like a pitch for the latest recreational drug, it may be. The drug is adrenaline, and it is automatically generated by your body when you are growing, risking, and discovering new worlds inside and outside your skin.

This book has started the process of discovery and intention, a powerful tool that can assist you in getting exactly what you want out of life. Following are several ways to reinforce the discovery and intention process.

> **" "**
>
> *Think wrongly if you please, but in all cases think for yourself.*
> –DORIS LESSING

> **" "**
>
> *Live as if you were to die tomorrow. Learn as if you were to live forever.*
> –GANDHI

> **" "**
>
> *Learning is not a task or a problem–it is a way to be in the world. Man learns as he pursues goals and projects that have meaning for him.*
> –SIDNEY JOURARD

"...use the following suggestions to continue..."

Keep a journal. Psychotherapist Ira Progoff[1] wrote that regular journaling can be a path to life-changing insights and based his Intensive Journal System on this idea. To begin this path, consider buying a bound notebook in which to record your private reflections and dreams for the future. Get one that will be worthy of your personal discoveries and intentions.

Write in this journal daily. Record what you are learning about yourself and the world.

Write about your hopes, wishes, and goals. Keep a record of significant events. Consider using the format of Discovery Statements and Intention Statements you learned in this book. For more ideas, see "Taking notes on your journey—The art of journal writing" later in this chapter.

Take a seminar. Schooling doesn't have to stop at graduation, and it doesn't have to take place on a campus. Workshops start each week in most cities about everything from cosmetology to cosmology. Use workshops to learn skills, understand the world, and discover yourself. Learn cardiopulmonary resuscitation (CPR), attend a lecture on developing nations, or take a course on assertiveness training.

Read, watch, and listen. Many books related to becoming a master student are recommended in the bibliography at the end of this chapter. Ask friends and instructors what they are reading. Sample a variety of newspapers and magazines. None of them has all of the truth; most of them have a piece of it.

In addition to books, many bookstores and publishing houses offer audio- and videotapes on personal growth topics. Record your most exciting discoveries in an idea file.

Take an unrelated class. Sign up for a class that is totally unrelated to your major. If you are studying to be a secretary, take a physics course. If you are going to be a doctor, take a bookkeeping course.

You can discover a lot about yourself and your intended future when you step out of old patterns. In addition to formal courses offered at your school, check into community education classes. These are a low-cost alternative that offers no threat to your grade point average.

Travel. See the world. Visit new neighborhoods. Travel to other countries. Explore.

Find out what it looks like inside buildings you normally have no reason to go into, museums you think you have little interest in, cities that are out of the way, forests and mountains that lie beyond your old boundaries, and far-off places that require planning and saving to reach.

Get counseling. Solving emotional problems is not the only reason to visit a counselor, therapist, or psychologist. These people are excellent resources for personal growth. You can use counseling to look at yourself and talk about yourself in ways that may be uncomfortable for anyone except a trained professional. Counseling offers a chance to talk about nothing but yourself without anyone's thinking you are rude.

Form a support group. Just as a well-organized study group can promote your success in school, an organized support group can help you reach goals in other areas of your life.

Today people in support groups help one another lose weight, stay sober, cope with chronic illness, recover from emotional trauma, and overcome drug addiction.

Groups can also brainstorm possibilities for job hunting, career planning, parenting, solving problems in relationships, promoting spiritual growth—for reaching almost any goal you choose.

Find a mentor—or become one. Seek the counsel of experienced people you respect and admire. Use them as role models. If they are willing, ask them to be sounding boards for your plans and ideas. Most people are flattered to be asked.

You can also become a mentor. If you want to perfect your skills as a master student, teach them to someone else. Offer to coach another student in study skills in return for childcare, free lunches, or something else you value. A mentor relationship can bridge the boundaries of age, race, or culture.

Redo this book. Start by redoing one chapter or maybe just one exercise. If you didn't get everything you wanted from this book, it's not too late.

You can also redo portions that you found valuable. Redo the quizzes to test your ability to recall certain information. Redo the exercises that were particularly effective for you. They can work again. Many of the exercises in this book can produce a different result after a few months. You are changing, and your responses change too.

The Discovery Wheel can be useful in revealing techniques you have actually put into practice. Redo the Journal Entries. If you keep your own journal, refer to it as you rewrite the Journal Entries in this book.

As you redo this book or any part of it, reconsider techniques that you skimmed over or skipped before. They may work for you now. Modify the suggestions or add new ones. Redoing this book can refresh and fine-tune your study habits.

Another way to redo this book is to retake your student success course. People who do so often say the second time was much different from the first. They pick up ideas and techniques they missed the first time and gain deeper insight into things they already know.

EXERCISE #39
DO SOMETHING YOU CAN'T

You can accomplish much more than you might think you can. Few significant accomplishments result when people stick to the familiar. Risk yourself.

Pick something that you don't know how to do and do it. Choose something you think you can't do and do it.

Be smart. Don't pick something that will hurt you physically, such as flying from a third-floor window.

This exercise has three parts.

Part 1

Select something that you have never done before, that you don't know how to do, that you are fearful of doing, or that you think you probably can't do. Describe below the thing you have chosen.

_____

_____

_____

_____

Part 2

Do it. Of course this is easier to say than to do. This exercise is not about easy. It is about discovering capabilities that stretch your self-image.

In order to accomplish something that is bigger than your self-perceived abilities, use all the tools you have. Develop a plan. Divide and conquer. Be willing to be a fool. Stay focused. Use all available outside resources. Let go of self-destructive thoughts.

Part 3

Write about the results of this exercise in your journal if you choose to start one.

Attitudes, affirmations & visualizations

"I have a bad attitude." People say this as if they were talking about having the flu. An attitude is certainly as strong as the flu, but it isn't something you have to succumb to or accept.

Some people see their attitudes the way they see their height or their eye color: "I may not like it, but I might as well accept it."

Acceptance is certainly a worthwhile approach to things you cannot change. Acceptance is not necessary when it comes to attitudes. If you have an attitude that you don't like, change it. You may have to go through life being too short or too tall. You don't have to live your life with an attitude that doesn't work.

Attitudes are powerful because they create behavior. If your attitude is that you're not very interesting at a party, then your behavior will probably match your attitude, and you can act like a bore. If your attitude is that you are fun at a party, then your behavior is more likely to be fun. Soon you are the life of the party. All that has to change is attitude.

You can change your attitudes by regular practice with affirmations and visualizations.

Affirm it

An affirmation is a statement describing what you want. The most effective affirmations are personal, positive, and written in the present tense.

Affirmations have an almost magical power. They are used successfully by athletes and actors, executives and ballerinas, and tens of thousands of people who have succeeded in their lives. Affirmations can change your attitudes and behaviors.

To use affirmations, first determine what you want, then describe yourself as if you already have it. For example, if you decide you want a wonderful job, you might write, "I, Susan Webster, have a wonderful job. I respect and love my colleagues and they feel the same way about me. I look forward to going to work each day."

Or if money is your desire, you might write, "I, John Henderson, am rich. I have more money than I can spend. I have everything I want, including a six-bedroom house, a new sports car, a 200-watt stereo system, and a videotape recorder with a satellite dish receiver."

What makes the affirmation work is detail. Use brand names, people's names, and your own name. Involve all your senses—sight, sound, smell, taste, touch. Be positive. Instead of saying, "I am not fat," say, "I am slender."

Once you have written the affirmation, repeat it. Practice saying it aloud several times a day. This works best if you say it at a regular time, such as just before you sleep or just after waking up.

Sit in a chair in a relaxed position. Take a few deep and relaxing breaths, and then repeat your affirmation with emotion. It's also effective to look in a mirror while saying the affirmation. Keep looking and repeating until you are saying your affirmation with conviction.

Visualize it

It would be difficult to grow up in our culture without hearing that practice improves performance. The problem is that most of us limit what we consider practice. Effective practice can occur when you are not moving a muscle.

You can improve a golf game, a tennis serve, or your skiing ability while lying in bed. You can become a better driver, speaker, or cook while sitting silently in a chair. In line at the grocery store, you can improve your ability to type or take tests. This is all possible through visualization—the art of seeing yourself be successful.

Here's how. Decide what you want to improve, and write down what it would look like, sound like, and feel like to have that improvement. If you are learning to play the piano, write down briefly what you would see, hear, and feel if you were playing skillfully. If you want to improve your relationships with your children, write down what you would see, hear, and feel if you were communicating successfully.

A powerful visualization includes not only seeing but other sense channels as well. Feel the physical sensations. Hear the sounds. Note any smells, tastes, textures, or qualities of light that accompany the scene in your mind.

Once you have a sketch of what it would be like to be successful, practice in your imagination—successfully. Rehearse in your mind. Include as many details as you can. Always have your practices be successes. Each time you toss the basketball, it will swish through the net. Every time you invite someone out, he will say yes. Every test will have an A on the top. Practice at least once per day.

You can also use visualizations to replay errors. When you make a mistake, replay it in your imagination. After a bad golf shot, stop and replay it in your head. Imagine yourself making that same shot again very successfully. If you just had a discussion with your lover that turned into a fight, replay it successfully. Get all your senses involved. See yourself calmly talking it over together. Hear the words, and feel the pleasure of a successful interaction.

Visualizations and affirmations can restructure your attitudes and behaviors. Be clear about what you want and then practice.

Attitude replacements

You can use affirmations to replace a negative attitude with a positive thought. There are no limits other than your imagination and practice. Here are some ideas to stir your imagination. Modify them to suit your individual hopes and dreams, and then add practice. The article "Attitudes, affirmations and visualizations" explains ways to use these attitude replacements.

I, _____, am healthy.

I, _____, have abundant energy and vitality throughout the day.

I, _____, exercise regularly.

I, _____, work effectively with many different kinds of people.

I, _____, eat wisely.

I, _____, plan my days and use time wisely.

I, _____, have a powerful memory.

I, _____, take tests calmly and confidently.

I, _____, am a great speller.

I, _____, fall asleep quickly and sleep soundly.

I, _____, am smart.

I, _____, learn quickly.

I, _____, am creative.

I, _____, am aware of and sensitive to people's moods.

I, _____, have relationships that are mutually satisfying.

I, _____, work hard and contribute to other people through my job.

I, _____, am wealthy.

I, _____, know ways to play and have fun.

I, _____, am attractive.

I, _____, focus my attention easily.

I, _____, like myself.

I, _____, am liked by other people.

I, _____, am a worthwhile person even though I am _____.

I, _____, have a slim and attractive body.

I, _____, am relaxed in all situations, including _____.

I, _____, make profitable financial investments.

I, _____, have an income that far exceeds my expenses.

I, _____, live a life of abundance and prosperity.

I, _____, always live my life in positive ways for the highest good of all people.

Name _____ Date _____/_____/_____

EXERCISE #40
REPROGRAM YOUR ATTITUDE

Affirmations and visualizations can be used to successfully reprogram your attitudes and behaviors. Use this exercise to change your approach to any situation in your life.

Step 1
Pick something in your life you would like to change. It can be about anything—relationships, work, money, or personal skills. Write a brief description of what you choose to change.

_____

_____

_____

_____

_____

_____

Step 2
Write how you would like your choice in Step 1 to change. Be outlandish. Write down your greatest wish about how you would like it to be. Imagine you are about to ask your fairy godmother for a wish you know she will grant. Be detailed in your description of how you want it to be.

_____

_____

_____

_____

_____

_____

_____

_____

_____

Step 3
Here comes the fairy godmother. Use affirmations and visualizations to start yourself on the road to creating exactly what you wrote about in Step 2. Below, write at least two affirmations that describe your dream wish. Also, briefly outline a visualization that you can use to picture your wish. Be specific, detailed, and positive.

_____

_____

_____

_____

_____

_____

_____

_____

_____

_____

_____

_____

Step 4
Put them to work. Set up a schedule of practice. Determine a time and place when you can practice your new attitudes. Set the first time to be right now. Then set up at least five other times that you intend to practice your affirmations and visualizations.

I intend to relax and practice my affirmations and visualizations for at least five minutes on the following dates and at the place(s) given.

	Date	Time	Location
1.			
2.			
3.			
4.			
5.			

Some Places Your Computer Can Visit

n your continuing search for resources to promote your academic and personal success, consider the Internet. Begin with some of the sites listed below, and they will lead you to others. Remember to type a site address exactly as written. Also keep in mind that sites often change, and some are deluged with visitors. If you can't connect to a site, check your typing, look for a more current address, or try again later. (Note that World Wide Web site addresses begin with the letters *http*.)

Critical Thinking Community Home Page
http://www.sonoma.edu/cthink/

E-mail address for members of the U.S. Congress
www.yahoo.com/Government/Legislative Branch/Congressional E Mail Addresses/

Federal Express (to track your shipment's progress)
http://www.fedex.com/

FinAid: FAQ (frequently asked questions about financial aid)
http://www.cs.cmu.edu/afs/cs.cmu.edu/user/mkant/ftp/finaid/finad.faq

First Lady of the United States
first.lady@whitehouse.gov

(her husband)
president@whitehouse.gov

Houghton Mifflin College Survival Home Page
http://www.hmco.com/hmco/college/ColSurviv.html

Lycos (to search the World Wide Web)
http://lycos.cs.cmu.edu

Multimedia Medical Reference Library
http://www.tiac.net/users/jtward/index.html

Public Broadcasting Service
http://www.pbs.org/

Webcrawler (to search the World Wide Web)
http://www.webcrawler.com

Yahoo (another way to search the World Wide Web)
http://www.yahoo.com

EXERCISE #41
THIS BOOK SHOUTS

"*Use me!*"

Becoming a Master Student *is* designed to be used for years. The success strategies presented here are not likely to become habits overnight. There are more suggestions than can be put into action immediately. Some of what is discussed may not apply to your life right now, but may be just what you could use in a few months.

Plan to keep this book and use it again. Imagine that your book has a mouth. (Visualize the mouth.) Your book has arms and legs. (Visualize them.)

Now picture your book sitting on a shelf or table that you see every day. Imagine a time when you are having trouble in school and struggling to be successful as a student. Visualize your book jumping up and down shouting, "Use me! Read me! I may have the solution to your problem, and I know I can help you solve it."

This is a memory technique to remind you to use a resource. Sometimes, when you are stuck, all you need is a small push or a list of possible actions. At those times, hear your book shout, "Use me!"

Other ideas for getting lasting value from Becoming a Master Student include:

- Keep it on the coffee table, in the kitchen, or in the bathroom.
- Keep it near your bedroom nightstand.
- Loan the book to someone else, then talk about it with that person.
- Teach your favorite suggestions from this book to your friends and family.
- Tear out specific articles and share them with family or friends.
- In your calendar or appointment book, schedule periodic times to review the book.

Taking notes on your journey—
The art of journal writing

If you've been writing Discovery and Intention Statements as you use *Becoming a Master Student*, you've already practiced the art of journal writing. This is a practice that you can do well beyond this course—for a lifetime, in fact.

Journal writing provides a host of benefits. To begin, it offers a chance to hone your writing skills and reflect on your course work. In addition, journals promote self-awareness. Through journal writing, we discover patterns in our lives. Our experiences take on the form of a story, with a beginning, middle, and end. We learn to step back from the daily hustle, spot recurring problems, and invent solutions.

Keeping a journal is a low-cost activity with a high return on investment. Begin with a pencil and a ream of the cheapest paper you can find. As your budget allows, you might wish to work with fancy pens and high-quality paper. You can also write journal entries at a computer.

Just jump in and start

One thing that stops people from keeping a journal is writer's block. To get past this problem, do a free writing exercise: Set a timer and write for five minutes without stopping to revise. Just keep your hand moving and write anything that pops into your head. Put yourself on automatic pilot until the words start happening on their own. For related suggestions, see the chapter on writing.

There are many other ways to get started. Write letters—including those you don't plan to send. The person you're "sending" the letter to can be famous or obscure, near or far, dead or alive. This can be a useful way to deal with anger or grief.

Also use leading sentences to jump-start your writing. For example, Journal Entries in this book start with *I discovered that I . . .* or *I intend to . . . .* Invent your own lead-ins.

Feel free to dream wildly. Create a compelling future. Include the details—what you want to have, do, and be five, 10, or 50 years from now. Write as if you've already attained your long-term goals. After this kind of brainstorm, focus on one goal and write an action plan to meet it.

Make lists

For example, write down the five most influential people in your life and what they taught you. If you're a parent, list the three most important skills you want to teach your children.

Keep a list of your favorite quotations. Record notable things that you and your friends say.

In addition, list new words and their definitions. Writing them down helps to make these words part of your working vocabulary.

You can make lists of anyone you've harmed and note how you plan to make amends. Listing resentments can rob them of their power and move us toward forgiveness.

Also make a list of what you've received from others. Record your thanks to people who have benefited you. You could well end up with "an attitude of gratitude."

Use a journal for critical thinking

There's a definition of note taking: Words that go directly from the instructor's mouth to the student's paper—without ever entering the student's mind.

You can avoid this fate by writing in a journal. Here is a chance for you to stretch out mentally. Reflect on the significance of your courses. Mine your own experiences for examples of the ideas you're learning about. Speculate about how you might apply what you're learning in class.

One technique recommended by writing teachers Richard Solly and Roseann Lloyd[2] is to imagine that you're sitting face to face with the author of your textbook. Write what you would say to this person. Argue. Debate. Note questions you'd want to ask this person and then pose them in class.

Play with learning styles

Journals don't have to be limited to paper. Draw. Paint. Create a collage or sculpture. Visualizing through art is a powerful way to remember our experiences. Write a piece of music. Dictate your journal entries into a tape recorder. Use a journal to take risks and explore new learning styles.

If you're shy about doing any of this, remember that no one has to see your work. Your journal is in safe hands—your own.

Reread your journal

Use journals to periodically get in touch with an old friend—yourself. Rereading a journal entry can transport us across the years and alter our emotional state in seconds. Reading about times when we excelled at work, school, or relationships can rekindle our zest for life.

To aid in locating important entries, create an index or table of contents for your journal notebook. If you use a computer for journal writing, see if your word processing software can do this automatically.

Use a journal to manage stress

Much stress has its source in negative self-talk—nagging voices in our heads that make dire predictions for the future and undermine our abilities: "This is the worst thing that could ever happen to me" or "I never finish what I start."

Getting these disempowering ideas outside our heads and onto paper is one way to defuse them. Begin by listing any irrational, self-defeating beliefs you have. Then write down more reasonable, empowering beliefs and Intention Statements.

Use a journal to increase writing skills

Writing in a journal can sharpen your powers of observation. To begin, list as many details as you can about a person or object in your environment. Make your description as complete, vivid, and detailed as you can.

Try your hand at fiction too. Create a character for a play or novel. Write poems, short stories, or articles you might submit for publication.

Mine your journal for writing topics. Perhaps you've already written something that could become the basis for a research paper.

Use a journal for personal growth

Visualizations and affirmations can begin on the pages of your journal. Also write about your fears, hopes, dreams, and ambitions. In this way a journal becomes a trusted confidant who always respects your safety and privacy. Here is a counselor who's available anyplace, anytime—free.

"But I don't know what I want to do"
—CHOOSING A MAJOR

One decision that troubles many students in higher education is the choice of an academic major. It's easy to put off this decision when we view it as an irrevocable choice that determines our future. Instead, choosing a major can be the start of a continuing path toward self-knowledge.

When it comes to choosing a major, it can pay to stay undecided for a time. This is not a decision that most of us can make on demand. Choosing a major calls for gathering facts, weighing alternatives, and allowing unhurried time for wondering, pondering, doodling, and daydreaming. You can use the following ideas to bring your options into focus.

Know thyself

Choosing a major can be more effective when you begin from a basis of self-knowledge. Your responses to the exercises and Journal Entries in this book are a place to start gaining this knowledge. After reviewing what you wrote, do any of them again with an eye to insights that bear on your choice of major.

Ask others

Other people might have valuable suggestions about a choice of major for you. Ask key people in your life for their ideas and listen without criticizing. You can always choose whether to follow up on what they say.

Plan your life

Your decision about a major can fall into place once you clarify the overall direction of your life. Consider your values—the personal qualities you consider to be most important in living effectively. Also decide what you want to accomplish in five years, 10 years, or even 50 years from today. After that, choosing your courses for next quarter might seem like a piece of cake.

Plan your career

There are many excellent materials that can assist you in planning your career. For an overview of the topic and an immediate chance to put ideas on paper, see "Career planning—Begin now" in this chapter. Also distinguish between careers that require specific majors and those that do not.

Consider further schooling

With some specific ideas for your life and career plans in hand, think about the possible need for an advanced degree in your field. Such degrees are required for many careers, such as medicine, counseling, law, and college teaching.

Draw on other resources

Remember that people commonly work in fields with little or no direct relationship to their major. Other experiences besides courses in your major can be tools for defining your skills and interests. Examples are part-time jobs, internships, work-study programs, and extracurricular activities.

Do some research

When the only tool you have for choosing a major is a few course listings in your school catalog, trying to decide on a major can seem like a pretty academic affair. Instead, go beyond the printed page. Talk to some people. Visit with instructors who teach the courses in a given major. Ask them about required course work and career options in the field. Also ask for the names of students currently taking courses in a given major and sit in on some of those courses. In addition, contact students who've graduated and are working in the field.

Choose a complementary minor

You can add flexibility to your academic program through your choice of a minor. That course of study can complement or contrast with your choice of a major. The student who wants to be a minister could opt for a minor in English; all those courses in composition can help in writing sermons. Or the student with a major in psychology might choose a minor in business administration with the idea of managing a counseling service some day.

Invent a major

When choosing a major, you may not need to limit yourself to those listed in your course catalog. Many schools now have flexible programs that allow for independent study. Through such programs you might be able to combine two existing majors, or even invent one of your own. Some people even graduate without a conventional major, creating instead a focus in the humanities or liberal arts studies.

Just choose

Chances are, you already know a lot about what your major's going to be. To verify this, do a short, playful experiment. Search your school's catalog for a list of available majors. Now cross out all those majors you already know are not right for you. You will probably eliminate well over half the list. Next, scan the remaining majors. Pretend that you have to choose a major today. Write down the first three ideas that come to mind.

Choose again

Changing majors is a natural result of getting to know yourself better. Consider, too, that you're likely to change jobs—as well as careers—several times in your life. As you discover more about your passions and potentials while in school, let your choice of a major reflect that ongoing quest.

Majors for the taking

The variety of majors available in higher education is staggering. Many schools also allow for double majors, individually designed majors, interdepartmental majors, and minors in various areas. Knowing this, you can create a course of study that matches your skills, interests, and passions.

To verify this, take a glance through the college catalogs in your local library. Or skim a reference work such as Peterson's Guide to Four-Year Colleges, *which describes schools with the following majors. Look through the list to see what you might have forgotten.*

Agribusiness
Agronomy
Airway science
Architectural drafting
Audiology
Botany
Building construction technology
Ceramics
Classical languages
Climatology
Criminal justice
Cytotechnology
Dance
Dietetics
Equestrian studies
Exercise and sport science
Fashion design and merchandising
Film studies
Forestry
Hospitality and tourism services
Human ecology
Kinesiology
Liberal studies
Machine shop welding
Medical records services
Music therapy
Office management
Paralegal studies
Pet-assisted therapy facilitation
Petroleum land management
Recreational leadership
Respiratory therapy
Retail management
Sculpture
Substance abuse counseling
Theology
Third World studies
Transportation technologies
Upholstery
Urban affairs
Water utilities operation
Wildlife fisheries
Zoological sciences

CHANGING SCHOOLS

Changing schools involves making a decision that will have a major impact on your education. Choosing a school for your higher education is much like choosing a career. You first define the profile of an ideal prospective school, much as you define an ideal job for you. Next you create a profile of yourself—your skills, background, experience, learning style, and other preferences. Then you seek a reasonable fit between yourself and your ideal school, just as you seek a fit between yourself and your job. The following suggestions can assist you in making this important decision.

Know key terms

As you begin researching schools, take a few minutes to review some key terms.

Transfer is an official term for changing schools.

Course equivalents are courses you've already taken that another school will accept as meeting its requirements. Since no two schools offer the same curriculum, determining course equivalents is often a matter of interpretation. In some cases, you might be able to persuade a registrar or admissions office to accept some of your previous courses.

Articulation agreements are official documents that spell out the course equivalents a school accepts.

Prerequisites are courses or skills that a school requires students to have before they enter or graduate.

Learn about the different types of schools

Schools differ in countless dimensions. Start by digging up key facts in the following ten areas about each school you're considering.

1. **Number of students.** The largest state universities can have a student body numbering 50,000 or more. Small private schools might have less than 1,000. Between these extremes are many options.

2. **Class sizes.** Large schools might enroll 1,000 in a general education course. At smaller schools, your largest class might number between 20 and 30 people. You might enroll in advanced seminars with a handful of students or take an individualized, guided reading course. Even within a single school, class sizes can vary between course levels and departments.

3. **Contact with instructors.** Some schools enlist faculty members who are dedicated to teaching. You could take most of your classes from associate or full professors. In other schools, graduate assistants teach lower level courses while professors focus mainly on graduate students, publishing, or research. If you value close contact with your instructors, this is a crucial factor to investigate.

4. **Admissions criteria.** Some schools are highly competitive, admitting only a small percentage of the students who apply each year. Other schools are relatively open, admitting most students with high school diplomas.

5. **Availability of degrees.** Community colleges and vocational-technical schools commonly offer associate arts (A.A) degrees, also called two-year degrees. Public and private colleges and universities generally offer four-year degrees, such as the bachelor of arts (B.A.) or bachelor of science (B.S.) Because their schedules vary so greatly, students might find that these degrees take longer than two or four years to complete. Many larger schools also offer graduate programs, leading to master's and doctoral degrees or specialized degrees in law, medicine, dentistry, or the ministry. If you want to make only one more transfer, then the availability of such degrees can be an important part of your decision-making process.

6. **Costs.** Schools that receive public funding generally have lower tuition than private schools. Even so, tuition is only one of the costs of attending school. Others include books, materials, residence hall fees, and laboratory fees. If you plan to live off campus, factor in the cost of living in the surrounding community.

7. Mission. Schools that emphasize liberal education could have fewer courses that prepare students for specific careers. In contrast, many community colleges offer degrees geared to a specific job field, such as dental assistance, real estate, or auto mechanics. Some schools have a reputation for their teacher education programs, while others excel in research or offer outstanding graduate programs.

8. Location. The school you choose might be nestled in an idyllic rural setting or thrive in the heart of a large city. The differences can greatly color your experience of higher education. Also consider the school's distance from your current home.

9. Religious affiliation. You might value contact with students who share your sense of spirituality. Or perhaps you want a school attended by people of many spiritual perspectives. Schools differ greatly along this continuum.

10. Diversity. This term can apply to faculty members as well as students. Some schools primarily serve women or people of color, while others enroll a highly diverse student body. Also consider the mix between full-time and part-time students, students who live on campus and those who commute, and graduate and undergraduate students.

Dig up other key facts

Before you transfer to any school, gather the facts about your current academic profile. This includes grades, courses completed, degrees attained, and grade point average (GPA). Standardized test scores are important also, such as those for the Scholastic Aptitude Test (SAT), the American College Test (ACT), Graduate Record Exam (GRE), and any advanced placement tests you've taken.

Also list each school's course requirements. Note all prerequisites, including those required for general education or your proposed major, and any other courses required for graduation. Check the availability of courses in your major, including any graduate courses and advanced degrees if you're planning for those.

With your requirements in hand, begin creating a list of course equivalents. Most schools will have specific worksheets for this purpose. The school's registrar or admissions office can answer your questions about how to complete these forms.

After totaling the costs of attending a school, check on financial aid. For more specific ideas, see "Education's worth it—and you can pay for it" in Chapter One.

Resources such as a counseling center, career planning center, or job placement office can be critical to your success in school. Check out the availability of these services at each school you consider.

Turn to three basic sources

So far this article has suggested what to ask about when you research a school. How to find this information is a separate question. Basically, you can turn to three sources: materials, people, and your own experience.

Materials include print sources, such as school catalogs. Also check more general guides, such as *Barron's Profiles of American Colleges*, *Peterson's National College Data Bank*, or the *Directory of Special Programs for Minority Group Members*.

People include instructors, academic advisers, counselors, and other school staff members. Also seek out current students at a school, as well as former students who are now working in your chosen field.

Your own experience includes a visit to your top two or three choices for schools to attend. Take a thorough tour of the facilities—the library, laboratories, residence halls, bookstores, cafeterias, and student center. Also ask about sources of entertainment, such as restaurants, theaters, galleries, and concert halls.

When you're done with "official" tours, just walk around and observe the school grounds. Your direct experience of a school can be more intensive if you work in the surrounding community for a summer or take a course at the school before you transfer.

Put this choice in context

Crucial to this process is the larger context that shapes your choice. To begin, consider the needs and wishes of your family members. Ask for their guidance and support. If you involve them in the decision, they can have more stake in your success.

Then broaden the context even more. Consider the purposes, values, and long-term goals you've generated through exercises and Journal Entries in this book, such as the lifeline exercise. All of these can have a bearing on the school you select.

Your experience of a school goes well beyond the facts listed in the catalog. After you gather facts, let them simmer in your subconscious. Then pay attention to your instincts—your attraction to one school or feelings of hesitation about another.

Finally, just choose. There is no one "right" school for you, and you could probably thrive at many schools (perhaps even your current one). Use the suggestions in this book to take charge of your education—no matter what school you attend.

Contributing:
The art of selfishness

This book is about contributing to yourself—about taking care of yourself, being selfish, and filling yourself up. The techniques and suggestions in these pages focus on ways to get what you want out of school and out of life. One of the results of all this successful selfishness is the capacity for contribution, for giving to others. Contributing is what's left to do when you're satisfied—filled up—and it completes the process.

People who are satisfied with life can share that satisfaction with others. It is not easy to contribute to another person's joy until you experience joy. The same is true for love. When people are filled with love, they can more easily contribute love to others.

Our interdependence calls for contribution

Every day we depend on contribution. We stake our lives on the sensibilities of other people. When you drive, you depend on others for your life. If a driver in the oncoming lane crosses into your lane, you might die. You depend upon the sensibilities of world leaders for your safety.

People everywhere are growing more interdependent. A plunge in the U.S. stock market reverberates in markets across the planet. A decrease in oil prices gives businesses everywhere a shot in the arm. A nuclear war would ignore national boundaries and devastate life on the planet. Successful arms negotiations allow all people to sleep a little easier.

In this interdependent world, there is no such thing as win/lose. If others lose, their loss directly affects us. If we lose, it is more difficult to contribute to others.

The only way to win and to get what we want in life is for others to win also.

A caution

The idea of contributing is not the same as knowing what is best for other people. We can't know. There are people, of course, who go around "fixing" others: "I know what you need. Here, do it my way." That is not contribution. It often causes more harm than good and can result in dependence on the part of the person we are "helping."

True contribution occurs only after you find out what another person wants or needs and then determine that you can lovingly support his having it.

How you can begin contributing

The world will welcome your gifts of time, money, and talent. The advantages of contributing are clear. When we contribute, the whole human family benefits in a tangible way. Close to home, contributing often means getting involved with other people. This is one way to "break the ice" in a new community and meet people with interests similar to your own.

When you've made the decision to contribute, the next step is knowing how. There are ways to contribute in your immediate surroundings. Visit a neighbor, take a family member to a movie, or offer to tutor a roommate.

Look for ways you can contribute to the organizations mentioned.

An additional benefit to volunteer work is that it is a way to explore possible career choices. Consider the following organizations.

Big Brothers and Big Sisters provide friendship and guidance to children who might have only one parent. Girls Club, Boys Club, Girl Scouts, and Boy Scouts of America all need large numbers of volunteers.

Sierra Club, Greenpeace, Audubon Society, World Wildlife Fund, and similar organizations are dedicated to protecting the environment and endangered species.

Amnesty International investigates human rights violations. It assists people who are imprisoned or tortured for peacefully expressing their points of view. You can participate in letter-writing campaigns.

Hospitals and hospice programs often depend on volunteer help to supplement patient care provided by the professional staff. Museums and art galleries need interested people to conduct tours and provide supervision.

Nursing homes welcome visitors who are willing to spend time listening and talking with residents.

Political parties, candidates, and special-interest groups need volunteers to stuff envelopes, gather petition signatures, and distribute literature.

The American Red Cross provides disaster relief. Local community care centers use volunteers to feed homeless people.

Service organizations like Cosmopolitan, Zonta, Jaycees, Altrusa, Kiwanis, Lions, American Association of University Women, Sertoma, Business and Professional Women, and Rotary want members who are willing to serve others.

Tutoring centers offer opportunities for competent students to help non–English-speaking people, grade school and high school students, and illiterate adults.

Churches of all denominations want volunteers to assist with projects for the community and the world.

World hunger groups want you to help feed starving people and to inform all of us about the problems of malnutrition, food spoilage, and starvation. These groups include Oxfam America, CARE, and The Hunger Project.

Our environmental problems are so serious that there's a chance the earth will be uninhabitable in 30 years. And there are so many nuclear warheads right now that if only 20 percent of them were detonated, human life might no longer exist. Over 13 million people die each year from hunger or hunger-related diseases.

The techniques and strategies in this book make no difference in all this. However, you can make a difference. You can use these techniques to work with others and choose a new future for our planet.

JOURNAL ENTRY #63
DISCOVERY STATEMENT

Recall a time when you contributed—for example, when you volunteered your time for an important cause or a worthy group. Write details of the contribution you made and how you felt afterward. Use an additional sheet of paper if necessary.

_____

_____

_____

_____

_____

_____

_____

JOURNAL ENTRY #64
INTENTION STATEMENT

Review the list of organizations in the article "Contributing: The art of selfishness." Choose one or two organizations which interest you. Also, think about people in your life to whom you could give time, money, or something of yourself.

Make a commitment to contribute. Make the commitment detailed and time-specific.

I intend to . . .

_____

_____

_____

_____

EXERCISE #42
DISCOVERY WHEEL—COMING FULL CIRCLE

This book doesn't work. It is worthless. Only you can work. Only you can make a difference and use this book to become a more effective student.

The purpose of this book is to give you the opportunity to change your behavior. The fact that something seems like a good idea doesn't mean that you will put it into practice. This exercise gives you a chance to see what behaviors you have changed on your journey to becoming a master student.

Answer each question quickly and honestly. Record your results in the Discovery Wheel, and then compare it with the wheel you produced in Chapter One. Your scores may be lower here than on your earlier wheel. That's OK. Lower scores might result from increased self-awareness and honesty— valuable assets.

The scores on this Discovery Wheel indicate your current strengths and weaknesses in becoming a master student. The last Journal Entries in this chapter provide space for writing about how you intend to change. As you complete this self-evaluation, ask yourself how you want to change. Your commitment to change allows you to become a master student.

5 points
This statement is always or almost always true of me.

4 points
This statement is often true of me.

3 points
This statement is some- times true of me (about half the time).

2 points
This statement is seldom true of me.

1 point
This statement is never or almost never true of me.

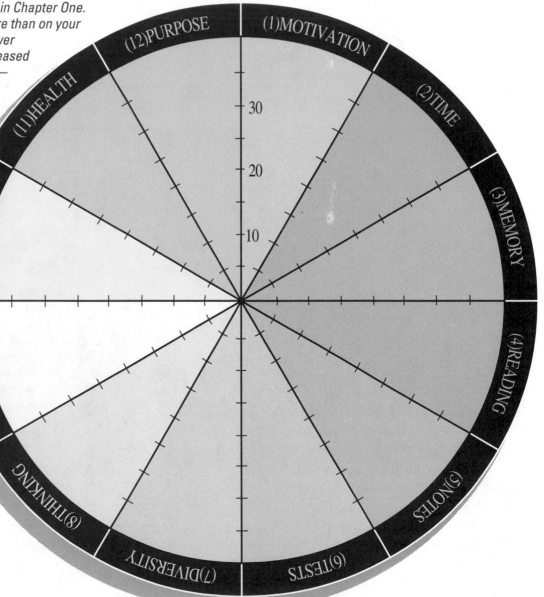

1._____I start each term highly motivated, and I stay that way.

2._____I know what I want to get from my education.

3._____I enjoy learning.

4._____I study even when distracted by activities of lower priority.

5._____I am satisfied with how I progress toward achieving goals.

6._____I budget my money and I am in control of my personal finances.

7._____I am excited about the courses I take.

8._____I have a clear idea of the benefits I expect to get from my education.

_____Total score (1) Motivation

1._____I periodically refine my long-term and short-term goals.

2._____I can efficiently use a computer to promote my success in school.

3._____I write a plan for each day and each week.

4._____I assign priorities to what I choose to do each day.

5._____I plan review time so I don't have to cram before tests.

6._____I plan regular recreation time.

7._____I adjust my study time to meet the demands of individual courses.

8._____I have adequate time each day to accomplish what I plan.

_____Total score (2) Time

1._____I am confident in my ability to remember.

2._____I remember people's names.

3._____At the end of a lecture, I can summarize what was presented.

4._____I apply techniques that enhance my memory skills.

5._____I can recall information when I'm under pressure.

6._____I remember important information clearly and easily.

7._____I can jog my memory when I have difficulty recalling.

8._____I can relate new information to what I've already learned.

_____Total score (3) Memory

1._____I preview and review reading assignments.

2._____When reading, I underline or highlight important passages.

3._____When I read, I ask questions about the material.

4._____When I read textbooks, I am alert and awake.

5._____I relate what I read to my life.

6._____I select a reading strategy to fit the type of material I'm reading.

7._____I take effective notes when I read.

8._____When I don't understand what I'm reading, I note my questions and find answers.

_____Total score (4) Reading

1._____When I am in class, I focus attention.

2._____I take notes in class.

3._____I am aware of various methods for taking notes and choose those that work best for me.

4._____My notes are valuable for review.

5._____I review class notes within 24 hours.

6._____I distinguish important material and notice key phrases in a lecture.

7._____I copy material the instructor writes on the board or overhead projector.

8._____I can put important concepts into my own words.

_____Total score (5) Notes

1._____I feel confident and calm during an exam.

2._____I manage my time during exams and I am able to complete them.

3._____I am able to predict test questions.

4._____I can examine essay questions in light of what I know and come to new and original conclusions during a test.

5._____I adapt my test-taking strategy to the kind of test I'm taking.

6._____I understand what essay questions ask and can answer them completely and accurately.

7._____I start reviewing for tests at the beginning of the term and review regularly.

8._____My sense of personal worth is independent of my test scores.

_____Total score (6) Tests

1._____ I am aware of my cultural biases and open to understanding people with different backgrounds.

2._____ I build rewarding relationships with people from other cultures and races.

3._____ I can point out examples of discrimination and effectively respond to them.

4._____ I study in a way that draws on my preferred learning styles.

5._____ I practice using several different learning styles when I study.

6._____ I take specific steps to make a successful transition into higher education.

7._____ I am in regular contact with instructors and students who share my academic interests.

8._____ I effectively integrate schooling with my family and work lives.

_____ Total score (7) Diversity

1._____ I have flashes of insight, and solutions to problems appear to me at unusual times.

2._____ I use brainstorming to generate solutions to a variety of problems.

3._____ When I get stuck on a creative project, I use specific methods to get unstuck.

4._____ I see problems and decisions as opportunities for learning and personal growth.

5._____ I am willing to consider different points of view and alternative solutions.

6._____ I can state the assumptions that underlie a series of assertions.

7._____ I can detect common errors in logic.

8._____ I approach courses in mathematics and science with confidence.

_____ Total score (8) Thinking

1._____ I approach writing with confidence.

2._____ I can effectively plan and research a large writing assignment.

3._____ I create first drafts without stopping to edit or criticize my writing.

4._____ I revise my writing for clarity, accuracy, and coherence.

5._____ My writing affirms women and is free of sexist expressions.

6._____ When writing, I accurately credit ideas and facts from other people.

7._____ I know ways to prepare and deliver effective speeches.

8._____ I am confident when I speak before others.

_____ Total score (9) Writing

1._____ I develop and maintain mutually supportive relationships.

2._____ I am candid with others about who I am, what I feel, and what I want.

3._____ Other people tell me that I am a good listener.

4._____ I communicate my upset and anger without blaming others.

5._____ I make and keep promises that stretch me to meet my potential.

6._____ I am able to learn from various instructors with different teaching styles.

7._____ I have the ability to make friends and create valuable relationships in a new place.

8._____ I am open to being with people I don't especially like in order to learn from them.

_____ Total score (10) Relationships

1._____ I have enough energy to study and still fully enjoy areas of my life.

2._____ I exercise regularly.

3._____ My emotional health supports my ability to learn.

4._____ If the situation calls for it, I have enough reserve energy to put in a long day.

5._____ I accept my body the way it is.

6._____ I notice changes in my physical condition and respond effectively.

7._____ I am in control of any alcohol or drugs I put into my body.

8._____ The food I eat contributes to my health.

_____ Total score (11) Health

1._____ I see learning as a lifelong process.

2._____ I relate school to what I plan to do for the rest of my life.

3._____ I learn by contributing to others.

4._____ I revise my plans as I learn, change, and grow.

5._____ I am clear about my purpose in life.

6._____ I know that I am responsible for my own education.

7._____ I take responsibility for the quality of my life.

8._____ I am willing to accept challenges even when I'm not sure how to meet them.

_____ Total score (12) Purpose

JOURNAL ENTRY #65
DISCOVERY/INTENTION STATEMENT

The purpose of this Journal Entry is to 1) review both of the Discovery Wheels you completed in this book, 2) summarize your insights from doing them, and 3) declare how you will use these insights to promote your continued success in school.

In addition, staff members at College Survival would like to know about your experience with this book. With that purpose in mind, your instructor will collect a copy of this Journal Entry and send it to College Survival for national data collection. Keep in mind that this is not a test of any kind, and that your responses will be held in confidence.

Begin by tearing out the blank sheet of paper that follows this page, then list your scores for the Discovery Wheel in Chapter One (pages 14-16) and in this chapter (pages 329-330). Remember that a lower score on the second Discovery Wheel does not necessarily indicate decreased personal effectiveness. Instead, the lower score could result from increased honesty and greater self-awareness.

	Chapter 1	Chapter 12
Motivation	_____	_____
Planning	_____	_____
Memory	_____	_____
Reading	_____	_____
Notetaking	_____	_____
Tests	_____	_____
Diversity	_____	_____
Thinking	_____	_____
Writing	_____	_____
Relationships	_____	_____
Health	_____	_____
Purpose	_____	_____

Comparing the Discovery Wheel in this chapter with the Discovery Wheel in Chapter One, I learned that I . . .

_____

_____

In the next six months, I intend to review the following articles from this book for additional suggestions I could use:

_____

_____

_____

_____

Please fill in the following
demographic information,
tear out this page, and turn
it in to your instructor.

GENDER:
❑ Male
❑ Female

AGE:
❑ 15-20
❑ 21-30
❑ 31-40
❑ 41-50
❑ 51-60
❑ Over 60

ATTEND SCHOOL:
❑ Full-time
❑ Part-time

TYPE OF SCHOOL:
❑ Technical
❑ Community college
❑ Four-year college
❑ University

SIZE OF SCHOOL:
❑ Under 5,000
❑ 5,000-10,000
❑ Over 10,000

WORK:
❑ Full-time
❑ Part-time
❑ Do not work

Instructors, please mail a
collection of these Discovery
Wheel forms to:

College Survival
2075 Foxfield Road, Suite 100
St. Charles, IL 60174

JOURNAL ENTRY #65
DISCOVERY/INTENTION STATEMENT

The purpose of this Journal Entry is to 1) review both of the Discovery Wheels you completed in this book, 2) summarize your insights from doing them, and 3) declare how you will use these insights to promote your continued success in school.

In addition, staff members at College Survival would like to know about your experience with this book. With that purpose in mind, your instructor will collect a copy of this Journal Entry and send it to College Survival for national data collection. Keep in mind that this is not a test of any kind, and that your responses will be held in confidence.

Begin by tearing out the blank sheet of paper that follows this page, then list your scores for the Discovery Wheel in Chapter One (pages 14-16) and in this chapter (pages 329-330). Remember that a lower score on the second Discovery Wheel does not necessarily indicate decreased personal effectiveness. Instead, the lower score could result from increased honesty and greater self-awareness.

	Chapter 1	Chapter 12
Motivation	_____	_____
Planning	_____	_____
Memory	_____	_____
Reading	_____	_____
Notetaking	_____	_____
Tests	_____	_____
Diversity	_____	_____
Thinking	_____	_____
Writing	_____	_____
Relationships	_____	_____
Health	_____	_____
Purpose	_____	_____

Comparing the Discovery Wheel in this chapter with the Discovery Wheel in Chapter One, I learned that I . . .

_____

_____

_____

In the next six months, I intend to review the following articles from this book for additional suggestions I could use:

_____

_____

_____

_____

This page intentionally left blank.

Career planning — *Begin now*

A satisfying and lucrative career is often the goal of education. It pays to clearly define both your career goal and your strategy for reaching it. Then you can plan your education effectively.

Career planning is an adventure that involves exploration. There are dozens of effective paths to planning your career. The *Career Planning Supplement to Becoming a Master Student* offers many suggestions on this subject and guides you to more.

You can begin your career planning adventure now by remembering five basic ideas.

1. You already know a lot about your career plan. When people learn study skills and life skills, they usually start with finding out things they don't know. That means discovering new strategies for taking notes, reading, writing, managing time, and the other subjects covered in this book.

Career planning is different. You can begin by realizing how much you know right now. You've already made many decisions about your career. This is true for young people who say, "I don't have any idea what I want to be when I grow up." It's also true for midlife career changers.

Take the student who can't decide if he wants to be a cost accountant or a tax accountant and then jumps to the conclusion that he is totally lost when it comes to career planning. It's the same with the student who doesn't know if he wants to be a veterinary assistant or a nurse.

These people forget that they already know a lot about their career choices. The person who couldn't decide between veterinary assistance and nursing already ruled out becoming a lawyer, computer programmer, or teacher. He just didn't know yet whether he had the right bedside manner for horses or for people. The person who was debating tax accounting versus cost accounting already knew he didn't want to be a doctor, playwright, or taxicab driver. He did know he liked working with numbers and balancing books.

In each case, these people have already narrowed their list of career choices to a number of jobs in the same field—jobs that draw on the same core skills. In general, they already know what they want to be when they grow up. So do you.

Find a long list of occupations. (One source is *The Dictionary of Occupational Titles*, a government publication available at many libraries.) Using a stack of 3x5 cards, write down about 100 job titles, one title per card. Sort through the cards and divide them into two piles. Label one pile "Careers I've Definitely Ruled Out for Now." Label the other pile "Possibilities I'm Willing to Consider."

It's common for people to go through a stack of 100 such cards and end up with 95 in the "definitely ruled out" pile and five in the "possibilities" pile. This demonstrates that they already have a career in mind.

2. Career planning is a choice, not a discovery. Many people approach career planning as if they were panning for gold. They keep sifting through the dirt, clearing the dust, and throwing out the rocks. They are hoping to strike it rich and discover the perfect career.

Other people believe they'll wake up one morning, see the heavens part, and suddenly know what they're supposed to do. Many of them are still waiting for that magical day to dawn.

We can approach career planning in a different way. It can be the bridge between our dreams and the reality of our future. Instead of seeing a career as something we discover, we can see it as something we choose. We don't find the right career. We create it.

There's a big difference between these two approaches. Thinking that there's only one "correct" choice for your career can lead to a lot of anxiety: "Did I choose the right one? What if I made a mistake?"

Viewing your career as your creation helps you relax. Instead of anguishing over finding the right career, you stay open to possibilities. You choose one career today, knowing that you can choose again later.

Suppose that you've narrowed your list of possible careers to five, and you still can't decide. Then just choose one. Any one. Many people will have five careers in a lifetime anyway. You may be able to do all your careers, and you can do any one of them first. The important thing is to choose.

One caution is in order. Choosing your career is not something to do in an information vacuum. Rather, choose after you've done a lot of research. That includes research into yourself—your skills and interests—and a thorough knowledge of what careers are available.

Career planning materials and counselors can help you on both counts. You can take skills assessments to find out more about what you like doing. You can take career planning courses and read books about careers. You can contact people who are actually doing the job you're researching and ask them what it's like. You can also choose an internship, summer job, or volunteer position in a field that interests you. There's no end to resources for gathering information about yourself and the job market.

After all the data has been gathered, there's only one person who can choose your career: you.

This decision does not have to be a weighty one. In fact, it can be like going into your favorite restaurant and choosing from a menu that includes all your favorite dishes. At this point, it's difficult to make a mistake. Whatever you choose, you can enjoy it.

3. Name names. One key to making your career plan real and to ensuring you can act on it is naming. Go back over your plan to see that you include specific names whenever they're called for. For example:

- Name your job. Take the skills you enjoy using and find out which jobs use them. What are those jobs called? List them. Note that the same job may have different names.

- Name your company, agency, or organization. If you want to be self-employed or start your own business, name the product or service you'd sell. Also list some possible names for your business.

- Name your contacts. Take the list you just compiled. What people in these organizations are responsible for hiring? List those people and contact them directly. If you choose self-employment, list the names of possible customers or clients.

- Name your location. Ask if your career choices are consistent with your preferences about where to live and work. For example, someone who wants to make a living as a studio musician might consider living in a large city such as New York or Toronto. This contrasts with the freelance graphic artist who conducts her business mainly by phone, fax, and mail. She may be able to live anywhere and still pursue her career.

4. Get back to your purpose. When we're deep into the details of planning, it's easy to lose sight of the big picture. Listing skills, researching jobs, writing résumés—all of this is necessary and useful. At the same time, attending to them can obscure our broadest goals. To get perspective, we can go back to the basics—a life purpose.

Your deepest desire might be to see that hungry children are fed, to make sure that beautiful music keeps getting heard, or to help alcoholics become sober. When such a large purpose is clear, smaller decisions about what to do are often easier.

Career counselor Richard Bolles[3] notes that a life purpose makes a career plan simpler and more powerful. It cuts through the stacks of job data and employment figures. Your life purpose is like the guidance system for a rocket. It keeps the plan on target while revealing a path for soaring to the heights.

5. Change your mind when appropriate. Career planning is not a once-and-for-all proposition. Rather, career plans are made to be changed and refined as you gain new information about yourself and the world. Career planning never ends. If your present career no longer feels right, you can choose again—no matter what stage of life you're in. The process is the same, whether you're choosing your first career or your fifth.

"Yes," says the skeptic, "but what if I spend two years going to school and then discover I'm in the wrong field? Think about all the time I'll waste!"

There are three responses to this. First, you might be killed in an earthquake or struck by lightning in those same two years. But it's unlikely. It's also unlikely that you'll choose a career that's totally off-base for you as long as you do your homework in career planning. Remember that you're working on the difference between your top four or five career possibilities—not the 95 cards you put in the "definitely not" pile.

Second, there is some risk associated with career planning, just as there's risk in being alive. Risk cannot be totally avoided. People change. Circumstances change. The idea of facing 30 fourth graders for 205 days each year, which sounded so good 10 years ago, may not be as appealing to you today.

Third, if you are a master student, learning, growing, and benefiting from every experience, there's no such thing as waste.

**PRACTICING
CRITICAL THINKING #23**

Review the master student profiles throughout this book. Then review the article "The master student" in Chapter One. Choose one of the people profiled and explain how this person embodies qualities of a master student. Summarize your conclusions below.

_____

_____

_____

_____

_____

_____

_____

_____

_____

_____

_____

_____

_____

_____

EXERCISE #43
APPLY THESE STRATEGIES TO YOUR WORK

For the most part, the suggestions in Becoming a Master Student *are geared to promoting your success in school. Most of these suggestions can apply to your career as well. Consider some possibilities:*

Suggestions for decreasing expenses (Chapter Two) can help you in preparing budgets.

Techniques for remembering names (Chapter Three) can help you in applying for jobs.

Strategies for reading (Chapter Four) can assist you in keeping up with journals in your field.

Ideas for note taking (Chapter Five) can assist you during meetings.

Techniques for managing test anxiety (Chapter Six) can help you relieve job-related stress.

With the suggestions for responding to diversity (Chapter Seven), you can relate more effectively with coworkers.

Strategies for creating and evaluating new ideas (Chapter Eight) can assist you in planning projects on the job.

Writing techniques (Chapter Nine) can assist you in preparing memos and reports.

Ideas for resolving conflict (Chapter Ten) can help you reduce tension among people on the job.

Suggestions for managing your health (Chapter Eleven) can help you achieve the mental and physical energy needed to perform to your full capacity.

And with the strategies for changing habits (Chapter One), you can choose and adopt any of the suggestions in this book.

Take about one hour to list one specific idea from each chapter that you could apply outside the classroom to your current or intended career. Also list a job-related payoff for each suggestion, such as opportunities for promotion, higher income, or increased job satisfaction.

1. _____
_____
_____

2. _____
_____
_____

3. _____
_____
_____

4. _____
_____
_____

5. _____
_____
_____

6. _____
_____
_____

7. _____
_____
_____

8. _____
_____
_____

9. _____
_____
_____

10. _____
_____
_____

11. _____
_____
_____

12. _____
_____
_____

**PRACTICING
CRITICAL THINKING #24**

Imagine that you are about to teach a student success course; then create a brief outline or syllabus for the course. Analyze the topic of student success, choosing the main subtopics you will cover, any texts or other materials you will use, and any guest speakers you'd invite. Write your ideas in the space below.

_____

_____

_____

_____

_____

_____

_____

_____

_____

        Now reflect on what you just wrote. What results did you want students to achieve in this course? What other ways could you, as a teacher, help them achieve these results?

_____

_____

_____

_____

_____

_____

_____

_____

_____

_____

_____

_____

_____

_____

**JOURNAL ENTRY #66
INTENTION STATEMENT**

Even if you are not sure of your career preference, write a career plan right now. Include three elements: a career title, a list of steps you can take to prepare for that career, and a time line for reaching that career goal.

        Your plan might be incomplete or tentative. No problem. You can change this plan later—even throw it out and start over. Career planning is a continual cycle of discovery and feedback.

        The point is to dive into the process and make career planning a lifelong habit. This habit can radically affect the quality of your life.

        You can plan now, with no further research. Go ahead. There's nothing to lose and lots of space to write in. Make an outline, do a mind map—use any format you like. Discover what you already know.

        Mind map, outline, or write your career plan below.

_____

_____

_____

_____

_____

_____

_____

_____

_____

_____

_____

_____

_____

_____

_____

_____

_____

_____

_____

_____

_____

_____

Learning the langu

AN INVESTMENT IN YOUR CAREER

Computers now play a role in almost every job, from auto mechanics to corporate accounting. Computer technology is also driving many of the new careers that are being added to our job pool. Learning the following terms is one way to promote your success in the next career you choose.

application A computer program designed to accomplish a specific task—for example, word processing.

Archie A tool for searching the Internet that locates files for you to download.

baud rate The speed with which a modem can send or receive data, expressed in bits per second (bps). The higher the baud rate, the faster the modem.

BBS Short for bulletin board system, a computer system with modems that allows users to post and read messages.

boot To start up a computer.

browser Software that allows you to search for files on the Internet. Examples are Lycos, Yahoo!, and WebCrawler.

byte In computer processing, the equivalent of one letter or number.

CD-ROM Short for Compact Disk–Read Only Memory. 1. A device that stores large amounts of computer data (about 600 megabytes). 2. A device that reads such devices.

central processing unit (CPU) The computer hardware and software that decodes and carries out instructions.

chat room An online service that allows people to carry on a real-time conversation by typing messages to each other at their computers.

cursor A line, bar, or dot that appears on a computer screen. It indicates where the next character to be typed will appear.

cyberspace The software, hardware, and community of people who use the Internet.

database A computer file including records that can be searched, sorted, and resorted in a number of ways.

desktop publishing Using computer hardware and software to produce books, brochures, newsletters, and other printed materials.

disk A device for storing computer data. Disks can be pieces of flexible plastic (floppy disks) or inflexible metal (hard disks).

disk operating system (DOS) 1. Any operating system that is loaded from disks when a computer is started. 2. An operating system used by IBM and IBM-compatible computers. See also *operating system*.

domain The part of an Internet address that indicates a type of institution. For example, *edu* denotes an educational institution. *Com* refers to a commerical organization, and *gov* denotes a government agency.

download To copy a file from another computer to your computer.

e-mail A system for sending and receiving messages over a computer network.

emoticon In e-mail, a combination of letters and numbers that indicates how the sender is feeling. For example, :-) (Turn this page horizontally and you will see a "smiling face" just before this sentence.)

FAQ Stands for Frequently Asked Questions; files that contain answers to common questions about a site on the Internet.

file A document, program, or other set of data used by a computer.

flame An e-mail message that insults the receiver. The act of sending such a message.

forum A chat room that centers on a particular topic.

FTP 1. Stands for File Transfer Protocol, a set of standards that allows computers to transfer files. 2. A method for transferring files. 3. A site on the Internet that allows you to download files.

age of computers

Gopher Software that allows you to search the Internet by using menus. See also *menu.*

hacker 1. A person who is almost obsessed with computer hardware and software. 2. Someone who invades computer files to tamper with data.

hardware Physical computer equipment, such as disk drives, screens, and keyboards.

home page The first screen available at a site on the World Wide Web.

host The main computer in a system of linked computers.

HTML Stands for Hypertext Markup Language, a computer language used to create documents on the World Wide Web.

hyperlink A word or phrase that you can use to connect to another site on the World Wide Web. Hyperlinks are usually highlighted or underlined.

icon A small visual image displayed on a computer screen, usually marking some software feature that a user can control.

link *See hyperlink.*

log on To type a series of characters that "identifies" you to a computer.

megabyte Approximately 1 million bytes (exactly 1,048,576 bytes), abbreviated as MB.

menu A list of files or options, along with a way for you to select an item on the list.

modem A hardware device that allows computers to send or receive data over phone lines.

multimedia Software that displays text, graphics, sound, and video.

Net Short for Internet.

network A group of computers connected by modem or cables.

newsgroup A part of Usenet containing messages on a particular topic.

online Able to communicate with another computer.

operating system Software that controls basic hardware functions—for example, communication between a central processing unit and a printer.

peripheral Devices that are connected to and controlled by a computer. Examples are disk drives, printers, and modems.

port The part of a central processing unit that can receive and send data to peripherals.

post To submit an article to a newsgroup.

RAM Stands for Random Access Memory; the region of computer memory that users can manipulate by using software.

site The location of a file on the Internet.

software Coded instructions that "tell" computer hardware what operations to perform. Also called programs or applications.

spam To send "junk" e-mail.

spreadsheet Software designed to complete financial tasks, such as accounting or forecasting expenses and income.

TCP/IP Short for Transmission Control Protocol/Internet Protocol, a set of standards for sending and receiving data on the Internet.

telecommute The ability to work at a remote site (usually a private home) and communicate by modem with a central computer and those connected to it.

teleconference A meeting between people who link to each other via their computers, even though they are separated geographically.

Telnet A protocol that allows you to log on to a remote computer on the Internet.

upload To copy a file from your computer to another computer.

URL Stands for Uniform Resource Locator, a series of letters and numbers that gives a document's location on the World Wide Web.

Usenet A worldwide computer network that allows users to exchange public messages.

username A set of letters, numbers, or both that denote your name in an e-mail address.

Veronica Software that helps users find Gopher menus. See also *Gopher.*

virus A program that destroys data or software by reproducing copies of itself, or by producing meaningless text. Viruses can be transmitted by computer networks or by computer disks that are "infected" with such a program.

Web Short for World Wide Web.

window A self-contained unit of text, images, or both that appears on a computer screen.

word processing Software that allows you to create and edit text.

World Wide Web A network of computer files that are connected by hyperlinks.

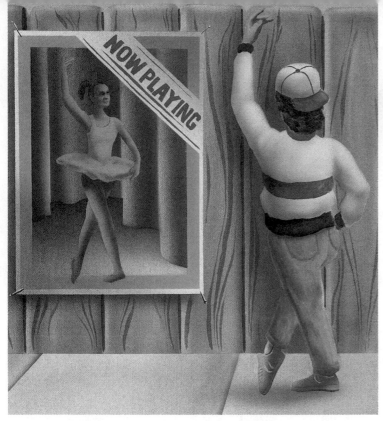

POWER PROCESS #12

Be it

All of the techniques in this book are enhanced by this Power Process. To tap into its full benefits, consider that most of our choices fall into three categories. We can:

1) increase our material wealth
   (what we have).
2) improve our skills
   (what we do).
3) develop our "being"
   (who we are).

Most people devote their entire lifetime to the first two categories. For example, many people act as if they are "human havings" instead of human beings. For them, the quality of life hinges on what they have. They devote most of their waking hours to getting more—more clothes, more cars, more relationships, more degrees, and more trophies. Human havings define themselves by looking at the circumstances in their lives—what they have.

Some people escape this materialist trap by adding another dimension to their identities. In addition to living as "human havings," they also live as "human doings." Their goal is to do everything well. They define themselves by how well they do their jobs, how effectively they raise their children, and how active they are in clubs and organizations. Their thoughts are constantly about methods, techniques, and skills.

Look beyond doing and having

In addition to focusing on what we have and on what we do, we can also focus on our being. Of course, it is impossible to live our lives without having things and doing things. This Power Process suggests that we balance our lives and give lots of attention to who we are—an aspect of our lives that goes beyond having and doing. Call it soul, passion, purpose, or values. Call it being. This word describes how we see ourselves—our deepest commitments, the ground from which our actions spring.

The realm of being is profound and subtle. It is also difficult to capture in words, though philosophers have tried for centuries. Christian theologian Paul Tillich described this realm when he defined faith as "ultimate commitment" and the "ground of being." In the New Testament, Jesus talked about being when he asked his followers to love God with all their heart, soul, and mind. An ancient Hindu text also touches on being: "You are what your deep, driving desire is."

If all this seems far removed from taking notes or answering test questions, then read on. Consider an example of how "be it" can assist in career choices. In a letter to her father, a young woman wrote:

We just went to see the Dance Theatre of Harlem. It was great!!! After the last number, I decided that I want to dance more than anything. I have a great passion to do it, more than anything else I can think or dream of. Dancing is what will make me happy and feel like I can leave this earth when my time comes. It is what I must do. I think that if I never fulfill this passion, I will never feel complete or satisfied with what I have done with my life.

In her heart, this woman *is* a dancer now, even before her formal training is complete. From her passion, desire, commitment, and self-image (her *being*) comes her willingness to take classes and rehearse (*doing*). And from her doing she may eventually *have* a job with a professional dance company.

Picture the result as you begin

The example of the dancer illustrates that once you have a clear picture of what you want to *be*, the things you *do* and *have* fall more naturally into place.

The idea is this: Getting where you want to be by what you do or by what you have is like swimming against the current. Have —> do —> be is a tough journey. It's much easier to go the other direction: be —> do —> have.

Usually we work against nature by trying to have something or do something before being it. That's hard. All of your deeds (what you do) might not get you where you want to be. Getting all the right things (what you have) may not get you there either.

Take the person who values athletics and wants to master tennis. He buys an expensive racket and a stylish tennis wardrobe. Yet he still can't return a serve. Merely having the right things doesn't deliver what he values.

Suppose that this person takes a year's worth of tennis lessons. Week after week, he practices doing everything "right." Still, his game doesn't quite make it.

What goes wrong is hard to detect. "He lost the match even though he played a good game," people say. "Something seemed to be wrong. His technique was fine, but each swing was just a little off." Perhaps the source of his problem is that he cannot see himself as ever mastering the game. What he has and what he does are at war with his mental picture of himself.

You can see this happen in other areas of life. Two people tell the same joke in what seems to be the same way. Yet one person brings a smile, and the other person has you laughing so hard your muscles hurt. The difference in how they do the joke is imperceptible. When the successful comedian tells a joke, he does it from his experience of already being funny.

To have and do what you want, be it. Picture the result as you begin. If you can first visualize where you want to be, if you can go there in your imagination, if you can be it today, then you set yourself up to succeed.

Be a master student now

Now relate this Power Process to succeeding in school. All the techniques in this book can be worthless if you operate with the idea that you are an ineffective student. You might do almost everything this book suggests. Yet you are likely to subtly sabotage your success and never have the success in school that you desire.

For example, if you believe you are stupid in math, then you are likely to fail at math. If you believe that you are not skilled at remembering, then all the memory techniques in the world might not improve your recall. Generally we don't outperform our self-concept.

If you value success in school, then picture yourself as a master student right now. Through higher education you are gaining knowledge and skills that reflect and reinforce this view of yourself.

This principle works in other areas of life. For example, if you value a fulfilling career, then picture yourself as already being on a path to a job you love. Use affirmations and visualizations to plant this idea firmly in your mind. Change the way you see yourself, and watch your actions and results shift as if by magic.

Define your values, align your actions

One key way to use this Power Process is to define your values. Values are the things in life that you want for their own sake. Values influence and guide your choices, including your moment-by-moment choices of what to do and what to have. Your values define who you want to be.

Some people are guided by values automatically adopted from others or by values that remain largely unconscious. These people could be missing the opportunity to live a life that's truly of their own choosing.

Investing time and energy to define your values is a pivotal suggestion in this book. As you begin to do this, consider those who have gone before you. In creeds, scriptures, philosophies, myths, and sacred stories the human race has left a vast and varied record of values. Be willing to look everywhere, including sources that are close to home. The creed of your local church might eloquently describe some of your values—so might the mission statement of your school, company, or club.

Also translate your values into behavior. Though defining your values is powerful, it doesn't guarantee any results. To actually get what you want, take action in ways that align with your values.

And while you're at it, remember that this Power Process is not positive thinking or mental cheerleading. "Be it" works well when you take a First Step—when you tell the truth about your current abilities.

In summary, define your values. Align your actions. Then watch your circumstances change. Flow with the natural current of be —> do —> have.

If you want it, be it.

EXERCISE #44
DEFINE YOUR VALUES

One way to define your values is to finish this sentence: "I value being . . . ." Complete the sentence with a single word or phrase that describes one of your deepest commitments. To gain further clarity, list synonyms for that word or phrase. For example:

"I value being accountable." This means being reliable, trustworthy, dependable, and responsible.
"I value being loving." This means being affectionate, dedicated, devoted, equitable, and accepting.
"I value being candid." This means being honest, authentic, genuine, frank, outspoken, and sincere.
"I value being involved." This means being committed, focused, attentive to detail, enthusiastic, and courageous.

On a separate sheet of paper, write about several of your own values. Begin each sentence with "I value being . . . ."

master student

r a u l   j u l i a

after receiving four Tony nominations for performances on Broadway, appeared in many films including One From the Heart, The Morning After, Moon Over Parador, Tequila Sunrise, Kiss of the Spider Woman, Havana, Presumed Innocent, *and* Romero. *He was also active in The Hunger Project, which is an international organization committed to the end of hunger.*

I've always known I was an actor. I acted in my first play when I was five years old. The play was in Spanish and I was the devil competing with a student, a farmer, and a hunter to capture the heart of a fair maiden. During the opening performance, I remember choosing to let go and risk being foolish. I fell to the floor and started rolling all over the stage like I was having a fit. No control. Everyone was stunned because this was not in the script. Suddenly I got up and started saying my lines. I've been acting and taking risks ever since.

I am committed to acting. Many years ago I had to choose between doing what I loved—acting—or going into my father's restaurant business in Puerto Rico. Choosing an acting career was a financial risk and besides, being a successful actor in the United States was as unlikely as being a prince in a fairy tale. I chose to do what I loved, no matter

what. What's the point of doing anything you don't love? It's not worth it.

I love acting and I'm very excited about making movies. And there's more to it. It's called The Hunger Project. Getting in touch with my work in The Hunger Project carries me through.

I was attracted to The Hunger Project in 1977, when for the first time in my life, I realized that we could actually end hunger on the planet.

I feel I have a responsibility beyond myself and my family to others who are starving. I have the good fortune to be able to feed my family. I imagine myself looking for work, not finding any, and not being able to provide food. This is happening right now for many people. All that is needed to end this tragedy is the commitment of people like you and me.

My commitment to end hunger inspires my acting. When I'm tired, disgusted, bored, or just don't feel like it, I remember that the more successful I become, the more of a difference I can make. Since I am now committed to something more than self-gratification, my work becomes finer. I am still learning and growing, of course, and contribution brings a different quality to my work.

Many of my high school Jesuit teachers had been tortured while they were imprisoned in China. The General of the Jesuit Order had been at Hiroshima when they dropped the bomb. The primary thing I learned from the Spanish Jesuits is that a hero is someone who goes beyond himself to make a difference for other people.

Going beyond yourself includes going beyond your cultural background. It is best to educate yourself about your background, be proud of who you are, and be accurate and knowledgeable when you communicate about it. Once you are knowledgeable and proud of your culture, you can go beyond yourself and become whatever you want to be. Transcending your background allows you to be free and proud.

I don't go around waving a flag saying that I am "Mr. Puerto Rico." I have that background and I am proud of it. I love Puerto Rico, I love my culture, and I love my background. But before anything else, I am a human being. My cultural heritage is in the background. I am first a human being who happened to be born into that background. If we see it that way, we can appreciate the diversity and, at the same time, enjoy our heritage even more. Then we don't need to use it as a shield in competition or as a prejudicial label.

The planet is small enough. It is time to put all that cultural and nationalistic kind of flag-waving in the background. It is now time for everyone on the planet to be human beings together.

1 Briefly discuss the meaning of "Now that you're done—Begin."

2 Which of the following affirmations does not follow the suggestions for an effective affirmation?

   (A) I have a healthy, fun, respectful relationship with my in-laws.
   (B) I am an artistic person.
   (C) I will stop putting off math assignments.
   (D) I speak clearly and concisely.
   (E) All of the above are affirmations.

3 Explain how career planning can be a process of choosing instead of a process of discovery.

4 What are three responses given in this chapter for the argument that making the wrong career choice will waste time?

5 Define the three main types of choices explained in the Power Process "Be it."

6 Using the Power Process "Be it" eliminates the need to take action. True or False. Explain your answer.

7 If your scores are lower on the Discovery Wheel the second time you finish it, that means your study skills have not improved. True or False. Explain your answer.

8 *Explain what Raul Julia learned about the meaning of the word* hero.

9 *Contributing to others does not involve:*

    (A) Telling people the best way for them to change.
    (B) Finding out what they want or need.
    (C) Determining if you can help them get what they want.
    (D) Giving your time, talent, or money.
    (E) Making sure that you experience satisfaction also.

10 *List at least three ways you can continue on your path of becoming a master student after completing this book.*

EXERCISE #45
MASTER MIND MAP (PART TWO)

On a separate sheet of paper, create a mind map of Chapters Seven through Twelve. If you did not read all of these chapters, then mind map the ones you did read. Again, do this without reviewing the chapters first. After creating your mind map, go back through the text and scan each chapter, spending no more than 10 minutes per chapter. Then revise your mind map based on this review.

JOURNAL ENTRY #67
DISCOVERY STATEMENT

Consider the benefits of doing this book one year from now. Imagine what you could gain by rereading the material, rewriting the Journal Entries, and redoing the exercises. Also, consider the cost of redoing the book. You would spend hours reading, writing, and experimenting. You might even feel uncomfortable looking at some aspects of yourself or discovering that you created your circumstances.

    Once you have thought about the potential costs and benefits of redoing this book, write your intention below with specific dates.

    I intend to . . .

_____

_____

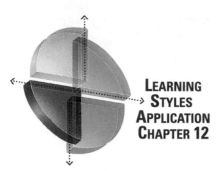

**LEARNING
STYLES
APPLICATION
CHAPTER 12**

Write your responses to these exercises on a separate sheet of paper.

Style 1
Consider your experience with this book and your student success class. Have any of your attitudes or actions changed as a result of this experience? Are you experiencing more success in school than you did before reading this book? Explain your answer.

Style 2
Brainstorm a list of the suggestions from this book that you've already applied. Rate each suggestion for its effectiveness on a scale of 1 to 5 (1 is most effective, 5 is least effective).

Style 3
Now list some suggestions you would like to apply but have not so far. Write Intention Statements describing how you will act on these suggestions.

Style 4
Imagine that you are going to lead your own student success course next term. Consider how you would design the course. What topics would you cover? What specific ideas and suggestions would you offer on each topic? Write a rough draft of your course outline.

Congratulations —
You have completed
a journey through a
book that is designed
to be the start of an
Adventure in becoming
a master student.
Dave Ellis

Bibliography

◼ Endnotes

[1] Ira Progoff, *At a Journal Workshop* (New York: Dialogue House, 1975).

[2] Richard Solly and Roseann Lloyd, *Journey Notes: Writing for Recovery and Spiritual Growth* (Center City, MN: Hazelden, 1989).

[3] Richard Nelson Bolles, *What Color Is Your Parachute*? (Berkeley, CA: Ten Speed Press, updated annually).

◼ Additional Reading

Bach, Richard. *Illusions: The Adventures of a Reluctant Messiah*, New York: Delacorte, 1977.

Bandler, Richard, and John Grinder. *Frogs into Princes: Neuro-Linguistic Programming*, Moab, UT: Real People, 1979.

Ellis, Dave, and Stan Lankowitz. *Human Being: A Manual for Happiness, Health, Love and Wealth*, Rapid City, SD: Breakthrough Enterprises, 1995.

Ellis, Dave, Stan Lankowitz, Ed Stupka, and Doug Toft. *Career Planning Supplement to Becoming a Master Student*, Rapid City, SD: College Survival, 1990.

Gawain, Shakti. *Creative Visualization*, Mill Valley, CA: Whatever, 1978.

Golas, Thaddeus. *The Lazy Man's Guide to Enlightenment*, Palo Alto, CA: Seed Center, 1972.

Keyes, Ken, Jr. *Handbook to Higher Consciousness*, Berkeley, CA: Living Love, 1974.

Rajneesh, Bhagwan S. *Journey Toward the Heart*, New York: Harper and Row, 1980.

Sher, Barbara, with Annie Gottlieb. *Wishcraft: How To Get What You Really Want*, New York: Ballantine, 1979.

Sinetar, Marsha. *Do What You Love, The Money Will Follow*, New York: Dell, 1987.

U.S. Department of Labor. *The Directory of Occupational Titles*, and *The Occupational Outlook Handbook*, Washington, DC: Government Printing Office, n.d.

Index